43
Inside the George W. Bush Presidency

Edited by

Michael Nelson, Barbara A. Perry, and
Russell L. Riley

University Press of Kansas

© 2022 by the University Press of Kansas
All rights reserved

Published by the University Press of Kansas (Lawrence, Kansas 66045), which was
organized by the Kansas Board of Regents and is operated and funded by Emporia
State University, Fort Hays State University, Kansas State University, Pittsburg State
University, the University of Kansas, and Wichita State University.

Library of Congress Cataloging-in-Publication Data

Names: Nelson, Michael, 1949– editor. | Perry, Barbara A. (Barbara Ann),
1956– editor. | Riley, Russell L. (Russell Lynn), 1958– editor.
Title: 43 : inside the George W. Bush presidency / edited by Michael
Nelson, Barbara A. Perry, and Russell L. Riley.
Other titles: Forty three
Description: Lawrence, Kansas : University Press of Kansas, 2022. |
Includes bibliographical references and index.
Identifiers: LCCN 2022007371
ISBN 9780700633753 (paperback)
ISBN 9780700633760 (ebook)
Subjects: LCSH: United States—Politics and government—2001–2009. |
Bush, George W. (George Walker), 1946–
Classification: LCC E902 .A14 2022 | DDC 973.931—dc23/eng/20220222
LC record available at https://lccn.loc.gov/2022007371.

British Library Cataloguing-in-Publication Data is available.

Printed in the United States of America

10 9 8 7 6 5 4 3 2 1

The paper used in this publication is acid free and meets the minimum requirements
of the American National Standard for Permanence of Paper for Printed Library Materials Z39.48-1992.

CONTENTS

PREFACE

In June 2008 two emissaries of President George W. Bush—ambassador Mark Langdale, who would soon head Bush's presidential library foundation, and Bush's longtime political adviser Karl Rove—made a quiet visit to Charlottesville to meet with the senior leadership of the Miller Center at the University of Virginia. Langdale and Rove had been dispatched by Bush during the final year of his administration to begin planning for his postpresidency, especially the construction of his presidential library and its activities. The purpose of this meeting at the Miller Center was to discuss a presidential oral history.

Although the Miller Center had conducted significant oral history projects on every president since Gerald Ford, a partnership with Bush was far from a given. Among other things, some members of his network harbored a confirmed skepticism about academics and their intentions. But as the conversation unfolded, including extended discussions about the non-partisan purposes and professional methods of the Miller Center's oral history work, the conditions for a productive partnership emerged.

That arrangement—later blessed by President Bush himself—would include major funding by the Bush Foundation to cover the cost of the interviews (then standard procedure for the Miller Center), paired with a commitment to allow the center's scholars complete academic independence in conducting and recording the oral histories. The shared purpose of this enterprise was simple: to create a lasting record of recollections by those who had served in the seniormost positions from Bush's 2000 campaign to his transition out of the presidency in January 2009—both the good and the bad. No questions were off-limits.

The chapters in *43: Inside the Presidency of George W. Bush* constitute the first thorough scholarly use of these oral histories. Some ninety interviews were recorded for the Bush project, and almost sixty of them were available to the contributors. Each session normally lasted seven to ten hours, with interviews conducted by teams of scholars. Typically, they explored the interviewees' memories of their service with and for President Bush, along with their careers prior to joining the administration. Interviewees also offered political and leadership lessons gleaned from being eyewitnesses to and often shapers of history. Following standard oral history protocols, each interview was conducted in confidence, and the subjects were allowed to stipulate conditions for the release of their own transcripts. That assurance helped foster candor at the interview table.

In drafting the chapters for 43, the contributing scholars mined these interviews for what they reveal about the inner workings and intentions of those serving in the Bush administration, but their research includes other public sources as well. Oral history provides invaluable inside evidence of White House behavior that can be captured in no other way. But it also suffers from the deficiencies of this intimacy. The chapters in this volume demonstrate how to make balanced use of these resources to enrich our understanding of recent presidential history.

In his introductory chapter, Russell L. Riley describes the three stages of the Bush presidency: pre-9/11, war, and postwar. Michael Nelson then chronicles Bush's elections—not only his own election and reelection in 2000 and 2004 but also the other elections that occurred during his administration: 2002, 2006, and 2008. Jesse H. Rhodes assesses Bush's domestic policy of "compassionate conservatism," with particular emphasis on education reform and his No Child Left Behind program, in chapter 2. Various aspects of Bush's interactions with the rest of the government are covered in chapters 4–7: Andrew Rudalevige analyzes the "unitary executive" aspects of the Bush presidency, John J. Pitney Jr. examines the president's relations with Congress, Barbara A. Perry offers an account of his Supreme Court nominations, and Joel K. Goldstein discusses the distinctive aspects of Dick Cheney's vice presidency. The wars of the Bush presidency are treated separately by Michael Nelson (9/11) in chapter 3 and Spencer D. Bakich (Iraq) in chapter 8. Robert F. Bruner (chapter 9) examines the last challenge of the Bush presidency: the financial crisis that marked his final months in office. In the concluding chapter, Sidney M. Milkis weighs Bush's presidency against the balance of presidential history.

This book and the larger project from which it emerged would not have been possible without the committed efforts of many people at several institutions. The late Gerald Baliles, former Virginia governor and then director of the Miller Center, chaired the initial 2008 meeting, and his even-tempered, inclusive approach to politics was undoubtedly instrumental in opening the door for this project to happen. His successor, William Antholis, provided valuable support and encouragement as the project progressed to completion. Credit also goes to the Miller Center's Governing Council, then chaired by Eugene Fife, who labored behind the scenes to convey the center's seriousness of purpose to critical people in the Bush network.

On the Bush side of the partnership, special thanks go to Karl Rove and Ambassador Langdale for their enthusiasm, voiced even as they were trying to build a state-of-the-art presidential library in Dallas. When Langdale stepped down as president of the Bush Foundation, Margaret Spellings succeeded him and continued to facilitate a model relationship between the Miller Center and the foundation. The productive character of that relationship radiated outward, making it vastly easier for the center to schedule interviews with busy Bush alumni. Special thanks to President Bush himself for agreeing to let his foundation fund the project and for encouraging cooperation among his "formers."

Within the Miller Center's Presidential Oral History Program, many hidden hands worked to move this project through to completion. Scheduling busy people for day-and-a half (or longer) interviews, plus making travel arrangements, is an extraordinarily complicated business, but it was done to perfection by Katrina Kuhn and Keri Matthews. The secret to maximizing the value of oral history is preparation, and the program benefited from the continuing labors of two longtime professional researchers: Rob Martin and Bryan Craig. Two supervising editors worked tirelessly on the thankless task of rendering spoken English into usable prose: Jane Rafal Wilson and Gail Hyder Wiley. In addition, teams of temporary student researchers, contract editors, and administrative aides made a very complicated machine run smoothly over several years. We are grateful for their labors. Michael Greco and his technology unit made the recording of the interviews a seamless task.

Finally, there are two groups of people who merit our highest praise for volunteering their time and energy to make this project possible. The first is the group of former public servants who agreed to sit and respond to endless questions, sometimes reflecting on unhappy or even tragic moments so that we could gain a better understanding of what life during the Bush years was like. Their sole compensation was an overnight stay at the Boar's Head Inn in Charlottesville. The second is the community of scholars who gave freely of their time to conduct these interview sessions. Team interviewing is an unorthodox activity for oral historians, but it is indispensable for the work we do. There is no substitute for collective wisdom when trying to pose questions that future generations are likely to have about the politics of our times. And there is no alternative to subject-matter expertise when digging deep into the experiences of a national security adviser proctoring internecine squabbles between the State and Defense Departments or delving into presidential options when credit markets freeze and the Dow drops 777 points in a single day. To the dozens of outside scholars who helped conduct these interviews, we extend our profound thanks for making this project possible. Future generations are indebted to you all.

There's a reason why scholars love to publish with the University Press of Kansas: the people who work so hard and well to bring our books into being. We especially thank Senior Editor David Congdon, Editor in Chief Joyce Harrison, Production Editor Erica Nicholson, Copy Editor Linda Lotz, Art Director Karl Janssen, and Indexer Elise Hess. And for their encouraging and helpful reviews of the manuscript, we thank Meena Bose and Stephen Knott.

43

INTRODUCTION

History and the Three Presidencies of George W. Bush

Russell L. Riley

No presidency in the lifetime of the republic will be more difficult for history to get right than the forty-third—that of George W. Bush. In part, this is a function of the extraordinarily controversial nature of Bush's tenure. The first person to win the office while losing the popular vote since Benjamin Harrison in 1888, Bush was encumbered from the beginning with questions about his political legitimacy. He was sworn in with chants of the so-called Brooks Brothers riot still reverberating through the land, his victory based on a Supreme Court decision so inventive that the justices felt compelled to proclaim that it shouldn't be taken as precedent for other cases. Then his watch was marked by an astonishing array of contentious developments, including the failure to detect and prevent the terrorist attacks of September 11, 2001, the invasion and occupation of Iraq, Hurricane Katrina, Abu Ghraib, and a massive expansion of the surveillance state at home and abroad. Few presidents have been more polarizing than Bush.

A decade after his departure from the White House, Bush was still politically radioactive. In October 2019 photographers captured images of the former president seated next to popular television personality Ellen DeGeneres at a Dallas Cowboys football game—which she made the mistake of visibly enjoying. The event caused a media firestorm, with criticism raining down on DeGeneres for not treating Bush as a pariah. She fell precipitously from public favor.[1] His unpopularity was contagious.

George W. Bush is not the first president to provoke strong, enduring, visceral reactions. But these predispositions are formidable obstacles to the kind of clear-eyed and dispassionate analysis required of those who endeavor to commit a president to history.

A second set of impediments confronting those attempting to create an authentic historical Bush arises from the archival resources necessary to discover what actually happened behind the closed doors of 1600 Pennsylvania Avenue. Here, paradoxically, are problems of feast as well as famine. The National Archives and Records Administration (NARA) reports, "The George W. Bush Presidential Library and Museum holds more than 70 million pages of paper records, 43,000 artifacts, 200 million emails and 4 million digital photographs."[2] That is a collection of almost unfathomable proportions. Historian Robert Caro, whose works on Lyndon Johnson set the standard for meticulous presidential research, has written that the core of his method, learned as a young investigative reporter, is to "turn every page."[3] What would doing so with the Bush documents entail? Let's assume for purposes of illustration that one could turn a thousand pages a day. At that pace, reviewing the paper records alone would require seventy thousand days of nonstop labor—191 years.[4] The collected email traffic is almost three times as voluminous. The search for needles in this colossal haystack will not be easy.

Yet the more immediate problem facing students of the forty-third presidency is actually one of scarcity. Because of the terms of the Presidential Records Act, which governs the disposition of official White House documents, all but a tiny fraction of these millions of pages is unavailable to outside eyes—pending their review, clearance, and release by a small cadre of overburdened archivists. Each line of those 270 million paper pages and emails must be examined to make sure they do not contain national security information or private personal data that should by law remain out of the public domain.[5] It will be a very long time before a significant percentage of this archival documentation is available to researchers.[6] In the interim—which will be measured in decades—those trying to paint an accurate historical portrait of the Bush presidency must do so on the basis of a fragmentary documentary record guaranteed to be least complete on the most delicate national security issues.

The problem of delayed release of records is not limited to Bush, of course. Each administration since Ronald Reagan's has been governed by these constraints. But the problem has been exacerbated for each successive presidency because of the exponential increase in the use of electronic communications, most prominently emails (which barely existed in Reagan's time). Accordingly, those who require written records to reconstruct the inner workings of each White House are compelled to reach conclusions fully aware that there are millions of pages of relevant evidence they have not examined—because they cannot.

Added to these familiar obstacles, however, is something unique to the Bush years—and, ironically, derived from his greatest accomplishment. The Bush administration's ability to prevent a follow-on attack after the catastrophe of September 11, 2001—an achievement continued by his successors—exerts a subtle but powerful adverse effect on our assessment of what Bush did in the Oval Office.

To be sure, historical review is always distorted by the prism of retrospection. It is never easy to practice willful forgetting when looking back at the past, to understand the problems and prospects of those who faced events in our history as their future. Because we know how things turned out, there is a common bias in historical assessments that affects every presidency—in fact, every historical episode we examine. As the German essayist Walter Benjamin once observed, "A man . . . who died at thirty-five will appear to *remembrance* at every point in his life as a man who dies at the age of thirty-five."[7] This kind of knowledge distorts the history we write in ways that typically go unremarked, because of both the manifest advantages of being able to examine the full consequences of past actions and the relatively benign (or at least latent) costs of that omniscience.

In Bush's case, however, this problem is singularly acute. At every point in his presidency after 9/11, the Bush of our remembrance is a man possessed by an event—a second terrorist attack—that never happened. Reliable sources—including national security adviser Condoleezza Rice and homeland security adviser Frances Townsend—inform us that for President Bush and his inner circle, every day that followed the initial attack was September 12.[8] The horror of those hours was the president's lasting preoccupation. He remained committed to doing anything he could, including stretching the capacious bounds of executive authority and military might, to prevent another life-threatening catastrophe. That reality defined his mission. "Everything had this incredible sense of urgency," Townsend reflected in her oral history, "and we all bore the weight of responsibility for the lives lost on 9/11. From the president on down, we felt a personal responsibility to make sure that never happened again."[9] In his interview, Robert Gates, who became secretary of defense during Bush's second term, reflected on what this meant for those serving on 9/11: "I was thinking to myself, *What would I be feeling if I were in their shoes today, September 12, 2001?* It is just this huge burden of failure, that thousands of people lost their lives because I didn't do my job right and a bunch of other people didn't do their jobs right. What's wrong with us? How do we fix this and how do we fix it overnight?" That was President Bush's reality. The full intensity of that preoccupation is not easy to recapture and convey to people today, who know the second wave of attacks never occurred.

Moreover, the absence of a second wave also subtly alters our ability to comprehend the nation's psychological state during those times. To be sure, the shock of September 11 is relatively easy to conjure again. Anyone old enough to have memories of that day can recall watching the Twin Towers collapse. Typically bundled with these memories are fragmented images of chaos and unity: masses of New Yorkers heading home on foot; chilling accounts of the doomed passengers aboard Flight 93; the grave countenances of the former presidents who supported the incumbent as he mourned the dead from the pulpit at the National Cathedral; Bush's spirited pledge of retaliation delivered through a bullhorn in the midst of the rubble in Lower Manhattan. It is not the shock of those days that is hard to recapture. It is the primal sense of suspense that followed—the deep anxiety over what would happen next.

Filmmaker Alfred Hitchcock made the distinction between shock and suspense central to his craft, and his methods are instructive. More than once, Hitchcock used the following film tableau to illustrate the point: Two men are seated at a table, carrying on an idle conversation. Without warning, a bomb goes off beneath them, killing both. The effect on the audience, Hitchcock notes, is shock. The sudden event stuns the viewer. But that effect is relatively short-lived: the film moves on to the next scene. Then Hitchcock suggests an alternative: At the moment the two men meet, show the audience that there is a bomb under the table that will detonate in five minutes. That knowledge manufactures suspense. There is a looming menace as the clock ticks. Unease mounts as each minute passes.[10] But according to Hitchcock, as a matter of art, the film works best if the bomb never goes off. If the danger lasts for the duration of the movie, the viewer gets no relief: tragedy could happen at any moment. That sustained anxiety was at the heart of Hitchcock's method. Yet for the film to work as intended, the audience could not know the ending in advance. That knowledge would ruin the effect, disarming the suspense.[11]

Hitchcock's commentary helps us understand something significant about the presidency of George W. Bush and how we recall it. Until September 11, most Americans had no idea that there might be a bomb under the table.[12] Indeed, the shock of that day was so great precisely because, until that moment, so few Americans had thought such an event was possible.[13] But for a considerable length of time thereafter, Americans were fearful of more bombs under other tables.[14] As Peter Baker later reported in the *New York Times*, in "the wake of the Sept. 11 attacks . . . further violent death on a mass scale seemed inevitable."[15] The clock was ticking. Today, however, we know how the story ended.

The distortions of that retrospective knowledge are exacerbated by a second factor: the failure to find weapons of mass destruction in Iraq. One of the strongest memories Americans have about the Bush era is that the threat from Iraq was overstated, so it is natural for those recollections to intrude on memories of the global war on terror. That being so, the absence of a follow-up attack on the United States can easily appear to be one more indicator that the whole threat was overblown. Any such predisposition makes it exceedingly difficult to gain an accurate picture of the tenor of the times—or the central motivating force of the Bush White House.

This volume represents one effort to compensate for such obstacles. In these pages, a group of accomplished scholars addresses some of the most controversial aspects of the Bush years, clarifying what happened and putting those developments in historical perspective. We also address the problems created by the constraints of the Presidential Records Act by drawing on an alternative source of evidence about the Bush years: presidential oral histories. For roughly ten years after George W. Bush left office, scholars associated with the University of Virginia's Miller Center of Public Affairs conducted scores of confidential interviews with senior officials from the Bush era, recording their memories. The chapters in this volume constitute a collective effort to mine that large cache of original historical materials. These interviews are not offered as the last word on any of the topics addressed. But they are among the most authoritative accounts available about a host of important political developments during the Bush administration.[16]

Finally, the insider accounts used throughout this book (best exemplified by Michael Nelson's curated interview passages recalling the terror of 9/11 in chapter 3, "Day of Fire") provide rich details about the inner workings of the Bush White House, including the tense character of the times. The oral histories thus convey nuances about hard decisions, choices that in retrospect may be too easily dismissed because the hunches of the decision makers turned out to be wrong or the policies based on them turned out badly. Our scholarly mission is to understand as best we can what happened and why, which usually requires an empathetic approach, the ability to see problems through the eyes of those who were there. If we dismiss from the outset the real plight of those who govern—including the suspense of their times—there is no way to learn from their experiences. These interviews are indispensable if we hope to gain an understanding of the roots of both success and failure—including decisions that today might seem inexplicable.

To be clear, acknowledgment of this extraordinary pressure does not amount to a blanket shield against criticism of Bush's presidency. There were dissenting voices—even among senior members of the administration— who urged more thorough diplomacy before invading Iraq or more realistic planning for the postwar period there. But a proper historical reckoning requires an understanding of why Bush acted as he did even when confronted with prominent voices urging caution and restraint. It is impossible to understand history if we discount the weight on one side of the scale.

Presidential scholar Richard E. Neustadt has observed that only the hardest problems get to the Oval Office. Presidential decisions are usually based on a 51–49 calculation of the benefits and costs, with just as many people arrayed on one side of the issue as the other.[17] Seldom is a presidential decision a "slam dunk"—even when some advisers may argue otherwise. Accordingly, one of the most important responsibilities of the presidential historian is to retrieve and account for this complexity and how the participants wrestled with it—in effect, to acknowledge the fog of war. In looking back, often our duty is not to simplify the decisions we assess but, to borrow from Cambridge classicist Mary Beard, "to make things seem more complicated."[18]

Every president governs within a deep institutional and cultural environment that limits what the incumbent can do and, at the same time, creates the basis for exercising presidential leadership. Normally this environment does not change much over time, although it is more protean than the language of the Constitution itself. For example, there was not much difference in the Constitution when Franklin Pierce and Abraham Lincoln held the presidency, but the circumstances of their times—what might generically be called their regimes—were dramatically different.[19] Lincoln was afforded far greater opportunities to exert vigorous and independent leadership. War required it.

What we find in George W. Bush's presidency is an anomaly. During Bush's eight years in the White House, he experienced three distinct leadership regimes. Framing these helps us better understand the historical forces at work in his time.

A Balanced System: January 20 to September 10, 2001

George W. Bush, reflecting on his own wisecracking ways, occasionally quipped that he had his father's eyes and his mother's (acerbic) mouth.[20] But he inherited something much more important from his father once he became president: an institution transformed by the successful conclusion of the Cold War.

During the Cold War, the presidency was an empowered institution in a state of continuous readiness for nuclear conflict.[21] Although it would be too much to say that the Cold War presidency was raised to the wartime heights of Lincoln (or Woodrow Wilson or Franklin Roosevelt), those presidents who served after World War II never returned to anything close to a status of power equality with the other branches of the federal government. "How could it . . . have," asked Sen. Daniel Patrick Moynihan (D-NY) in 1991, "in the course of 30 to 40 years in which Presidents knew they would have 10 minutes at most to decide whether to launch a thermonuclear second strike."[22] That persistently elevated threat, punctuated by hot wars in Korea and Vietnam and the unnerving jolts of *Sputnik* and the Cuban missile crisis, created two generations of presidents who dominated the American political system and the global landscape.

But the victory in the Cold War that President George H. W. Bush helped secure brought an end to that quasi-wartime presidency, ushering in a decade of constitutional readjustment. Such periods are commonly characterized by painful institutional contraction. That was certainly true for the elder Bush and his successor, Bill Clinton. Bush's reelection failure in 1992, Clinton's loss of a "permanent" Democratic majority in the House of Representatives and the Senate in 1994, and Clinton's 1998 impeachment can all be traced to the conventional postwar impulses to rightsize the presidential institution and restore something approaching a constitutional balance.[23]

By the time George W. Bush entered the White House, those post–Cold War contractions had left the presidency in an institutionally diminished state.[24] The office he was expected to fill was neither a place of grand public designs nor a seat of soaring global leadership. That kind of office would have called for a president with expansive ambitions. Instead, Bush had more modest aims. He would replicate what he had done as governor of Texas.

In 2001 Texas's governor was ranked thirty-ninth out of fifty in terms of statutory powers.[25] Thus, what Bush had been able to accomplish in Texas was largely the product of cooperation with the state legislature. He had developed an especially fruitful—and colorful—relationship with Democratic lieutenant governor Robert Bullock, which allowed Bush to tell national voters that his style was consensual. Observers often commented on the bipartisan character of their partnership and what it meant for Bush. "The relationship with Bullock," reported Paul Burka of *Texas Monthly* in 1999, "was the foundation of Bush's national image as a politician who values consensus and goodwill over partisanship."[26] But in the prevailing institutional environment of the times, the relationship may have been equally important for what it said about Bush's valuing of consensus and goodwill over getting his own way as governor. He was a political executive who succeeded in a state where the legislature was the dominant institution.[27] As president, Bush would thus be practiced in the art of deferring to legislative ways.

In her oral history, domestic policy adviser Margaret Spellings—who had worked for Bush in Texas—offers a telling anecdote revealing the governor's indifference to his formal stature:

When . . . [Bush] had been probably a week in office, Bob Johnson, the parliamentarian of the Texas Senate and the best friend of Bob Bullock, died very suddenly. There was a memorial thing at the Capitol. Bush . . . barely knew Bob Johnson, they'd met each other but were not even acquaintances. In the Senate chamber Bush was up there on the dais with Bullock, who was just bereft. And Betty King, the Secretary of the Senate, was reading this memorial resolution to Bob Johnson.

She started crying and couldn't get through the thing. I can't even tell the story without crying myself. [Bush] gets down off the dais and goes and puts his arm around her and finishes reading the thing. That's not something that a staff person says, "You know, that would be a really smart political thing to do." It's just how he reacts to people.

Bush subsequently featured his relationship with Bullock in his acceptance address at the Republican convention in August 2000. And when Bush finally appeared in public to claim the presidency after the Supreme Court ruled in his favor on the Florida recount, he chose to speak in the chamber of the Texas House of Representatives. "Here, in a place where Democrats have the majority, Republicans and Democrats have worked together to do what is right for the people we represent," Bush said. "We had spirited disagreements, and in the end, we found constructive consensus. It is an experience I will always carry with me, and an example I will always follow."[28] This would be a president comfortable with the prerogatives of Congress.

Moreover, the way Bush depicted his approach to the job in his 2000 presidential campaign betrayed a relatively modest conception of his aims in office. Bush's five major priorities, according to domestic aide Kristen Silverberg in her oral history (with Josh Bolten), were No Child Left Behind, tax cuts, Social Security reform, Medicare reform, and faith-based initiatives. But, Bolten noted, "from the President's perspective there was no question that two things had to come first. One . . . was the tax cuts, and the other was his top priority, which was education reform. . . . He ran to be the education President."[29]

Selling tax cuts to a Republican Congress was not a heavy lift—and had the added benefit of constraining the size of the national government. Education reform was another small-bore policy that, for most Americans, did not betray imperial aspirations on the part of the president. It made him look like the nation's governor. In pursuing No Child Left Behind, Bush closely replicated his Austin experience by finding an unlikely Democratic leader to help sell his plan: Sen. Edward M. Kennedy of Massachusetts. Karl Rove reported in his oral history that the day after his victory speech in the Texas house chamber, Bush asked Kennedy to work with him on education. That partnership was indispensable in getting the reforms passed.

It was clear from the beginning of Bush's presidency that he—unlike his immediate predecessor, who reportedly said he would have preferred to be president during World War II—was content to lead in ways that were more transactional than transformational.[30] As John Dickerson observed, "In 2001, President George W. Bush's staff talked about how he was going to be an A4 president, not always in the center of the day's news on page A1 of the newspaper."[31] Indicative of these intentions, the administration announced just days before the September 11 attack that it would follow up its earliest initiatives with a "national campaign . . . to get people to be nicer" to one another. A major Canadian paper described the program as "politicians and Hollywood stars united together in a public campaign to eliminate gossip from the American landscape and restore some sort of dignity to public debate."[32] In Indiana, one press account correctly identified Bush's commitment as "part of a broader package of low-cost proposals designed to promote stronger communities."[33]

Another instructive—and amusing—measure of the relatively tranquil and accommodating state of the first phase of the Bush presidency arises from the oral history of one of the most influential figures of the post-9/11 period: John Yoo. Yoo was appointed to a senior position in the Justice Department's Office of Legal Counsel (OLC), which unexpectedly became the nerve center of the Bush administration's legal efforts to prosecute the war on terror. In one of the great accidents of history, Yoo's scholarly work had been in the (then) backwaters of presidential studies: executive war powers. Given his unique facility with this arcane legal history and his embrace of the unitary executive theory, Yoo was perfectly positioned to provide the White House with exactly what it needed in the way of robust authorities to counterattack America's enemies. But the job certainly didn't start that way.

Yoo arrived at the Justice Department in July 2001, and rather than reveling in the experience of being the formal dispenser of executive powers under a forward-leaning Republican president, he found himself completely bored:

> There was really not enough work for the day. I spent some time on a Vacancies Act issue, which always happens at the beginning of an administration: When can you appoint people who aren't confirmed yet, how long can they be in office, and what are they allowed to do? I remember working on the Presidential Executive Order on federalism. I remember reviewing a treaty about marine mammals and thinking Antarctica and things like this. There was a case about a Russian on an American ship who might have killed an American. . . . I was thinking I'd probably go back home after a year because I thought the job was pretty dull. It wasn't that the issues themselves were inherently dull, there just weren't many things coming in for work.

Beyond Yoo's interview, the other oral histories generally reaffirm the conventional wisdom that terrorism was not a major preoccupation of the Bush administration prior to the al Qaeda attacks. Philip Zelikow, who served on Bush's foreign policy transition team and later directed the 9/11

Commission, noted, approvingly, a characterization attributed to White House national security staffer Dick Clarke: for the Bush administration, "counterterrorism was an important problem, but not urgent."[34] Without any indicators of presidential urgency, the matter of terrorism was committed to the ordinary slog of the policymaking process.[35] "We had a series of deputies committee meetings," reported National Security Council legal adviser John Bellinger, which "concluded that we couldn't just decide on a policy toward al-Qaeda until we decided on a policy toward Afghanistan, and we couldn't decide on a policy toward Afghanistan until we had decided on a policy toward Pakistan, and we couldn't decide on a policy toward Pakistan until we decided on an Indo-Pak [India-Pakistan] policy."[36]

Then airplanes began to fly into buildings.

A War President: September 11, 2001, to November 7, 2006

Unlike some other democratic charters, the US Constitution does not have formal provisions for an alternative means of governance in times of emergency. Article 16 of the French Constitution, for example, explicitly allows the president to take exceptional measures "where the institutions of the Republic, the independence of the Nation, the integrity of its territory or the fulfillment of its international commitments are under serious and immediate threat."[37] In the United States, the resort to emergency government is mainly behavioral. Americans, both within and without the government, act differently when emergency conditions threaten the nation. The US Constitution only obliquely suggests that a different kind of government—mainly under presidential direction—is possible when the institutions of the republic are under serious and immediate threat. Yet there have been multiple instances of this type of emergency government, or what Clinton Rossiter called "constitutional dictatorships."[38]

In the aftermath of 9/11, Bush could not single-handedly institute a crisis government. He had no Article 16 to invoke. Rather, an emergency regime would require significant behavioral changes outside as well as inside the White House. And in 2001 there were good reasons to wonder whether the nation would comply.

The last time the United States had experienced a full-scale, protracted episode of crisis government ended on VJ Day—fifty-six years earlier.[39]

That was only slightly longer than the interval between Appomattox and the sinking of the *Lusitania*. But the fundamental social, economic, and political changes in the more recent interval were vastly more pronounced than those that occurred between Lincoln and Wilson. The escalation of political polarization and cultural atomization—defining traits of the decades leading up to 9/11—made the creation of a unity government more complex than at any time in American history.[40]

Then there were questions about the president himself. The George W. Bush who took office in January 2001 showed few signs of being a Lincoln or an FDR. Until that time, Bush's success as a political figure had been built primarily on his Everyman qualities: he was jocular and accessible, a Texas oilman turned baseball promoter who wore cowboy boots and spun off a constant stream of nicknames. In small meetings, his charm commanded the room. But there was little indication that he was capable of commanding national leadership. Bush's aides could never figure out, for example, how to capture his in-person communications skills when the television cameras were running—a critical tool for modern public leadership. White House counselor Edward Gillespie noted the persistent staff frustration that "the person you . . . saw in the Oval Office or individual settings . . . never came across on television." On camera, Bush all too often seemed to channel Johnny Carson's hapless Floyd R. Turbo.[41] In sum, a person ideally suited to be a post–Cold War transactional president was not easily envisioned as a towering source of national unity.

It didn't matter. After 9/11, Americans willingly divested themselves of the usual protections of separate, jealously independent governing institutions and stifled their usually robust impulse to dissent. They would follow the president's lead. Their conversion was initiated by what House minority leader Richard Gephardt (D-MO) called, in his oral history, an event more transformative than Pearl Harbor. But it should be recalled that the turn to presidential leadership under Bush was fueled by serial attacks on Washington: American Airlines Flight 77 was crashed into the Pentagon on September 11; one week later, letters containing anthrax began to show up on Capitol Hill, among other places, killing several and raising a scare that Vice President Cheney was "about to die";[42] and one year later, in October 2002, the Washington area was terrorized by snipers who killed ten in thirteen separate shooting incidents.[43] As secretary of homeland security Michael Chertoff later recalled in his oral history, "If you look at all that stuff together—9/11, anthrax and the sniper—it really began to look as if we were in a dangerous state of affairs unlike people have had in the United States maybe since the Civil War."

A Gallup poll that closed on September 10, 2001, showed that 51 percent of Americans approved of the job Bush was doing as president. Within two weeks, his approval numbers had jumped to 90 percent.[44] The magnitude and duration of Bush's favorable ratings, as he directed an aggressive national response from the White House, were unprecedented. His approval ratings remained elevated, not returning on a sustained basis to pre-9/11 levels until nearly the second anniversary of the attacks, when public attention shifted to the war in Iraq.

Congress was equally supportive. Gephardt's oral history provides evidence of an earnest willingness among members to cooperate. For the duration, obstruction would no longer be his party's default setting:

> I remember looking down at the Pentagon and seeing it in flames and smoke and thinking, *The Germans and Japanese fought us for five years and if they could have done this, it would have been their fondest wish, and four people did this.* It was a wake-up call of the first order. . . . The next day, maybe the day after . . . we met in the White House: the leadership, and the President, the Vice President. Everybody said their piece. When I got a chance to talk, I said something that I felt very strongly. I said, "Mr. President, the most important thing now is that we all trust one another. This is about life and death. Our first responsibility is to keep the people safe. We failed; we all failed and we have to do better. . . . I know politics intrudes in everything that happens here, as it should, but with this we have to keep politics out. We cannot play politics with this. We have to do whatever we can to do the right things to keep the county safe and to avoid anything like this happening again."

A sign of the trust and unity prevailing on Capitol Hill was Congress's prompt action on the Authorization for Use of Military Force (AUMF), which was the functional equivalent of a declaration of war against those who initiated the September 11 attacks or harbored the perpetrators. By September 18, the Senate had voted 98–0 and the House 420–1 in favor of the joint resolution. Similarly, President Bush signed into law the more controversial USA Patriot Act on October 26, which had passed in the House 357–66 and in the Senate 98–1. David Hobbs, a deputy White House congressional relations specialist, later recalled that this period was characterized by "a real spirit of bipartisanship. [I] remember the scene when [the members of Congress] came together and sang "God Bless America" on the [Capitol] steps." One study of House roll-call votes confirms that congressional support for President Bush rose dramatically after the attacks and remained high for the rest of 2001; although levels of support settled back somewhat in 2002, they were still significantly above his pre-9/11 experience. For the balance of the 107th Congress, there were eighteen bills easily identifiable as related to the war on terror. The White House lost only four of those.[45]

The American form of constitutional dictatorship has never meant Congress's wholesale and indiscriminate allegiance to the president.[46] In practice, emergency government has been more subtle, more emergency specific. Some measure of congressional independence is thus completely consistent with past behavior.[47] But two realities from the Bush years confirm that this president enjoyed an exceptional consonance of interests between the White House and Congress.

First, when American voters were given an opportunity in November 2002 to enhance the check on Bush in the midterm congressional elections, they refused to take it. Rather, they rewarded Bush by increasing the Republican majority in the House and returning control of the Senate to the president's party, after the defection of Vermont's Jim Jeffords had flipped control earlier in the term. This midterm result (adding seats to the president's party in both houses) had happened only twice since the Civil War.[48] Second, Bush served his entire first term without using the veto power. Before Bush, the most recent example of a full presidential term without a single veto was the shared presidency of Zachary Taylor and Millard Fillmore in the 1850s.[49] The rarity of this occurrence makes it notable. What makes it extraordinary—conspicuously so—is that in prosecuting the war on terror, Bush armored up the presidency with a prodigious array of executive authorities, using them, it sometimes seemed, just to demonstrate that he could.[50] Not so, tellingly, with the veto. When congressional liaison David Hobbs was pressed on this point during his oral history, he replied that the administration did not need to use the veto because "we weren't losing anything."

Independent executive authorities are themselves an important part of the story. Much of the enhanced presidential power in wartime occurs because so much of the nation's agenda shifts from the normal domestic preoccupations, which, in a system of separated institutions, tends to occupy each branch equally, to matters of defense and national security, which the presidency dominates.

By the time Bush became president, the accumulated executive authorities on the shelf for wartime situations were already substantial. Moreover, he had people working with him—including Vice President Dick Cheney, the vice president's counsel David Addington, and Yoo at the OLC—who were past masters in presidential maximalism, experts at helping the president work right up to the boundaries of the law and even nudging that line when doing so was, by their lights, desirable.[51]

In sum, the center of gravity of the American constitutional system shifted dramatically in the direction of the presidency after 9/11 because so many of the central issues of the national response involved activities that, by constitutional design, law, and informal practice, tended to gravitate toward the president. These included the prosecution of the war against the terrorists and those who supported them; the elevated threat to the homeland caused by external forces; the management of diplomatic alliances to facilitate both the war effort and the protection of international security; the disposition of enemy combatants; and the detection and prevention of future threats. It was the last matter—perceived dangers on the horizon—that led the president into his gravest error: the invasion of Iraq.

The Iraq War can only be touched on here. (Spencer D. Bakich deals with it extensively in chapter 8.) But two points about Iraq relate directly to the broader core arguments about the Bush presidency. First, for all that is noteworthy about Bush's constitutional dictatorship and his exploitation of the office's unilateral powers, his administration did not take a strictly unilateralist approach to the invasion of Iraq. In other words, the president did not, based on available evidence and relying on his office's teeming authorities, decide on his own to invade Iraq and then execute his plan narrowly through the military chain of command. Instead, Bush engaged and sought the support of the legislative branch and the nation's global allies. Karl Rove attributed this in part to Bush's sensitivity about his own political legitimacy, "a special burden" imposed by "Florida and the 36 days from hell" after the 2000 election. Whatever the reasons—absence of clear authority in existing law or prudent concerns about going it alone (which had motivated his father to seek congressional approval for the first Gulf War)[52]—the fact that Bush did not invade Iraq based solely on his own institutional powers is an important datum about crisis government in America. Presidents operating in a crisis are usually at their maximum powers, but again, constitutional dictatorships in the American model are not completely unconstrained. Here, substantial congressional minorities initially voted against authorizing force in Iraq—opposition that would swell precipitously when things went badly. (In addition, the United Nations Security Council refused to adopt a resolution explicitly authorizing an Iraq invasion in early 2003, requiring Bush to fall back on an October 2002 resolution to justify the use of force.) So the consent to follow Bush's lead, though robust, was not unlimited. Indeed, if Bush had been more attentive, he might have taken the magnitude of that opposition as a warning that he was nearing the limits of his license to lead.

Second, the history of the Iraq invasion has been singularly haunted by the failure to find weapons of mass destruction (WMD) there, one of the main reasons cited to justify the invasion.[53] That failure has fed a popular narrative that the president and his team manufactured the rationale: the existence of WMD was a lie, concocted by hard-liners to justify something they had wanted to do even before 9/11. That some national security specialists inside the administration had long wanted to go after Saddam Hussein is undeniable. Insider accounts confirm that this option was raised during a Camp David meeting of Bush's senior advisers on the first weekend after the attacks.[54] Moreover, some individuals within the administration, including key figures in the vice president's office, tried to move marginal evidence about WMD to the center of the president's arguments for war, hoping to solidify the case for an invasion that otherwise might not happen.

But the oral history evidence suggests that the president had legitimate reasons to be worried about WMD, even if the threat may have been hyped to convince the outside world. Based on these oral histories, the core problem was an intelligence failure. Minority leader Gephardt, who was skeptical of the White House's intentions when talk about Iraq first surfaced in early 2002, revealed how his misgivings were overcome when the president arranged for Gephardt to examine the intelligence himself:

> I went out to the CIA. I think I went three times at least and talked to everybody there, alone. I said to [director] George Tenet, "This is not about Saddam Hussein for me. This is not about trying to go change the Middle East forever," which some of the neocons [neoconservatives] thought this should be about. Even though that's understandable to try to do, I said, "For me it boils down to one simple fact: Does he have weapons of mass destruction, especially components of nuclear weapons, or does he not? Do we worry that some components could wind up in the hands of terrorists?" Tenet and everybody else I talked to—they

said the other world intelligence services agreed that he did. It was a real problem. So I came back and told the President, "I'll speak for and vote for and cosponsor the resolution [to invade]."

Director of the National Security Agency (and later CIA director) Michael Hayden specifically confirms this point in his oral history:

When we look back on it, I think no one disagrees that it was mishandled. But I also point out that it's our fault, not the President's, not the Vice President's. This is tradecraft on the part of the intelligence community. [Former Clinton chief of staff] Leon Panetta had written a little bit when he was out of government about the [Bush] administration cooking the intel, and the very last thing I said to him as I left the building [to turn the job over to him] was, "Leon, that's just not right. We just got it wrong. . . . You've got to stop saying it [was Bush's fault]. It was our fault. We just got it wrong."

On November 2, 2004, George W. Bush was reelected over Sen. John Kerry (D-MA), making him the sole Republican (as of this writing) to win a majority of the popular vote since his father did it in 1988. The Republicans also gained seats in both the House and the Senate. These results plainly vindicated Bush's wartime leadership.[55]

A month after the president's reelection, some senior Pentagon officials began referring publicly to the "long war" against global terrorism, acknowledging the growing reality that theirs would be the work of a generation.[56] Although their sense of the conflict's scale proved to be accurate, the presidential crisis regime that had arisen to fight it would be over in two years.

A "Postwar" President: November 8, 2006, to January 20, 2009

On November 7, 2006, something else unusual occurred: Bush's Republican Party lost both houses of Congress in the midterm elections, giving up five seats in the Senate and thirty-one in the House.[57] Presidents have rarely seen their party lose control of both chambers in a single midterm election. Historically, there have been only six clear instances, four of which were postwar elections: 1918 (World War I), 1946 (World War II), 1954 (Korea), and

1994 (the Cold War).[58] In addition, something similar happened after both the Civil War (1866) and Vietnam (1974), but neither of those elections resulted in a complete shift in partisan control. Even so, the Congresses created by these postwar midterm elections were transformed into historically obstreperous governing partners for their presidents.[59]

All these elections were political manifestations of Newton's Third Law: for every action in nature there is an equal and opposite reaction. In times of war or other major crisis, the typical action has been to license the president to exercise extraordinary powers to meet the challenge. But under the operational dynamics of American politics, such emergency powers should endure only as long as necessary. Once the threat has been met, a return to something approximating the status quo antebellum should occur. In the American model, crisis government has been largely behavioral, and the end has followed suit. Postwar midterm elections are behavioral signatures of that process—a Newtonian-style reaction. The end of emergency government under presidential direction has always featured the seating of an oppositionist—even hostile—legislature committed to what Warren Harding famously called the "return to normalcy." Constitutional dictatorships in the United States typically conclude, then, with a distinctive form of "American regicide."[60]

The election of the opposition-controlled 110th Congress in 2006, however, is a puzzle. What war ended? There was no armistice with Osama bin Laden; no peace was declared in Baghdad. The violence in Iraq actually worsened through 2006, with American deaths reaching three thousand before the close of the year.[61] How, then, should we read this peculiar election result?[62]

Ironically, one possibility is to see it as a sign of Bush's success in his main mission. At a very early moment after the 9/11 attacks, the president offered a surprisingly detached observation to congressional liaison Nick Calio about the nation's impatience with intrusions into its daily affairs. Calio shared that exchange in his oral history:

> At one point I asked him how he was doing. He said, "I'm good, I'm ready. You need to be ready; we all need to be ready." He told us all, "We're at war. It's a different kind of war. In three weeks, or four weeks, or six weeks, rest assured, people are going to want to forget about this. They're going to watch the World Series; they're going to want to watch football games. They're not going to want to think about this. We're go-

ing to have to stay on it. We're going to have to keep harping on it and we're going to have to watch because our number-one job is to make the United States and its citizens secure."

Not long thereafter, Bush publicly encouraged people to go back to their normal activities as soon as possible. That he would use the bully pulpit to urge Americans to go shopping or visit Disney World made him a target for ridicule, especially among those who thought greater public sacrifice was in order. But Bush's underlying argument was that resuming enjoyable, even mundane activities would combat the "atmosphere of fear" the terrorists intended to create.[63]

By late 2006, Americans had reestablished most of their normal routines—going to amusement parks and watching the World Series and the Super Bowl without incident. Moreover, although the cost in public treasure and human sacrifice in Iraq was high, the immediate burdens were felt by a relatively small portion of the population. There was no military draft, for example, to spread those costs around.

The sum of these developments, then, might reasonably have led some voters to believe that the global war on terror had been won—especially since the long-feared second attack never happened. With popular worries successfully assuaged through the effective use of presidential powers enhanced for precisely this purpose, they may have judged that it was time to return to constitutional normalcy.

There is, of course, a contrary interpretation, one that seems more broadly consistent with the available polling data. The magnitude of President Bush's failures—especially in Iraq—had convinced voters that he was no longer a reliable steward of the extraordinary powers entrusted to him. The midterm election was thus condign punishment for the accumulated failures of his empowered presidency. During his years in the White House, Bush often quoted to his staff the wisdom of St. Luke: "To whom much is given, much shall be required."[64] He understood that with greater empowerment came heightened expectations for the use of that power—and more severe judgment for its failure or misuse.

Between his reelection in 2004 and the midterm rebuke, Bush's standing with the American people collapsed. His job approval ratings routinely hovered in the 30s in the months before the 2006 election.[65] Exit polls from 2006 reveal that 57 percent of voters disapproved of Bush's job performance, 41 percent strongly so[66]—despite the fact that unemployment was only

4.5 percent. And a historically high 36 percent of voters claimed that opposition to Bush was a motivating factor in their choices for Congress.[67] Moreover, by November 2006, only 41 percent of Americans thought the nation was generally on the right track, down from 59 percent at the time of Bush's first midterm in 2002. (On the day in 2008 that Barack Obama was elected to succeed Bush, that right-track number had cratered to 21 percent.)

Several specific events contributed to Americans' accumulating dissatisfaction. In August 2005 Hurricane Katrina made a devastating direct hit on New Orleans. Although the administration later asserted that much of the blame for the poor governmental response rested on ill-prepared state and local officials, the president suffered public censure—an outcome the White House partly invited when it decided to publish a photo of Bush looking down on the devastated region from the safety of Air Force One. Then the president agitated his conservative base with a quickly reversed Supreme Court nomination for fellow Texan Harriet Miers, somebody the proprietary Federalist Society viewed with suspicion on the grounds that she was not known to be doctrinally sound.[68] Vice-presidential aide Lewis Libby was subsequently indicted for perjury and obstruction of justice in an arcane cloak-and-dagger effort to punish an intelligence agent who was thought to be feeding damaging information about WMD to the press. Then the *Washington Post* published reports of detainees being held at black-site prisons. This array of problems only punctuated the flow of bad news out of Iraq.[69]

Taken together, these events were debilitating, bringing an unprecedented end to a wartime leadership regime. Presidential empowerment was terminated before the shooting stopped. They also set the stage for the most unusual episode of emergency government in the history of the republic: the financial crisis of 2008, which threatened to destroy the very foundations of the global economy. As such, it was precisely the kind of peril that normally would have precipitated a crisis government under presidential direction, along the lines of FDR's first New Deal. Bush's discredited wartime leadership, however, precluded that option and left him in a compromised position to direct the nation's response. What arose instead was a heterogeneous improvisation.

The main source of national leadership in dealing with the economic emergency was an unelected troika of financial bureaucrats: treasury secretary Henry Paulson; Federal Reserve chairman Benjamin Bernanke; and Timothy Geithner, president of the Federal Reserve Bank of New York. For most of 2008 they handled the crisis on a daily basis and made the most consequential decisions to stave off catastrophe. White House chief of staff Josh Bolten recalls, "We didn't view them, and they certainly didn't view themselves, as subject to the direction of the President." Indeed, they exploited an astonishing array of independent legal authorities that gave them life-or-death influence over vast portions of the private-sector economy, in some cases using regulatory powers that exceeded the president's. In effect, they were running—at least insofar as the economy was concerned—a supercharged experiment in emergency cabinet government. For much of the year, the locus of the American response shifted away from the Oval Office to the Treasury Building and even, for a time, to Federal Reserve headquarters in Manhattan. That fall, emergency teams were convened on weekends—when the financial markets were closed—to invent ways to save the economy before business reopened on Monday.

In March 2008, using creative interpretations of its authority, this group put $30 billion of US taxpayer money at risk to help save the Bear Stearns investment firm. When housing finance giants Fannie Mae and Freddie Mac started swaying in July, the group sought from Congress what Paulson called "an unlimited blank check" to stabilize them.[70] The resulting Housing and Economic Recovery Act (HERA) "was perhaps the most expansive power to commit funds ever given to a Treasury secretary." Using a provision of the Federal Reserve Act that permitted extraordinary action under "unusual and exigent circumstances," the group made an $85 billion bridge loan to insurance giant AIG (American International Group), prompting Sen. Harry Reid (D-NV) to observe that "Congress has not given you formal approval to take action. This is your responsibility and your decision" alone. And in September, when a full economic meltdown seemed possible because of a freeze in credit markets, their response was the Troubled Asset Relief Program (TARP)—a $780 billion plan originally presented to Congress as a three-page bill promoting maximum discretion and including no provision for judicial review. The Republican nominee to succeed Bush, Sen. John McCain (R-AZ), publicly objected that the plan "gives a single individual the unprecedented power to spend one trillion—one trillion—dollars without any meaningful accountability. Never before in the history of our nation has so much power and money been concentrated in the hands of one person." He was referring not to the president but to Paulson. Although Congress subsequently added an elaborate set of constraints to the package, the bill still placed an enormous sum of money at the disposal of the Treasury Department to use at its discretion.[71]

Where was *presidential* leadership in this emergency? Although Bush appointed many of the officials responsible for crisis management, he then, as Robert F. Bruner describes in chapter 9, "extensively delegated decisions about policy implementation." Indeed, according to Josh Bolten, Bush appointed Paulson to head Treasury largely because Bolten (who had known Paulson at Goldman Sachs) sensed that a financial crisis was overdue. Clay Johnson, the president's personnel chief, remarks, "If you had 10 years of hindsight to think about who would have been perfect to have in there [for this crisis], . . . those three people . . . were the best you could imagine." Bush then monitored their activities—mainly through direct reports by Paulson—and provided them with moral support and, where he could, political support at key moments.[72] Undoubtedly the president deserves credit for assembling an expert team seemingly constructed with this kind of crisis in mind and for giving it the latitude to work. Yet this does not amount to a vigorous exercise of presidential leadership. His acts were more nearly the doings of a prime minister.[73]

What is striking in reading close accounts of the financial crisis is the extent to which Bush was reduced to what Richard Neustadt identifies as a presidential "clerk": an enabler of others' activities.[74] At one critical moment in congressional negotiations, Bush announced his decision rule for the crisis: "If Hank Paulson and Ben Bernanke say it's going to work and help stabilize the financial system, we are for it."[75] He deferred to them "99 times out of 100," National Economic Council director Keith Hennessey recalls in his oral history.[76] And Bush's direct contributions to their decision making was minimal. He was persistently presented with faits accomplis by his team—"a gun to his head," in the memorable words of counselor Edward Gillespie— and dutifully signed off on them, with the whole economic system at risk.

Bush's compromised public standing left him with little leverage over Congress, a dangerous situation in a national emergency. Paulson's claim about the congressional reaction to fixing Fannie Mae and Freddie Mac is representative of the entire year: "the response ranged . . . from skeptical to hostile." Later, at a critical moment in discussions about TARP, the president told Paulson, "Maybe I can help with the House Republicans," a remarkable confession of uncertainty about his own party. As it happened, even this was an overly optimistic assessment. Josh Bolten recalls that the White House economic team was booed when it spoke before the House Republican conference. And when the TARP bill first came up for a House vote, it lost, mainly because two-thirds of the president's own party rejected it. That vote was later reversed, but only after the markets tanked again and the Senate voted overwhelmingly in favor.[77] Still, Karl Rove says, "At the end of the day we would not have passed this had [Bush] not been able to take some members . . . and convince them," relying on a personal form of retail politics built on an eight-year relationship.[78]

Emblematic of the president's role in the crisis was a hastily convened White House meeting in late September—called not by the president or anyone in his administration but by John McCain. The Republican nominee for president had announced that he was leaving the campaign trail to focus on a solution to the financial crisis. Without outlining a plan, he asked the president to host the meeting. Nobody in the White House thought this was a good idea. But, Paulson said, "the president felt he had no choice but to accommodate him." The meeting was by all accounts a fiasco. Looking back, Bolten called it "probably the worst meeting I've ever been in as a senior government official." The president followed protocol and asked the Democratic congressional leadership to open the discussion. They deferred to their party's presidential nominee, Sen. Barack Obama, who said the Democrats were willing to act boldly. McCain deferred to his party's congressional leaders, and in the absence of an agreed-on approach, the meeting quickly devolved into a chaotic shouting match. When it became evident that nothing productive would be accomplished, Bush abruptly dismissed himself: "Well, I've clearly lost control of the meeting. It's over." In a fitting coda, Paulson tracked Speaker of the House Nancy Pelosi into a neighboring room and theatrically dropped to his knees, pleading with her not to let this ill-advised intervention by McCain and the White House ruin their chances of success.[79]

What might have happened had the nation followed a more conventional course of presidential leadership in response to what was by any measure a system-threatening crisis? The skilled team President Bush assembled still would have been on the job, expertly handling the daily response. But the primary center of activity would have been in the White House—most likely in the Oval Office itself. Had the president not been distracted by the quagmire in Iraq, he might have found it possible to devote his full attention—and political capital—to early signs of trouble, perhaps even sufficient to take some effective preemptive action. Admittedly, this is highly speculative.[80] Less so is the observation that, had Bush not been mired in an Iraq-induced political trough, the financial emergency would have boosted his public support to crisis-induced heights. The absence of that rallying effect in this instance had profound implications. Bush lacked the stature to do anything other than let his administrators manage their way through the crisis.

Any full accounting of the opportunity costs of the Iraq intervention must therefore include its adverse effects on the execution of national leadership as the economy collapsed in 2008. And those costs may have been more extensive than they appeared at first glance. The enfeeblement of the presidency in 2008 affected not just the technical application of government powers to preserve the economy or the president's ability to move Congress. It also undermined the president's ability to construct a national narrative about what was at issue in that emergency.

Crisis-empowered presidents are uniquely situated to define for the American people what their historic moment is about. The Civil War evolved into a fight against slavery because of what Lincoln eventually did and *said*. The nation's reaction to the Great Depression was shaped as much by the power of Franklin Roosevelt's words as by his deeds. In contrast, the politically weakened George W. Bush did not have the nation's confidence, nor its ear, at the end of his presidency. Consequently, the cultural meaning of the financial crisis—that is, the definition of its origins and how the nation ought to conceptualize, organize, and remember the response—was left to others, as nature abhors a vacuum.

One dimension of Bush's response illuminates this point. Throughout 2008 and into 2009, the troika fended off persistent recommendations by angry constituencies that the president force a reckoning with those in the housing and financial markets whose greed or bad judgment had wrecked the economy while leaving them fabulously wealthy. Timothy Geithner frequently counseled in those days against exacting what he called "Old Testament justice." Even righteous anger, he argued, was counterproductive when the economy desperately needed both stability and the assistance of people with the expertise to manipulate the arcane levers of the financial markets to right them. Accordingly, when some wanted to impose limits on executive compensation as a condition for providing federal bailout money, the troika objected that such limits would impair their efforts to get maximum cooperation from the people they needed to turn the markets around.

As an economic matter, this counsel may have made perfect sense. But it was politically toxic. Although George W. Bush was a commerce-friendly

Republican whose first career had been as an oilman, his blood boiled over the excesses and irresponsibility of those who had helped break the financial markets. "He was mad," observes Ed Gillespie. "He has always had a strong populist streak; he doesn't trust the bankers. He thinks the credit default swaps and these instruments that got set up were all suspect and half illusory and . . . he was mad at the notion of having to bail these guys out." Yet the president stifled the urge to exact retribution or point fingers of blame, assured by his team that this would undermine their ability to restore confidence, their top priority. He felt powerless to do otherwise.

If Bush had been operating from the commanding heights of a crisis-empowered presidency, it would have been easy to see an alternative way. As with Richard Nixon's opening to China, Bush's established history as a free-market Republican probably would have given him the stature to take aggressive action toward those who had engaged in financial excess without being seen as either too hard on the bankers or too intrusive in the markets. At a minimum, an empowered Bush would have been able to shape popular perceptions of the governmental response with his rhetoric (or other symbolic action); he would have been able to explain in a convincing way why Old Testament justice, while warranted, had to be deferred in the interest of recovery. In this scenario, those who felt abused by the financiers would have known that their president was equally offended and was committed, at the proper time, to balancing the scales. Their grievances would have been fully acknowledged.

Instead, the opposite happened. A diminished Bush muddled through. His relative silence fueled criticism that his government was interested only in advantaging the financial interests that had torpedoed the system in the first place. His successor, who did not have the benefit of Bush's market bona fides and who inherited the presidency in a diminished state (and elevated Geithner to secretary of the treasury), felt compelled to stay the course. He, too, was advised to commit to stabilizing an economy that was hemorrhaging jobs as he took office—to avoid Old Testament justice.[81] This he did.[82] Small wonder, then, that loud political movements on both the extreme right (the Tea Party) and the extreme left (Occupy Wall Street) soon arose, energized by Americans with jaded and charged views of what their presidents—clerks rather than champions—had done to meet the crisis. Their punitive narratives filled the void. And, by some persuasive accounts, it was this complex of grievances directed at both parties that lifted Donald Trump to power in 2016.[83] When George W. Bush chose to go into

Iraq fourteen years earlier—based on evidence we may not see in full for a very long time—he surely did not foresee *this* among the opportunity costs.

Notes

1. Emily Yahr, "The Downward Spiral of Ellen DeGeneres's Public Persona: A Complete Guide," *Washington Post*, August 3, 2020, https://www.washingtonpost.com/arts -entertainment/2020/08/03/ellen-degeneres-show-reputation/.

2. See the Bush library website: https://www.bushcenter.org/plan-your-visit/conduct -research.html#:~:text=214)%20346%2D1557The%20George%20W.,records%200f%20 any%20presidential%20library.

3. Robert Caro, "Turn Every Page," *New Yorker*, January 28, 2019, https://www.newy orker.com/magazine/2019/01/28/the-secrets-of-lyndon-johnsons-archives.

4. Political scientist Paul Musgrave has calculated that the backlog of Freedom of Information Act (FOIA) requests alone at the Bush library constitutes 240 years of work, based on NARA's reporting. See Paul Musgrave, "Trump's Presidential Library Will Be a Shrine to His Ego," *Washington Post*, November 18, 2020, https://www.washingtonpost .com/outlook/trump-presidential-library-narrative/2020/11/17/fcd27b9e-1edd-11eb -ba21-f2f001f0554b_story.html; NARA memorandum to David Ferriero, archivist of the United States, from Gary M. Stern, general counsel, on "Reducing FOIA Backlogs and Improving FOIA Management Oversight at NARA," July 18, 2019, 14, https://www .archives.gov/files/foia/images/foia-management-oversight-and-backlog-reduction.pdf.

5. White House visitors, for example, are usually asked for their Social Security numbers to allow a security check, and these sometimes show up on internal paperwork.

6. Researchers can make use of the FOIA to request specific files, but anyone entering this portal must be prepared to wait years to have requests acted on—and may find significant redactions when they finally receive the documents. By law, FOIA requests have to be given priority treatment, so in practice, NARA staff spends all its time complying with these requests rather than working in a rational, systematic way to maximize the release of presidential records. For example, NARA staff is inundated by FOIA requests from UFO enthusiasts seeking any unpublished government revelations about extraterrestrials.

7. Walter Benjamin, "The Storyteller: Reflections on the Works of Nikolai Leskov," [1936], in *Illuminations* (New York: Harcourt Brace Jovanovich, 1968).

8. All direct quotes or citations in this chapter not otherwise identified by source are drawn from interviews conducted for the George W. Bush Oral History Project. All open transcripts can be found at https://millercenter.org/the-presidency/presidential -oral-histories/george-w-bush. In this case, Townsend is the source about Rice, as Rice's own interview has not yet been released.

9. Barack Obama's speechwriter Ben Rhodes affirms this point in "The 9/11 Era Is Over," *Atlantic*, April 6, 2020. Rhodes reports that he saw a sign declaring "Every day is September 12" hanging in CIA headquarters when he was getting oriented at the beginning of the Obama years.

10. For this scenario, see https://www.youtube.com/watch?v=-Xs111uH9ss.

11. Alfred Hitchcock was an early advocate of the use of spoiler alerts and controlled access to theaters where his films were showing.

12. This public ignorance is worthy of exploration as an instance of ineffective national leadership—or Americans' resistance to living in a security state without a clear and present danger. On Bill Clinton's watch, for example, there were two incidents of domestic terrorism that might have lodged in the popular consciousness as ill portents: a prior, often forgotten, attack by Middle Eastern radicals on the World Trade Center in 1993, killing six and wounding over one thousand; and the destruction of the Alfred P. Murrah Federal Office Building in Oklahoma City in April 1995, the result of a truck bomb set off by domestic terrorists, killing 168. These events—as well as mounting intelligence about threats from abroad—had convinced some key Washington policymakers that more was to come, however vague the nature of the threat. But there was little public anxiety about the prospect of terrorism. See https://www.state.gov/1993-world-trade-center-bombing/; https://www.fbi.gov/history/famous-cases/oklahoma-city-bombing.

13. One of the great historical questions of the forty-third presidency is how seriously the new administration took the threat of foreign terrorism before September 11. A final verdict will be a long time coming because of the slow release of relevant documents. But the work of the 9/11 Commission provided a preliminary conclusion: there was a lack of imagination among the newcomers about the character of the threat. See *The 9/11 Commission Report: Final Report of the National Commission on Terrorist Attacks upon the United States: Authorized Edition* (New York: W. W. Norton, 2004).

14. The Gallup organization has a helpful web page devoted to this subject under the general heading "Terrorism" at https://news.gallup.com/poll/4909/terrorism-united-states.aspx. The print version runs forty-five pages, mainly focused on the period after 2001.

15. Peter Baker, "A Preordained Coda to a Presidency," *New York Times*, January 14, 2021, https://www.nytimes.com/2021/01/13/us/politics/donald-j-trump-impeachment-second-time.html?action=click&module=Spotlight&pgtype=Homepage.

16. All involved with this project are acutely aware of the limitations of oral history as a form of historical documentation. For an extended discussion, see Russell L. Riley, "The White House as a Black Box: Oral History and the Problem of Evidence in Presidential Studies," *Political Studies* 57 (2009): 187–206.

17. Lecture notes from Richard E. Neustadt, "The American Presidency," Government 1540, Harvard University, December 18, 1984.

18. Quoted in Rachel Poser, "He Wants to Save Classics from Whiteness: Can the Field Survive?" *New York Times Magazine*, February 2, 2021, https://www.nytimes.com/2021/02/02/magazine/classics-greece-rome-whiteness.html.

19. I reluctantly employ the term *regime* here because, in presidential studies, it is almost exclusively associated with the designs in Stephen Skowronek's *The Politics Presidents Make: Leadership from John Adams to Bill Clinton* (Cambridge, MA: Belknap, 1997). Most fundamentally, Skowronek uses the term in a generic sense. But the book develops a highly stylized rubric, asserting repetitive historical patterns of regime change and leadership behavior, that has become broadly accepted as definitive in describing the evolution of the presidency. I employ the term here without invoking all that Skowronek

attaches to it. A brief critique appears in Russell L. Riley, *The Presidency and the Politics of Racial Inequality: Nation-keeping from 1831 to 1965* (New York: Columbia University Press, 1999), 19–21. See also James Sterling Young, "Power and Purpose in 'The Politics Presidents Make,'" *Polity* 27, 3 (Spring 1995): 509–516.

20. Susan Page, "Bush's 'Love Letter' to Dad and Message to Jeb: Run," *USA Today*, November 10, 2014, https://www.usatoday.com/story/news/politics/2014/11/09/george-w-bush-book-about-his-dad/18720877/.

21. John Kenneth White, *Still Seeing Red: How the Cold War Shapes the New American Politics* (Boulder, CO: Westview Press, 1997).

22. Daniel Patrick Moynihan, "Dialogue: Next Step in the Gulf—It's Almost Midnight: Restraint, Mr. Bush," *New York Times*, January 15, 1991, A19.

23. These developments are discussed extensively in my own contributions to Michael Nelson and Barbara A. Perry, eds., *41: Inside the Presidency of George H. W. Bush* (Ithaca, NY: Cornell University Press, 2014), and Michael Nelson, Barbara A. Perry, and Russell L. Riley, eds., *42: Inside the Presidency of Bill Clinton* (Ithaca, NY: Cornell University Press, 2016).

24. I date the culmination of those post–Cold War contractions of presidential power to November 3, 1998, when Bill Clinton's Democrats gained seats in the House, the first time an incumbent president's party had done so in a midterm election since 1934. The Republicans overplayed their hand in impeaching Clinton for personal misbehavior, marking a bottoming out of presidential standing in this era. There is, however, a ratcheting effect in successive episodes of crisis government, with each leaving the president's power at a higher plateau than previous levels. On this theory, see Robert Higgs, *Crisis and Leviathan: Critical Episodes in the Growth of American Government* (New York: Oxford University Press, 1987).

25. Stevenson Swanson, "Governors' Powers Ranked," *Chicago Tribune*, September 2, 2001, https://www.chicagotribune.com/news/ct-xpm-2001-09-02-0109020193-story.html.

26. Paul Burka, "The Dominator," *Texas Monthly*, August 1999, https://www.texasmonthly.com/politics/the-dominator/.

27. See Janice May, "Texas Legislature," in *Texas State Historical Association: Handbook of Texas*, https://www.tshaonline.org/handbook/entries/texas-legislature.

28. Quoted in Ian Christopher McCaleb, "Bush, Now President-elect, Signals Will to Bridge Partisan Gaps," CNN.com, https://www.cnn.com/2000/ALLPOLITICS/stories/12/13/election.wrap/index.html.

29. This set of dual priorities was confirmed, ironically, by Philip Zelikow as a sign of President Bush's relative emphasis on domestic rather than international concerns.

30. "I am a person out of my time," Clinton claimed, according to Bob Woodward. Another close student of Clinton, David Maraniss, reported the same basic observation. Both are cited in Russell L. Riley, "The Limits of the Transformational Presidency," in *Presidential Power: Forging the Presidency for the Twenty-First Century*, ed. Robert Y. Shapiro, Martha Joynt Kumar, and Lawrence W. Jacobs (New York: Columbia University Press, 2000), 447.

31. John Dickerson, "Build Back Boring," *Atlantic*, January 20, 2021, https://www.theatlantic.com/ideas/archive/2021/01/biden-should-build-back-boring/617740/.

32. Susan Martinuk, "Good Words Should Come from Within, Not from a Rule Book," *Vancouver Province*, October 3, 2001, A28. Among the celebrities committed to the effort were Tom Cruise and Bette Midler. See also Jennifer Harper, "Celebs Sign on with Talk-Nice Effort," *Washington Times*, September 5, 2001, A3.

33. Scott Richardson, "National Campaign Tries to Get People to Be Nicer," *[Bloomington, IN] Pantagraph*, September 5, 2001, A1.

34. Zelikow, however, claimed this was true of both the Clinton and the Bush presidencies. Some senior Clinton officials have objected to this characterization, including national security adviser Sandy Berger: "I said to Condi [Rice] during the transition . . . that the number one issue that she would deal with as National Security Advisor was terrorism in general and al-Qaida specifically. The President said to President Bush during their meeting that there were five priorities, in his judgment. The first one was terrorism." Sandy Berger interview, March 24–25, 2005, William J. Clinton Presidential History Project, Miller Center, University of Virginia. Then–deputy national security adviser Stephen Hadley effectively confirms that Berger identified terrorism as his own most important priority.

35. Clarke's fate as White House counterterrorism czar—in effect, demoted by the new administration—has fueled perceptions that there was a significant diminution of interest in the issue under Bush. Zelikow disagreed, explaining at length (both in his interview and in the *9/11 Commission Report*) the origins of Clarke's idiosyncratic standing in the national security apparatus under Clinton and how Bush's decision not to indulge that arrangement was mainly a commitment to a more orderly policymaking process—not a sign that terrorism was less important. Indeed, the fact that the Bush administration retained the prickly, famously independent Clarke can be read as an indication of its desire to get counterterrorism right. The *9/11 Commission Report* thus observed "significant continuity in counterterrorism policy" from one administration to the next (200).

36. Bellinger's account of this process is echoed with remarkable consistency by Stephen Hadley's oral history. Hadley held that Clarke's thinking was too tactical and thus needed to be embedded in a more strategic approach to the region. Clarke evidently chafed at the pace of that deliberative review, fearing an immediate threat.

37. French Constitution, https://www.constituteproject.org/constitution/France_2008. This version, commonly referred to as the Fifth Republic, was enacted in 1958.

38. Clinton Rossiter, *Constitutional Dictatorship: Crisis Government in the Modern Democracies* (1963; reprint, New Brunswick, NJ: Transaction Publishers, 2002). Signaling how unimportant this general topic had become before 9/11, Rossiter's book had gone out of print—but was republished soon thereafter.

39. At issue here is not simply a so-called rallying event, although such events have probably sparked the beginning of some emergency regimes: the secession crisis for Lincoln, the resumption of unrestricted U-boat warfare for Wilson, and Pearl Harbor for FDR. But what makes these cases distinctive—and separates them from dozens of others, including the *Sputnik* launch or the Bay of Pigs invasion—was the emergence of a *protracted* exercise in presidential leadership, with the conventional norms of checks and balances substantially suspended for the duration. These are more profound changes than the momentary imbalance created during a rallying event, however one defines

it. For an early analysis of this question and how the forty-third presidency fit into the existing literature, see Marc J. Hetherington and Michael Nelson, "Anatomy of a Rally Effect: George W. Bush and the War on Terrorism," *PS: Political Science and Politics* 36, 1 (January 2003): 37–42, https://www.jstor.org/stable/pdf/3649343.pdf?refreqid=excels ior%3A89bad47aa6d9241dae79212b53c0e7d3.

40. The divisions that produced civil war in 1861 were more severe, of course, but the departure of the rebellious states meant that Lincoln no longer had to deal with their disruptive representatives in Washington. They had literally abandoned the field. This simplified Lincoln's immediate governing environment during the war.

41. For an example of Carson's character, see https://www.youtube.com/watch?v =AOKofZe_FWg.

42. Peter Baker, *Days of Fire: Bush and Cheney in the White House* (New York: Doubleday, 2013), 168.

43. The sniper shootings were unrelated to the earlier terrorist attacks, but that was unknown until the domestic perpetrators were caught after weeks of nerve-racking disruption in the lives of capital region residents.

44. Gallup poll, https://news.gallup.com/poll/116500/presidential-approval-ratings -george-bush.aspx.

45. See Michael S. Rocca, "9/11 and Presidential Support in the 107th Congress," *Congress & the Presidency* 36, 3 (2009): 272–296. There were three defeats by huge margins on bills related to victims of terrorism, the arming of pilots, and military retiree benefits. There was also a narrow loss on the bill establishing the 9/11 Commission.

46. In subsequent years, Rossiter confessed that the rhetorical force of his title overwhelmed the nuances of his argument in the American context. See his "Preface to the 1963 Edition" in the 2002 reprint of *Constitutional Dictatorship.* There, Rossiter claims that, in retrospect, he should have used the subtitle alone.

47. Legislative independence remains most pronounced on matters not directly related to the emergency response. For example, in the weeks after 9/11, Congress refused to follow President Bush's lead on the 2001 farm bill. There was a modest effort by the Office of Management and Budget to tie this legislation to the crisis of the moment, but it was unsuccessful. This is typical of what Rossiter has to say about constitutional dictatorships in the American model. Thus, when David Hobbs observed that the "spirit of comity" lasted only "a good month or so," that is not inconsistent with conventional wartime practice and may, in retrospect, be an observation influenced by the severity of the reaction to Bush's later problems.

48. The other two were also historically notable elections: 1934, in the middle of the New Deal, and 1998, as Bill Clinton's impeachment unfolded.

49. See https://www.presidency.ucsb.edu/statistics/data/presidential-vetoes.

50. The best example of this flexing of presidential muscle came in the promiscuous use of signing statements.

51. See Charlie Savage, *Takeover: The Return of the Imperial Presidency and the Subversion of American Democracy* (New York: Little, Brown, 2007).

52. William Barr interview, April 5, 2001, George H. W. Bush Oral History Project, Miller Center, University of Virginia.

53. There were other rationales, including Saddam's failure to comply with multiple United Nations resolutions. In fact, some in Bush's orbit claimed his big mistake was not emphasizing that issue rather than WMD.

54. That meeting is described in detail in Bob Woodward, *Bush at War* (New York: Simon & Schuster, 2002), 72–92.

55. It is worth noting that, at the time of the election, Americans who supported the decision to send troops to Iraq outnumbered those who thought it was a mistake. See Gallup poll, https://news.gallup.com/poll/1633/iraq.aspx.

56. The first major news account attributing the "long war" terminology to a senior administration official was a profile of Central Command (CENTCOM) commander John Abizaid in David Ignatius, "Bound for the Future: Achieving Real Victory Could Take Decades," *Washington Post*, December 26, 2004. In some quarters, it was replacing "global war on terror."

57. The injury was compounded by a Democratic gain of six governors' seats in thirty-eight contested races.

58. The 1918 midterm election actually preceded the armistice ending World War I by six days. By Election Day, however, the end of the conflict was assured, and Wilson had explicitly nationalized the election beforehand, asking voters in October to enable him to rule in peacetime as he had during the war. He miscalculated badly.

59. The Congress elected in 1866 impeached Andrew Johnson. The "Watergate babies" Congress of 1974 was famously reformist in reasserting congressional equality after the excesses of earlier "imperial presidents."

60. See Russell L. Riley, "American Regicide: Postwar Presidents and the Bitter Politics of Returning to Normalcy," in *The Presidency: Facing Constitutional Crossroads*, ed. Michael Nelson and Barbara A. Perry (Charlottesville: University of Virginia Press, 2021).

61. These accelerating difficulties led to Bush's internal review of Iraq, which ultimately generated the troop surge the following year.

62. For an early attempt to deal with this question, see Russell L. Riley, "Divided We Stand," *Politico*, January 30, 2007. Of course, it is possible that this election was another of the outliers, unrelated to war and empowerment.

63. "At O'Hare, President Says 'Get on Board,'" remarks by the president to airline employees, O'Hare International Airport, Chicago, September 27, 2001, https://georgewbush-whitehouse.archives.gov/news/releases/2001/09/20010927-1.html. See also Peter Feaver, "Now I Remember Why President Bush Urged People to Go about Their Daily Lives," *Foreign Policy*, April 17, 2013, https://foreignpolicy.com/2013/04/17/now-i-remember-why-president-bush-urged-people-to-go-about-their-daily-lives/; George W. Bush, *Decision Points* (New York: Crown, 2010), 444.

64. This specific language is from the Revised Geneva Translation of the Bible. Josh Bolten jokingly said the president quoted it "three hundred times." The verse was also cited in Mark Dybul's interview.

65. Gallup poll, https://news.gallup.com/poll/116500/presidential-approval-ratings-george-bush.aspx.

66. Exits polls are not easy to use for comparative purposes because the questions tend to change from election to election. For example, voters in 2002, 2004, and 2008

were asked how worried they were about another major terrorist attack—but not, for some reason, in 2006. So that information, which would be relevant to this discussion, is missing. For the 2006 results, see https://ropercenter.cornell.edu/ipoll/study/31093360.

67. In 1990 exit pollsters began asking whether midterm votes were motivated by opposition to the incumbent president. The results: 1990 (G. H. W. Bush), 15 percent responded affirmatively; 1994 (Clinton), 28 percent; 1998 (Clinton), 20 percent; 2002 (G. W. Bush), 18 percent; 2006 (Bush), 36 percent; 2010 (Obama), 31 percent; 2014 (Obama), 33 percent. Bush's 2006 number was finally exceeded in the 2018 midterm elections, with 37 percent reporting that their congressional votes reflected opposition to President Donald Trump.

68. Michael Chertoff's oral history is especially illuminating about Hurricane Katrina. And Harriet Miers's interview provides inside details about her failed Supreme Court nomination.

69. Josh Bolten says the 2006 election was the product of multiple forces, with Iraq being "by far the largest thing."

70. The following account of the financial crisis is largely based on Henry M. Paulson Jr., *On the Brink: Inside the Race to Stop the Collapse of the Global Financial System* (New York: Business Plus, 2010). This is by far the most detailed report of the internal workings of the government's response. Bush's own account in *Decision Points* tellingly includes few instances in which he was proactive. And neither Geithner nor Bernanke places Bush at the center of the story. In his oral history, Josh Bolten makes special note of the veracity and comprehensiveness of Paulson's reporting on the crisis. Paulson's oral history was opened after publication deadlines for this book closed.

71. Paulson, *On the Brink*, 153, 155, 266, 279.

72. On at least one occasion, the president broadcast a speech to the nation urging Congress to adopt the emergency plan his people had devised.

73. See Michael Nelson's observation on this same point in Keith Hennessey's oral history interview.

74. Richard Neustadt, *Presidential Power and the Modern Presidents: The Politics of Leadership from Roosevelt to Reagan* (New York: Free Press, 1990), 7.

75. Paulson, *On the Brink*, 296.

76. Hennessey adds that, as a matter of principle, the president did not wish to get involved in narrow financial decisions because it meant selecting winners and losers among specific firms.

77. Paulson, *On the Brink*, 150, 295.

78. Hennessey and Paulson both credit Josh Bolten with doing much of the key legwork to reverse the TARP vote. But Hennessey also repeatedly emphasizes the importance of the markets crashing after the first vote failed.

79. Paulson, *On the Brink*, 288, 296–299.

80. Hennessey addresses this question in his oral history, noting the standard criticism that the administration should have moved to a TARP-style response much earlier. He says, "There was not a snowball's chance in hell that we could have gotten Congress to agree to it" in May or June. That might not have been the case had the president been operating in a more conventional crisis empowerment mode.

81. President Obama was a bit more vocal than his predecessor in criticizing execu-

tive compensation packages, but Geithner reports in his memoir that Obama "once told me that he felt uncomfortable playing a populist, like he was wearing clothes that didn't fit. He wasn't going to be a convincing Teddy Roosevelt lambasting the 'malefactors of great wealth.'" Timothy Geithner, *Stress Test: Reflections on Financial Crises* (New York: Broadway Books, 2014), 330.

82. For a thorough critique of the new administration's response to the financial crisis, see Reed Hundt, *A Crisis Wasted: Barack Obama's Defining Decisions* (New York: Rosetta Books, 2019).

83. Pew Research Center, "Trump's Staunch GOP Supporters Have Roots in the Tea Party," May 2019, https://pewresearch.org/politics/2019/05/16/trumps-staunch-gop-supporters-have-roots-in-the-tea-party/; Jeremy W. Peters, "The Tea Party Didn't Get What It Wanted, but It Did Unleash the Politics of Anger," *New York Times*, August 28, 2019, https://www.nytimes.com/2019/08/28/us/politics/tea-party-trump.html.

CHAPTER ONE

George W. Bush's Elections: 2000, 2002, 2004, 2006, and 2008

Michael Nelson

Commentators on twenty-first-century presidential elections often note that they include two of the five contests in American history in which the candidate who received the most popular votes was defeated in the Electoral College. George W. Bush's victory over Al Gore in 2000 was one of those two elections. Observers also note that as of 2020, the Republican nominee won more popular votes than his Democratic opponent in only one election since then. Bush's reelection in 2004 was that one election.

Taking an even broader historical perspective, students of American political parties and elections have made much of the fact that no long-lasting partisan realignment—such as those that made the Republicans the nation's majority party starting in the 1890s and the Democrats the majority party starting in the 1930s—has occurred in nearly a century. Of the six presidential elections in the period from 2000 to 2020, Democrats and Republicans each won three. Democrats controlled Congress for four years during this period, Republicans for eight and a half years, and control was divided between the parties—one with a majority in the House of Representatives and the other with a majority in the Senate—for the remaining seven and a half years.

Arguably, Bush's election and reelection constitute the century's most serious effort to bring about a partisan realignment. Indeed, despite losing the 1992 and 1996 elections to Bill Clinton and seeing Clinton's Democratic Party actually gain seats in the 1998 midterm election, the Republican Party was on a steep upward course during the first three contests of Bush's presidential career: his election in 2000, his party's gains in the 2002 midterm, and his reelection in 2004.

This chapter explores the Bush-inspired Republican ascent, as well as the subsequent Bush-related Republican decline that followed on the heels of his reelection and became apparent in the 2006 midterm election and the 2008 presidential election. It draws extensively on the Miller Center's George W. Bush Oral History, the Center for Presidential History's Elections of 2004 oral history, and multiple published accounts.

2000: Bush v. Gore becomes *Bush v. Gore*

Although the Democrats dominated Congress from the 1930s to the 1980s, they lost control of the presidency to the Republicans in the late 1960s. Starting in 1968, the GOP won five of six presidential elections, four of them by landslides. Bush's father, George H. W. Bush, won the last of these in 1988 with a popular vote majority of 53.4 percent to 45.6 percent and an electoral vote majority of 426 to 111. At the start of the 1992 election year, pundits confidently predicted an easy reelection for the elder Bush, based in part on the prevailing "electoral lock" theory, which held that because of his party's recent victories, Bush could count on at least 300 electoral votes from states that had always (or nearly always) voted Republican in recent presidential elections.[1]

In 1992 Clinton found a way to pick the lock. Less dogmatically liberal than his party's defeated predecessors, Clinton ran as a "New Democrat" who tempered the Democrats' usual emphasis on opportunity with a corresponding demand for responsibility. Carrying recent Republican strongholds such as California, Georgia, and Ohio, he defeated Bush handily and was reelected even more impressively in 1996, beating Senate Republican leader Bob Dole. Despite his frustrations with Congress, which went Republican in 1994 and impeached (but did not remove) him in 1998, Clinton left office after two terms with a job approval rating of 66 percent, the highest ever recorded for an outgoing president.

Like eight of the nine most recent vice presidents who sought their party's presidential nomination, Clinton's vice president, Al Gore, won the Democratic nod in 2000. Along with the growing prominence and influence of the office, the Twenty-Second Amendment offered an edge to Gore and other recent vice presidents by imposing a two-term limit on presidents starting in 1951. The two-term limit made it possible for the vice president to step forward as a candidate early in the president's second term rather than waiting in the wings until the president decided what he wanted to do.[2] Gore took advantage of the opportunity, and with ample funds, a strong organization, and Clinton's clear (albeit condescending) endorsement of Gore as "the next best thing" to himself, he fended off a primary challenge from Sen. Bill Bradley of New Jersey and wrapped up the nomination in early March.[3] Political scientists who forecast the outcome of presidential elections based on models of economic growth and presidential approval unanimously predicted that Gore would win the general election by a popular vote margin of anywhere from 6 to 20 percent.[4]

But vice presidents who win their party's presidential nomination carry burdens into the general election that are as surely grounded in their office as the advantages they derive. Years spent fertilizing the party's grass roots with fervent campaign rhetoric that rallies fellow partisans may alienate voters who look to the presidency for leadership that unifies rather than divides. The unfailing public loyalty a vice president must display toward the president—in Gore's case, for the past eight years—can undermine the message that he is capable of providing the strong leadership people also look for in a president. Blurting to a postimpeachment rally of Democratic members of Congress that Clinton "will be regarded in the history books as one of our greatest presidents" doubtless raised the spirits of Gore's fellow Democrats, but it seemed wildly excessive to almost everyone else.[5] Election modelers in 2000 also overlooked the four-percentage-point "time for a change" penalty that voters usually impose on a nominee whose party has been in office for two consecutive terms.[6]

Like Gore's capture of the Democratic nomination, George W. Bush's march to the top of the Republican ticket in 2000 followed the modern script closely. Service as governor had recently become the other leading stepping-stone to a presidential nomination, supplanting the senatorial experience that had been politically valuable in the post–World War II era.[7] Starting with former Georgia governor Jimmy Carter in 1976 (the first Democrat to win the presidency after 1964), governors benefited from the nation's post-Vietnam, post-Watergate disillusionment with Washington, as well as from the value voters placed on governors' experience as chief executives.

Unlike Gore, who grew up in Washington as the son of a congressman-turned-senator and then served in the House, the Senate, and the vice presidency, Bush had no Washington experience—and little else to show for much of his life. "Bush's resumé begins at age forty-five," said civil rights leader Jesse Jackson. "Everything before that is just youthful indiscretion."[8]

By 1989 (at age forty-three), however, Bush had turned his life around and was part owner and managing partner of the Texas Rangers baseball team. Five years later, he was elected governor of Texas, unseating a popular Democratic incumbent, and then won a landslide reelection in 1998. Like nearly all Republicans, Bush was a conservative committed to cutting taxes and easing government regulation of business. But at the time, "there was a view of the Republicans as kind of harsh, serrated-edged, too antigovernment," recalls speechwriter Pete Wehner.[9] Bush's emphasis on education reform, juvenile justice, and faith-based social services enabled him to claim the label "compassionate conservative." According to chief campaign strategist Karl Rove:

> He talked about welfare as a system that kept people from achieving all that they could be in life [instead of] saying the problem is we've got too many people who are freeloading. . . . The same on education, where . . . Bush's attitude was that the system is failing you if you're Black, if you speak Spanish at home, and you're poor. . . . The same goes for juvenile justice reform. If you talk about crime and you're a Republican, you're a hard ass most of the time. . . . Instead he said, "We're at risk of losing a generation of young people and we can't afford, as a compassionate society, to do that."

"A lot of it is about love, in a way, even Christian love, coupled with a sense of accountability, but support," according to historian Philip Zelikow. And a lot of it "was a brand," says Republican political consultant Ed Gillespie, "given where we were with the Republican brand at the end of the '96 campaign, all about slashing spending and all that."

Governors who run for president find it easy to raise a great deal of money in their states, much of it from contractors that do business with the state government. Bush raised so much additional money for his nomination campaign from what Rove called "his Yale connections, his baseball work [as owner of the Texas Rangers], the oil patch, Texas, and then his father's connections" that he could eschew federal campaign funding and the spending ceiling that went with it.

The challenge for governors seeking the presidency is to demonstrate a mastery of national issues, both foreign and domestic. Bush worked to overcome this challenge during the spring and summer of 1999 by inviting small groups of respected members of the Washington policy community to Austin to engage him on national matters. "For the first six months of the campaign we ran George W. Bush University," says campaign policy director Josh Bolten. Policy advisers "would simultaneously be instructors for somebody who was relatively new to a lot of these issues, . . . formulators of both campaign and governing policy, and, very importantly, credentialers" who, upon their return to Washington, would tell their colleagues and the press that Bush was "a serious person." "He knew he was performing for them as much as they were performing for him," Bolten adds.

Bush's father paid a political price for abandoning his 1988 "no new taxes" campaign pledge, losing reelection four years later. From that loss, the younger Bush learned to run "a campaign that was designed for governing, not just for winning." In September 1999, for example, Bush gave a major address at the Citadel outlining his plan to transform the Cold War-designed military into one that was lighter and more mobile. When Stephen Hadley, one of Bush's defense advisers, said, "I think you have to stay at a pretty good level of generality" to avoid stirring controversy, Bush replied:

> Let me tell [you] how I think about elections. If I run for president of the United States and don't say anything about how I want to transform the Defense Department and I become president, and I then meet with the Joint Chiefs and say, "By the way, I want to transform how we do defense business in this country," they'll think, "Hmmm, this is this guy who may only be here for four years. He's got his opinions, but his opinions are his opinions and maybe as an institution we're going to be here long after he leaves office. . . . "
>
> On the other hand, if I make that a campaign issue, and I campaign across the land and say we need to transform how we do the business of defense, and I get elected president and I go to the Joint Chiefs and say, "I have a mandate from the American people to transform how we do defense," they're going to have . . . a different attitude toward what I ask. So I intend to campaign on the basis of what I'm going to do and I intend to do what I campaign on.

When the primaries began, Bush was able to pursue compassionate conservatism and defense reform without facing serious charges that he was diluting the party's ideology. After two terms out of power, most Republicans believed that the best path to regaining the White House ran through the center-right of the ideological spectrum rather than the hard right. In addition, all the leading contenders for the Republican nomination were moderate conservatives like Bush, including former secretary of labor Elizabeth Dole, former Tennessee governor Lamar Alexander, and Bush's main rival, Sen. John McCain of Arizona. Unlike the senior Bush's three bids for his party's nomination in 1980, 1988, and 1992, George W. Bush did not have to worry about securing his right flank.

Nonetheless, on February 1, 2000, Bush stumbled out of the gate in New Hampshire. He took the state for granted even though McCain campaigned there ardently as a political reformer. "We might have done 20 [town hall meetings]," recalls Bush's chief supporter in the state, Sen. Judd Gregg; "McCain probably did 100." And then the campaign "made a big mistake. They brought his father in and his father said, 'You have to help my boy,' and that really hurt, because he shouldn't have been running as 'my boy' [but] as an individual who had been a really good governor of Texas." Just as Bush derived advantages from being the son of a former president, he suffered disadvantages as well. "McCain was running against him as, 'This is just a kid; this is somebody who thinks he's owed it because his father was president.'"

As soon as the New Hampshire votes were tallied, Bush told his campaign staff that "this loss is on my shoulders, not yours," recalls Rove—the last thing staffers expect to hear from a defeated candidate. "He was absolutely calm," says press secretary Ari Fleischer—"no temper, no finger-pointing—and he said, 'We're going to pick ourselves up and go to South Carolina and we're going to win in South Carolina.'" Contrasting himself with McCain as "a reformer with results," Bush swept to victory in the February 19 South Carolina primary. After Bush won nine of thirteen contests on March 7, including those in California, New York, and Ohio, McCain withdrew his candidacy on March 9. Bradley ended his challenge to Gore on the same day after suffering a similar number of defeats. With eight months to go before the November election, the field was set.

Just as Bush derived both advantages and disadvantages from being the son of a former president, so did Gore—not from his real father (Albert Gore had been out of public life since 1970) but from his political "father," President Clinton. Gore's eight years as vice president in the Clinton administration were the basis of his successful campaign for the Democratic nomination, and politically, there was little reason to change course in the general election. The economy was booming, the world was largely at peace, and Clinton's job approval rating was high. The obvious strategy for Gore was to embrace the administration's record of accomplishment while asking voters to judge him on the basis of his own straitlaced character, not Clinton's rakish one. As Clinton himself told Gore, "Al, there's not a single person in the country who thinks you messed around with Monica Lewinsky."[10]

Instead, Gore ham-handedly distanced himself from both Clinton the president and Clinton the person. He told a prime-time television audience that Clinton's affair with Lewinsky was "inexcusable."[11] He chose as his vice-presidential running mate Sen. Joseph Lieberman of Connecticut, who had publicly condemned the president's conduct as "immoral."[12] Even worse, instead of embracing the prosperity that marked his and Clinton's time in office, Gore ran a campaign better suited to an outsider challenging an incumbent in hard times than a vice president seeking to extend his party's control of the presidency in good times. Gore's approach was "consultant populist bullshit," Clinton privately complained; in addition, wrote historian Michael Kazin, it lacked "any policies to back it up."[13] Bush's "compassionate conservatism" was close enough thematically to Clinton's "third way"–style liberalism that voters did not have to reject the Democrat's popular policies to feel comfortable voting for the Republican.[14]

As Bush campaign consultant Stuart Stevens summarized the tone-deaf theme of the Gore campaign, "Times have never been better—Vote for change."[15] In his three debates with Bush, Gore never mentioned Clinton. He refused the president's repeated offers to campaign for him. "I will never understand," says Rove, "on a tactical level, why he didn't say to Clinton, I want you to go to every small town in Arkansas; and if you get tired of doing that, go to Tennessee, Kentucky, and West Virginia." All four states had voted for the Clinton-Gore ticket in 1992 and 1996. None of them voted for Gore in 2000. As it turned out, support from any one of them would have given him the electoral votes he needed to become president.

Bush's national party convention was aimed squarely at the centrist swing voters he needed to woo back from the Democrats in order to win. Other than himself and his vice-presidential running mate Richard Cheney, nearly all the speakers featured in prime time were African Americans, Latinos, women, or, in one case, a gay Republican member of Congress. Bush sincerely hoped to expand his party's support among Latinos, with whom he had done especially well in his 1998 reelection as governor of Texas. But his main purpose in choosing these speakers was to assure moderate and independent white voters that he was not a hard-edged conservative. As his gubernatorial policy adviser Margaret Spellings points out, Bush "talked about education reform when the standard Republican orthodoxy was: abolish the Department of Education."[16]

Bush's selection of Cheney as his running mate served multiple purposes. Cheney's long, deep, and broad experience in Washington as President Gerald Ford's chief of staff, George H. W. Bush's secretary of defense, and the third-ranking Republican leader in the House of Representatives was meant to assuage any doubts voters might have about gaps in Bush's resumé. Cheney's rock-ribbed conservatism—"I'm *really* conservative," he warned Bush—appealed to party members who were concerned that compassionate conservatism was a way of dismissing their own brand of conservatism as extreme.[17] Bush's interest in Cheney was long-standing. In 1992 he urged his father to replace Vice President Dan Quayle with Cheney.[18] As for Cheney, he played hard to get, refusing Bush's initial offer to join the ticket but agreeing to head up the vice-presidential selection process. Eventually, recalls Bush's friend and gubernatorial chief of staff Clay Johnson, "Cheney came back to report to the governor the results of the search, and we talked about a couple of people, but nobody was obvious. The governor noticed something different about Dick's body language and suggested, 'Dick, maybe you've changed your mind. Are you interested in doing it?'" It turned out he was.

In an otherwise close election, the presidential debates loomed as potentially decisive. Gore carried a reputation into the 2000 campaign as an aggressive, experienced, and skillful debater, a reputation that Bush lacked.[19] As a result, Gore wanted more debates and Bush fewer, a stance that made Gore appear confident and Bush timid in the minds of voters. Realizing this, Bush reluctantly agreed to three debates in early and mid-October. "Bush was fairly diligent about preparation," says Bolten, "but I thought he had not been diligent enough. . . . He didn't like to practice." Gore campaign adviser Tad Devine predicted that in the first debate "people would see two candidates on stage, but only one president."[20]

Surprisingly, Bush benefited more from the debates than Gore did. In their first encounter, a formal affair in which both candidates stood behind podiums, Gore treated his opponent in an unattractively disdainful way, often speaking condescendingly and arrogantly when it was his turn and sighing and grimacing while Bush spoke. Chastened by the adverse public response, Gore was deferential to the point of seeming obsequious during the second debate, a more loosely structured event at which the two candidates sat around a table with PBS's Jim Lehrer, who moderated all the presidential debates. In the town meeting–style third debate, Gore generally hit his stride, despite an ill-conceived decision to lumber across the stage in an effort "to use his size to physically intimidate" Bush—which, according to Bolten, Bush had been coached to expect and shrug off dismissively. But the inconsistency of Gore's approach and manner from one debate to the next fed voters' doubts about who he really was. Bush was not strongly impressive in any of the debates, but voters saw the same Bush in all three.

Gore's verdict on his performance in the three presidential debates was that, like the three bears' porridge, he had been "too hot" in the first one, "too cold" in the second, and "just right" in the third.[21] One could just as easily say that Gore performed well in only one of the three debates and performed consistently in none of them. Bush, who had entered the debates trailing Gore by around five points in the polls, came out of them with a five-point lead.

Seemingly headed for a clear victory, Bush forfeited that advantage during the weekend before the election. A news story appeared revealing that he had been convicted of drunk driving in 1976 while visiting his parents in Maine. According to Alberto Gonzales, who was a Texas Supreme Court justice when Bush was governor, Bush had previously said, "I need to tell my daughters and we need to get this out"—but he never did. Rove had also "known about it for a long time," but once the presidential campaign was under way, he and Bush decided to keep the incident under wraps. "I think in his heart of hearts he didn't think it would get out," says communications director Dan Bartlett. "There had been investigative reporters, op[position] research guys digging all over Texas. . . . 'They'll never look in Kennebunkport, Maine.'" Concealment was "the single biggest mistake of the campaign," says Rove, because instead of rolling out the story "on our own terms" so that voters had time "to absorb it, digest it, and to move on, instead it was this last-minute surprise" that raised questions about what else Bush might be hiding. According to Rove, the story was especially demoralizing to Bush's evangelical Christian supporters, many of whom wondered, "[if] he's not the guy I thought he was . . . what else is he hiding?"—and decided not to vote at all.

The closeness of the election underscores how winnable it was for the Democrats. It remained unresolved until December 12, when the Supreme Court's bitterly contested decision in *Bush v. Gore* ended the process of recounts and litigation that had kept Florida's twenty-five electoral votes in limbo.[22] Gore nearly swept the Northeast, the upper Midwest, and the Pacific coast. The national exit poll revealed that he ran more strongly among certain demographic groups—including women (54 percent), African Americans (90 percent), members of union households (59 percent), liberals (80 percent), gay and lesbian voters (70 percent), poor and working-class voters (55 percent), city dwellers (61 percent), voters who seldom or never attended religious services (56 percent), and highly educated voters (52 percent)—than any Democratic presidential candidate since Lyndon B. Johnson in 1964.[23] In all, Gore surpassed Bush by nearly half a million popular votes, the first time the losing candidate outpaced the winner since 1888.

But Gore clearly paid a price for his decision to distance himself from the peace and prosperity of the Clinton years, as well as for a campaign organization that, in contrast to Bush's, "set a new low for backbiting and political drama," according to Gore campaign manager Donna Brazile.[24] Voters who said world affairs was their greatest concern supported the considerably less experienced Bush 54 percent to 40 percent. And although voters who thought the economy was in "excellent" condition supported Gore 53 percent to 46 percent, those who said it was only "good" favored Bush 53 percent to 38 percent. "More than anything else," political scientist Gary Jacobson concluded, "Gore's inability to exploit his biggest asset, the Clinton economy, effectively cost him a clear-cut victory."[25]

For his part, Bush won nearly all the traditionally Republican Plains and Rocky Mountain states, three of the four border states, and Ohio, all of which Clinton had carried in 1996. Bush also swept the South, including four states—Arkansas, Florida, Louisiana, and Gore's home state of Tennessee—that Clinton had won four years earlier. The loss of Tennessee, which had voted for Gore all five times he appeared on the statewide ballot, was especially significant. The only reason Florida's electoral votes mattered was that Gore failed to carry his own state. Tennessee's 11 electoral votes would have raised Gore's total to 278, a clear majority even without Florida. In truth, Gore's neglect of Tennessee during his tenure as vice president, and the Bush campaign's understanding that, with enough effort, it could snatch the state away from him, turned out to be decisive.

Among groups of voters, Bush did nearly as well among men (53 percent) as Gore did among women. He enjoyed stronger support from white voters (54 percent), college-educated voters (51 percent), and conservatives (81 percent) than any Republican presidential candidate since his father in 1988. Bush's 35 percent support among Latino voters marked a strong advance from 1996, when Dole received just 21 percent.

Other major divisions between Bush and Gore voters were economic and, perhaps more important, cultural. A strong correlation existed between voters' annual incomes and their support for Bush. He won the votes of 37 percent of those who earned $15,000 per year or less, but 54 percent of those who earned $100,000 or more. The more religious voters claimed to be, the more likely they were to vote for Bush: 59 percent of those who attended services at least once a week supported him, compared with 38 percent of those who seldom or never attended church. Married women supported Bush (53 percent), as did gun owners (61 percent), self-identified members of the religious right (80 percent), Protestants (63 percent), voters who valued "moral leadership" in a president more than "managing the government" (70 percent), small-town and rural residents (59 percent), opponents of stricter gun-control laws (74 percent), and opponents of legalized abortion (71 percent). Roman Catholics, who had supported Clinton in both 1992 and 1996, narrowly swung to Bush (52 percent).

Partly because he had his hands full waging his own campaign, Bush's narrow victory was accompanied by disappointing results in the congressional elections. Democrats gained one seat in the House, which was not enough to retake control of that chamber, and five seats in the Senate, creating a 50–50 division that made Vice President Cheney's tie-breaking vote decisive. For the first time since 1954, a Republican president governed with a Republican Congress, but only for a few months. In May 2001 Republican senator James Jeffords of Vermont joined the Democrats, giving them a 51–49 majority.

The contested nature of the incredibly close 2000 election—including the irregularities in ballot design and vote counting in Florida, Bush attorney Ted Olson's determination to take the case to "federal court right from the beginning," and the strict partisan divide among the Supreme Court justices, who voted 5–4 in Bush's favor—left Democrats angry and bitter. On January 6, 2001, Gore "was very good . . . presiding over his own defeat" when, as president of the Senate, he announced the official tally of the electoral votes submitted by the states and declared Bush the winner, according to House Republican Dennis Hastert. But House Democratic leader Richard Gephardt recalls that the close and controversial nature of the election "was a huge impediment for many of my members to accept this president and want to deal with him in any way. They just thought it was stolen."

Republican attorney Fred Fielding remembers the "really deep, deep sense of anger and mistrust" among Democrats, who felt, "'We wuz robbed!'"

2002: Midterm Momentum

The controversy surrounding Bush's election shadowed him when he entered the White House on January 20, 2001. Still, he made progress on most of the policies he had emphasized during the campaign: a tax cut (a record $1.35 trillion after several rounds of negotiations with Congress), education reform (with bipartisan support, his No Child Left Behind bill was on the road to enactment) and, largely through executive action, defense reform and faith-based involvement in social services delivery. According to Margaret Spellings, who joined the administration as Bush's domestic policy adviser, Jeffords's defection to the Democrats and the loss of Republican control in the Senate "ended up being the best things that ever happened to No Child Left Behind, *no doubt about it*, . . . because Ted Kennedy believed in the stuff more than Jim Jeffords did by a country mile."[26] "The Republican leadership did not like the bill," says White House legislative liaison Nick Calio; "the conservatives did not like the bill from the start." But the combined support of a Republican president and a Democratic Senate made it hard for House Republicans to resist education reform.

By September 10, Bush's job approval rating was 51 percent, the lowest of any elected president in modern history less than eight months into his term. Denied the traditional "honeymoon" by the controversial nature of his election, Bush failed to earn the support of those who had voted against him. The terrorist attacks on New York and Washington that occurred the next morning changed all that. Within days, Bush's approval rating shot up 35 points, cresting soon afterward at 90 percent. The rally-round-the-flag effect sparked by the attacks was steeper (his immediate 35-point jump was nearly double the previous record), higher (90 percent is the highest any president has ever achieved), and longer lasting (he stayed above his pre–September 11 peak for more than a year) than any in recorded history.[27]

Because Bush's surge in popular support was tied to September 11, he got his way on nearly all matters related to national security during the remaining sixteen months of the 107th Congress. Democrats united with Republicans to support the president's September 20 declaration of a "war on terror" with a resolution authorizing him to "use all necessary and appropriate force" against those involved in any way with the attacks on the World Trade Center and the Pentagon. A year later, in October 2002, Congress approved the president's request to support the use of force against the Saddam Hussein regime in Iraq "as he determines to be necessary and appropriate." Every Democrat in Congress who was thinking of running for president in 2004 or 2008 voted to endorse Bush's course in Iraq, for fear of being on the wrong side of a popular war. These included Gephardt and senators John Kerry of Massachusetts, John Edwards of North Carolina, Joeseph Biden of Delaware, and Hillary Clinton of New York. As late as November 2002, Congress was still considering Bush's June proposal for a massive new Department of Homeland Security, and during the fall midterm election campaign he browbeat Democrats and their union supporters for resisting a provision that would grant managers within the department extensive latitude to hire, transfer, and fire employees.

Unlike any of his predecessors, Bush experienced both united and divided party government during his first two years in office. Despite the Democrats' cooperation on education reform and national security, he resolved that his best strategy going forward—both to win reelection in 2004 and to lead Congress until then—was for Republicans to regain control of the Senate and increase their narrow majority in the House in the 2002 midterm elections. Convinced that low turnout by Christian conservatives had nearly cost Bush his 2000 victory, Rove immediately began to field-test various methods to increase participation. "In Virginia in 2001 we were doing mail and phone tests on precinct levels, lots of A/B testing," Rove says. "Make these kind of phone calls in this precinct and don't make them in this precinct and then evaluate the difference." He focused on microtargeting—using what eventually became "250 pieces of household-level information" to identify individuals who would support Bush. For example, Rove says, "if you have a Volvo, you're a Democrat; if you have a pickup truck, you're a Republican." "Advertising on the Golf Channel or the Outdoor Channel because that's where our people were," adds Bartlett.

The political challenge of attaining Republican majorities in both houses of Congress was formidable. In the post–World War II era, the president's party had lost an average of twenty-six House seats in midterm elections. Since the Civil War, only two presidents had seen their party gain House seats at midterm. In 2002 the loss of just six seats would turn over control of that chamber to the Democrats. Senate elections were more variable, but the average loss for the president's party was four seats. Even worse from the Republicans' standpoint, they were more "exposed" in 2002 than the Democrats: twenty Republican seats were contested, compared with only fourteen Democratic seats.[28] Because four Republicans (and no Democrats) were retiring, their Senate seats were open in 2002 and thus more vulnerable to capture by the opposition party than seats defended by incumbents. As for the president's party wresting control of the Senate from the other party in a midterm election, that had not happened since 1882.

From the start of his first term, Bush was a party builder. At two important milestones—the first after he was declared the winner of the divisive 2000 election and the second after the September 11 attacks—Bush was counseled by many political pundits (and Democrats) to govern in a broadly bipartisan manner. On both occasions he refused to do so, choosing instead to pursue his own agenda. To be sure, he adopted some policies traditionally supported by Democrats, including expanded farm subsidies, increased tariffs on imported steel, and a new prescription drug benefit as part of Medicare. He also made some demographically diverse appointments to his staff and cabinet. In making these exceptions, however, Bush's purpose was to increase support for the GOP in particular regions of the country (especially the Farm Belt and the steel-reliant states of Ohio, West Virginia, and Pennsylvania) or among specific groups of voters, especially women, seniors, and Latinos.

Preparing for the 2002 midterms, Bush personally recruited strong Republican challengers to incumbent Democrats, even intervening in some states to make it clear which candidate he wanted the party to nominate. "Being able to recruit—to have the power of the White House to lend—the credibility of the White House to go after somebody, I mean that's a big thing," says Chris LaCivita, who was political director of the National Republican Senatorial Committee (NRSC) in 2002. In every instance but one (John Thune lost very narrowly in South Dakota but ran again and won in 2004), the Bush-recruited Republican nominee was elected, including Norm Coleman in Minnesota, Lamar Alexander in Tennessee, Saxby Chambliss in Georgia, John Cornyn in Texas, and John E. Sununu in New Hampshire.

Bush raised a record $141 million for his party in 2002. Cheney raised an additional $40 million, a record for a vice president. Added together, this $181 million nearly accounted for the $184 million margin by which the GOP outspent the Democrats. Bush also campaigned hard for Republican candidates throughout the country. He knew that campaigning typically reduces the president's approval rating because it brings his partisanship into sharp relief. But he was willing to pay that price to help the Republican Party.[29]

The results of the 2002 election vindicated Bush's decision to become actively involved. The Republicans not only gained six seats in the House, doubling the size of their majority in that chamber, but also added the two seats they needed to take control of the Senate. For the first time since 1934—and the first time ever for a Republican—the president's party gained seats in both chambers in a first-term midterm election. Also for the first time ever, the president's party made midterm gains in state legislatures. Republicans picked up about 200 state legislative seats instead of losing 350, the average loss for the president's party in a midterm election. For the first time since 1952, the GOP had a majority of state governors and legislators. Political analysts were quick to credit Bush with his party's success, pointing out that twelve of the sixteen Senate candidates for whom he campaigned were victorious, as were all but two of the twenty-three House candidates he actively supported.

2004: Prospects for Realignment

Having laid a strong foundation for his party in all the elected branches of the federal government and, closer to the grass roots, in most state governments, Bush almost immediately focused on 2004. He instructed his political strategists to plan and execute a campaign that would reelect him and also make the Republican Party "stronger, broader, and better."[30] "Don't give me a lonely victory," he told his political team. "I don't want what Nixon had. I don't want what Reagan had." According to one Bush aide, "He was explicit that he doesn't want to win with 55 percent and have a 51–49 Senate. He wants to expand the governing coalition."[31] Bush "was a highly partisan leader who relied upon partisan majorities in Congress, on most of the policy initiatives that he cared about, once he became president," says political scientist Mark Rozell. "He didn't really see a bipartisan vehicle for moving much of his agenda through, so he needed his victory to be a party victory, not just a Bush victory."

Bush and his campaign team developed and executed a remarkably successful strategy to secure the sweeping Republican victory he sought. Unusual for a reelection-seeking president, says Rove, "we made generous transfers from the Republican National Committee to the Senate Congressional Campaign Committee."[32] Just as important to Bush and his party's success were the public policies he pursued as president. In foreign policy, Bush's declaration of a prolonged war on terror assured that, as had been the case during the Cold War but not in the decade afterward, voters would remain attentive to national security issues, traditionally the Republicans' greatest electoral strength. When the first president Bush defeated Iraq in the first Gulf War, he portrayed it as an isolated event. When the second president Bush drove Saddam Hussein from power in the second Gulf War, he described it as merely one battle in an ongoing war that, like the Cold War, had no clear end in sight.

Economically, Bush's strongly pro-business tax and regulatory policies energized both large and small companies to support the GOP in 2004 more than ever before with campaign contributions and efforts to rally their employees.[33] Bush also successfully identified himself and his party as the chief defenders of traditional social values, based on both what he upheld (religious faith, unabashed patriotism, restrictions on abortion) and what he opposed (sexual permissiveness, gun control). In eleven states, popular measures to ban same-sex marriage were on the ballot, and voters approved the ban in all eleven. Most of them were red states that Bush was bound to carry anyway, such as Kentucky and Mississippi. Others were blue states he was bound to lose, notably Michigan and Oregon. Electoral vote–rich Ohio, however, was very much up for grabs, and the referendum's presence on the ballot surely drove up turnout among its Republican, conservative Christian supporters.

In contrast to 2000, the Democrats waged a wide-open contest for the 2004 presidential nomination. An obscure small-state governor, Howard Dean of Vermont, raced to an early lead in 2003 by "captur[ing] the anger of Americans . . . specifically, Democrats [and] liberals . . . about the Iraq war," says political scientist John Geer. At the initiative of senior campaign adviser Joe Trippi, Dean became the first presidential candidate to use a campaign website to raise money and Meetup.com "to organize the concentric-circle campaign"—thousands of web-organized meetings of Dean supporters around the country. "Because of his antiwar stance," says political journalist Walter Shapiro, the Dean campaign "hit a gusher. I mean, this is what it must have been like to be in Sutter's Mill in 1848." Dean entered the January 19, 2004, Iowa caucuses as the front-runner against a field of candidates who had voted in Congress to authorize Bush's use force against Iraq. But Dean's effort faltered when the inexperienced candidate made several politically off-key remarks—for example, that "the capture of Saddam Hussein has not made America safer."[34] Another Democratic challenger, Rep. Richard Gephardt, "attacked Dean in television ads, so Dean attacked back," and with both candidates discredited, "they end[ed] up finishing third and fourth," notes longtime Democratic campaign strategist Bob Shrum.

The Democratic contenders who finished first and second in Iowa were Shrum's candidate, Senator Kerry, and Senator Edwards, who later joined the ticket as Kerry's running mate. Kerry's background in the late 1960s "as a [Vietnam] war hero and a war protester, at the same time, was really brilliantly suited for the times," says Mark Mellman, his campaign's pollster. Victory in the Iowa caucuses and, eight days later, in the New Hampshire primary essentially sealed Kerry's nomination. As Mellman points out, "There was no one who had won both Iowa and New Hampshire and lost in the history of the process." All the other candidates withdrew by March 3.

Even as he worked hard for his candidate, Mellman recalls, "I said to my colleagues and Senator Kerry when I was talking about taking the job, 'Look, I believe that George Bush is going to be reelected.'" In "the first presidential election post September 11," Bush "was certainly seen by the public as strong and able to deal with terrorism." Further, he "was seen as a regular guy who was in touch with people."

Bush had other advantages as well. His 2000 campaign team remained intact and met regularly on Saturday mornings at the home of lead strategist Karl Rove (the so-called breakfast club). They planned a reelection campaign centered on mobilizing the party's core constituencies to turn out at a higher rate than in 2000 and on increasing support for Bush among generally pro-Democratic women and Latinos. Kerry farmed out his voter turnout effort to the independent political group Moveon.org. In contrast, Bush campaign manager Ken Mehlman notes that, "watching Governor Dean and watching what Joe Trippi put together—we learned something about the power of neighbor mobilizing and influencing neighbor." The Bush campaign's microtargeting techniques, which Rove had been field-testing since 2001, enabled the team to identify individual supporters in battleground states and connect them with local Bush activists they knew personally. Bush's "small, disciplined group" of managers was "well ahead of us as far as voter contact and technology, and the mechanics of campaigns," concedes Kerry campaign adviser Joe Lockhart.

Far from a surefooted campaigner, Kerry blundered in several ways. In

March he took the bait when a Bush ad accused the senator of letting down the troops in Iraq by voting against an $87 billion appropriations bill to fund the war. "I actually did vote for the $87 billion before I voted against it," Kerry told a West Virginia audience. "That was a gift," says Vice President Cheney. According to deputy campaign strategist Mike Shannon, "It cemented the charge we were making against Senator Kerry that he flip-flopped." When an independent anti-Kerry group, the Swift Boat Veterans for Truth, challenged the legitimacy of his Vietnam heroism right after the generally successful Democratic convention in July, the Kerry campaign was slow to respond. According to Mellman, there were two reasons for letting the charges go unanswered: First, "Kerry had been attacked in all his previous races on something to do with foreign policy and military service, and it had always boomeranged. Second, . . . the story was just not getting that much attention." The latter soon ceased to be true.[35] "You have to address these things when it's still in a liquid or gelatinous state, before it gets rock hard," says political analyst Charlie Cook. "And [Kerry] didn't do it."

The Swift Boat Veterans were hardly unique in 2004. Republican campaign lawyer John Ryder says their involvement was the beginning "of the phenomenon of outside groups—the 527s—so-called because of section 527 of the Internal Revenue Code, which permits a political organization to raise money without disclosing much about its donors" and to spend "unlimited amounts." The reason 527s rose to prominence in 2004 was that the 2002 Bipartisan Campaign Reform Act (better known as McCain-Feingold) banned large "soft money" donations to political parties, which had the effect of channeling these funds to independent groups. "No way" the Bush campaign itself would have attacked Kerry's war record, says principal Swift Boat Veterans media adviser Chris LaCivita. "Because they wouldn't have had the credibility to deliver that message, because it would have been the campaign doing it. And because George Bush didn't serve in Vietnam."

Kerry had good moments as well as bad. In their first debate, says political scientist and Bush campaign adviser Daron Shaw, "the president looked kind of peevish and small," while Kerry "showed he had command and mastery of the facts." It was a "crappy performance" by Bush, says Rove. "I think that happens to every second-term president. They say, 'I don't need to prep, I'm doing this stuff every day.' What they forget is that for three and a half years they have not been confronted in either the context or the way that a political opponent will confront them." A few days later, however, Cheney demolished Edwards (whom he later described as a "scumbag") in the vice-presidential debate. Both Edwards and Kerry, in the final presidential debate, mentioned that Cheney's daughter Mary is a lesbian, which Mellman concedes allowed the Bush campaign to do "an effective job trying to mitigate the victories that Senator Kerry had in the debates with those individual nuggets."

On November 7, Election Day, Bush became a majority president. He won more than half the electoral votes: 286 for Bush, 251 for Kerry.[36] Bush also won a majority of the national popular vote: 62 million (50.7 percent) to Kerry's 59 million (48.3 percent), the first time in sixteen years that any presidential candidate secured a popular majority. Equally important, the president's party retained control of both houses of Congress, increasing the Republican majority by three in the House and four in the Senate. Bush was the first president since FDR in 1936 to be reelected with accompanying gains for his party in both congressional chambers. The fruits of his efforts were apparent in the 55–44 Republican Senate and the 232–202 Republican House.

Bush was the fifth president to be elected to a second term in the postwar era. Each of his victorious predecessors—Dwight Eisenhower (1956), Richard Nixon (1972), Ronald Reagan (1984), and Bill Clinton (1996)—had been reelected by a larger margin than Bush. But in every case, theirs were isolated triumphs in which the president did well—partly because he focused on himself—but the party's congressional candidates did not. None of them did what Bush and the Republicans did in 2004: gain seats in both the House and the Senate while securing the president's reelection. Nor did Eisenhower, Nixon, Reagan, and Clinton begin their second terms as the head of a united party government that controlled the White House and both houses of Congress.

"We tried very hard to avoid a lonely victory," says Mehlman, "to run a campaign that was very much focused on collaborating with Republicans around the country." According to consultant Mike Shannon, the Bush campaign ran "joint advertising with the Republican National Committee where we were able, in a sense, to make the case for President Bush and congressional Republicans." The same was true of the GOP congressional campaign committees. Bush "was very interested in building that majority," says NRSC executive director Jay Timmons. "He gave a lot of time to the House and Senate candidates on the road during the last month." Equally important, Bush, like Kerry, relied on public financing in the general election, which allowed Republican donors to focus on supporting the party's congressional nominees. "Bush was a good party leader," says chief speech-writer Michael Gerson. "I think he cared about the party; he knew that his fate was tied to theirs, as far as effectiveness."

A majority president himself, Bush was well on his way to becoming the leader of the nation's new majority party. His reelection meant that from 1968 to 2004, Republican candidates had won seven of ten presidential elections, cumulatively amassing 3,381 electoral votes (63 percent) to the Democrats' 1,949 (36 percent). Neither of the two Democrats elected in this period, Clinton and Carter, ever exceeded the 50.7 percent of the national popular vote that Bush won in 2004.

The budding Republican majority extended to Congress as well as the presidency. The party's victories in the 2004 congressional contests marked the sixth consecutive election in which the Republicans won control of both the House and the Senate. In 1946 and 1952, the only other congressional elections since the 1920s in which the Republicans were victorious, they lost their majority just two years later. As for the third branch of government, by 2004, the judiciary had also become a Republican bastion. Control of the presidency and the Senate enabled the Republicans to choose a large majority of judges at all levels of the federal court system. By 2004, Republican presidents had made nine of the eleven most recent Supreme Court appointments (82 percent), 218 of 335 federal appeals court appointments (65 percent), and 834 of 1,342 district court appointments (62 percent).[37]

At the state level, Republicans held a majority of governorships starting in 1994, and in 2002, for the first time in the post–*Baker v. Carr* era of "one person, one vote" in legislative apportionment, they attained a majority of state legislators. By 2003, more voters were registered as Republicans than Democrats in the states that allowed party registration.[38] A December 2004 Gallup poll showed that Republicans led Democrats 37 percent to 32 percent among voters who claimed a party affiliation,[39] constituting "the most Republican electorate America has had since random-sample polling was invented" in the 1930s.[40] The dramatic surge in voter turnout from Bush's first election to his second—from 54 percent of eligible voters in 2000 to 60 percent in 2004—helped him secure 10.5 million additional votes. Histori-cally, surges in voter turnout, such as those that occurred in 1860 and dur-ing the 1930s, often mark the appearance of a new majority party.[41]

Geographically, the embryonic Republican majority was grounded in the twenty-nine states that Bush carried in both 2000 and 2004. These states constituted all or most of every region of the country except the Northeast,

Pacific coast, and upper Midwest. Demographically, Republican strength rested mainly on a foundation of white men (who voted 62 percent for Bush in 2004) and married women (55 percent) living in suburban or rural (58 percent) communities. Bush's sustained efforts to earn support from Latino (44 percent) and elderly (54 percent) voters were rewarded with strong showings in 2004. Ideologically, Republicans tended to be philosophically conservative on most issues related to culture, economics, and national security. In religious faith and practice, they were, for the most part, churchgoing Christians (70 percent). Bush even carried Catholic voters (52 percent) against the first Catholic nominee for president since John F. Kennedy in 1960.[42] From 2000 on, says Catholic-focused Republican strategist Leonard Leo, Bush aimed his appeal not at "the whole Catholic vote" but, with frequent references to "the culture of life," at "mass-going Catholics," whose "lingo and language is very different from evangelical and Protestant lingo and language."

The prospect of an emerging Republican majority did not come about through a dramatic realigning election.[43] Instead, a "rolling" (or, to use the preferred term of political scientists, a "secular") realignment was under way,[44] tied mostly to the gradual transformation of the conservative South from a pillar of the Democratic coalition to a mainstay of the Republican majority. Bush and Rove "had seen Texas go from a one-party dominated Democratic state to a state that, by the time he left office as president, had become a very red Republican-dominated state," says Dan Balz of the *Washington Post*. "Their goal was not simply to win reelection, but to put a foundation that, over succeeding years, they could create what they described as a durable Republican majority."

Some argued that Bush's reelection was entirely an artifact of the public's approval of his leadership in the aftermath of September 11. In truth, far from being a passing effect, the continuity in his support from election to election suggested something more solid. With one exception, every state that Bush carried in 2000 supported him again in 2004,[45] even though the issues that dominated the two elections shifted radically from domestic policy in 2000 to war and terrorism in 2004. And, as is often the case, in 2004 the nation's minority party fought the election on issues defined by the majority party. Kerry ran less as the champion of a Democratic agenda than as the anti-Bush, promising to pursue Bush's war on terror more effectively and to make Bush's tax cuts fairer. Bush ran as himself, defending his record. On Election Day the great majority of Bush's votes came from people who said they were for him. Nearly half of Kerry's votes came from people who said they were against Bush.[46]

2006 and 2008: Thwarted Realignment

The GOP was not going to win every election after 2004, no matter how well things went for Bush and his party. Whether measured by policy achievements or political standing, presidents' second terms are almost always less successful than their first terms.[47] No one doubts that Franklin D. Roosevelt brought about a Democratic realignment in the 1930s, but that did not prevent him from experiencing second-term difficulties when it came to passing new laws and fending off a major Republican comeback in the 1938 midterm elections. But as was the case for FDR and the Democrats, the foundation for a Bush-led Republican realignment was in place as he began his second term. Republicans were en route to becoming the default setting in American politics, perhaps for a generation.

Yet actions by the same President Bush who had worked so hard and so well to bring his party to the brink of majority status thwarted the incipient realignment, resulting in the Democrats regaining Congress in 2006 and the White House in 2008. Bush's second term was a cascading series of bad choices and bad fortunes, starting with his decision to place Social Security reform at the top of his legislative agenda.

Reforming Social Security in any way, much less in the direction of privately managed individual accounts, was always going to be a hard sell. Social Security has long been regarded as the notorious "third rail" of American politics, the one that harms anyone who gets too close. Bush had campaigned on the issue in 2000, only to discover that Republican leaders in Congress wanted no part of it. "The president would come in," recalls legislative liaison Nick Calio, "he'd talk to the House leadership about it at these meetings. You'd get not a word of response." "Afterward, you'd get all this bellyaching," adds Jack Howard, a member of Calio's staff, as in: "You've got to quit talking about Social Security." Bush shelved the issue for the next four years, barely mentioned it during his reelection campaign, and then revived it as his major legislative initiative in 2005. "By that time the ability to do social security reform the way he wanted to was lost," says Gillespie.

According to Bartlett, Bush completely misread the voters after his re-election. He declared, "'I have a mandate. We're going to do social security reform,' and everybody went, 'Huh?' . . . I remember telling President Bush and Karl, 'You had a 53-minute stump speech. We had it down to 51 minutes of how we're going to kill those bastards overseas, and then two minutes where you would tick off all these other things we were going to do, like social security reform.' . . . We had not prepared the public for a debate about social security. Nor did we have a mandate." Nevertheless, claiming to have "the will of the people at my back," Bush spent weeks touring the country on behalf of his proposal, only to find out how wrong he was. Once again, congressional Republicans wanted no part of it. "They said, 'You know, we're right behind you,'" says National Economic Council director Keith Hennessey, "'Way behind you.'" Not only did Social Security reform sink without a trace—"it just turned out to be a total dud," says Bolten—but it wasted time and effort that could have been spent showcasing immigration reform, an issue riper for enactment and one that would have helped lock in the expanded Latino support Bush had long cultivated.

Woe followed woe for the president. In August 2005 the administration's response to Hurricane Katrina was painfully inadequate, and the president was judged to be insensitive to the suffering of the poor of New Orleans. All year long, and well into 2006, the situation in Iraq deteriorated, rousing strong public opposition to Bush's conduct of the war and its aftermath. As with Social Security reform, Bush overinterpreted his reelection mandate with regard to Iraq. According to Bush defense adviser Peter Feaver, "The administration had this view that the 2004 election had decided the matter. . . . Is the Iraq War a mistake? No. How do we know? Because the president went before the American people, [they] decided in 2004, end of story, we're moving forward. That was a mistake." More generally, recalls Secretary of Labor Elaine Chao, "You have the A team at the beginning [of an administration], and then they get tired or they want to monetize their government experience and they move on."

"Move on" meant "push out" in one prominent case. Immediately after the 2006 midterm elections—not before Election Day, when it might have done Republican candidates some good—Bush announced his decision to replace Secretary of Defense Donald Rumsfeld with former CIA director Robert Gates. Few quarreled with the decision—in fact, Bush's first-term secretary of state, Colin Powell, had told him, "After the election of 2004—'you need to get rid of all of us, bring in an entirely new team.'" But, according to Gates, Bush delayed the announcement because he "did not want to have the decision interpreted in political terms. In a way it was a kind of head-in-the-sand approach, because he had to know everybody would interpret it that way, regardless of when he did it. It would actually look worse the day after the election than had he done it—at least people would have said that's a politically smart move—six weeks before. The Republicans would have all applauded up on the Hill—'You gave us a fighting chance.'" Instead, "Republicans, in the Senate in particular, were pissed as hell on the timing." The GOP lost thirty-one seats in the House and five seats in the Senate, thereby ceding control of Congress to the Democrats.

In 2007 Gates and Bush launched a new strategy in Iraq—an increased deployment of forces with a redefined mission called the "surge"—that bore some fruit, but by then, the public had written off the president. The same was true when Bush and Secretary of the Treasury Henry Paulson adroitly managed the financial crisis of 2008. Rescuing major banks and investment houses was unpopular, even though, as Paulson recalls, Neither John McCain nor Barack Obama, the 2008 Republican and Democratic presidential candidates, respectively, "came out against what we were doing, and Obama was quite positive and constructive." Paulson adds, "McCain was hurt by it, and he could have demagogued it, but he didn't. And he voluntarily helped get some House Republicans on board." In the end, Bush left office with the highest disapproval rating—71 percent—of any president in modern history, his reputation and that of his party in steep decline.

Seldom in demand, Bush did little campaigning in 2008 and, to McCain's relief, did not even attend the Republican National Convention after his scheduled speech was washed out by Hurricane Gustav. Hobbled by Bush's severe unpopularity, McCain was handily defeated, as were about two dozen congressional Republicans. The party lost even more ground in both chambers to the Democrats.

The thwarted Republican realignment of the 2000s did not, however, turn into a Democratic realignment. The GOP regained control of the House in 2010, the Senate in 2014, and the presidency in 2016. Indeed, in the aftermath of the 2014 midterm elections, there were more Republicans in the House than in any Congress since 1946. The New Deal Democratic realignment of the 1930s was long gone, but no other realignment has arisen to take its place.

Notes

1. In the six presidential elections from 1968 to 1988, the Republicans carried twenty-one states with 187 electoral votes in every election and fourteen states with 157 electoral votes in every election but one. The Democrats won only the District of Columba (3 electoral votes) in every election and Minnesota (10 electoral votes) in every election but one. Michael Nelson, *Clinton's Elections: 1992, 1996, and the Birth of a New Era of Governance* (Lawrence: University Press of Kansas, 2020), 2.

2. Sidney M. Milkis and Michael Nelson, *The American Presidency: Origins and Development, 1776–2021* (Washington, DC: Congressional Quarterly Press, 2023), chap. 15.

3. David E. Sanger, "After 'Next Best Thing,' Clinton Carefully Praises Gore," *New York Times*, November 4, 2000.

4. Robert G. Kaiser, "Academics Say It's Elementary: Gore Wins," *Washington Post*, August 31, 2000.

5. Bill Turque, *Inventing Al Gore* (Boston: Houghton Mifflin, 2000), 356.

6. Samuel L. Popkin, *The Candidate: What It Takes to Win—and Hold—the White House* (New York: Oxford University Press, 2012), 198.

7. Michael Nelson, "Who Can Be President?" in *The Elections of 2020* (Washington, DC: Congressional Quarterly Press, 2021).

8. Quoted in Andrew Rice, *The Year that Broke America* (New York: HarperCollins, 2022), 292.

9. Unless otherwise noted, all quotations in this chapter are from one of two sources: the Miller Center's George W. Bush Oral History or Southern Methodist University's Center for Presidential History's Elections of 2004 oral history. The Miller Center interviews were with Dan Bartlett, Josh Bolten, Nick Calio, Elaine Chao, Peter Feaver, Fred Fielding, Ari Fleischer, Robert Gates, Richard Gephardt, Ed Gillespie, Alberto Gonzales, Judd Gregg, Stephen Hadley, Dennis Hastert, Keith Hennessey, Clay Johnson, Ted Olson, Henry Paulson, Colin Powell, Karl Rove, Margaret Spellings, Frances Townsend, Pete Wehner, and Philip Zelikow. The Center for Presidential History interviews were with Dan Balz, Richard Cheney, Charlie Cook, John Geer, Michael Gerson, Jack Howard, Chris LaCivita, Joe Lockhart, Ken Mehlman, Mark Mellman, Mark Rozell, John Ryder, Mike Shannon, Walter Shapiro, Daron Shaw, Bob Shrum, Margaret Spellings, Jay Timmons, and Joe Trippi. Because Margaret Spellings was interviewed for both projects, each time she is quoted, a note indicates the source.

10. John F. Harris, *The Survivor: Bill Clinton in the White House* (New York: Random House, 2001), 389.

11. Sidney Blumenthal, *The Clinton Wars* (New York: Farrar, Straus & Giroux, 2003), 716.

12. Bob Woodward, *Shadow: Five Presidents and the Legacy of Watergate* (New York: Simon & Schuster, 1999), 454.

13. Jake Tapper, *Down and Dirty: The Plot to Steal the Presidency* (Boston: Little, Brown, 2001), 24–25; Michael Kazin, *What It Took to Win: A History of the Democratic Party* (New York: Farrar, Straus & Giroux, 2022), 292.

14. Rice, *Year that Broke America*, 84.

15. John Robert Greene, *The Presidency of George W. Bush* (Lawrence: University Press of Kansas, 2021).

16. Spellings, Center for Presidential History.

17. Greene, *Presidency of George W. Bush*.

18. Greene.

19. James Fallows, "An Acquired Taste," *Atlantic Monthly*, July 2000, 33–53.

20. Quoted in Rice, *Year that Broke America*, 285.

21. "What a Long, Strange Trip," *Newsweek*, November 20, 2000, 126.

22. The ins and outs of *Bush v. Gore* and the Florida dispute in general are superbly chronicled in Charles L. Zelden, *Bush v. Gore: Exposing the Growing Crisis in American Democracy*, 3rd ed. (Lawrence: University Press of Kansas, 2020).

23. Michael Nelson, "The Election: Ordinary Politics, Extraordinary Outcome," in *The Elections of 2000*, ed. Michael Nelson (Washington, DC: CQ Press, 2001), 55–92.

24. Donna Brazile, *Cooking with Grease: Stirring the Pots in American Politics* (New York: Simon & Schuster, 2004), 232.

25. Gary C. Jacobson, *The 2000 Elections and Beyond* (Washington, DC: CQ Press, 2001), 26.

26. Spellings, Miller Center.

27. Marc J. Hetherington and Michael Nelson, "Anatomy of a Rally Effect: George W. Bush and the War on Terrorism," *PS: Political Science and Politics* 36 (2003): 37–42.

28. Bruce I. Oppenheimer, James A. Stimson, and Richard W. Waterman, "Interpreting U.S. Congressional Elections: The Exposure Thesis," *Legislative Studies Quarterly* 11 (1986): 227–247.

29. Michael Nelson, "George W. Bush and Congress: The Electoral Connection," in *Considering the Bush Presidency*, ed. Gary L. Gregg II and Mark J. Rozell (New York: Oxford University Press, 2004), 141–159.

30. Dan Balz and Mike Allen, "Four More Years Attributed to Rove's Strategy," *Washington Post*, November 7, 2004.

31. Dan Balz, "GOP Aims for Dominance in '04 Race," *Washington Post*, June 22, 2003; Balz and Allen, "Four More Years."

32. Rove meant the National Republican Senatorial Committee.

33. Tom Hamburger, "Business Groups Invested in Races, Now Wait for Return," *Los Angeles Times*, November 8, 2004.

34. "Dean: America Not Safer after Saddam's Capture," foxnews.com, http://www .foxnews.com/story/2003/12/16/dean-america-not-safer-after-saddam-capture/.

35. According to Bob Shrum, the problem was that "Mark Mellman's polling was telling us that this wasn't having much impact," a recollection with which Mellman strenuously disagrees.

36. A Minnesota elector who was pledged to support Kerry voted instead for his running mate, John Edwards.

37. Calculated from data provided by the Federal Judicial Center (www.fjc.gov).

38. John Micklethwaite and Adrian Wooldridge, *The Right Nation: Conservative Power in America* (New York: Penguin Press, 2004), 231.

39. Harold F. Bass, "George W. Bush, Presidential Party Leadership Extraordinaire?" *Forum* 2 (2004), http://www.beprss.com/v012/iss4/art6.

40. Michael Barone, "Reshaping the Electorate," *U.S. News and World Report*, November 29, 2004, 32.

41. See, for example, V. O. Key, "A Theory of Critical Elections," *Journal of Politics* 17 (1955): 3–18; Walter Dean Burnham, *Critical Elections and the Mainsprings of American Politics* (New York: W. W. Norton, 1970), 7–8.

42. Michael Nelson, "George W. Bush, Majority President," in *The Elections of 2004*, ed. Michael Nelson (Washington, DC: CQ Press, 2005), 1–17.

43. Even David Mayhew, a strenuous critic of realignment theory, urges acceptance of "a stripped-down version" that "keeps[s] using the term *realignment* to characterize the two genuine outlier eras of American political history—the 1860s and 1930s." David Mayhew, *Electoral Realignment: A Critique of an American Genre* (New Haven, CT: Yale University Press, 2002), 162.

44. "Rolling realignment" is the term used by Bush political strategist Karl Rove. According to political scientist V. O. Key, a "secular realignment . . . may be regarded as a movement of the members of a population category from party to party that extends over several presidential elections." V. O. Key, "Secular Realignment and the Party System," *Journal of Politics* 21 (May 1959): 199.

45. New Hampshire supported Bush in 2000 but not in 2004. This loss was more than offset by Iowa and New Mexico, which Bush lost in 2000 but won in 2004.

46. Nelson, "George W. Bush, Majority President."

47. Michael Nelson, "1997 and Beyond: The Perils of Second-Term Presidents," in *The Elections of 1996*, ed. Michael Nelson (Washington, DC: Congressional Quarterly Press, 1997), 1–13.

CHAPTER TWO

George W. Bush and Compassionate Conservatism: Rhetoric and Reality

Jesse H. Rhodes

"We are a generous and caring people. We don't believe in a sink-or-swim society." Encountering these words without context, a reader would be forgiven for assuming they were spoken by a Democratic politician. After all, generosity and solidarity with disadvantaged members of society have been hallmarks of Democratic presidential rhetoric for decades.[1] But these words were spoken by Republican president George W. Bush in 2002 in a speech promoting his philosophy of compassionate conservatism in San Jose, California.[2]

Compassionate conservatism is the idea that policymakers should "put conservative values and conservative ideas into the thick of the fight for justice and opportunity," as Bush stated when he launched his campaign for the 2000 Republican presidential nomination.[3] This was a matter of both high principle and political calculation for Bush. As an evangelical Christian, he believed a compassionate approach to public policy was a requirement of his faith. At the same time, Bush the politician perceived that compassionate conservatism would appeal to moderate voters alienated by the usual themes of individual achievement and material success featured in Republican rhetoric. Compassionate conservatism was a central refrain during Bush's first run for the White House and remained an important strand of his rhetoric throughout his presidency.

Compassionate conservatism was not simply a rhetorical gloss on conventional Republican approaches to policymaking. It left a distinctive and enduring mark, particularly in the areas of education and health care. Bush's signature No Child Left Behind policy, though significantly altered over time through legislative amendments, administrative maneuvers, and state government actions, wrought enormous changes in K–12 education, and his advancement of prescription drug coverage under Medicare substantially increased the scope and costs of that program. Of course, not every domestic initiative associated with compassionate conservatism had lasting consequences. Bush's faith-based initiatives program had few long-term effects, and his crusade to introduce individualized retirement accounts into the Social Security system ended in political failure. Even so, long after Bush departed the political scene, the philosophy of compassionate conservativism remains embedded in major public policies that affect the lives of millions of Americans.

Whatever the merits of compassionate conservatism in theory, in practice it largely failed to achieve its lofty objectives. In elementary and secondary education, student achievement has increased modestly, if at all, and racial and economic differences in educational outcomes remain substantial. Medicare is still a vitally important social program, but its financing is severely strained, and the reforms Bush spearheaded have arguably added to its political and fiscal vulnerability. More pointedly, Bush's commitment to other, more mainstream conservative ideas undermined much of the promise of compassionate conservatism. The growing economic precariousness of middle- and working-class Americans, exacerbated by Bush's pursuit of large tax cuts for the wealthiest Americans; the human catastrophe wrought by the administration's botched response to Hurricane Katrina; and the denigration of minority voting rights and LGBTQ+ rights enabled by Bush's pursuit of conservative votes all undermine the notion that his presidency was truly "compassionate" to the disadvantaged.

In the long run, and despite its undeniable influence on public policy, compassionate conservatism left little lasting imprint on the ideology of the Republican Party. Today, in the words of former Republican Party chairman Ed Gillespie, compassionate conservatism "has a bad name" within GOP circles.[4] Instead of expressing solidarity with the disadvantaged, many in the Republican Party have embraced an increasingly extreme ideological conservatism and, during the presidency of Donald Trump, endorsed conspiracy theories, white ethnonationalism, and authoritarianism. Confronted with an openly antidemocratic Republican Party, it is understandable why many Americans might be nostalgic for a conservatism that at least acknowledges the importance of compassion toward marginalized members of society.

The Philosophy of Compassionate Conservatism

The compassionate conservatism of George W. Bush drew on ideas that had long percolated in Republican circles. Several Republican politicians experimented during the 1970s and 1980s with rhetoric that framed policy proposals in terms of compassion toward less fortunate members of society. Most notable was New York congressman and George H. W. Bush–era secretary of housing and urban development Jack Kemp, who was fond of saying, "No one cares what you think unless they think that you care."[5]

Bush borrowed liberally from Kemp's playbook and surpassed Kemp as the most prominent advocate of the compassionate conservative philosophy within the Republican Party during the 1990s. Bush presented compassionate conservatism as a response to both the perceived failures of New Deal–Great Society liberalism and the limitations of the doctrinaire conservatism of Barry Goldwater and Ronald Reagan. As Bush explained in "The Duty of Hope," the speech that launched his first campaign for the presidency:

> Our nation must get beyond two narrow mindsets. The first is that government provides the only real compassion. A belief that what is done by caring people through church and charity is secondary and marginal. . . . There is another destructive mindset: the idea that if government would only get out of our way, all our problems would be solved. An approach with no higher goal, no nobler purpose, than "Leave us alone."[6]

In opposition to both these failed paradigms, Bush envisioned a "carefully limited" but "strong and active and respected" government that "appl[ies] our conservative and free-market ideas to the job of helping real human beings."[7] Or, as he explained in another address, "the truest kind of compassion doesn't only come from more government spending, but from helping citizens build lives of their own. The aim of this philosophy is not to spend less money, or to spend more money, but to spend only on what works. The measure of compassion is more than good intentions—it is good results."[8]

Compassionate conservatism sought to advance a more individualistic society in which "more of our citizens have a *personal* stake in the future of our country," Bush explained.[9] At the same time, he claimed that government programs that advanced this vision would also address enduring social problems such as economic and racial inequality in new and better ways. It would do so by forcing government bureaucracies to be more receptive to the needs of individual citizens and more accountable for their efforts to attain their stated objectives. This attempt at synthesis took the form of significant proposals in Bush's speech accepting the GOP presidential nomination in 2000. He proposed that parents of children in failing school districts should be able to use federal funds to send their children to other schools, including private schools; that young workers should be empowered to put part of their Social Security contributions into individualized private investment accounts; and that low-income Americans should be granted tax credits to purchase health insurance on the private market.[10] These proposals required individuals to take greater responsibility for decisions about education, retirement planning, and health care, respectively. But they also sought to make government agencies (schools, the Social Security system, and federal and state health care bureaucracies) more responsive to the particular needs of individual citizens through a combination of performance measurement, market competition, and accountability for results. To Bush, this combination of individual responsibility and government accountability would yield superior outcomes for individuals—better education for young people (particularly those trapped in so-called failing schools), higher rates of return on retirement savings, and more extensive and personalized health insurance—and thus advance social justice. Whether any of these claims is true is highly debatable. The point is that each initiative wedded the "conservative" themes of individual responsibility and government accountability to the "compassionate" motive of "helping people," as Bush later put it. Taken together, they would maintain, if not expand, government's role in citizens' lives.[11]

The Principles and Politics of Compassionate Conservatism

Despite coming from a family of great wealth and political influence, Bush achieved no distinction in his youth and struggled with business failures and alcohol abuse into his forties. His efforts to recoup his business and political fortunes, quit drinking, and renew his religious faith informed the distinctive approach to policymaking that became compassionate conservatism. According to Margaret Spellings, a close ally who served as domestic policy adviser and then secretary of education during Bush's presidency, compassionate conservatism "has a lot to do with [Bush's] own personal story and drinking and recovery and all that. . . . It was so personal with him. You can't really get in somebody's chili about their faith experience when it's so authentic."

The personal conviction that supported Bush's compassionate conservative philosophy was reinforced by a program of conscious study and deliberation. During his tenure as governor of Texas, Bush met repeatedly with and studied the works of conservative philosopher Marvin Olasky—coiner of phrase *compassionate conservatism*—to develop his own governing philosophy and policy agenda.[12] In the words of John Bridgeland, Bush's Domestic Policy Council director, he also held "deep dive, almost educational seminars" with prominent conservative intellectuals to expand his understanding of important national issues. Among those invited to advise Bush was John DiIulio, a University of Pennsylvania professor and leading advocate of infusing social policymaking with Christian values (and future head of Bush's Office of Faith-Based Initiatives).

Yet Bush's public embrace of compassionate conservatism was also influenced by political calculations. Bush rose to national prominence in the late 1990s, a period of considerable uncertainty and doubt within the GOP. Bill Clinton's convincing win in the 1996 presidential election, followed by the Democrats' unexpected gains in the House of Representatives in 1998, raised concerns among Republicans that the party's traditional agenda of tax cuts, spending reductions, and regulatory relief was alienating moderate voters whose support was essential to the party's electoral success. Peter Wehner, Bush's director of the Office of Strategic Initiatives, described the circumstances surrounding Bush's run for the White House in 2000: "On the domestic side and intellectually, there was a sense of running out of energy [in the Republican Party], which was not simply or even primarily or even because of George H. W. Bush, but maybe circumstances. . . . With George W. Bush, this came after two terms of Clinton, after the [Newt] Gingrich revolution had crashed and burned. Gingrich lost the Speakership and there was a sense of the Republican Party casting about."

In this context, Bush needed to establish a distinctive political identity with appeal beyond the Republican base. Claiming the mantle of compassionate conservatism helped him do that. Ed Gillespie, who served as chairman of the Republican National Committee during Bush's presidency, later argued that "compassionate conservatism was a brand. It was a smart brand, given where we were with the Republican brand at the end of the '96 campaign, all about slashing spending and all of that." Rather than recycle the divisive themes that had characterized Republicanism—particularly Gingrich-style Republicanism—during the 1990s, Bush "offered an inclusive message that [would] draw people together," Karl Rove suggested.

Bush's public commitment to compassionate conservatism also enabled him to present a potent political contrast with the brilliant but undisciplined Bill Clinton and, by association, with Clinton's vice president and protégé Al Gore, Bush's Democratic opponent in 2000. Bush shrewdly perceived that Gore's major political weakness was his close relationship with Clinton, who was seen as a dazzling but unprincipled and self-serving politician. On the campaign stump, Bush frequently argued that, in an era of failed moral leadership, his staunch commitment to principle made him the best choice for the presidency.[13] As he explained in one campaign speech, "When we tell you something, we mean it. When we say we're going to do something, we're going to do what we say. That's what America hungers for."[14] In an indication of this strategy's effectiveness, Americans surveyed during the 2000 campaign deemed Bush the superior candidate on most personal traits, particularly honesty, strength of leadership, and integrity, even though they preferred Gore on the issues.[15]

The Domestic Policy Achievements of Compassionate Conservatism

Compassionate conservatism influenced a number of modest successes (as well as a few policy failures). In this chapter I focus on two major initiatives—No Child Left Behind and Medicare prescription drug coverage—that were powerfully shaped by compassionate conservatism and left long, important, but also fraught legacies in national politics. Concentrating on these two major initiatives serves two important purposes: to highlight areas where compassionate conservatism had the greatest effects, and to draw attention to areas where compassion was absent or lacking.

No Child Left Behind

During his tenure as governor of Texas, Bush made a name for himself as an important figure in the accountability movement in K–12 education, leading the charge for more testing of students and accountability for schools that failed to demonstrate improvements in learning.[16] For Bush, a straight line connected his compassionate conservative philosophy and schools' responsibility for student achievement. It involved the application of a conservative principle, government accountability for results, to an important social justice issue, racial and economic equity in educational outcomes. Karl Rove recollects that "Bush's attitude was that the [education] system was failing, and it's failing you if you're black, if you speak Spanish at home, and you're poor. . . . The idea of accountability, holding the system responsible for results, comes from it failing too many people and, as a society, we couldn't afford that; it was a conservative but compellingly compassionate view of how life ought to be."

During his campaign for president, Bush embraced the then-controversial idea that the federal government could play a leading role in promoting high standards, regular testing, and accountability for results in public schools.[17] He insisted that "when a school district receives federal funds to teach poor children, we expect those children to learn," and he proposed "an annual testing requirement that would tell parents which schools do better and which do worse," as well as exit options for children in "failing" schools.[18] Such ideas put Bush at odds with many congressional Republicans, conservative activists, and GOP-affiliated intellectuals. As Margaret Spellings tartly recalled, "We were so far ahead of them [the Republican establishment] it wasn't even funny. . . . The old Republican orthodoxy on education, was about choice, vouchers, vouchers, and furthermore vouchers. Big whoop."

Of course, electoral politics also played a central role in Bush's decision to prioritize education reform. At the time of Bush's election, education had reached a high-water mark in terms of public interest, with more Americans perceiving it as the most important problem facing the nation than at any previous point in history.[19] Surveys also suggested that Americans were concerned that low-performing schools were an obstacle to both individuals' achievement of the American dream and the nation's global economic competitiveness. In this context, spearheading a federal initiative that promised to solve the nation's education problems made good political sense.

Given the Republican establishment's opposition to a strong federal role in education, Bush enlisted alternative allies in his quest for a major legislative breakthrough. In formulating the legislative proposal that became No Child Left Behind (NCLB), Bush largely froze out orthodox Republican think tanks and activists in favor of a coalition of business leaders and civil rights activists who had been advocating similar policies at the federal level for some time.[20] Bush also carefully courted moderates within the Democratic Party, who had grown dissatisfied with the track record of traditional education programs. In the words of Richard Gephardt, the House Democratic leader at the time, "We're not succeeding here. . . . You have to try something." The product of this collaboration was an initiative to expand the role of the federal government in K–12 education policymaking beyond anything the Republicans or most Democrats had previously imagined. In its essentials, NCLB leveraged the largest federal education program—the Elementary and Secondary Education Act, which had previously funded programs to assist disadvantaged students—to induce states to adopt statewide, integrated systems of educational standards, mandatory student testing, and escalating sanctions against schools whose students failed to meet performance goals. To broaden its appeal, NCLB included an unprecedented infusion of federal funds for elementary and secondary education. Bush praised the deal for "includ[ing] monumental reforms that promote real accountability, annual testing and funding flexibility."[21]

The scope and costs of NCLB made it a difficult pill for Republican leaders in Congress to swallow. But because Bush had made education reform the centerpiece of his domestic agenda, virtually all Republicans eventually fell in line to support the legislation. According to Nick Calio, Bush's legislative director, "The [Republican] leaders didn't want to do No Child Left Behind. But for the fact that we'd had Clinton for eight years and they'd [Republicans] been out in the wilderness and they were so happy that George Bush was now President, they probably never would have accepted and put through No Child Left Behind at that opportunity." Despite private grumblings, Republicans ultimately joined hands with Democrats—many of whom were mollified by the historic increase in K–12 spending—to pass the legislation by an overwhelming bipartisan vote.

The No Child Left Behind Act transformed federal education policy by requiring states to adopt standards, testing, and accountability reforms as conditions for receiving federal funds under the Elementary and Secondary Education Act. Under the law, states were required to test students in reading and math each year in grades three through eight and once in high school; report the test results for all students, as well as for subgroups such as racial or ethnic groups, English learners, and children from low-income families; demonstrate "adequate yearly progress" toward a standard of academic proficiency for all student groups by 2013–2014; and implement a series of escalating sanctions against schools that failed to show that students were making progress toward proficiency. States were also supposed to guarantee that all teachers and paraprofessionals were "highly qualified" and possessed appropriate credentials and licenses.

In signing NCLB into law, Bush invoked the language of compassionate conservatism to frame the meaning of the act: "There's no greater challenge than to make sure that . . . every single child, regardless of where they live, how they're raised, the income level of their family, every child receive[s] a first-class education in America. . . . As of this hour, America's schools will be on a new path of reform, and a new path of results."[22] Bush's belief that federal leadership in standards, testing, and accountability was necessary to advance racial and economic equity in education has remained central to federal education policymaking—for good or for ill—ever since, although the precise policy mechanisms have evolved significantly in the two decades since the enactment of NCLB. Bush's successor, Democrat Barack Obama, continued to endorse federal leadership by establishing a "Race to the Top" initiative that provided federal funds in exchange for states' promises to adopt a prescriptive menu of standards, testing, and accountability reforms.[23] Growing popular backlash against some features of NCLB—in particular, its stringent sanctions against schools that failed to demonstrate "adequate yearly progress" in students' achievement—ultimately led Congress to pass the Every Student Succeeds Act (ESSA) in 2015. But this law, widely described as a "replacement" for NCLB, still required states to establish accountability systems with performance targets and interventions for low-performing schools, to articulate challenging academic standards, and to test students in reading and math in grades three through eight and in high school, even though states were given somewhat more flexibility in how they met these requirements.[24]

Five years after passage of the ESSA, *Education Week*, the premier journal of K–12 education politics, reported that "the universal expectation on Capitol Hill is that [ESSA] will effectively be the law of the land for years to come."[25] In no small part, the durability of NCLB's successor is attributable to extreme partisan polarization in Congress, which presents a huge obstacle to efforts to amend the law. But the resilience of federal leadership in educational standards, testing, and accountability also points to a broader consensus around the fusion of educational accountability and educational equity that Bush regarded as central to the philosophy of compassionate conservatism.

There is little doubt that compassionate conservatism has wrought major changes in K–12 education in the United States. Whether these changes are positive or negative is debatable. If the measure of success is student achievement, it can be argued that the reforms initiated by NCLB and elaborated in subsequent decades have had a modest impact at best. As evaluated by the National Assessment of Educational Progress (NAEP), the nation's premier measure of student achievement, average test scores in reading have held steady since NCLB was enacted in 2002, while average scores in mathematics have improved slightly.[26] But achievement gaps between whites and students of color have remained stubbornly large.[27] Meanwhile, reforms have had some educationally dubious consequences, including an overemphasis on rote test preparation, a preoccupation with tested subjects to the detriment of nontested subjects, the imposition of stringent and disruptive sanctions on schools based on low standardized test scores, and (in some instances) gaming and cheating behavior by school officials to avoid harsh accountability measures.[28]

To be fair, Bush deserves credit for making racial and economic differences in student achievement visible and forcing states and schools to take steps to reduce educational inequities when and where they occur. Since the enactment of NCLB, federal and state policymakers have largely worked within the parameters Bush brought to national prominence, even as they have expended considerable energy to soften the many sharp edges of the policy he signed into law.

The Medicare Prescription Drug Benefit

During the 1990s Medicare, the nation's health care system for the elderly, encountered increasing fiscal strain, even as it faced criticism for failing to meet the needs of seniors. In particular, Medicare failed to keep pace with a revolution in the pharmaceutical industry and changes in medical practice that led practitioners to emphasize outpatient treatments involving expensive medications that were not covered under the law. Perhaps it is no surprise, then, that Medicare reform was one of the Bush campaign's "five big domestic priorities," along with NCLB, a tax cut, Social Security reform, and faith-based initiatives, according to Kristen Silverberg, who held a number of senior positions in the Bush White House before serving as US ambassador to the European Union. Although Bush hoped to restrain Medicare's overall growth, he also sought to expand seniors' access to outpatient prescription drugs. On the campaign trail, he promised that "every senior will get help paying for prescription drug coverage—and every low-income senior will get prescription coverage for free."[29]

Like NCLB, Bush's focus on Medicare reform as part of his compassionate conservative agenda blended high principle and political calculation. According to legislative liaison David Hobbs, Bush was personally committed to reforming Medicare and, in particular, to increasing seniors' access to outpatient prescription drugs. Hobbs recalls, "I was at one meeting on Medicare and [Bush] said, 'This is what I want to do.' I said, 'They're [congressional Republicans] going to hate it, they don't want to do it, they want to run from it.' There was a policy meeting in the Roosevelt Room. I remember [Bush] said, 'We're only here for a short time. Shouldn't we try to do the right thing?'"

Bush's approach to Medicare reform was conservative as well as compassionate because—at least initially—he intended to expand needy seniors' access to prescription drugs through block grants to the states rather than through a traditional federal entitlement program. In his first budget, which included $400 billion for Medicare reform, Bush proposed a block grant for states to provide drug coverage for Medicare beneficiaries with incomes up to 175 percent of the poverty level, as well as "catastrophic coverage" to limit individuals' out-of-pocket costs for all medical services to $6,000, regardless of income.[30] Another conservative dimension of Bush's push for prescription drug reform was, as Josh Bolten explained, his intention to use it as "leverage" to "improve [Medicare's] efficiency and make its costs more sustainable over the long term." In other words, Bush hoped prescription drug reform would be so politically attractive to members of Congress that they would accept constraints on spending, as well as an expanded role for private-sector insurers, to get it.[31]

But Bush's proposal to enhance access to prescription drugs also represented a calculated appeal for support from elderly Americans, particularly the large number of seniors residing in pivotal Electoral College states such as Florida and Ohio. Polls from the early 2000s indicated that a clear majority of seniors wanted a prescription drug benefit added to the Medicare program. Enjoying Republican majorities in the House and, for a time, in the Senate after the 2000 election, Bush perceived a chance to turn a traditionally Democratic issue to the GOP's political advantage.[32]

Still, Bush shied away from a sweeping prescription drug benefit early in his first term. The funding for prescription drug coverage proposed in the president's fiscal year 2002 budget "was only one-tenth of what the Congressional Budget Office projected that the Medicare population would spend on prescription drugs."[33] In fact, Bush soft-pedaled Medicare reform in general early in his first term, an approach attributable to his focus on education reform and tax cuts and the huge political disruption caused by the September 11 terrorist attacks and the war on terror. In 2002 a tepid administration effort to expand prescription drug benefits by executive order stalled in the face of court opposition, while dueling congressional proposals by Republicans and Democrats failed to secure broad support.[34]

After the 2002 midterm elections, which restored GOP control of the Senate, the president and Republican congressional leaders pressed forward with plans to expand prescription drug coverage within the Medicare program as well as increase its market orientation. Bush highlighted the issue and rhetorically linked prescription drug coverage to his compassionate conservative agenda in his 2003 State of the Union address, declaring, "Medicare is the binding commitment of a caring society. We must renew that commitment by giving seniors access to preventive medicine and new drugs that are transforming health care in America."[35] Bush offered $400 billion in new Medicare spending over ten years (not all of it for prescription drug benefits), federal support for drug expenses, and increases in catastrophic coverage. Notably, Bush's new framework offered prescription drug coverage to all seniors, not just the neediest.[36] But he paired this compassionate expansion of benefits with conservative inducements that "openly encouraged Medicare beneficiaries to leave the traditional fee-for-service program . . . by offering additional prescription drug coverage to those who joined private, Medicare-approved health plans."[37]

Both the Senate and the House versions of the legislation departed from Bush's proposal somewhat, but they each significantly increased federal funding, expanded prescription drug coverage and catastrophic coverage, and enhanced the role of Medicare-approved private health plans and care providers. Because the Senate and House bills both advanced the administration's overarching policy and political objectives, Bush was happy to overlook differences in the details in the interest of securing a big Republican win going into the 2004 presidential campaign.[38]

For the most part, Senate Republicans were convinced of the electoral advantages of enacting Medicare reform, even though it created a huge new entitlement program.[39] The political situation was more difficult in the House. Although he had the support of the GOP leadership, Bush had to contend with the reality that "there were some Republicans who were just against the whole thing—don't expand the Medicare program," as Josh Bolten recalls. With the support of the House Republican leadership, the Bush administration used unusually aggressive tactics to address the problem and secure legislative victory. While the leadership kept the vote on the conference committee report open for three hours, rather than the normal fifteen minutes, administration negotiators and GOP leaders twisted arms to secure support from conservative Republican legislators. Bush personally called Republican holdouts from Air Force One, and his emissaries engaged in more hard-hitting tactics. Nick Calio recalls, "An unnamed [Republican] Member [of the House] . . . wasn't going [to support the bill], was [saying] no, no, no. Karl [Rove] called up his biggest fundraiser and said, 'You're dead to me if you don't vote with us.' I remember seeing him [and asked], 'Are you with us?' It was like a [raised middle finger]—and he voted yes." Even more ruthlessly, the Bush administration suppressed evidence from the Department of Health and Human Services revealing that the true cost of the legislation was far above the official $400 billion price tag, meaning that representatives were voting for the legislation without an accurate understanding of its effect on the budget.[40]

In the end, the Bush administration and the GOP congressional leadership exploited narrow partisan majorities in both chambers to eke out a legislative victory for Medicare reform. Most Democrats ultimately voted against the legislation on the grounds that its benefits were too modest and its privatizing features too destabilizing. Although the politics surrounding enactment were ugly, the law was the most significant reform of Medicare since its creation in 1965. Consistent with Bush's desire to expand prescription drug coverage, the Medicare Modernization Act of 2003 (MMA) allowed Medicare beneficiaries to purchase government-guaranteed but privately provided drug plans.[41] Those who voluntarily enrolled in these plans paid a monthly premium of $35 and an annual deductible of $250 and were responsible for 25 percent of drug costs between $250 and $2,250, 100 percent of drug costs between $2,250 and $5,100, and 5 percent of drug costs over $5,100.[42] Additionally, and in keeping with Bush's objective to reshape Medicare in a more conservative direction, the MMA introduced new privatizing features, such as requiring beneficiaries who chose to enroll in the drug benefit program to select among private prescription drug plans and expanding private health savings accounts within Medicare. Given its distinctive combination of expanded government benefits and increased private-sector participation, it is fair to say that the MMA represented a major compassionate conservative achievement that rivaled if not exceeded NCLB in significance.

Unlike NCLB, however, the MMA was very unpopular because of the huge donut hole in coverage between $2,250 and $5,100 in prescription drug costs and the bruising partisan politics surrounding its enactment. And although the MMA deserves substantial credit for increasing 43 million seniors' access to outpatient prescription drugs, there were significant limitations. The MMA destabilized Medicare's social insurance orientation by reducing the uniformity of benefits, assisting some seniors more than others, and requiring beneficiaries to anticipate their own needs and choose plans accordingly.[43] The MMA also specifically forbade the federal government to use its purchasing power to constrain the exponential growth in the cost of many drugs. In consequence, the prescription drug benefit has been incredibly expensive, imposing additional strain on an already stressed federal budget.[44] Thus, arguably even more than NCLB, the MMA illustrates the ambiguous policy consequences of Bush's compassionate conservatism.

The Limits of Compassion

The principles of compassionate conservatism were in serious tension—if not outright conflict—with Bush's enthusiasm for cutting taxes, particularly for the wealthy. His advancement of a series of massive tax cuts tilted toward the most affluent Americans significantly increased economic inequality and eroded the federal government's capacity to address the challenges facing ordinary Americans, such as the high costs of health care and college education, during a period of mounting economic insecurity. Additionally, although compassionate conservatism seemed to speak to the concerns of historically marginalized groups, Bush declined to grapple with the systemic inequality affecting people of color, women, and the LGBTQ+ community. Indeed, Bush's troubling record on voting rights, his wholly inadequate response to Hurricane Katrina, and his advocacy of a constitutional amendment to ban same-sex marriage belied his promise of compassion toward the most vulnerable Americans.

Tax Cuts and Economic Inequality

Bush was a true believer in the power of tax cuts to stimulate economic growth and create jobs. As he proclaimed in a speech shortly before his election in 2000, "The momentum of today's prosperity began in the 1980s—with sound money, deregulation, the opening of global trade and a 25 percent tax cut. . . . The success of our economy is not a tribute to politicians, hungry for praise. It is a tribute to the effort and risk-taking of Americans. It is a tribute to the power and possibilities of freedom."[45]

During the 2000 campaign, Bush argued that the presence of a federal budget surplus meant that the time had come for a new round of tax cuts, as a means of both returning "the people's money" to them and stimulating investment and job creation. Having made the pledge to cut taxes central to his campaign, Bush focused on achieving tax legislation early in his first term.[46]

Publicly, Bush claimed his tax proposals provided substantial benefits to middle- and working-class Americans. In reality, the tax-cut packages he and congressional Republicans advanced were tilted overwhelmingly toward the wealthiest Americans. The Economic Growth and Tax Relief Reconciliation Act of 2001, which cost the federal government as much as $2.1 trillion over ten years, allocated 36 percent of its tax cuts to the richest 1 percent of Americans, almost as much as the share received by the bottom 80 percent. Another major tax cut for individuals in 2003 (the Jobs and Growth Tax Relief Reconciliation Act), with an estimated price tag of more than $1 trillion, showered a similar share of benefits on the wealthiest.[47] As a result of these two acts, the top 1 percent of households received an average tax cut of over $570,000 per year between 2004 and 2012, effectively increasing their annual after-tax income by more than 5 percent.[48] Two additional tax cuts between 2003 and 2004—one for individuals and another for corporations—also disproportionately benefited affluent individuals.

The Bush tax cuts contributed directly to the growing economic chasm between the most affluent Americans and everyone else—without significantly boosting the economy as a whole.[49] More problematic, given Bush's ostensible commitment to helping the needy, the cumulative magnitude of the tax cuts contributed substantially to persistent deficits in the federal budget, thereby depriving the federal government of the revenue needed to combat major social problems such as the rising cost of higher education, exploding health care costs, expensive and unobtainable child care, a dearth of affordable housing in many parts of the country, and stagnant or declining incomes. From 2001 through 2010, Bush's 2001 and 2003 tax cuts cumulatively added $2.6 trillion to the national debt, accounting for almost 50 percent of the total debt amassed during this period.[50] Extension of most of the Bush tax cuts during the Obama era increased the cumulative total to roughly $5.9 trillion through 2018. In no small part due to these losses, federal revenue is inadequate to fund current government obligations, a state of affairs that not only hamstrings efforts to address emergent social problems but also creates political pressure to cut existing services.[51]

Harsh Treatment of Marginalized Groups

The limits of Bush's compassionate conservatism are further illustrated by his harsh treatment of marginalized groups in three important areas: voting rights, response to Hurricane Katrina, and same-sex marriage.

During his presidency, Bush took momentous steps that undermined voting rights, particularly for people of color. Most importantly, he appointed two Supreme Court justices, chief justice John Roberts and associate justice Samuel Alito, who consolidated a conservative majority that has been skeptical of—if not openly hostile to—the vigorous federal enforcement of voting rights.[52] This majority has issued a series of decisions that seriously limited the capacity of the Voting Rights Act to safeguard the rights of voters of color. Most devastatingly, in *Shelby County v. Holder* (2013), the Roberts court effectively terminated the "preclearance" process by which the Department of Justice or the federal courts reviewed proposed changes in voting and election procedures prior to their implementation in jurisdictions with histories of discrimination. Since that time, states released from preclearance requirements have adopted an array of new policies that make it harder for people to vote, from stringent voter identification laws to purges of the voter registration rolls.[53]

No less than his lackluster record on voting rights, Bush's mismanagement of the Hurricane Katrina tragedy contradicted his claims of compassion for the disadvantaged. The August 2005 storm devastated the New

Orleans area and the Gulf coast of Mississippi, displacing hundreds of thousands of people and causing billions of dollars in damage. At least 1,833 people perished as a result of the storm, 1,577 of them in Louisiana alone.

From the beginning, the Bush administration mismanaged the crisis, particularly in New Orleans. Although the administration had sought to harden the American response to natural and man-made disasters after 9/11 by coordinating federal emergency agencies under the new Department of Homeland Security (DHS), the DHS was still an untested organization in 2005 and was unsure how to deploy its authority and resources in an emergency.[54] In the years running up to the Katrina disaster, the Bush administration weakened the Federal Emergency Management Agency (FEMA), the organization charged with coordinating federal, state, and local responses to natural disasters. Bush's appointees to top leadership positions at FEMA were chosen for their loyalty to the president rather than their expertise in emergency management, contributing to an exodus of competent staff during Bush's first term.[55]

Weakened by poor leadership and drained of bureaucratic capacity, the Bush administration in general and the DHS in particular were caught flat-footed by Katrina and responded lethargically to the unfolding crisis. Despite warnings that the storm was likely to devastate New Orleans, DHS chief Michael Chertoff failed to take appropriate action to coordinate a national response and mobilize federal emergency resources before the hurricane arrived.[56] After Katrina made landfall, early reports of levee breaches in New Orleans were discounted by DHS officials, leading to a substantial delay in the allocation of federal disaster response assets while New Orleans drowned.[57] FEMA's efforts were similarly inept. For example, it failed to secure buses to evacuate New Orleans residents from the Superdome and convention center in a timely fashion, leaving thousands stranded for days without food or water. And while federal troops were eventually deployed to quell looting and violence, hesitation and delays meant that a dangerous situation on the ground did not begin to stabilize until a full five days after the storm made landfall.[58]

These bureaucratic failures, compounded by state and local officials' misjudgments, exacerbated the effects of the storm and unnecessarily increased human suffering. Of central importance, this suffering was concentrated among the most vulnerable residents of New Orleans and the Gulf coast—impoverished African Americans. Thus, regardless of the intentions of administration officials, mismanagement of the Katrina crisis both reflected and deepened the structural racism in American society.[59]

Bush's arguably cynical promotion during the 2004 presidential campaign of a constitutional amendment to prohibit same-sex marriage further undermines the compassionate character of his presidency. Historically, exclusion from the right to marry both reflected and contributed to the marginalization of the LGBTQ+ community within mainstream American society.[60]

Even though Bush seemed to harbor no personal animus toward LGBTQ+ individuals, he knew that fear of them and of the "homosexual political agenda" was deeply entrenched among evangelical Christians and conservative Catholics, two of the GOP's most important political constituencies.[61] Indeed, opponents of same-sex marriage orchestrated a powerful political movement that placed initiatives banning gay marriage on the ballot in eleven states in 2004, which increased voter turnout among white evangelical Protestants and helped fuel Bush's reelection.[62] Additionally, according to Peter Wehner, Bush believed that the Massachusetts Supreme Judicial Court's 2003 decision recognizing gay marriage in that state required him to take a stand against liberal judicial activism that "takes this [issue] away from the public."

Thus, while Bush endorsed "civil unions" for same-sex couples, he simultaneously advocated a constitutional amendment to define marriage as a union between one man and one woman. On the 2004 campaign trail, Bush engaged in misleading fearmongering to bolster his position, arguing that the amendment was essential to protect the "most fundamental institution of civilization" from destruction by a few "activist judges."[63] "The union of a man and woman is the most enduring human institution . . . honored and encouraged in all cultures and by every religious faith," Bush intoned. "Marriage cannot be severed from its cultural, religious and natural roots without weakening the good influence of society."[64] Although opposition to gay marriage was not a major motivating factor for the average voter in 2004, it apparently stimulated support for Bush among white evangelical Protestants in crucial swing states where gay marriage bans were on the ballot.[65]

Bush undoubtedly knew that the proposed amendment was destined for political failure in a country where support for a constitutional ban on same-sex marriage was neither broad nor deep enough to secure its enactment. The fact that Bush essentially dropped his advocacy of the amendment after the 2004 election—much to the chagrin of conservative Christian activists—is powerful evidence that the proposal was merely a campaign gambit.[66]

A Post-Compassionate Republican Party

As we have seen, the compassionate conservatism of George W. Bush was deeply flawed. Despite its promise of a new framework for policymaking that transcended old political divisions and offered new hope for vulnerable Americans, compassionate conservative policies were often unwieldy, disruptive, and divisive, without offering any dramatic improvement in either government performance or social outcomes. During Bush's presidency, the promise of compassionate conservatism was further undermined by conventional conservative policies that increased economic insecurity and eroded the rights of vulnerable groups.

And yet—in light of what the Republican Party became during the presidency of Donald Trump—it is hard not to look back on the compassionate conservative agenda with nostalgia. Despite its many limitations, compassionate conservatism at least attempted to speak directly to the hopes and needs of marginalized Americans. Today, the resurrection of a compassionate conservatism may be a central task for Republicans seeking to reestablish a healthy and vital Republican Party in a complex and diverse America.

Notes

1. Jesse H. Rhodes and Kaylee T. Johnson, "Welcoming Their Hatred: Class Populism in Democratic Rhetoric in American Presidential Campaigns, 1932–2012," *Presidential Studies Quarterly* 47, 1 (2017): 92–121.

2. White House, "President Promotes Compassionate Conservatism," Parkside Hall, San Jose, CA, April 30, 2002.

3. George W. Bush, "The Duty of Hope," Indianapolis, July 29, 1999.

4. Unless otherwise noted, all quotations are from the Miller Center's George W. Bush Oral History. The Miller Center interviews were with Josh Bolten, John Bridgeland, Nicholas Calio (with David W. Hobbs, John W. Howard, and Ziad S. Ojakli), Richard Gephardt, Edward Gillespie, Karl Rove, Margaret Spellings, and Peter Wehner.

5. Steven M. Teles, "The Eternal Return of Compassionate Conservatism," *National Affairs* (2009): 112.

6. Bush, "Duty of Hope."

7. Bush, "Duty of Hope."

8. White House, "President Promotes Compassionate Conservatism."

9. White House, "President Discusses Education, Entrepreneurship, and Home Ownership at Indiana Black Expo," Indianapolis, July 14, 2005.

10. George W. Bush, "Address to the Republican National Convention: Compassionate Conservatism," Philadelphia, August 3, 2000.

11. "President George W. Bush on Compassionate Conservatism: A Conversation with President George W. Bush," *Catalyst* 12 (Fall 2018), https://www.bushcenter.org /catalyst/opportunity-road/george-w-bush-on-compassionate-conservatism.html.

12. Anthony Sparacino, "Compassionate Conservatism in the Spiral of Politics," *American Political Thought* 7 (Summer 2018): 480–513.

13. Stephen Skowronek, "Leadership by Definition: First Term Reflections on George W. Bush's Political Stance," *Perspectives on Politics* 3, 4 (2005): 817–831.

14. George W. Bush, campaign speech, Naperville, IL, September 4, 2000.

15. Gerald Pomper, "The 2000 Presidential Election: Why Gore Lost," *Political Science Quarterly* 116, 2 (2001): 201–223.

16. Patrick J. McGuinn, *No Child Left Behind and the Transformation of Federal Education Policy, 1965–2005* (Lawrence: University Press of Kansas, 2006).

17. Jesse H. Rhodes, *An Education in Politics: The Origins and Evolution of No Child Left Behind* (Ithaca, NY: Cornell University Press, 2012), chap. 5.

18. George W. Bush, address to California Republican Party Convention, September 16, 2000.

19. See Patrick J. McGuinn, "Swing Issues and Policy Regimes: Federal Education Policy and the Politics of Policy Change," *Journal of Policy History* 18, 2 (2006): 205–240.

20. See Jesse H. Rhodes, "Progressive Policy Making in a Conservative Age? Civil Rights and the Politics of Federal Education Standards, Testing, and Accountability," *Perspectives on Politics* 9, 3 (2011): 519–544.

21. George W. Bush, "President Commends House Education and Workforce Committee," White House, Office of the Press Secretary, May 9, 2001.

22. Quoted in Valerie Strauss, "Why It's Worth Re-reading George W. Bush's 2002 No Child Left Behind Speech," *Washington Post*, December 9, 2015.

23. Patrick J. McGuinn, "Stimulating Reform: Race to the Top, Competitive Grants and the Obama Education Agenda," *Educational Policy* 26, 1 (2012): 136–159.

24. Patrick J. McGuinn, "From No Child Left Behind to the Every Student Succeeds Act: Federalism and the Education Legacy of the Obama Administration," *Publius: The Journal of Federalism* 46, 3 (2016): 392–415.

25. Andrew Ujifusa, Evie Blad, and Daarel Burnette II, "ESSA Voices: The Every Student Succeeds Act, Four Years Later," *Education Week*, September 25, 2020.

26. Thomas S. Dee and Brian Jacob, "The Impact of No Child Left Behind on Student Achievement," *Journal of Policy Analysis and Management* 30, 3 (2011): 418–446; Jennifer L. Jennings and Douglas Lee Lauen, "Accountability, Inequality, and Achievement: The Effects of the No Child Left Behind Act on Multiple Measures of Student Learning," *RSF: The Russell Sage Foundation Journal of the Social Sciences* 2, 5 (2016): 220–241.

27. Nick Huntington-Klein and Elizabeth Ackert, "The Long Road to Equality: A

Meta-Regression Analysis of Changes in the Black Test Score Gap over Time," *Social Science Quarterly* 99, 3 (2018): 1119–1133.

28. Derek Neal and Diane Whitmore Schanzenbach, "Left behind by Design: Proficiency Counts and Test-Based Accountability," *Review of Economics and Statistics* 92, 2 (2010): 263–283; Thomas S. Dee, Brian Jacob, and Nathaniel L. Schwartz, "The Effects of NCLB on School Resources and Practices," *Educational Evaluation and Policy Analysis* 35, 2 (2013): 252–279.

29. Bush, address to California Republican Party Convention.

30. Thomas R. Oliver, Philip R. Lee, and Helene L. Lipton, "A Political History of Medicare and Prescription Drug Coverage," *Milbank Quarterly* 82, 2 (2004): 307.

31. Henry J. Aaron, "Medicare: The Good, the Bad, and the Ugly," *Washington Spectator*, January 15, 2004.

32. Theda Skocpol, "A Bad Senior Moment," *American Prospect*, December 15, 2003.

33. Oliver, Lee, and Lipton, "Political History of Medicare," 308.

34. Robert Pear and Elisabeth Bumiller, "Doubts Are Emerging as Bush Pushes His Medicare Plan," *New York Times*, January 30, 2003.

35. George W. Bush, State of the Union address, January 8, 2003.

36. Douglas Jaenicke and Alex Waddan, "President Bush and Social Policy: The Strange Case of the Medicare Prescription Drug Benefit," *Political Science Quarterly* 121, 2 (2006): 226.

37. Oliver, Lee, and Lipton, "Political History of Medicare," 309.

38. Jonathan Oberlander, "Through the Looking Glass: The Politics of the Medicare Prescription Drug, Improvement, and Modernization Act," *Journal of Health Politics, Policy and Law* 32, 2 (2007): 190.

39. Jaenicke and Waddan, "President Bush and Social Policy," 225.

40. Jonathan Chait, "Power from the People: The Case against George W. Bush, Part II," *New Republic*, July 25, 2004.

41. Jacob S. Hacker and Theodore R. Marmor, "Medicare Reform: Fact, Fiction and Foolishness," *Public Policy and Aging Report* 13, 4 (2003): 1–23.

42. Rick Mayes, "Medicare and America's Healthcare System in Transition: From the Death of Managed Care to the Medicare Modernization Act of 2003 and Beyond," *Journal of Health Law* 38, 3 (2005): 417.

43. Marsha Gold, "Medicare Part D's Importance Extends Far beyond the Drug Benefit It Provides," Health Affairs blog, January 15, 2016, https://www.healthaffairs.org/do/10.1377/hblog20160115.052694/full.

44. Priya Vedula, "What to Do about the High Cost of Pharmaceuticals?" Loma Linda University health blog, September 25, 2018, https://ihpl.llu.edu/blog/what-do-about-high-cost-pharmaceuticals-part-2.

45. "Text of Remarks Prepared for Delivery Wednesday, December 1, 1999, by Texas Gov. George W. Bush in Des Moines, Iowa," *Washington Post*, December 1, 1999.

46. Scott Greenberg, "Looking Back at the Bush Tax Cuts, Fifteen Years Later." Tax Foundation, June 7, 2016, https://taxfoundation.org/by/scott-greenberg.

47. Jacob S. Hacker and Paul Pierson, "Abandoning the Middle: The Bush Tax Cuts and the Limits of Democratic Control," *Perspectives on Politics* 3, 1 (2005): 33.

48. Emily Horton, "The Legacy of the 2001 and 2003 'Bush' Tax Cuts," Center on Budget and Policy Priorities, October 23, 2017.

49. Marc Labonte, "What Effects Did the 2001 to 2003 Tax Cuts Have on the Economy?" Congressional Research Service Report for Congress, January 16, 2008; Danny Yagan, "Capital Tax Reform and the Real Economy: The Effects of the 2003 Dividend Tax Cut," *American Economic Review* 105, 12 (2015): 3531–3563; William G. Gale and Andrew A. Samwick, "Effects of Income Tax Changes on Economic Growth," Brookings Institution and Tax Policy Center, February 1, 2016.

50. Andrew Fieldhouse and Ethan Pollack, "Tenth Anniversary of the Bush-Era Tax Cuts," Economic Policy Institute, June 1, 2011, https://www.epi.org/page/-/EPI_Policy Memorandum_184.pdf.

51. Steve Wamhoff and Matthew Gardner, "Federal Tax Cuts in the Bush, Obama, and Trump Years," Institute on Taxation and Economic Policy, July 2018, https://itep.org /federal-tax-cuts-in-the-bush-obama-and-trump-years/.

52. Jesse H. Rhodes, *Ballot Blocked: The Political Erosion of the Voting Rights Act* (Palo Alto, CA: Stanford University Press, 2017), 153–161.

53. Desmond Ang, "Do 40-Year-Old Facts Still Matter? Long Run Effects of Federal Oversight under the Voting Rights Act," Harvard Kennedy School Faculty Research Working Paper RWP18-033, October 2018; Scot Schraufnagel, Michael J. Pomante, and Quan Li, "Cost of Voting in the American States: 2020," *Election Law Journal* 19, 4 (2020): 503–509.

54. Donald P. Moynihan, "The Response to Hurricane Katrina," IRGC case study for "Risk Governance Deficits: An Analysis and Illustration of the Most Common Deficits in Risk Governance," 2009, 1.

55. Donald P. Moynihan and Alasdair S. Roberts, "The Triumph of Loyalty over Competence: The Bush Administration and the Exhaustion of the Politicized Presidency," *Public Administration Review* 70, 4 (2010): 575.

56. Dwight Ink, "An Analysis of the House Select Committee and White House Reports on Hurricane Katrina," *Public Administration Review* 66, 6 (2006): 801.

57. Anihita Gheytanchi et al., "The Dirty Dozen: Twelve Failures of the Hurricane Katrina Response and How Psychology Can Help," *American Psychologist* 62, 2 (2007): 118.

58. Saundra K. Schneider, "Administrative Breakdowns in the Governmental Response to Hurricane Katrina," *Public Administration Review* 65, 5 (2005): 515–516.

59. Paul Frymer, Dara Z. Strolovitch, and Dorian T. Warren, "New Orleans Is Not the Exception: Re-politicizing the Study of Racial Inequality," *Du Bois Review* 3, 1 (2006): 37–57.

60. See William N. Eskridge Jr. and Christopher R. Riano, *Marriage Equality: From Outlaws to Inlaws* (New Haven, CT: Yale University Press, 2020).

61. Carin Robinson and Clyde Wilcox, "The Faith of George W. Bush: The Personal, Practical, and Political," in *Religion and the American Presidency*, ed. Mark J. Rozell and Gleaves Whitney (London: Palgrave Macmillan, 2007), 227–228.

62. D. Sunshine Hillygus and Todd G. Shields, "Moral Issues and Voter Decision Making in the 2004 Presidential Election," *PS: Political Science and Politics* 38, 2 (2005): 201–209.

63. Quoted in David Stout, "Bush Backs Ban in Constitution on Gay Marriage," *New York Times*, February 24, 2004.

64. George W. Bush, "President Calls for Constitutional Amendment Protecting Marriage," White House, Office of the Press Secretary, February 24, 2004.

65. David E. Campbell and J. Quin Monson, "The Religion Card: Gay Marriage and the 2004 Presidential Election," *Public Opinion Quarterly* 72, 3 (2008): 399–419.

66. Robinson and Wilcox, "Faith of George W. Bush," 228.

CHAPTER THREE

Day of Fire: An Oral History of 9/11

Michael Nelson

Crises present themselves to presidents in a variety of forms. Some are slow-acting, and are not obviously and indisputably regarded as crises by the political community until they reach a critical mass. Climate change offers one example. The coronavirus pandemic that began in early 2020 offers another.

Other crises arrive suddenly but their approach is visible to all. The British attack on Washington, DC, in the summer of 1814 was clearly going to happen; only the precise date, which turned out to be August 24, was uncertain. In the spring of 1861 President Abraham Lincoln knew that his strategically provocative resupply of Fort Sumter would cause the South to fire the first shots of the war, but he did not know that April 12 would be the day the Confederate cannoneers fell into his trap. Still other crises are of the president's unintentional making. No one forced John F. Kennedy to authorize the failed Bay of Pigs invasion, Franklin D. Roosevelt to propose packing the Supreme Court, or Richard Nixon to attempt to use the CIA to prevent the FBI from investigating the Watergate break-in.

A final kind of crisis is exemplified by the one examined in this chapter: a sudden *event* whose timing is *unanticipated* and that indisputably *requires* an *urgent response* by the president. Examples from American history marked by all four italicized elements are few—notably, the Japanese attack on the US naval base at Pearl Harbor on December 7, 1941; the discovery in Cuba of Soviet-deployed nuclear missiles aimed at the United States on October 14, 1962; and the potential domino effect of the collapse of Lehman Brothers on September 15, 2008. A perverse and historically unique variation was the January 6, 2021, assault on the US Capitol, an event that, far from being unanticipated by President Donald Trump, was incited by him. In this case, the urgent response required when, for example, Trump learned that Vice President Mike Pence was in danger of assassination was not forthcoming.

When it comes to this kind of crisis, Pearl Harbor most resembles what happened on September 11, 2001, universally known as 9/11. In both 1941 and 2001, attacks on the United States were expected in a general way at an unknown (albeit not distant) time against an unforeseen location, but no one saw them coming in any specific form or at any particular time or place. Like Pearl Harbor, there was no playbook—no comprehensive and widely familiar set of standard operating procedures—to prescribe how the president should respond to the 9/11 attacks. To be sure, some warnings—notably, National Security Council counterterrorism staff member Richard Clarke's famous "Bin Laden Determined to Attack Inside the United States" memo of August 6, 2001—had been issued, and they took on retrospective significance, despite their lack of specificity. Some procedures and protocols related to continuity of government came in handy, even though they had been designed during the Cold War with a Soviet nuclear strike in mind. But no one woke up on the morning of September 11, 2001, expecting to deal with the attacks that occurred that day or equipped with an instruction manual telling them how to respond when they did. As Gen. George Casey said in his oral history interview, 9/11 was "what [Albert and Roberta] Wohlstetter said about Pearl Harbor; it wasn't so much an intelligence failure as a failure of imagination. We just couldn't imagine some guys coming out of caves, being able to inflict that much damage on the United States."[1]

Much of value has been written about 9/11 in memoirs, in *The 9/11 Commission Report*, and in accounts such as Garrett Graff's *The Only Plane in the Sky* and Peter Baker's *Days of Fire*, from which this chapter adapts its title.[2] The distinctive approach I offer here is to chronicle the day's events as White House staff and other officials experienced them, drawing on the Miller Center's presidential oral history project. Oral history, like all historical methods, is an imperfect instrument. Memories are fallible, incomplete, and subject to conscious self-aggrandizement and unconscious bias. But as historian Philip Zelikow has argued from long experience both serving in and studying government, "In weighing the value of oral histories, consider that there are only two kinds of primary sources about the past. There are the material remnants of what happened—documents, coins, statues. Then there are the preserved recollections of the human observers."[3]

As I have argued elsewhere, oral history has two advantages that are lacking in "material" sources.[4] First, scholars can ask questions of an interviewee, probing deeply for elaboration, clarification, and context and seeking comment on apparent contradictions with the written record or the accounts of others. In contrast to journalistic treatments of events based on unattributed quotations, oral history interviewees are placed on the record. Andrew Card, President George W. Bush's chief of staff and a high-ranking official in several other Republican administrations, says that, based on his experience, oral history is sometimes more accurate than the history recorded in documents. Card offers this example from personal observation: A foreign leader was asked by an American president to do something that might cause the leader domestic political difficulties. He responded by telling the president no for the record while emphatically nodding yes.

The second advantage of oral history is availability. Fewer written records concerning sensitive or important matters are being created nowadays, the result of reasonable fears of congressional or judicial subpoenas. "I didn't keep notes," says Donna Shalala, Bill Clinton's secretary of health and human services.[5] According to former Clinton national security adviser Anthony Lake, "More and more officials are loath to put anything in writing." Bush's White House counsel Alberto Gonzales laments that, "as people become more and more concerned about investigation and discovery, more and more is going to be oral." After being instructed by "the White House counsel's office . . . about what records . . . could be subpoenaed," homeland security adviser Fran Townsend says she understands why "people did not take notes. And they did not take notes very consciously." Former national archivist Don Wilson describes the modern White House "climate for avoiding documentation or perhaps even destroying it."[6] Consequently, argues political scientist Russell L. Riley, "The White House operates largely as an oral culture" in which "much of the most important business occurs only in spoken, not written, words."[7]

Nearly every memoir of the Bush presidency includes an extended treatment of the author's experiences on September 11. Unlike this chapter, each of these accounts is individual and freestanding rather than juxtaposed with the accounts of others. Unlike the oral history interviews that provide the raw material for this chapter, no scholars were present during the memoir-writing process to ask follow-up questions about matters that were unclear or incomplete.

What follows is, quite literally, an account of the Bush presidency on 9/11—the day itself, not the events or the institutions (with the partial exception of

Congress) that surrounded and bracketed it. This account is chronological, narrative, and grounded entirely in the words of participants. Its purpose is to portray how these individuals experienced the sudden, unanticipated events that marked the crisis, as well as the president's urgent responses as they unfolded in the uncertain, terrifying circumstances of that day.

Bush in Florida

Dan Bartlett, White House deputy communications director: We were getting slammed on education. We're trying to regain the narrative on education. . . . As events go, it was a pretty cookie-cutter playbook we'd done a gazillion times. Go to the school, read to the children, make remarks.

Mike Morell, president's daily briefer, CIA: I walked into his suite for the president's morning intelligence briefing. . . . The second intifada was well under way then, and the briefings at that time were very heavy on Israeli-Palestinian stuff. There was nothing in the briefing about terrorism. It was very routine.[8]

Bartlett: As we're pulling up to the [Emma E. Booker Elementary] school the first tower had been hit. We're all, like most people, puzzled by that. . . . [Bush] said, "The weather must be bad up there or something." I said, "No, it's a clear day." He said, "Well, that doesn't make any sense." We were all left with, "Keep me posted."

Frances Townsend, director of Office of International Programs (OIPR), Department of Justice: Given what I did at OIPR, when the first plane hit, I knew immediately that it was terrorism. If it had been a little plane, it would have bounded off the side of the World Trade Center building. Any commercial pilot of a plane that size would have put the plane down in the Hudson, and done everything to avoid a building. There is no version of this that is explainable by a professionally trained pilot.

Andrew Card, White House chief of staff: [While the president was reading to the students, the] navy captain who was the acting national security adviser on the trip . . . came up to me and said, "Oh my God, another plane hit the other tower." . . . I made a conscious decision to pass on two facts and make one editorial comment and to do nothing to invite a conversation because I assumed [Bush] was sitting under a boom microphone.... I whispered into his ear, "A second plane hit the second tower. America is under attack." He did not turn around and talk to me, which I was pleased. I could tell he was thinking and thinking, and then I went back to the door, looked at him again, he was still—his head was kind of bobbing up and down. The students ... were taking out their books to read with the president. The press pool was all turned around talking to Ari Fleischer.[9]

Ari Fleischer, White House press secretary: I took my legal pad, where I take my notes, and I wrote on the back of it, "Don't say anything yet," in big letters and maneuvered over, putting my back to the press and holding it up. And Bush gave me a nod. I didn't want him to say anything until he had a proper briefing.

Everywhere presidents go a hold is set up, and inside the hold are two secure phones. In my eight or nine months, I had never seen the president use the hold.... He went into the hold that day and Condi [national security adviser Condoleezza Rice] was waiting for him on the phone. She didn't really have any information.... We were just working the phones—he was working the phones, Andy [Card] was working the phones—all trying to get information.

Karl Rove, White House senior adviser: When the president walked back into the staff hold, he said, "We're at war—give me the FBI and the vice president."[10]

Fleischer: I started to write what I thought President Bush should say, because he was going to go to the gymnasium, where he had been scheduled to give a big speech to everybody outside the classroom. . . . But I had a hard time writing it; nothing was coming to me. The president started to write, Dan [Bartlett] started to write, and it was just cobbled together. . . . [He] was basically talking off the cuff. He called them "those folks" and his remarks, in many people's eyes—I think deservedly so—weren't terribly strong. The "those folks" line raised eyebrows about why he was being so informal about it, and then he also said, "This will not stand," which is what his father had said [in reaction to Iraq invading Kuwait in 1990]. At a time when people were still questioning whether [Vice President Dick] Cheney was in charge and whether Bush was smart, for him to say what his father said created more doubts in the mind of cynics: "Can the president stand on his own two feet?"

President George W. Bush (addressing the nation from the Emma E. Booker Elementary School, Sarasota, Florida): I, unfortunately, will be going back to Washington after my remarks. . . . Terrorism against our country will not stand.

Morell: I was really worried that someone was going to fly a plane into that school. This event had been on the schedule for weeks.[11]

Bartlett: We get to the airport. . . . At this point we do believe we're going back to Washington.

Fleischer: The president heard about the third plane hitting the Pentagon in the motorcade.

Philip Smith, army branch chief, Pentagon: It was truly a miracle that the plane hit the strongest part of the Pentagon—it had been completely renovated—it was virtually unoccupied. In any other wedge of the Pentagon, there would have been 5,000 people, and the plane would have flown right through the middle of the building.[12]

Col. Mark Tillman, Air Force One pilot: President Bush comes up the stairs in Sarasota. We watched him come up the stairs with that famous Texas swagger. That day, no swagger. He was trucking up the stairs. As soon as the passengers are on board, I fired engines 1 and 2.[13]

Fleischer: The first thing he said when he got on board was to Eddie [Lorenzo], the lead Secret Service agent: "Are my wife and kids safe?"

From Florida to Barksdale Air Force Base, Bossier Parish, Louisiana

Ryan Crocker, former ambassador to Lebanon, Kuwait, and Syria: The War on Terror for me did not start on 9/11. It started on April 18, 1983, when the Embassy of Beirut was blown up and I was in it. . . . [But] I have to say, in all honesty, I never imagined a 9/11-style attack. . . . I think many American officials, including myself, were trapped in the assumption that terrorism is a threat to America, but it's a threat to America overseas.

Tillman: The initial conversation was that we'd take him to an air force base, no less than an hour away from Washington. Maybe we'd try to get him to Camp David. That all changed when we heard there was a plane headed for Camp David.[14]

Fleischer: One of the president's quotes was, "I don't want some tin-horned terrorist keeping me out of Washington. The American people want to know where their dang president is."

Richard Clarke, counterterrorism adviser, National Security Council: We did not want to bring the president back into what, frankly, was a war zone. There were F-15s circling the White House, armored vehicles, light tanks. . . . We didn't know what was yet to happen.[15]

Josh Bolten, White House deputy chief of staff: At least once, and probably more, the vice president got cut off while he was talking to the president. I remember him getting mad about that. . . . There was a huge challenge under the primitive circumstances of both communicating with the rest of the government but probably more importantly, communicating with the American public. We realized that we had no way to communicate with the American public.

Bush: One of my greatest frustrations on September 11 was the woeful communications technology on Air Force One. The plane had no satellite television. We were dependent on whatever local feeds we could pick up. After a few minutes on a given station, the screen would dissolve into static.[16]

Fleischer: Aboard Air Force One . . . the first word we got about the fourth plane was that it went down near Camp David. Karl [Rove] actually corrected that and said it was south of Pittsburgh. We got reports about the Mall being on fire, a car bomb at the State Department. . . . What goes wrong on a day like that is that bureaucracies are trained to filter information so only the most important and verified information gets to the top. Except on a day of reckoning. Except on a day of horrible crisis. In this case, people's instincts change and you pass it up to the top because, after seeing those attacks, everything becomes credible. The filters vanish and your job is to let your boss know what you just picked up because, God forbid, it could be true. That's why people call it the "fog of war." . . .

[Bush] gave the order to go to DEFCON 3, which was the first time we had been at that level of readiness since the Yom Kippur War.

Eric Edelman, principal deputy assistant to the vice president: [In the Presidential Emergency Operations Center (PEOC)], I told the vice president, "We probably need to let the Russians know why we're doing this, so they don't misinterpret. . . . Condi [Rice] was sitting there at the time and she said, "That's a good idea." She said, "I'll go call Sergei Ivanov." She called and they actually put her through to Putin.

Card: [Bush] said, "We're going back to the White House." He was pretty hot with me. I kept saying, "I don't think you want to make that decision right now." He went back and forth. It wasn't one conversation—it was five, six, seven conversations.[17]

Dave Wilkinson, Secret Service agent: We basically refused to take him back. The way we look at it is that by federal law the Secret Service has to protect the president. The wishes of that person that day are secondary.[18]

Fleischer: At 10:32, he turned to the mil[itary] aide, who said they had just received a report saying, "Angel is next." "Angel" is the code name, at least it was back then, for Air Force One.

Harriet Miers, White House staff secretary: [We] headed to Barksdale, where they know there is already a secure situation there where we could land, and [the president] started preparing his next set of remarks.

Bush (addressing the nation from Barksdale Air Force Base): Make no mistake, the United States will hunt down and punish those responsible for these cowardly acts.

Gordon Johndroe, assistant White House press secretary: No one really remembers the president's statement there. It was bad lighting, bad setting, but it was important to have him say something to the nation.[19]

Bartlett: We were fearing that what it was looking like was Bush is on the run.

The Scene in Washington

Bolten: I remember it as being an unusually relaxed day because people were still sort of filtering back from vacation. The intensity of the congressional calendar and so on had not yet taken hold.

Nick Calio, White House legislative liaison: I'm thinking it's a gorgeous day, it's the congressional picnic, we're finally doing an outdoor event where it's not going to rain or be 400 degrees.

Pete Wehner, presidential speechwriter: I remember consciously thinking, "Boy, this is one of the most boring days of the Bush presidency." . . . I wrote an email to Mike [Gerson, chief speechwriter]. . . . The first line of my note was, "There's nothing much going on today." I sent it exactly five minutes before the first plane hit.

Clay Johnson, White House personnel director: I have a meeting at 9:00 with Tim Flanigan, who was the deputy to [White House counsel] Al Gonzales. . . . At about 9:10 or something his assistant knocks on the door, hands him a note. . . . He said, "A second plane has flown into the World Trade Center towers." A minute later, 30 seconds, 20 seconds later, she opens the door again and says, "We've been told to go to the White House Mess. Don't go back to your office. Right now walk directly to the White House Mess," which was considered to be safest if we got hit by a plane because it's the lowest floor. . . . We go in there and five minutes later someone comes in and says, . . . "Leave the White House as fast as you can."

Fleischer: Hector Irastorza, who ran White House administration, said to them, "Walk out orderly, walk out calmly." All of a sudden a Secret Service agent came running in and said, "Get the hell out of here. Run! Run now.

Women, take off your shoes. Take off your heels. Run!" Because the Secret Service had word that a plane is coming.

Johnson: [First Lady Laura Bush's chief of staff] Anita McBride's husband worked for Daimler Chrysler, and their offices were a couple blocks way. She said, "Let's go to my husband's offices. They've got a lot of free space and we can congregate there. Everybody in the White House staff, let's go." We stayed over there watching television, watching the stuff unfold, until about noon.

Bolten: The second plane hit. I thought, "Okay, this is not an accident." So I went into the large conference room in the Situation Room where Condi [Rice] was having her staff meeting with all her senior directors. That's a lot of people, it's like 20 people or something. I'd never walked in on one of her meetings before, so she immediately said, "Oh, and here's the deputy chief of staff, Josh Bolten." She started to introduce me. . . . I made the time-out sign. I motioned her out of the room and I told her there was a second plane hitting the other trade tower so this was clearly an attack of some kind. . . . We went up to the vice president's office, which is right next to the chief of staff's office, to talk with Cheney about what was going on. While we were standing there talking, a large Secret Service guy came in and said to the vice president, "We have to go *now*." He got around behind the vice president, put his arms around him, all the way around him, picked him up, and started running with him with Cheney's feet barely touching the ground.

Vice President Dick Cheney: [Once in the Presidential Emergency Operations Center] I didn't spend a lot of time thinking about it; I just began to operate. Everybody responded to me; everybody came to me. I didn't have to say, "I'm in charge here." I think part of it had to do just with the way I'd been operating as vice president, the way the president has treated me.[20]

Edelman: Even before "who did it" was the question of "what is this?" How big is this? What else is out there that we don't know about? [Cheney] and the president talked and made the decision to ground all aviation in the United States. I remember Secretary [of Transportation Norm] Mineta was there and he had a legal pad and he had a direct link to the FAA [Federal Aviation Administration] operations center and he was literally taking down the tail number of every plane as it got on the dock until he could assure us that literally, . . . "Everything is on the ground."

Johnson: Norm [Mineta] was on the phone saying, "Yes, okay, okay, good, good." He gets off the phone—it's maybe one o'clock or one thirty—and he said, "Mr. Vice President, we have it on good authority that the plane that hit the Pentagon was a private plane." As he's saying that, CNN on a TV directly behind Norm Mineta, reports, "Yes, it's been verified that the plane that hit the Pentagon was American Airlines Flight—." Or Delta Flight—whatever it was. Here's the head of Transportation, and CNN has better intel than the secretary of transportation. The fog of war.

John Bellinger, principal legal adviser, National Security Council: I ultimately spent a good part of the day in the Situation Room. . . . There were all these reports coming into the Situation Room about hundreds of planes; there were at least seven planes that were all heading toward different places. It looked like there were multiple planes flying everywhere.

Bolten: The FAA was frantically trying to get everybody out of the air as quickly as possible so that anybody left in the air could be identified as a danger. . . . Eventually as time went on each of them got resolved except for this one that was headed for DC from the northwest. It became clearer that this one plane might be another one the terrorists had taken over. So the military aide was shuttling in saying how far out, what its trajectory was. . . . The vice president very calmly gave the order to shoot down, to scramble fighter craft that were available and intercept, United Flight 93.

Scooter Libby, chief of staff to the vice president: We "learn" that a plane is five miles out and has dropped below 500 feet and can't be found; it's missing. You look at your watch and think, "Hmmm, five miles out, 500 miles an hour. Tick, tick, tick."[21]

Elaine Chao, secretary of labor: We didn't know how to use the PA [public address] system. We didn't know what to say. We didn't know where the controls of the PA system were! We were trying to call the White House; no one was answering. . . . They finally found the PA system and this shaky voice goes on. . . . It was not calming.

Bolten: Scooter Libby's notes reported me, after the vice president issued the shoot-down order, saying to the vice president, "You need to notify the president." . . . The 9/11 Commission thought that reflected doubt that the vice president had the authority to do that. I actually wasn't doubting that, I was just saying that even assuming he had that authority—which I thought he did—the president needed to know that he had executed that authority. The vice president said, "Oh, of course, of course" and tried to get him on the line, which I'm not sure he was able to do very quickly.

Cheney: It had to be done. Once that plane became hijacked—even if it had a load of passengers on board who, obviously, weren't part of any hijacking attempt—having seen what had happened in New York and the Pentagon, you really didn't have any choice. It wasn't a close call.[22]

Philip Zelikow, director of the Miller Center and later executive director of the 9/11 Commission: Some of the [9/11 Commission] staff leaned toward the view, though they couldn't prove it, that . . . basically, Cheney really ordered it and Bush ratified it. But they couldn't prove that and there was countervailing evidence. . . . To this day I'm not really sure what happened.

Bolten: The military aide came back in. He was periodically reporting on the progress of Flight 93 and then came in and said, "Flight 93 is down." At that time we assumed that our fighters had brought it down.

Stephen Hadley, White House deputy national security adviser: When we get news that an airplane had gone down in Pennsylvania, . . . the first thing that goes through my mind is, "My God, we've shot down an airplane and we've killed a bunch of people."

Edelman: The vice president was actually several steps ahead of everybody else in the room. . . . He said, "I think an act of heroism just took place on that plane."

Mike Hayden, National Security Agency director: [CIA director] George [Tenet] called me about 10:30, 11:00 . . . and he said, "What do you have," and I said, "It's al-Qaeda." He said, "Do you have proof?" I said, "Well, we're hearing the celebratory gunfire on the network."

Edelman: We knew it was al-Qaeda very quickly. We had a SVTS [Secure Video Teleconference System] with George [Tenet], and he told us that very quickly. George also told some member of Congress, and [Sen.] Orrin Hatch and a couple of others actually went out and said it.

Mary Matalin, assistant to the vice president: [In the PEOC] I did not have the perspective seeing what the American public was seeing. . . . We weren't watching TV. We weren't watching people jumping out of buildings. We didn't see all the chaos that the American people were seeing.[23]

Bartlett: We learned that [Solicitor General] Ted Olsen's wife was on Flight 93. . . . So now we've lost somebody we all know. It's not a vague tragedy.

Congress

Richard Gephardt, House Democratic leader: I'm in the Capitol early on 9/11, early in the morning, 8:00. We had a meeting on the budget. I had my leadership team. . . . I'm sitting here looking at them, talking. I can see their eyes were going to the TV and they weren't listening to what anybody else was saying. So they said, "Looks like a small plane hit the World Trade Center." Whatever, it's another mess. Then soon after that the second plane hit and the police, the Capitol Police, came in and said, "We think there is a plane on the way to the Capitol; we have to get you out of here." . . . They took me [to my condo].

Calio: Nobody knew where the members of Congress were. There is a system in place that certain of the leadership get scooped up in any kind of emergency like that and taken to an undisclosed location.

Cheney: I sort of immediately began to respond based on my training in the continuity-of-government program . . . how you would maintain the government, a legitimate, constitutionally-based government, in the event of an all-out nuclear exchange with the Soviet Union. . . . One of the first things you've got to do, certainly one of the top priorities for me, was: how do we preserve the constitutional power of the presidency? If something happens to the president, I'm next; something happens to me, Denny Hastert is next, the Speaker, and so forth. And so that led me to do things such as contact the Speaker. Where was he? Well, we got him out to Andrews Air Force base and then relocated him to another secure facility.[24]

Dennis Hastert, Speaker of the House: All of a sudden, two of my security guys—one on each side of me—picked me up and whisked me away. I said, "What's going on?" They said, "We think there's a fourth plane and we think it's headed for the Capitol."

Gephardt: An hour or so later they said, "We're exercising the survival of government plan in case of nuclear war or whatever. You have to come close to the Capitol right away; they're going to take you and the three other leaders to an undisclosed location in Virginia." . . . They had an individual helicopter for each of us because they didn't know what was going to happen.

Sen. Edward M. Kennedy (D-MA): Mrs. [Laura] Bush was coming up to testify on early education before the Education, Health, Labor Committee. . . . She was going to come in around 9:15 and meet me and Senator Judd Gregg. . . . I saw her walking down. She was completely unaware; she was walking by herself. . . . She came into the office. Judd Gregg had just arrived, and we filled her in as to what was happening.[25]

Sen. Judd Gregg (R-NH): The Secret Service comes running up and says, "We can't take you back to the White House." . . . We sat there and talked for probably 30, 40 minutes. We were just talking about what was happening and what it meant, hoping that our kids were okay. Then they cleared the buildings because they knew there was another plane, and at the time the plane had hit the Pentagon. Finally, the Secret Service came in and said, "We're going to take you off."

Calio: I was able to find out because I had somebody's number, one of the assistant sergeant-at-arms in the House, where the members were and where their leadership was [at the Mount Weather Emergency Operations Center near Bluemont, Virginia]. We arranged a phone call for the vice president with the leadership asking them to please stay put because they were growing antsy and wanted to come back.

Steve Elmendorf, chief of staff to Gephardt: Don Nickles, who was the Senate Republican whip at the time, suggested that we ought to leave. He was agitated, asking, "Why are we all here? The situation is clear. We need to get back." Cheney was clearly annoyed with this, and his voice came out of the speakerphone in the middle of the table and said, "Don, we control the helicopters. We'll decide when you leave."[26]

Gephardt: Senator [Patrick] Leahy [and I] commiserated and he said something I've never forgotten. He said, "The balance between freedom and security is forever changed." He was right.

From Barksdale Air Force Base to Offutt Air Force Base, Sarpy County, Nebraska

Bush (to Cheney): Unless they tell me something I haven't heard, this ass is going back to Washington. . . . I'm gonna entertain this continuity-of-government thing a bit longer. But we're going back.[27]

Fleischer: We flew out to Offutt Air Force Base in Nebraska.

Morell: On the way from Barksdale to Offutt, the president asked to see me alone—it was just me, him, and Andy Card. He asked me, "Michael, who did this?" I explained that I didn't have any actual intelligence, so what you're going to get is my best guess. He was really focused and said, "I understand, get on with it." . . . Iran and Iraq . . . would have everything to lose and nothing to gain from the attack. When all was said and done, the trail would lead to Osama bin Laden. I told him, "I'd bet my children's future on that."[28]

Fleischer: Offutt was chosen because it had . . . incredible communications facilities where the president could convene a secure video teleconference with anybody around the world. . . . There was this little brick outhouse, kind of, not very big, 10 feet by 10 feet with a door, and that's what we went into. Down. Down. Down. Down. Deep into the earth . . . and then— whoosh. We were in something like a *WarGames* set and the president went into one side of it to convene a meeting of the National Security Council.

Bartlett: That's the first time that [Bush] is truly able to convene what is now being viewed almost as a war cabinet.

Bolten: I think I and many others were in more of a stunned state than any-thing else, managing our different roles but not really comprehending what had happened and what it meant for the country. The president seemed to get that right away. The very first thing he said when he got on both that conference call and a conference call with the relevant members of the cabi-net and the FBI director and stuff like that was that he had a pretty clear sense that everything had changed, that the United States was now entering a war that was likely to be a protracted struggle against a grave threat to the homeland. . . . He addressed [FBI director] Bob Mueller directly and said, "Your job has now changed. You're not trying to catch people after they do bad things; your job is now to catch them before."

Edelman: The president seemed actually quite calm and self-possessed . . . in the secure video conference, in the SVTS. He was pretty good, very calm, and very clear that we were going to have to approach this not as a criminal matter but as a war, one in which we had to bring all the elements of national power together.

Calio: He told us all, "We're at war. It's a different kind of war. In three weeks, or four weeks, or six weeks, rest assured, people are going to want to forget about this. They're going to watch the World Series; they're going to want to watch football games. They're not going to want to think about this. We're going to have to stay on it. We're going to have to keep harping on it."

From Offutt Air Force Base to Washington

Bartlett: "At Offutt, [Bush] got the review from the Secretary of Transporta-tion and the FAA that the US airspace is under control under the command of the military. Once that was determined, that was the big turning point to say yes, . . . it's absolutely critical to get the president back to the White House, back to Washington. . . . We spent a significant portion of that trip on the way back to Washington working on the speech that he would deliver. We were on the phone with those back at the White House, Mike Gerson and [White House communications director] Karen [Hughes] and those. A lot of debate back and forth about what tone to strike, how declaratory should we be. . . .

It was probably one of the more surreal images I've ever seen, coming into DC airspace with two F-16s on each side of Air Force One. . . . We're looking out the window and [the F-16 pilot's] giving the president the thumbs-up. The president salutes him. You pull into DC airspace and it's abandoned. There is no one except for the emergency personnel around the Pentagon. Smoke is billowing out of the Pentagon. You think, "In America, in 2001? How?" It looked like a movie. I could not believe it.

Fleischer: Out of the front left of the chopper [en route] from Andrews Air Force Base to the White House, the president had a clear view of the Pentagon. The president said to nobody and everybody, "The mightiest building in the world is on fire. This is the face of war in the twenty-first century."[29]

Bolten: He landed on the south lawn in the early evening. . . . There was supposed to have been some sort of congressional party on the south lawn because there were a lot of tables, big round ones out there. But he came directly into the Oval Office and talked to some of us in the Oval for a bit and I think went directly back to the private dining room with Mike and Karen to work on his remarks.

Alberto Gonzales, White House counsel: Sometime late in the evening I ran into Karen Hughes, and she and I went down to the Oval Office because the president was returning in Marine One. Karen and I were standing outside the Oval Office when Marine One landed. I remember him coming up to us. Of course Karen and I have known him from his days in Texas. I don't know what we said, something like "Welcome home" or "I'm glad you're home, Mr. President." He didn't say anything. He just looked at us and walked into the Oval Office. He was being readied to address the nation.

Bartlett: There was a definite tension. Karen really felt that we're still kind of in comforter, calming-of-the-nation mode as opposed to commander in chief and preparing for war. . . . [The speech] wasn't one of his better moments. Now a distracted mind, a fatigued mind and all that on top of everything else and we're doing this on a whim when you're used to being able to have a lot of preparatory work for an address to the nation. It was all on full display.

Bush (addressing the nation from the Oval Office): We will make no distinction between the terrorists who committed these acts and those who harbor them.

Wehner: I don't think the speech on the evening of 9/11 was bad. It just wasn't memorable. Things seemed a little bit off balance, but that's because they were.

Bolten: After he made the remarks, . . . we went back down to the bunker and he convened a conference call with various international security players. He was in full war president—he didn't seem panicked. He didn't seem exhausted. He just seemed like, "Okay, I've got this. That's why they put me here."

Cheney: The night of 9/11, Lynne [Cheney] and I had been evacuated—Liz and the family—evacuated to Camp David. And they put us in Aspen Lodge, the president's lodge, because that was the most secure and at that point Secret Service didn't know how extensive the attack might be.[30]

Col. Matthew Klimow, executive assistant to the vice chair of the Joint Chiefs of Staff: Secretary [of Defense Donald] Rumsfeld said, "I want the chain of command to notify everybody that tomorrow, 12 September, is a normal workday at the Pentagon," . . . which was, at the time, a pretty startling announcement.[31]

Kennedy: That night, we went back into the Senate. It was 8:00. I talked to [Senate Majority Leader Tom] Daschle, to urge him to go back in—to have the Senate go back into session. We all went back and the House went back in. . . . They weren't going to stop the functioning of government. . . . But through all this, people believed that [Iraqi dictator] Saddam Hussein was behind it.[32]

Gen. Hugh Shelton, chairman of the Joint Chiefs of Staff: The night of September 11, [Deputy Secretary of Defense Paul] Wolfowitz and Rumsfeld had me up in Rumsfeld's office. They knew we [the Joint Chiefs] were going to the White House the next morning. They were trying to get me to pull out the Iraq war plans and recommend, as a part of their recommendation, that we go to Iraq and use this as an opportunity to get rid of Saddam. I told them, "Not until I see some evidence that says Saddam was involved in this, and I don't think there is any. I think it will be al Qaeda."[33]

Zelikow: The notion of invading Afghanistan—on the morning of 9/11 the invasion of Afghanistan was inconceivable. Literally inconceivable. It is inconceivable in the sense that no one could even conceive it enough to write it down as an option on a piece of paper—no one, not even Dick Clarke, no one. By the afternoon of 9/11 not only was it conceivable, it was the obvious policy option we should have thought of six months or a year ago.

Richard Armitage, deputy secretary of state: My view is [Bush] didn't know why he was president. Then 9/11 happened and all of a sudden he figured, well, I was here for a reason. He was very spiritual and all that—I'm here for a reason.

Colin Powell, secretary of state: As Rich [Armitage] says, with something moving inside of him that was something spiritual. Very often [Bush] made very good decisions, but often they were instinctive.

The Aftermath

Surprise, fear, confusion, misinformation, uncertainty, malfunction, tension, exhaustion—all of these fog-of-war qualities marked 9/11, capped by a false alarm that prompted the Secret Service to roust the Bushes out of bed late that night and take them back to the PEOC. Nothing seemed more certain on the morning of September 12 than that additional international terrorist attacks against the United States were coming. "For those who were part of the Bush White House," says Townsend, "every day they were there post-9/11 was September 12, and every decision, every crisis, all went through that filter. . . . Everyone walked away from 9/11 with a sense of personal responsibility." Yet two decades later, foreign terrorists have carried out no other attacks against the United States approaching the scale of 9/11—or, for that matter, the scale of the August 7, 1998, American embassy bombings in Kenya and Tanzania or the October 12, 2000, attack on the USS *Cole*. Although hard to prove, it seems likely that at least some of the measures taken in the aftermath of 9/11 helped forestall such attacks.

These measures, many of them adopted in response to the report of the National Commission on Terrorist Attacks upon the United States—the 9/11 Commission—fall into two main categories relevant to the kind of crisis defined at the start of this chapter: a sudden, unanticipated event that indisputably requires an urgent presidential response. Specifically, these measures involved reforms designed to prevent such events in the future and, in the case of failure to do so, reforms designed to allow the president and other policymakers to respond effectively.

According to Zelikow, the executive director of the 9/11 Commission, the commission's members abandoned the "pattern of doing these sorts of things that I think of as the model of the IG [inspector general] report. That is a 'what went wrong' style of report" in which "the lawyers basically are writing as if they're writing a brief for a tort case: 'We can see the following breaches of duty.' It is very hindsight driven. Instead . . . we actually tried to write the report without letting the hindsight suffuse it too much: Here's what people understood, here are the choices we made."

Prevention-Related Reforms

Most of the reforms—and especially the most publicized reforms—were intended to forestall future 9/11s. "The one recommendation that several commissioners had in their head from the start," recalls Zelikow, "we ended up calling a DNI [director of national intelligence]—the intelligence consolidation idea." The CIA resisted losing its supervisory role in the intelligence community, and according to Townsend, "to say there was a dogfight in the policy process about the three military components— National Geospatial-Intelligence Agency, NSA [National Security Agency], and DIA [Defense Intelligence Agency]—would be an understatement." At Bush's request, Congress authorized the DNI to be the president's principal intelligence adviser and to direct and coordinate the efforts of the sixteen agencies of the intelligence community. It left ambiguous the DNI's authority over budget and personnel, however, which reduced the position's preeminence. Nonetheless, intelligence budgets expanded, agencies did a better job of sharing information and coordinating their efforts, and the FBI redefined its organizational culture to emphasize counterterrorism and intelligence gathering.

Additional preventive reforms enacted after 9/11 included the creation of a National Counterterrorism Center as part of the Office of the DNI, the merging of multiple executive agencies and personnel into the newly created Department of Homeland Security, and the implementation of Real ID driver's licenses to remedy the lack of security that allowed eighteen of the nineteen 9/11 hijackers to obtain state-issued IDs.

Response-Related Reforms

Problems that arose as events unfolded from morning to night on September 11 spurred certain obvious reforms. Communications aboard Air Force One were dramatically improved to allow television and internet reception, as well as videoconferencing that, according to Bartlett, would permit the president "to speak live to the nation . . . so we're never in a situation where he can disappear." Within the White House, significant and long overdue upgrades were made to the underground PEOC and the ground-level Situation Room. Within the new Department of Homeland Security, the Federal Emergency Management Agency enhanced its continuity-of-government planning and operations, and a Central Locator System was established to keep track of individuals in the presidential line of succession in the event of an attack. In a less publicized response, Bush signed National Security Presidential Directive 5 in 2007, consisting largely of classified plans to ensure continuity of government in times of crisis.

Although the appropriateness of these responses to a crisis like 9/11 is clear, none is foolproof. This became obvious during the January 6, 2021, attack on the Capitol, when the president himself was a major part of the problem and continuity-of-government plans were not effectively activated, despite the physical vulnerability of Vice President Mike Pence, Speaker of the House Nancy Pelosi, and Senate president pro tempore Patrick Leahy—the first three officials in the line of succession. As became clear on 9/11, when an air defense system aimed at averting airborne attacks from overseas was slow to respond to airborne attacks launched within the United States, focusing on threats from one kind of enemy can lower defenses against another. When the next crisis occurs in its own unanticipated form, another real test will occur.

Notes

1. Unless otherwise indicated, all quotations are from oral history interviews conducted by the University of Virginia's Miller Center as part of the George W. Bush Oral

History. The transcribed interviews are available at https://millercenter.org/the-presi
dency/presidential-oral-histories/george-w-bush.

2. Garrett M. Graff, *The Only Plane in the Sky: An Oral History of 9/11* (New York: Avid Reader Press, 2019); Peter Baker, *Days of Fire: Bush and Cheney in the White House* (New York: Doubleday, 2013).

3. Philip Zelikow, foreword to *41: Inside the Presidency of George H. W. Bush,* ed. Michael Nelson and Barbara A. Perry (Ithaca, NY: Cornell University Press, 2014), vii–xi.

4. See Michael Nelson, "Bill Clinton and Welfare Reform: A Perspective from Oral History," *Congress and the Presidency* 42 (2015): 243–263; Michael Nelson, "Redivided Government and the Politics of the Budgetary Process in the Clinton Years: An Oral History Perspective," *Congress and the Presidency* 43 (2016): 300–323.

5. Donna Shalala, interview for the Miller Center's William J. Clinton Oral History, https://millercenter.org/the-presidency/presidential-oral-histories/bill-clinton.

6. Jill Lepore, "The Trump Papers," *New Yorker,* November 23, 2020, 24.

7. Russell L. Riley, "Presidential Oral History: The Clinton Presidential History Project," *Oral History Review* 34 (2007): 86.

8. Graff, *Only Plane in the Sky,* 12.

9. Transition Lab, "The George H. W. Bush Transition to Power," Center for Presidential Transition, April 27, 2020, https://podcasts.apple.com/us/podcast/the-george-h-w
-bush-transition-to-power/id1495404153?i=1000472759358.

10. Graff, *Only Plane in the Sky,* 78.

11. Graff, 76.

12. Graff, 229.

13. Graff, 80.

14. Graff, 209–210.

15. PBS, "George W. Bush," *American Experience,* May 5, 2020.

16. George W. Bush, *Decision Points* (New York: Crown, 2010), 130.

17. Graff, *Only Plane in the Sky,* 215.

18. Graff, 213.

19. Graff, 282.

20. Dick Cheney with Liz Cheney, *In My Time: A Personal and Political Memoir* (New York: Threshold Editions, 2011), 210.

21. Graff, *Only Plane in the Sky,* 84.

22. James Rosen, *Cheney One on One: A Candid Conversation with America's Most Controversial Statesman* (Washington, DC: Regnery, 2015).

23. Graff, *Only Plane in the Sky,* 417.

24. Rosen, *Cheney One on One,* 211–212.

25. Miller Center's Edward M. Kennedy Oral History, https://millercenter.org/the
-presidency/presidential-oral-histories/edward-kennedy.

26. Graff, *Only Plane in the Sky,* 315.

27. Robert Draper, *Dead Certain: The Presidency of George W. Bush* (New York: Free Press, 2007), 142.

28. Graff, *Only Plane in the Sky,* 308.

29. Graff, 368.

30. Rosen, *Cheney One on One,* 110.

31. Graff, *Only Plane in the Sky*, 362.

32. Miller Center's Edward M. Kennedy Oral History.

33. Hugh Shelton, interview for the Miller Center's William J. Clinton Oral History, https://millercenter.org/the-presidency/presidential-oral-histories/bill-clinton.

CHAPTER FOUR

"On My Own": George W. Bush, the Unitary Executive, and Unilateral Action

Andrew Rudalevige

In March 2004 President George W. Bush spoke in Los Angeles to a friendly crowd he described as "people of faith . . . helping meet social objectives." Bush touted his creation, by executive order, of the White House Office of Faith-Based and Community Initiatives, then turned to a second directive boosting religious charities' efforts to win federal grants to provide human services. He had been trying to achieve this goal by statute, Bush said, but "got a little frustrated in Washington because I couldn't get the bill passed out of the Congress." He added, in mock disbelief, "They were arguing *process*." But no problem. "Congress wouldn't act, so I signed an executive order. That means I did it on my own."[1]

To be sure, every president is tempted to do things "on my own." Long before Bush took office, scholars stressed that a key element of contemporary presidential power lay in the "administrative presidency," a tool kit of managerial mechanisms by which presidents seek to control policy change in the executive branch. The idea, as former White House staffer Elena Kagan put it, is to enhance "the President's ability to provide energetic leadership in an inhospitable political environment" characterized by gridlock across the branches of government and even within the executive branch itself.[2]

Kagan's notion of "presidential administration" was particularly important to the George W. Bush administration. That focus flowed from both intent and circumstance. Bush entered office determined to strengthen the presidency against a series of post-Watergate congressional incursions that, in his opinion, had weakened the office. This belief was wed to an expansive theory of executive authority: even in domestic policy, Bush frequently referred to a "unitary executive branch" housed in a "zone of autonomy" subject solely to presidential direction and control, whatever Congress might assert.[3] Indeed, the administration argued that congressional intervention was not only wrongheaded but often unconstitutional. Thus, for eight years Bush used an array of unilateral instruments, including executive orders, signing statements, regulatory reviews, and directive memoranda, to execute policy in a manner congruent with presidential preferences, sometimes with controversial results. As White House counsel Harriet Miers later put it, "We had strong views about the role of the executive."[4]

The preference for unilateralism was bolstered by the events of the 2000s, which ensured that many of the most salient decisions of the Bush administration were necessarily executive centered. From the reaction to the terror attacks of September 11, 2001, to the management of Hurricane Katrina, to the attempts to rebuild postwar Iraq, to the implementation of massive late-second-term financial-sector bailouts, the roles and responsibilities of the federal government grew greatly on Bush's watch—and with them, the scope for executive action.

At the same time, especially as Bush's tenure progressed, divided government and partisan polarization made legislative relations increasingly difficult. Thus, both opportunity and motive added to the appeal of unilateralism. One result was that a strengthened administrative presidency became a crucial aspect of the Bush administration and his legacy.

This chapter assesses what this development meant for the Bush presidency, both in theory and in practice. It begins by reviewing the unitary executive's implications for presidential power, then turns to the people and processes involved in extending managerial control over the departments and agencies of the executive branch—the bureaucracy. The Bush presidency was as consistent and systematic in its approach as any recent administration. Still, the desire to act "on my own" did not always lead to well-implemented policy; the tactic prompted political pushback, and as subsequent administrations have found, executive action can have a short half-life. "We did more management stuff . . . than anybody's ever done," Bush management czar Clay Johnson later said. "It's sickening that—I was naïve about it, as on a lot of things—I didn't push to have more of it immortalized in legislation."

Strength from Weakness: The Unitary Executive

Article II of the Constitution begins with a seemingly simple assignment of authority: "the executive Power shall be vested in a President of the United States of America." That "does not mean *some* of the executive power," Justice Antonin Scalia wrote two hundred years later, "but *all* of it." As the Supreme Court put it in 1959, Congress cannot "supplant the Executive in what exclusively belongs to the Executive."[5]

Such is the heart of the unitary executive theory, which beat strongly and steadily throughout the Bush administration. The theory has inspired a slew of academic literature and even made a cameo appearance in Hollywood via the Dick Cheney biopic *Vice*.[6] Yet its premise prompts a question: even if "all" the executive power "belongs to" the president, what exactly is the executive power? The Constitution certainly does not define it. Instead, its meaning has been worked out in practice through interbranch contestation over time. Scalia's comment was made in just such a context, as he dissented from a 1988 decision holding that the independent counsel's office created by Congress to police executive ethics after Watergate was a pragmatic compromise that did not violate the separation of powers. If anything, the presidential office, as strictly defined by the Constitution, is obstructed rather than omnipotent. At the Constitutional Convention of 1787, James Wilson of Pennsylvania downplayed worries about what presidents might do with "the executive power," stating that "the only powers he conceived [as] strictly Executive were those of executing the laws, and appointing officers."[7] Alexander Hamilton defended the framers' work by arguing that the president—unlike tyrants throughout history—would be hemmed in by a long list of checks, from veto overrides to treaty ratification to impeachment and removal from office.[8] "Presidential weakness," as Richard Neustadt observed in his classic 1960 book, is "the underlying theme of *Presidential Power*."[9]

Yet (as Neustadt recognized) presidents have long sought to leverage historical context and their vantage within the government to overcome the limits on their authority. Edward Corwin called the arc of the presidency "a history of aggrandizement."[10] Over time, executive authority and autonomy have grown as the American national state has grown. And since the 1930s, thanks to depression, war, globalization, alliances, social movements, and widespread regulatory zeal, that growth has been immense. This makes what Kagan called the president's "directive authority" over the bureaucracy more effective and also more appealing. Indeed, recent presidents have relied on precisely the two functions James Wilson identified. Shaping how laws are executed and carefully selecting who executes those laws are crucial to presidential power.

George W. Bush's contributions to this development came from the confluence of two firmly held ideas: that the presidency was weak when he took office, and that it should be institutionally strong (both in theory and in practice).

Restoring Presidential Strength

Bush's first belief flowed from the impeachment of his immediate predecessor, Bill Clinton, as well as a series of laws passed in the 1970s. Responding to the "imperial presidency" of the Vietnam and Watergate era, Congress enacted a number of interlaced statutes and procedures designed to strengthen its authority in interbranch relations. In areas ranging from the use of force to a requirement for executive transparency, legislators sought to reshape vital policy processes and rein in presidential discretion.[11] For observers like Vice President Dick Cheney, who had entered public life as a Nixon aide and later served as Gerald Ford's chief of staff, these "concerted efforts to place limits and restrictions on presidential authority" were "misguided," even at the time. "For the 35 years that I've been in this town, there's been a constant, steady erosion of the prerogatives and the powers of the president of the United States, and I don't want to be a part of that," he told an interviewer in 2003.[12] Cheney's running mate (whose father had also been a high-ranking appointee under Nixon and Ford) was himself quite enamored of the strength of the executive office, even before the brutal catalyst of the September 11 terrorist attacks. "The President and Vice President always made clear that a central administration priority was to maintain and expand the President's formal legal powers," wrote Jack Goldsmith, who headed the Office of Legal Counsel in the Bush Justice Department. As the president himself put it in early 2002, "I'm not going to let Congress erode the power of the executive branch. I have a duty to protect the executive branch from legislative encroachment."[13]

The perception was that Clinton had failed on that front. White House counsel Fred Fielding noted broadly that, "coming into the Bush administration there was a feeling that there had been an abrogation, a diminution of executive power"—specifically, "a real feeling that, especially in the last couple years of the Clinton administration, they had given away the store to make peace. This was in part due to events, not Monica Lewinsky necessarily, but other events as well." Regarding the Lewinsky affair, which had prompted Clinton's impeachment, Bush artfully promised to restore "honor and dignity to the Oval Office" during the 2000 campaign. His chief political strategist, Karl Rove, argued that Bush "was conscious that the prerogatives of the Presidency had been worn away principally through scandal and disuse, but he wanted to restore that."

In fact, presidents had pushed back almost immediately against Congress's "resurgence regime" of the 1970s and met surprisingly little resistance.[14] Ronald Reagan was notable in this regard; as legal scholar and Bush-era Justice Department official John Yoo observed, "The Bush administration, in many ways philosophically [is] a continuation of Reagan views of presidential power."[15] In some cases, legislators themselves backed away from using the processes they had created to challenge the president or could not make them work. The shortcomings of the War Powers Resolution and the Congressional Budget Act, for instance, have received bountiful attention. Not every piece of the regime crumbled at once or forever; still, one key institutional result of the Clinton impeachment was to kill off the independent counsel statute. And a headline from 1998—referring to summer air strikes ordered by Clinton—credited him with "Perfect[ing] the Art of Go-Alone Governing."[16]

Even so, the Bush administration found room for improvement when it came to unilateralism. The clarity and scope of its claims and capacities were new, and they occurred across the spectrum of governance. It may seem odd to discuss presidential power in terms of regulatory policy rather than terrorism or to treat domestic management similarly to policies applicable to Guantánamo Bay, but all these elements reflect a particular approach to the use of presidential power and the place of the presidency in the constitutional structure. The notion of the unitary executive, as expanded by the Bush administration, was very consistently applied.

Again, unitary executive theory centers on the idea that other political actors cannot infringe on the executive power vested in the president. The implications that flow from this idea follow from one's definition of the executive power. For example, the pardon power is clearly a purely executive function in the Constitution. It would be hard to imagine a legitimate statutory intrusion on this power.[17] But what Article II means with regard to the executive bureaucracy is hardly so straightforward. That link is so complicated that it "has haunted the relationship between the president and Congress from the very beginning of their history together."[18] The most impressive scholarly exegesis of the unitary executive concludes that the vesting clause must mean "that the president retains supervisory control over all officers exercising executive power."[19]

But how far does that control extend? Can it overturn a reporting requirement? Can it overturn a statutory directive? Are large swaths of the regulatory state—populated by independent agencies whose decisions are often insulated from presidential influence by design—constitutionally problematic? Such conclusions are appealing to presidents, but they go against Supreme Court decisions that allow pragmatic ambiguity in such structural arrangements.[20] The bureaucracy was created by Congress, and agencies' basic missions are written into the law, subject to legislative overseers and their funding decisions. The Constitution in turn demands that the president "take care that the laws be faithfully executed."

Yet fidelity in such cases is a contested quality. That was clear in the Bush administration's systematic use of substantive signing statements. Bush issued 126 such statements, appended to bills newly signed into law and challenging an unprecedented 1,139 provisions of law. (He made 116 separate objections to the Consolidated Appropriations Act of 2005 alone.)[21] The rationale was that Congress frequently adopted statutory requirements that exceeded its powers, raising the question, as White House chief of staff Josh Bolten put it, "whether it was properly within the legislature's authority to direct the President to do a particular thing." Strongly encouraged by Cheney and the vice president's general counsel David Addington, Bush often decided that it was not. "Bush's attitude," Rove said, "was, 'I'm going to be very explicit in the signing statements so that the Congress knows what I believe my constitutional obligation requires me to ignore.'"

The signing statements aimed to provide a new boilerplate rationale for bureaucratic control, repeated so frequently as to become routine. The general formulation was as follows: "The executive branch shall construe this provision in a manner consistent with the President's exclusive constitutional authority, as head of the unitary executive branch and as Commander in Chief"—in this case, attached to a Homeland Security appropriations act in 2005.[22] The legalistic, even formulaic nature of the language used to assert executive claims tended to conceal the breadth of their avowal. In late 2006 Bush's signing statement attached to an act regulating atomic energy cooperation between the United States and India claimed that because Congress could not "purport to establish U.S. policy with respect to various international affairs matters," he would consider the law's ban on the transfer of certain nuclear materials to India merely "advisory."[23] The legitimacy of that claim depends on how plenary and exclusive one believes the president's foreign policy authority to be. But treating the law as "advisory" led to controversy in late 2005 when Bush asserted that he would construe the Detainee Treatment Act's ban on "cruel, inhuman, or degrading treatment or punishment" of prisoners captured in the war on terror "in a manner consistent with the constitutional authority of the President to supervise the unitary executive branch and as Commander in Chief and consistent with the constitutional limitations on the judicial power."[24]

Such claims were not limited to foreign policy or the war powers. In every substantive realm, Congress only "purported" to act, and the president had "the Constitutional authority to supervise the unitary executive branch." The meaning was not intended to be formulaic, despite the bureaucratese: these statements asserted the centralized direction of what executive departments and agencies did, the qualifications of their personnel, what information they released, and with whom they communicated. Where necessary, presidential preferences in these matters were intended to override the language of the law he had just signed.

How often these claims moved beyond theory to practice remains disputed. Bolten suggests that the statements were rhetorical as much as real: "The ones I was most familiar with were circumstances in which we were going to do it, whatever the legislation directed, but rejected the notion that legislation could force the President to do X, Y, and Z." Rove suggests that the statements were a courtesy to Congress, alerting legislators to a difference of opinion over which they were welcome to sue.[25] A Government Accountability Office (GAO) examination of the fiscal year 2006 appropriations bills found mixed results regarding signing statements' effect on the way statutory provisions were implemented.[26] Still, as a systematic claim of presidential power, those statements were important. The administration "waved around the vesting clause like a talisman," one observer later put it.[27]

As Bush counsel Brad Berenson said about powerful Cheney aide Addington's role in systematizing signing statements, such efforts united "two of Addington's passions. One is executive power. And the other is the inner alleyways of bureaucratic combat. It's a way to advance executive power through those inner alleyways."[28]

Expanding the Zone of Autonomy

A second element of the unitary executive theory swelled to wall off those alleyways against intrusion. This was the administration's new stress on exclusivity: the assertion that the scope of the executive power was defined entirely by the president. If the executive power was the indivisible purview of the president, and if the president defined what the executive power actually was, it was a short jump to conclude that Congress could not infringe on any presidential preferences flowing from his self-defined constitutional authority. As Justice Scalia argued in *Morrison*, any statute that constrained the president's "exclusive control" over a "purely executive" power must be invalid. The Bush Justice Department held that the Constitution allowed the president a "zone of autonomy"[29]—a region whose boundaries would be determined by the president himself but clearly lay in newly occupied interbranch territory.

Not surprisingly, these claims crystallized after the September 11, 2001, terrorist attacks. When Congress passed the sweeping Authorization for the Use of Military Force (AUMF) a few days later, the Justice Department's Office of Legal Counsel (OLC) said this might be helpful politically but had no practical import:

> In the exercise of his plenary power to use military force, the President's decisions are for him alone and are unreviewable. . . . It is clear that Congress's power to declare war does not constrain the President's independent and plenary constitutional authority over the use of military force. . . . [Whatever the text of the AUMF], military actions need not be limited to those . . . that participated in the attacks on the World Trade Center and the Pentagon.[30]

In keeping with that logic, President Bush promptly and unilaterally approved a wiretapping program that allowed the National Security Agency (NSA) to bypass the warrant requirements of the Foreign Intelligence Surveillance Act; designated and detained hundreds of "unlawful enemy combatants," including American citizens arrested within the United States;

issued orders limiting the applicability of the Geneva Conventions and creating a system of military tribunals; and approved interrogation techniques that many considered torture, which was prohibited by both treaty and domestic statute.

Congress ultimately passed laws authorizing some of these presidential actions. But in certain cases, such as the 2001 AUMF, the administration argued that although such statutory grounding was welcome, it was not necessary, given the breadth of the executive power in wartime. When the NSA initiative was revealed in late 2005, the Justice Department claimed in a lengthy justification submitted to Congress that "the NSA activities are supported by the President's well-recognized inherent constitutional authority of Commander in Chief."[31] Thus, any efforts to legislate in the broad field of war powers might themselves be "unreviewable" or even unconstitutional. When it came to the interrogation program, the Defense Department argued, "In order to respect the President's inherent constitutional authority to manage a military campaign [the laws against torture] as well as any other potentially applicable statute must be construed as inapplicable to interrogations undertaken pursuant to his Commander-in-Chief authority."[32] Attorney general Michael Mukasey denied that this claim "put the President above the law," arguing that it positioned "the President within the law because the law includes the Constitution . . . and if the President has a power under the Constitution, he's obligated to exercise it, and if a statute infringes on that, then the statute is unconstitutional."[33]

The administration's stance attracted much skepticism.[34] Its elevation to doctrine disturbed even sympathetic scholars like the OLC's Goldsmith, who would later write, "When one concludes that Congress is disabled from controlling the President . . . respect for separation of powers demands a full consideration of competing congressional and judicial prerogatives," which did not always occur.[35]

People and Processes: The Plot that Succeeded?

The same theory of the unitary executive, with complementary methods, underwrote the rest of Bush's administrative strategy. As those close to the Oval Office saw it, that approach flowed from both norm and necessity. The notion of "unitary control of the executive branch" translated into a firm stance in areas where prior administrations might have sought compromise with Congress. Josh Bolten, for example, recalled that the "secrecy stuff" that prompted a Supreme Court case involving the transparency required of presidential task forces originated with Cheney and his staff—who were "very attuned to protecting the prerogatives of the executive and often attuned to making a point of principle in circumstances where other people would just say, 'Let that go.'" On the practical side, as Domestic Policy Council chair Karl Zinsmeister put it, the wider bureaucracy was riddled with "human inertia . . . All their incentives and structures are built up to avoid risk and dodge problems." Zinsmeister went on to argue that "overcoming this inertia . . . is what you have a White House staff for." Thus, building that staff and upgrading its managerial resources were crucial.

Bush and his team did not start from scratch, of course. The creation of the administrative state did not take place at a single moment, and the "administrative presidency" is usually traced to the Nixon administration.[36] Nixon, too, saw a recalcitrant permanent bureaucracy over which he needed to assert control. His strategy innovated many now-familiar tactics: efforts to centralize regulatory review in the Executive Office of the President (EOP); direct executive branch implementation through such tools as signing statements, executive orders, and budget impoundment; and build a "counterbureaucracy" in the White House—a large staff that could lengthen the president's reach into different policy arenas, such as through the new Domestic Council. In Nixon's second term, this approach was complemented by a push to make appointments that would allow "Nixon loyalists" to retake the departments.[37]

But Nixon aide Martin Anderson would conclude that this was too little, too late: "Nixon lost his opportunity to govern before he started." Richard Nathan, who worked in Nixon's Office of Management and Budget (OMB), summed up the effort as a "plot that failed."[38] Yet before long, thanks to Ronald Reagan—helped by some of Nixon's staff (not least Anderson)— the plot thickened. His efforts led to a "sea change" in the administrative presidency.[39] For example, Reagan successfully institutionalized centralized review of agency regulations in OMB.[40] He also learned a lesson from Nixon's belated efforts to coordinate executive branch appointments, adopting at the outset the credo "personnel is policy."[41] The Reagan team systematically removed every holdover from the Carter administration and vetted appointees at both the cabinet and subcabinet levels for "ideological fortitude" in dealing with departmental inertia.[42] The general idea was to be vigilant against what one OLC opinion termed "common legislative encroachments on executive authority."[43]

With these developments refined by the administrations preceding his, George W. Bush inherited a robust set of administrative tools linked to both people and processes.[44] Given the motivations arising from unitary executive theory, his interpretation of interbranch history, his background as the nation's first president with an MBA, and the external shocks facing the administration, Bush did not hesitate to use these tools. In many (but not all) ways, his was the plot that succeeded.

People: The President's DNA

From the outset of the Bush administration, great care was taken to install presidential loyalists throughout and deep within the executive branch.[45] As one staffer later put it, the president sought to "implant his DNA throughout the government"—and he did so systematically.[46]

Transition (and later Presidential Personnel Office) director Clay Johnson was charged with finding appointees who were competent but also loyal to presidential preferences. Johnson clearly fit that bill himself; his ties to the president extended back to high school, and he had served a similar vetting role during Bush's governorship. Bush paid personal attention to the process and was "one of the few presidents who actually met with his personnel staff on a weekly basis," Johnson said. "It was important for President Bush to be directly involved and he wasn't doing it for my benefit. That's the way he wanted to run the railroad."

Such staff meetings began in the White House just two days after the 2001 inauguration, but the selection process was already under way. During the transition, Bush elevated the role of the Presidential Personnel Office, and most members of the cabinet were given a choice of subordinates who had already been vetted by the White House personnel and political teams. Bush's more high-profile cabinet picks, such as Donald Rumsfeld and Colin Powell, were people with long experience and their own political capital. But Johnson advised Powell that the centralized process was "to protect you and the President," if mostly the latter: the idea was to ensure "a consistency of product that went to the president."[47] Even a parallel recruiting effort by the vice president's transition team was apparently shut down.[48]

The aim was to ensure that the far-flung executive branch would be responsive to presidential preferences and that core programmatic functions received consistent support across the government. Thus, key positions within each department and agency received special scrutiny: not just the secretary at the top of the pyramid but also the deputy secretary (who often handles departmental administration), the general counsel, the legislative liaison, and the head of the press office. As chief of staff Andrew Card told an interviewer, "I made sure our communications team is not just a team in the White House. It is a communications team for the executive branch of government. Our legal team is a legal team for the government."[49] That practice started with the cabinet secretaries, who, according to Johnson, needed to understand they were "not *the* secretary, but Bush's Secretary."[50] If loyalty was demanded, it was a two-way street, to the extent that, in Johnson's view, it became an Achilles' heel of the Bush presidency. "Some people were promoted to jobs within the administration who shouldn't have been," he conceded. Bush was "in some cases loyal to a fault."

The administration's original set of appointees came partly from Texas, of course—and more than a third had worked on the 2000 campaign—but even more came from Washington, DC. One shared trait was administrative experience: some 43 percent had worked for President George H. W. Bush. Another 20 percent came from trade associations or lobbying firms—the Interior Department, for example, included new officials who had lobbied for mining, cattle, and oil and gas interests.[51] Such appointments indicated the new president's interest in regulatory policy, usually with an eye toward deregulation. Bush aggressively used his recess appointment powers when senators objected to his appointees.[52] One prominent recess appointment was John Bolton, nominated in August 2005 to serve as Bush's envoy to the United Nations but the subject of a long-stalled confirmation process.

Over time, attention was given to the "farm team" as well. White House staff were sent to serve in the cabinet departments (such as Margaret Spellings to Education and Alberto Gonzales to Justice), and younger staff were given increasing responsibility within the White House (not always, as Johnson notes, with happy results). Like his predecessors, Bush focused his ideologically oriented appointments on agencies he considered ideologically distant, hoping to gain a foothold in their decision-making processes.[53] But even the General Services Administration (GSA)—the normally nonpartisan agency that deals with matters such as cleaning federal buildings and maintaining the motor pool—was expected to be responsive. The head of the GSA attracted unwelcome public attention when she asked the White

House what her organization could do "to help our candidates" in 2008.[54] Journalist Charlie Savage detailed the systematic modification of the Civil Rights Division of the Department of Justice (DOJ), perceived as a bastion of liberal careerists: first, the division changed hiring procedures to shut out civil service influence, then it restored civil service protections once the makeup (and thus preferences) of the careerists had been transformed.[55] In another wing of Justice, controversy erupted over the dismissal of a number of US attorneys alleged to be "underperforming" and who were not, as one DOJ official put it, "loyal Bushies."[56] The administration held that the president could remove appointed personnel for any reason or for no reason at all—this was "clearly within the authority and discretion of the president," as Attorney General Gonzales later wrote—and it invoked executive privilege to block White House staff from providing information on the matter to the House Judiciary Committee.[57] When lawmakers responded by voting to refer criminal contempt-of-Congress charges to the DOJ, the administration replied that since prosecutors reported to the president, he could order them not to pursue such charges. None were proffered.[58]

None of this meant complete presidential control over the bureaucracy. The US attorney imbroglio contributed to Gonzales's unwilling resignation as attorney general in the summer of 2007. Even more dramatic was a showdown in March 2004 between DOJ and White House officials over the legality of "Stellarwind," part of the NSA's warrantless surveillance program.[59] Top White House aides went to then–attorney general John Ashcroft's hospital room to pressure him to sign off on continuing the program. He refused. The president then continued the program on his own authority: "I decide what the law is in the executive branch," he said.[60] But when as many as a dozen high-ranking Justice appointees, including FBI director and acting attorney general James Comey, threatened to resign over the matter, the president, facing a potential political disaster, allowed DOJ to rework the program to its legal satisfaction. (In the end, despite the behind-the-scenes theatrics, much of it remained in place.)[61]

Managerial Processes

More often, though, bureaucratic control foundered not on overt resistance but on different transaction costs—and sometimes on simple math. No matter how many political appointees there are in a given department, they are a small minority of the whole. The Environmental Protection Agency (EPA), for example, had sixty-four political appointees in 2004, midway through the Bush administration—but nearly eighteen thousand employees, giving those appointees a rather expansive span of command.[62] Elaine Chao, who served in multiple cabinet posts over her career (including as Bush's secretary of labor), observed that the Department of Transportation had fifty-five thousand employees and twenty thousand contractors but a statutory cap of only 110 political appointees: "I'm sure somewhere in the last 30 years, someone ticked off some congressional Member who imposed this ceiling." Further, the bureaucratic "blob" targeted by the White House is rich in expertise and valuable institutional memory, and it is subject to legal constraints that require or prevent certain actions, no matter what the president believes his mandate may be. "There is certainly room for judgment and discretion and choices," domestic aide Karl Zinsmeister noted, "but it's not nearly as wide as most people think."

Agency control can rarely be obtained purely by fiat. Coordinated action is difficult even within the EOP, given its own growth, much less across the entire executive branch.[63] In some cases, the challenges facing the Bush administration involved structural issues close to the Oval Office; after Hurricane Katrina, for instance, Bush aides used the president's "unflattering term [that] started with 'cluster' and ended with four more letters" to describe White House management of the disaster.[64] And there were spans of attention as well as of command. Although (as discussed later) the President's Management Agenda was the beneficiary of sustained presidential follow-through, that did not extend to tracking the day-to-day performance of political appointees, including cabinet secretaries. There was "no interest in the White House" for that, Johnson lamented, when there were more "hot and spicy [things] on the menu." In the end, "so much of what gets done in any White House is just fast," Zinsmeister recalled. "Not optimal. Just adequate—and done, thank goodness."

To account for these limitations, the White House monitored and managed agency behavior through a wide range of procedural means, with an eye toward imposing centralized control over how bureaus executed the law.

DIRECTIVES

Bush had great "focus on how stuff is being implemented," according to

Johnson. That made perfect sense: because new laws are hard to pass, the implementation of existing laws is key to policymaking.

Presidents use an array of methods to tell agencies how they expect that implementation to occur. These include the signing statements noted earlier, but many other administrative tools as well. In a 2008 report, the Congressional Research Service identified twenty-seven different types of presidential directives, and even that is an incomplete count.[65] Executive orders (EOs) are probably the best known. Phillip Cooper describes EOs as "directives issued by the president to officers of the executive branch, requiring them to take an action, stop a certain type of activity, alter policy, change management practices, or accept a delegation of authority under which they will be responsible for the implementation of law."[66]

Realizing the importance of such directives, the Bush administration was quite disciplined in planning an executive action agenda. "The use of presidential directives has grown to become a vital component of executive power," read a cover memo from a group tasked with "reviewing presidential directives" during the 2000–2001 transition, adding that "neither Congress nor the judiciary has shown much enthusiasm for curbing" their use.[67] Bush domestic policy adviser John Bridgeland said, "I think you could make an argument that the President was not only an agenda setter but through executive action did an extraordinary amount."[68]

The group assigned to review presidential directives assessed extant executive orders, memoranda, proclamations, and their kin and then made recommendations whether to retain, revoke, or amend them. Archival records show that the group, which included former OMB officials, considered both political and substantive arguments. Some decisions were easy. The "Mexico City Policy" linking foreign aid to family planning, put in place in the Reagan-Bush years but reversed by Clinton, was marked as something to restore on the "1st day," as "Bush is on record supporting reversal." Orders such as EO 12836, requiring union labor on federal contracts, were also tagged for revocation. Examining Clinton's EO 13132 dealing with federalism, the group urged, "Reinstate Reagan E.O. [in] Week 1."[69] On regulatory planning and review, it noted, "Cheney will lead."

Other decisions were trickier. Some Clinton memoranda, such as those protecting "roadless" areas in the national forest system, had already led to the promulgation of new regulations that could not be unilaterally rescinded. The group noted that the "Agriculture transition group recommends modifying the rule," and it urged legal challenges ("file lawsuits before the 20th" [of January 2001] read a scrawled reminder in the margins).[70]

Still other orders were "politically difficult to revoke," such as one issued just ten days before Bush's inauguration, dealing with disabilities in the workplace. "It would have been nice if President-elect Bush had the opportunity to issue this E.O., not President Clinton," the group noted. EO 13166, issued in August 2020 to provide services to people with limited English, teed up "a politically sensitive issue" that could impose "a true burden . . . depending on how it is implemented. Revocation would probably be unwise, but amendment could be possible." "Have new A.G. [attorney general] review," someone else noted. By contrast, a Clinton order extending specific protections against workplace discrimination to gay and lesbian federal workers was tagged as something to "revoke and replace," since (the reviewer managed to conclude) "there is no record of discrimination against homosexuals in federal employment." In addition, social conservatives would see it as "approval of the gay lifestyle," which could be used to extend such protections to the private sector. In the end, Bush ignored that recommendation, and the order stayed in place.

On January 29, 2001, Bush issued the first of his own EOs, indicating the priority he placed on the role of faith-based and community initiatives in his administration.[71] A pair of orders created a new White House Office of Faith-Based and Community Initiatives (OFBCI) and mandated that five federal departments establish "centers" (with directors chosen in conjunction with OFBCI) to identify and eliminate "regulatory, contracting, and other programmatic obstacles to the participation of faith-based and other community organizations in the provision of social services."[72]

As subsequent executive action developed, the EOP kept a close watch on the formulation process.[73] In contrast with prior administrations, the White House–based policy councils were the key points of contact with OMB, which continued its long-standing job of gathering governmentwide comments on proposed orders, proclamations, and executive memoranda. The increasing size of the government (including a new Department of Homeland Security during the Bush years) meant that twenty to forty agencies and entities had to be canvassed about possible directives. But some clearly had more sway than others, such as the Office of the Vice President, which was particularly sensitive to any orders that might have implications for presidential power. In August 2001, when asked to comment on a proposed order creating a board to coordinate government policy on critical infrastructure for information technology, David Addington responded with eight single-spaced pages of revisions. "The proposal to have the Board Chair report to three people," he grumbled, "is essentially a proposal that the Board Chair report to no one." His suggestions reduced the board membership and sought to maintain the broadest degree of presidential discretion with regard to its advisory processes. Few details were overlooked. In February 2003, for instance, in response to a fairly trivial order dealing with medals to be issued by the armed services in conjunction with the war on terror, Addington urged that "nothing" in the order "be construed for any purpose as . . . fixing the dates of initiation or termination of armed hostilities between the United States and terrorists of global reach."[74]

The number of EOs issued by Bush was not particularly impressive compared with other presidents. His total of 291 over two terms is similar to Obama's (276) and lags Clinton's (364). However, this accounts for only a fraction of Bush's executive actions, which include military orders (e.g., the November 2001 order creating military commissions to try those detained in the war on terror), guidance documents (including one setting aside the Geneva Conventions when defining the "humane treatment of al Qaeda and Taliban detainees"), and at least 131 other presidential memoranda.[75] And although the transition review group criticized the Clinton administration for "using their executive powers to pick up where their legislative agenda faltered," Bush would soon follow suit. As OFBCI director James Towey put it, the legislative debate on later faith-based initiatives was "so toxic and partisan that [Democrats] were not going to give [Bush] a victory. Then I thought, 'OK, we have to pivot to executive action. What can he do? . . . What can you do with executive action?' So we developed an Executive Order."[76] Indeed, that order was the subject of the boast by Bush that opens this chapter. His decision on federal funding for research using human stem cells—the topic of his first televised address from the Oval Office—was another variant on unilateral action. "There was never any discussion that it was going to be anything but a Presidential initiative," domestic policy chief Margaret Spellings recalled.

The executive order covering LGBT workplace rights, mentioned earlier, also provides a sense of how creative administrative tactics can affect the substance of federal policy. Although Bush did not revoke Clinton's executive order, federal workers' unions and LGBT interest groups soon realized that the Bush administration was not enforcing it, and they claimed that the new appointee charged with doing so had removed relevant materials from the agency's website.[77] Similarly, when tort reform legislation stalled in Congress, Bush told federal agencies to look for other methods to prevent what the administration saw as frivolous lawsuits. In some cases, agencies asserted their authority to forestall cases brought under state law by asserting that compliance with federal regulatory requirements would be a viable defense against tort claims; by 2008, more than fifty federal rules contained this kind of "preemption" language.[78]

Another means of customizing implementation involved how agencies spent their appropriated funds. OMB director Mitch Daniels, for instance, "sent out this missive to agencies saying you're not authorized to spend any money on any project that is listed in [legislative] report language without coming to the OMB for permission, which will not be forthcoming." This policy set aside congressional earmarks and earned Karl Rove a tongue-lashing from House majority whip Roy Blunt (R-MO).[79] Daniels kept a tight rein on agency behavior in general, in terms of both spending and (as discussed later) management issues, his aim being to "establish OMB as a very effective tool for [the president]." Signing statements, said Republican House Speaker Dennis Hastert, were not the issue; it was that "once you wrote the law, you never knew how the administration would implement the law. . . . The implementation, the rules and regs, that was the instruction of how to do it."

RULE MAKING

"Rules and regs" are indeed critical to the administrative presidency. As noted earlier, a centralized process of regulatory review was formalized under Ronald Reagan, despite pressure from pro-regulatory interests. Bill Clinton endorsed that review process and the cost-benefit analyses it required. Bush considered new legislation to formalize regulatory limits, but ultimately he made "a strategic decision . . . to focus regulatory reform efforts on executive actions."[80] Although Clinton's process was more generous than Reagan's in evaluating benefits over costs, the Bush transition group reviewing presidential directives noted that "the OMB policy group believes it can operate within" that framework. "They believe improved regulatory review can be accomplished more effectively by changes in personnel than changes in policy."[81]

Bush's first regulatory czar, John Graham, did give cost-benefit analyses increased emphasis, issuing new formal guidance (OMB Circular A-4) on

methods and analytical rigor. Even when agencies faced statutory prohi-
bitions against relying on such calculations, OMB required at least their
publication. Graham also took a strict line on agencies' scientific claims,
rejecting them if they did not meet OMB standards of "quality, objectivity,
utility, and integrity." Rules that fell short of these standards were returned
to the agencies for reconsideration (OMB cannot flatly reject rules if the
power to promulgate them is vested directly in an agency). Within a year,
some two dozen proposed rules had been returned, more than in the eight
years under Clinton. Critics complained that OMB was ignoring agency
expertise and rejecting conclusions that did not match the administration's
policy preferences.[82]

In 2007 the Bush administration became worried that agencies were
evading regulatory clearance by issuing guidance documents that laid out
statutory interpretations without actually engaging the formal rule-making
process. The president therefore issued an executive order on regulatory
planning and review that placed such guidance within OMB's purview. The
new order also emphasized that regulation should address a specific "market failure." Clinton had required agencies to designate a regulatory policy
officer; Bush's order required that officer to be a presidential appointee and
dictated that, unless directly authorized by the agency head, "no rulemaking
shall commence nor be included" in agency regulatory plans without that
officer's approval.[83]

As a backstop, presidential staffers energetically involved themselves in
a wide range of agency activities that threatened to diverge from presidential policy preferences. This led a variety of scientific groups to charge that
ideology was trumping research in areas ranging from climate change to
workplace safety standards to the evaluation of toxic chemicals. After the
Supreme Court ruled that the EPA could regulate carbon dioxide emissions
from auto tailpipes under the 1970 Clean Air Act, the White House refused
to acknowledge the agency's memorandum reporting its decision to do so.[84]
EOP staff even weighed in to block a Commerce Department measure seeking to lower maritime speed limits in shipping lanes populated by right
whales.[85] On the flip side, White House aides prompted new rule-making
processes to substitute for "doomed" legislation or to "block (or delay) overly
ambitious legislative proposals in the Congress or in the states."[86] The Clear
Skies environmental and energy regulations, administrative reforms to the

Endangered Species Act, and auto mileage rules were part of that agenda. And events mattered too: the September 11 attacks resulted in a flood of new regulations, and another "frenzy of executive policymaking" occurred in 2008 as the administration prepared to leave office and sought to cement its policy legacy. David Shafie calculates that "far more economically significant final rules were submitted . . . in 2008 and the first three weeks of 2009 than in the last year of any previous administration."[87]

THE PRESIDENT'S MANAGEMENT AGENDA

OMB's arsenal for shaping agency management practices was upgraded by the August 2001 President's Management Agenda (PMA). The PMA aimed to improve government performance in five areas: human capital, competitive sourcing, e-government, financial management, and budget and performance integration. Starting with the fiscal year 2003 budget, OMB classified each major government agency as either "effective" or "ineffective" and gave each agency an overall management grade on each of the five dimensions. The grades were like stoplights: green, yellow, or red. Most grades were poor: more than three-quarters were red, for failing, and of 130 scores (twenty-six agencies times five categories), just 5 percent were green, indicating full marks. By June 2003, several agencies had at least managed to improve to yellow; by March 2004, additional green lights were scattered across the agencies. Others, however, such as the Department of Housing and Urban Development (HUD), remained wholly red.

From the first PMA scorecard to the last, there was notable improvement—even HUD moved from "totally dysfunctional" to "totally functional," Clay Johnson claimed. The last PMA scorecard was 57 percent green. (Johnson rejected charges of grade inflation: "that doesn't mean we just ran out of red [ink] here and had to use green.")[88]

Added to the PMA in the budget for fiscal year 2004 and beyond was a more detailed analysis of programs within each departmental jurisdiction— some 1,200 in all. "This budget makes an unprecedented effort to assess the effectiveness of specific federal programs," Bush's budget message claimed. A questionnaire called the Program Assessment Rating Tool (PART) was used to evaluate each program. Again, many programs fell short—only 6 percent of federal programs were deemed "effective," with another 24 percent "moderately effective." For more than half, the rating was "results not demonstrated."

In the case of both the PMA and PART, the veiled (or not so veiled) threat was that programs that failed to meet effectiveness benchmarks were prime targets for cuts in funding or for privatization—the second main approach stressed by the Bush OMB. One study did find a small but significant correlation between higher PART scores and higher budget requests by the administration, as well as less robust evidence that programs associated with Democratic administrations received consistently smaller funding recommendations.[89]

By most accounts, the process did prompt change. Overall, agencies paid closer and more sustained attention to PART in particular, and to the PMA in general, than to most of the other management reform efforts that have periodically gripped Washington. This was partly because OMB took pains to publish its assessments. As Johnson noted, "When you highlight the degree to which it doesn't work, people reprioritize and work on it and find solutions. There were hundreds of examples of this in the management agenda world."[90] Further, the president took a personal interest, asking agency heads about their progress on these issues—especially about their "red lights."[91] Even the notoriously insulated Army Corps of Engineers was motivated by the president's involvement. "'Right now, you're red across the board,'" Johnson remembers telling its commander. "'What does that mean? It means the President will be looking at you.' . . . All of a sudden he became Mr. Go Get 'Em. It helped to say that the president sees this."

In short, Bush officials aggressively combined centralization and politicization in a way that extended the administration's control of bureaucratic outputs. One study suggests, for example, that the combination of appointments and centralized rule making decreased enforcement actions by the EPA.[92]

An additional tool was the control of information within and between the executive and legislative branches, which went far beyond the regulatory arena. Decision making was tightly controlled within the administration, eliminating layers of potential dissent; often, the president was "dead certain" (as Robert Draper titled his book on Bush).[93] And when facing external pressures, the White House staked out aggressive legal ground on issues of executive privilege from the outset of the administration, refusing to release records pertaining to Vice President Cheney's energy task force to the GAO and issuing administrative orders restricting access to federal documents requested through the Freedom of Information Act (FOIA) and those governed by the Presidential Records Act.[94] The court case involving the energy task force provides a telling summary of the administration's attitude toward the other branches of government. Efforts by Congress and the courts to gather information on White House proceedings, argued the solicitor general, amounted to "unwarranted intrusion" into "vital Executive Branch functions."[95]

To be sure, the president did not get everything he wanted. Although the cohesive singularity of the executive branch is assumed in unitary executive theory, the reality is far more fragmented. As George Krause and Brent Dupay observe, "although Congress suffers from well noted collective action problems, presidents suffer internal executive branch coordination problems of their own."[96] Even creating executive orders requires bargaining with the bureaucracy—a process that, as White House counsel Fielding said, can be "like giving birth to a pineapple."[97]

Still, if there is inevitable slippage between the demands voiced in the Oval Office and the action taken in an agency's San Diego field office, it is reasonable to conclude that the Bush administration tested the limits of the tactics that might reduce that gap.

Political Checks and Contingencies

As should be clear by now, the success of Bush's administrative unilateralism was contingent on the absence of political checks restricting its execution. Where the administration's claims to presidential autonomy stepped into shared constitutional ground, Congress often had the authority to push back. Whether it did so varied with partisan and institutional incentives.

For example, the political salience of the investigation into the 9/11 attacks meant that legislators were willing to wage a high-profile battle with the White House over whether national security adviser Condoleezza Rice would testify publicly before the 9/11 Commission. She did. "The president just got beaten down," Gonzales recalled, even though he and others had urged Bush, "for the institution of the White House and future Presidents, don't do this." As noted earlier, Gonzales himself was forced out of office by another congressional investigation, this one into the firing of US attorneys. That probe was spurred in part by the desire of a new Democratic majority in Congress to score points against the administration; however, it was also the result of legislators' broader institutional anger at perceived interference in state-level (and thus constituency-related) law enforcement, changing testimony about the rationale for the firings, and the administration's perceived willingness to use interim appointment powers to evade the Senate confirmation process.[98] Yet Congress had specifically authorized the president to fill vacant US attorney positions without Senate confirmation on an interim basis in a provision of the 2001 Patriot Act. The idea was to allow such posts to be filled in an emergency, such as another terrorist attack; thus, it was the purported abuse of that power rather than its existence that angered legislators.

Indeed, in matters more closely linked to national security Congress often chose to underwrite or even explicitly endorse presidential action. In 2007 and 2008 Democratic majorities amended the Foreign Intelligence Surveillance Act to legalize the administration's broad program of collecting communications data and to provide new tools for gaining the cooperation of private-sector tech firms.[99] Institutional incentives tend to differ across the domestic and foreign policy arenas; in this case, both public opinion and global events mattered in activating Congress's desire to delegate authority (or, put another way, to avoid blame). Democratic losses in the 2002 midterms led to legislative support for enhanced presidential control of personnel in the new Department of Homeland Security. Recall, too, that terrorists killed nearly two hundred people in a series of coordinated bombings in Madrid in March 2004, the same week the Justice Department was revisiting the legal standing of the expansive Stellarwind data-gathering program. The new attacks cemented the congressional leadership's private support for such surveillance long before the program was publicly revealed.[100]

The intersection of party loyalty and congressional procedure also hampered efforts to constrain the administration, even after Democrats regained majorities in both chambers. The president's ability to use unilateral action as "first mover"—that is, to require Congress to overcome its inherent collective action challenge and react to a new policy status quo—proved powerful in this regard. In the Senate, especially, a sizable Republican minority was able to use the filibuster to forestall the passage of Democratic priorities—or, when they did pass, to unite against a veto override. After using the veto just once in his first six years, Bush issued eleven in 2007–2008. Majority leader Harry Reid (D-NV) was driven to grumble that Bush was "pulling the strings on the 49 puppets he has here in the Senate."[101]

The judiciary, by contrast, was better able and more willing to push back against broad claims of unilateral executive discretion, even in national security cases. A sequence of high-profile decisions gave prisoners detained at Guantánamo Bay access to American courts, required congressional approval for the president's imposition of military commissions, and—when that case led to the quick passage of the Military Commissions Act of 2006—set aside parts of that new law as unconstitutional.[102] Gonzales notes that the administration never really considered going to Congress in advance, given its certainty about presidential power: "I don't recall discussion about going to Congress and getting additional authorization beyond the AUMF."[103] He conceded that "we miscalculated where we thought the Court would draw the line between the protection of civil liberties and the protection of our own security in certain cases."

Implementing the Administrative Presidency

George W. Bush was son to one president but, in terms of his managerial tactics, heir to another. Reagan was the progenitor. Having entered the Oval Office determined to reinforce the executive's autonomy from legislative constraints—and, crucially, to extend its control over the behavior of the executive branch more generally—President Bush extended the precedents of his predecessors and bequeathed to his successors a stronger office in institutional, administrative terms.

The rise of the unitary executive as a justification for unilateral action, shrugging off or disavowing the legitimacy of constraints imposed by the other branches of government, achieved some impressive short-term results. And, with "the vision thing" in (over?)abundance, the Bush administration could make a coherent case that carrying out its vision required careful discipline. Its centralized management presupposed suspicion of its agenda by risk-averse experts in the departments and sought to overcome their recalcitrance by blunt force. Bureaucratic pushback—by the EPA or even (eventually) the Justice Department—merely reinforced the Oval Office's view that outside actors could not be trusted unless they could be controlled.

The Bush administration and its legal craftsmen pushed their theories of executive power in good faith: they believed that the only way the nation could meet the threats it faced was by enhancing the president's authority over government policy. And in some ways, the growth of executive responsibility has been a natural and even laudable development. One cannot

phatic (if rather simplistic) view of unitary executive theory. In a speech to the Federalist Society in November 2019, William Barr (attorney general under both George H. W. Bush and Donald Trump) complained that it was a "horrible movie." For a transcript of his speech, see https://www.americanrhetoric.com/speeches/williambarrfederalistsociety.htm.

7. See James Madison's minutes from June 1, 1787, available at https://press-pubs.uchicago.edu/founders/documents/a2_1_1s4.html.

8. See "Cato," Letter V (November 22, 1787); Alexander Hamilton, Federalist 69, in Alexander Hamilton, James Madison, and John Jay, *The Federalist Papers*, ed. Clinton Rossiter (New York: Mentor Books, 1961). *The Federalist Papers* is also available through the Library of Congress at https://guides.loc.gov/federalist-papers/full-text.

9. Richard E. Neustadt, *Presidential Power and the Modern Presidents* (1960; New York: Free Press, 1990), ix. The expanded 1990 edition contains the 1960 original in its entirety.

10. Edward S. Corwin, *The President: Office and Powers, 1787–1957* (New York: New York University Press, 1957), 307.

11. Andrew Rudalevige, *The New Imperial Presidency: Renewing Presidential Power after Watergate* (Ann Arbor: University of Michigan Press, 2005), chap. 4. See also James Sundquist, *The Decline and Resurgence of Congress* (Washington, DC: Brookings Institution, 1981).

12. Dick Cheney, NBC interview, January 27, 2003, in Tom Curry, "Executive Privilege Again at Issue," MSNBC.com, February 1, 2003.

13. "The President's News Conference," March 13, 2002, https://www.presidency.ucsb.edu/node/212036; Jack Goldsmith, *The Terror Presidency: Law and Judgment Inside the Bush Administration* (New York: W. W. Norton, 2007), 132. In his oral history, Alberto Gonzales pushed back against the idea that Vice President Cheney was the prime force behind efforts to enhance presidential power: "The President subscribed to that as well though."

14. Rudalevige, *New Imperial Presidency*, 101.

15. Unfortunately, given his role in applying this philosophy to public policy during the Bush administration, the most relevant portions of Yoo's oral history are redacted as of this writing.

16. Francine Kiefer, "Clinton Perfects the Art of Go-Alone Governing," *Christian Science Monitor*, July 24, 1998, 3. See also David Gray Adler, "Clinton in Context," in *The Presidency and the Law: The Clinton Legacy*, ed. David Gray Adler and Michael Genovese (Lawrence: University Press of Kansas, 2002).

17. The Supreme Court held in *Zivotofsky v. Kerry* (2015) that the diplomatic recognition power is similarly exclusive. The pardon power, perhaps ironically, is one that Bush used relatively little. Karl Rove, in the second interview of his oral history, argues that this meant Bush wanted to limit his power: "It showed Bush's attitude, which was, 'I want to put it in a process and constrain it because I'm concerned about unlimited power.'" But Alberto Gonzales's oral history implies that Bush's sparing use of pardons was more about the president. Despite being "a very forgiving guy," he wanted to be careful about the political sensitivities of pardons and set a high bar for what offenses and offenders deserved clemency.

18. Francis E. Rourke, "Whose Bureaucracy Is This, Anyway?" *PS: Political Science and Politics* 26 (December 1993): 687.

19. Steven G. Calabresi and Kevin H. Rhodes, "The Structural Constitution: Unitary Executive, Plural Judiciary," *Harvard Law Review* 105 (1992): 1215. See also Jeffrey Rosen, "Power of One," *New Republic*, July 24, 2006; Steven G. Calabresi and Christopher S. Yoo, *A History of the Unitary Executive* (New Haven, CT: Yale University Press, 2008).

20. See, e.g., *Morrison v. Olson*; *Humphrey's Executor v. United States*, 295 U.S. 602 (1935).

21. Figures from Christopher Kelley and Bryan Marshall, "Going It Alone: The Politics of Signing Statements from Reagan to Bush II," *Social Science Quarterly* 91 (March 2010): table 2. See also Joel Aberbach, "Supplying the Defect of Better Motives? The Bush II Administration and the Constitutional System," in *The George W. Bush Legacy*, ed. Colin Campbell, Bert Rockman, and Andrew Rudalevige (Washington, DC: CQ Press, 2008), 116–120; Charlie Savage, *Takeover* (Boston: Little, Brown, 2007), chap. 10.

22. "Statement on Signing the Department of Homeland Security Appropriations Act, 2006," October 18, 2005, https://www.presidency.ucsb.edu/node/212936.

23. "Statement on Signing the Henry J. Hyde United States–India Peaceful Atomic Energy Cooperation Act of 2006," December 18, 2006, https://www.presidency.ucsb.edu/node/272569.

24. "President's Statement on Signing of H.R. 2863," December 30, 2005, https://www.presidency.ucsb.edu/node/214177.

25. Rove said: "Bush's attitude was, 'I'm going to be very serious about these signing statements and be very explicit about what I'm not going to do in that law so that I constrain the power of the Presidency by giving people a chance to go sue me in court and force me to do it if the courts hold that I'm acting in an inappropriate manner.'"

26. "Presidential Signing Statements Accompanying the Fiscal Year 2006 Appropriations Acts," letter from Gary L. Kepplinger, GAO general counsel, to Rep. John Conyers and Sen. Robert Byrd, reference B-308603, June 18, 2007.

27. Barton Gellman, *Angler: The Cheney Vice Presidency* (New York: Penguin, 2008), 324.

28. Quoted in Savage, *Takeover*, 236. Note that the Reagan staff anticipated the potential for a broader impact. Ralph Tarr, acting head of the Office of Legal Counsel, suggested in 1985 that signing statements were "presently underutilized and could become far more important as a tool of Presidential management of the agencies." See Savage, *Takeover*, 233.

29. Greenhouse, "Administration Says 'Zone of Autonomy' Justifies Its Secrecy."

30. US Department of Justice, Office of Legal Counsel, "The President's Constitutional Authority to Conduct Military Operations against Terrorists and Nations Supporting Them," September 25, 2001. See also Crouch et al., *Unitary Executive Theory*, 22.

31. US Department of Justice, "Legal Authorities Supporting the Activities of the National Security Agency Described by the President," January 19, 2006.

32. US Department of Defense, "Working Group Report on Detainee Interrogations in the Global War on Terrorism: Assessment of Legal, Historical, Policy, and Operational Considerations," April 4, 2003, 21, section III generally. See also US Department of

Justice, Office of Legal Counsel, "Re: Standards of Conduct for Interrogation under 18 U.S.C. §§2340–2340A," August 1, 2002.

33. Mukasey's fellow attorney general, William Barr, would extend this to the courts, calling the role of the judicial branch in the so-called enemy combatant cases "the most blatant and consequential usurpation of Executive power in our history." Barr, Federalist Society speech, November 2019.

34. See, e.g., Louis Fisher, "Presidential Inherent Power: The 'Sole Organ' Doctrine," *Presidential Studies Quarterly* 37 (March 2007): 139–152; Harold H. Bruff, *Bad Advice: Bush's Lawyers in the War on Terror* (Lawrence: University Press of Kansas, 2009); Crouch et al., *Unitary Executive Theory*.

35. Goldsmith, *Terror Presidency*, 149.

36. Nathan, *Administrative Presidency*; Richard Nathan, *The Plot that Failed* (New York: Wiley, 1975); Robert V. Percival, "Presidential Management of the Administrative State," *Duke Law Journal* 51 (2001): 963–1013. For a look at earlier developments, see Stephen Skowronek, *Building a New American State* (New York: Cambridge University Press, 1982).

37. Memo to the president, "The Second Administration Team: A Concept," 1972, 6, Frederick Malek Papers, Hoover Institution, Stanford, CA.

38. Martin Anderson, *Revolution: The Reagan Legacy*, expanded ed. (Stanford, CA: Hoover Institution Press, 1990), 195; Nathan, *Plot that Failed*.

39. Kagan, "Presidential Administration," 2277.

40. Andrew Rudalevige, "Beyond Structure and Process: The Early Institutionalization of Regulatory Review," *Journal of Policy History* 30 (October 2018): 577–608.

41. Thomas J. Weko, *The Politicizing Presidency* (Lawrence: University Press of Kansas, 1994), 89.

42. Dick Kirschten, "White House Strategy," *National Journal*, February 21, 1981, 302; Anderson, *Revolution*, 193–205; Don Moran to Ed Harper, December 26, 1981, National Archives II, Record Group 51 [OMB Files], Deputy Director's Subject Files: Ed Harper, 1981–82 (FRC 51-82-50), box 3, "Reorganization."

43. Common Legislative Encroachments on Executive Branch Authority, 13 Op. Off. Legal Counsel 248 (1989). The battle over the legislative veto (leading to its 1983 rescission in *INS v. Chadha*) was one example.

44. For a more detailed discussion, see Andrew Rudalevige, "George W. Bush's Administrative Presidency," in *The George W. Bush Presidency*, vol. 1, *The Constitution, Politics, and Policymaking*, ed. Meena Bose (New York: Nova, 2016). The "people and process" framework used here is adapted from Rudalevige, "Presidency and Unilateral Power."

45. John Burke, *Becoming President: The Bush Transition, 2000–2003* (Boulder, CO: Lynne Rienner, 2004); David E. Lewis, "Personnel Is Policy," in *President George W. Bush's Influence over Bureaucracy and Policy*, ed. Colin Provost and Paul Teske (New York: Palgrave Macmillan, 2009); Sheryl Gay Stolberg, "Bush Friends, Loyal and Texan, Remain a Force," *New York Times*, February 21, 2007.

46. Quoted in Mike Allen, "Bush to Change Economic Team," *Washington Post*, November 29, 2004, A1. See also Andrew Rudalevige, "'The Decider': Issue Management and the Bush White House," in Campbell et al., *George W. Bush Legacy*; James A. Barnes,

"Selecting the Players," *National Journal*, June 25, 2001; Shirley Anne Warshaw, "The Administrative Strategies of President George W. Bush," *Extensions: Journal of the Legislative Studies Section* (Spring 2006): 19–20.

47. Johnson stressed that the process was a joint effort—"you've got to do it with them, not to them." But even someone the secretary proposed needed to be vetted, as part of a wider conversation about what the job entailed, what skills it required, and "who else might be qualified but not recommended." Johnson added, "I could be more candid with [Bush] than others could be."

48. Johnson oral history.

49. Martha Joynt Kumar, "Recruiting and Organizing the White House Staff," in *The White House World: Transitions, Organization, and Office Operations*, ed. Martha Joynt Kumar and Terry Sullivan (College Station: Texas A&M Press, 2003), 368.

50. Johnson notes that Paul O'Neill at Treasury was particularly unsatisfactory in that regard. Robert Draper writes that it "wasn't enough for White House job seekers to be Republicans, or even friends of the Bushes—they had to agree with George W. Bush's ideology." Robert Draper, *Dead Certain: The Presidency of George W. Bush* (New York: Free Press, 2007), 105.

51. James Barnes, "Bush's Insiders," *National Journal*, June 23, 2001; Warshaw, "Administrative Strategies," 20.

52. Henry B. Hogue and Maureen Bearden, *Recess Appointments Made by President George W. Bush, January 20, 2001–January 31, 2008*, Report RL33310 (Congressional Research Service, 2008). The strategy angered Senate majority leader Harry Reid to such an extent that he kept the Senate in continuous pro forma sessions in 2007 to prevent recess appointments. This practice continued in the Obama administration and led to the Supreme Court decision in *NLRB v. Noel Canning* (2014), invalidating certain Obama recess appointments.

53. See Lewis, "Personnel Is Policy."

54. Robert O'Harrow Jr. and Scott Higham, "Doan Ends Her Stormy Tenure as GSA Chief," *Washington Post*, May 1, 2008.

55. Savage, *Takeover*, 294–300. The idea, according to one careerist who left in 2005, was "to leave behind a bureaucracy that approached civil rights the same way the political appointees did" (Savage, 300).

56. Dan Eggen and Paul Kane, "Justice Department Would Have Kept 'Loyal' Prosecutors," *Washington Post*, March 16, 2007.

57. Alberto R. Gonzales, *True Faith and Allegiance* (Nashville: Nelson Books, 2016), 404.

58. Dan Eggen and Amy Goldstein, "Broader Privilege Claimed in Firings," *Washington Post*, July 20, 2007. The claim rested on a Reagan-era Justice Department opinion, but the closer parallel was the president's argument in *U.S. v. Nixon* (1974). With some justification, Gonzales blames a "Democrat-led drumbeat" drowning out "the truth" with "raw politics" (Gonzales, *True Faith*, 442, 430), but the ultimate calls for his resignation were bipartisan, and the House vote to hold Josh Bolten and Harriet Miers in contempt of Congress was 223–32.

59. Peter Baker, *Days of Fire* (New York: Doubleday, 2013), 314–319; James Comey,

A Higher Loyalty (New York: Flatiron Books, 2018), 84–92; Gellman, *Angler,* 299–326; Gonzales oral history; Gonzales, *True Faith*, chaps. 26–29.

60. Gellman, *Angler*, 318.

61. See Charlie Savage, *Power Wars*, paperback ed. (New York: Back Bay Books, 2017), 190–194; Comey, *Higher Loyalty*, 98–99; Gonzales oral history.

62. EPA figures in Lewis, "Personnel Is Policy," table 2.1.

63. George Krause, "Organizational Complexity and Coordination Dilemmas in U.S. Executive Politics," *Presidential Studies Quarterly* 39 (March 2009): 74–88.

64. George W. Bush, *Decision Points* (New York: Crown, 2010), 95. See also Johnson's oral history, which isn't shy about mentioning the final four letters of that word.

65. For instance, it does not include presidential memoranda, which can be used as substitutes for executive orders. See Harold Relyea, *Presidential Directives: Background and Overview*, Report 98-611 GOV (Congressional Research Service, November 26, 2008).

66. Phillip J. Cooper, *By Order of the President: The Use and Abuse of Executive Direct Action*, 2nd ed. (Lawrence: University Press of Kansas, 2014), 21.

67. Cited documents in this section are from the Records of the OMB General Counsel 2001–2009, "Review of Presidential Directives," accession 051-11-0012, boxes 1–2, Washington National Records Center, Suitland, MD. The review is mentioned in John Bridgeland's oral history, 41.

68. Bridgeland added, "The legislative process had its peaks and valleys." It is perhaps worth noting that one important legislative success of the Bush presidency was preventing Congress from reining in its executive autonomy.

69. This did not happen: executive action can be constrained as well as prompted by broader events. As Gonzales notes in his oral history, the federalism executive order "died because of 9/11 when all of a sudden everyone was expecting the federal government to do everything. The thought was that we would delay it. . . . But after 9/11 everybody's mindset changed. It just wasn't the right time to push it."

70. The date was important so the suit would be filed against the Clinton administration, not the Bush administration.

71. Bush, *Decision Points*, 279.

72. EO 13198 (January 29, 2001).

73. Executive order "clearance files" from 2001 through 2004 are available in the OMB archives. This section is drawn from OMB materials held in accession 51-06-0013 [OMB: OGC: Ex. Orders/Proclamations 2001–2004] and accession 051-05-0006 [EO/Proclamations 2004], Washington National Records Center, Suitland, MD. For a broader discussion of the formulation of executive orders, see Andrew Rudalevige, *By Executive Order: Bureaucratic Management and the Limits of Presidential Power* (Princeton, NJ: Princeton University Press, 2021).

74. Gonzales marveled at Addington's attention span and work rate: "You asked me what David is focused on. David is focused on everything. Every Executive order, every speech, David would read and mark up. I was amazed. I think everyone else was amazed."

75. See "Detention, Treatment, and Trial of Certain Non-Citizens in the War against Terrorism," November 13, 2001, https://fas.org/irp/offdocs/eo/mo-111301.htm; "Humane Treatment," February 7, 2002, https://nsarchive2.gwu.edu//NSAEBB/NSA

EBB127/02.02.07.pdf. Thanks to Kenneth Lowande for additional memoranda data; see https://dataverse.harvard.edu/dataset.xhtml?persistentId=doi:10.7910/DVN/OAM 0IN.

76. Margaret Spellings adds: "We beat our heads against the wall legislatively. . . . We ended up eventually doing a lot of things, as much as we could, by Executive order." See also Josh Bolten's oral history.

77. See, e.g., American Federation of Government Employees, "Fact Sheet on the Employment Non-Discrimination Act," 2007, http://afgecouncil222.com/Lg/07afgeissue prs7.pdf.

78. John D. Graham, *Bush on the Home Front: Domestic Policy Triumphs and Setbacks* (Bloomington: Indiana University Press, 2010), 255.

79. Rove continues, "This just drove Congressmen and Senators up the wall."

80. Graham, *Bush on the Home Front*, 256.

81. "Review of Presidential Directives," January 9, 2001, 4, in Records of the OMB General Counsel 2001–2009, Washington National Records Center, Suitland, MD.

82. Graham, *Bush on the Home Front*, 257–259; Amy Goldstein and Sarah Cohen, "Bush Forces a Shift in Regulatory Thrust," *Washington Post*, August 15, 2004, A1; Rick Weiss, "'Data Quality' Law Is Nemesis of Regulation," *Washington Post*, August 16, 2004, A1. Note that Graham's formal title was director of the Office of Information and Regulatory Affairs (OIRA), a Senate-confirmed position within the Office of Management and Budget.

83. EO 13422 (January 18, 2007).

84. As a result, the EPA would not begin to regulate in this area until the Obama administration took office in 2009.

85. "Toxic Chemicals," testimony of John Stephenson, GAO, before Senate Committee on Environment and Public Works, April 29, 2008; Felicity Barringer, "White House Refused to Open Pollutants E-Mail," *New York Times*, June 25, 2008; Rep. Henry Waxman, "Responses to 16 November Questions from White House on Right Whale Ship Strike Reduction Final Rule" (National Oceanic and Atmospheric Administration document formerly on Waxman's website). See also https://www.ucsusa.org/resources /white-house-politics-collide-endangered-right-whale. More generally, see Christopher Lee, "Scientists Report Political Interference," *Washington Post*, April 24, 2008; Gellman, *Angler*, chap. 8.

86. Graham, *Bush on the Home Front*, 326, 327.

87. David M. Shafie, *Eleventh Hour: The Politics of Policy Initiatives in Presidential Transitions* (College Station: Texas A&M Press, 2013), 138.

88. Johnson became OMB's deputy director for management in June 2003.

89. John Gilmour and David Lewis, "Does Performance Budgeting Work? An Examination of the Office of Management and Budget's PART Scores," *Public Administration Review* 66 (September–October 2006): 742–752.

90. Johnson added, "You can't fix it if you don't put a little light on it."

91. Jonathan D. Breul, "Three Bush Management Reform Initiatives," *Public Administration Review* 67 (January–February 2007): 21–26; author's interviews with OMB staff. For previous efforts, see Paul C. Light, *Tides of Reform* (New Haven, CT: Yale University Press, 1997).

92. Colin Provost, Brian J. Gerber, and Mark Pickup, "Flying under the Radar? Political Control and Bureaucratic Resistance in the Bush Environmental Protection Agency," in Provost and Teske, *President George W. Bush's Influence*, 169–186.

93. Rudalevige, "'The Decider.'"

94. At one stage, the vice president argued that the visitor logs for his residence should be considered presidential rather than Secret Service records, thus making them immune from FOIA. A federal judge rejected this argument in late 2007.

95. Greenhouse, "Administration Says 'Zone of Autonomy' Justifies Its Secrecy."

96. George Krause and Brent M. Dupay, "Coordinated Action and the Limits of Presidential Control over the Bureaucracy: Lessons from the Bush Presidency," in Provost and Teske, *President George W. Bush's Influence*, 100.

97. Rudalevige, *By Executive Order*, 47.

98. For some of the bipartisan criticism (which Gonzales naturally disputes), see Gonzales, *True Faith*, 432–435. The issue came to a head over the interim appointment of a former Rove aide to fill a US attorney position in Arkansas, which angered Sen. David Pryor (D-AR). Gonzales argued that the plan had always been to submit the appointment to the Senate, and in his memoir he slammed "Pryor's inflammatory, false statements." Gonzales, 421.

99. Savage, *Power Wars*, 211–214.

100. As Gonzales notes, "That morning the Madrid train bombings had occurred. So now Congressional leadership is damn happy that they've said go forward, they're happy about it."

101. David Herszenhorn, "Reid's Chilly Relationship with Bush Enters Deep Freeze," *New York Times*, December 19, 2007.

102. See *Rasul v. Bush*, 542 U.S. 466 (2004); *Hamdan v. Rumsfeld*, 548 U.S. 557 (2006); *Boumediene v. Bush*, 553 U.S. 723 (2008).

103. Indeed, Gonzales stressed his "fundamental disagree[ment]" with the court's reasoning, adding, "it is not at all clear as times goes by that he could have gotten [congressional] approval, certainly not without compromising some of the things he wanted to do to protect our country."

104. Alexander Hamilton, Federalist 70, in *Federalist Papers*. Generally, see Rudalevige, *New Imperial Presidency*, chap. 8.

105. Gonzales is referring to an early Bush executive order seeking to rewrite the Presidential Records Act to expand executive privilege. The order was rescinded by Barack Obama on his first day in office in 2009. "In hindsight I wish we'd never done it," Gonzales says.

106. Despite Alexander Hamilton's role as patron saint of executive unitarians, he reached similar conclusions in Federalist 66, in *Federalist Papers*.

107. Calabresi and Yoo, *History of the Unitary Executive*, 411–412. See Hamilton, Federalist 70.

108. The Obama and Trump administrations would soon learn this lesson as well.

109. See, e.g., Rudalevige, "'The Decider.'"

110. Lawrence Wright, "The Spymaster," *New Yorker*, January 21, 2008, 56.

CHAPTER FIVE

George W. Bush and Congress

John J. Pitney Jr.

Having lost a 1978 House race to Texas Democrat Kent Hance, George W. Bush never served in Congress. Instead of firsthand experience, his beliefs about dealing with the legislative branch drew from other sources. One was Harvard Business School. Hance had successfully attacked Bush as an elitist, so he was always leery of talking too much about his Ivy League pedigree. But he was the first president with an MBA, and he carried his business school lessons to the White House. Harvard had taught him that managers could not know everything, so they had to build strong teams, set clear goals, and focus on the big picture rather than minutiae.[1] Said Josh Bolten, who served as director of the Office of Management and Budget (OMB) and later as Bush's chief of staff: "He was disinclined to engage in a lot of nitty-gritty horse-trading. He viewed it as his job to lay out the principles, lay out a plan that met those principles in the best way possible from his standpoint. . . . He'd say, 'I put out what I'm for, you tell me what you're for, and then we'll see what we can work out' That's the way it ended up going."[2]

During his father's presidency, the younger Bush had served as an informal adviser. In his memoir he wrote: "In 1991, Dad asked me to study the operation of the White House. After interviewing all his senior staffers, a common theme emerged: People were dissatisfied. Most felt that Chief of Staff John Sununu had denied them access to the Oval Office and limited the flow of information to Dad." He concluded: "I was determined to avoid that problem in my White House."[3] Jack Howard, deputy director of the forty-third president's legislative affairs office, had worked in the forty-first president's administration. He noted the difference between the two:

One of the first things that 43 did was sit down with the entire Legislative Affairs staff in the Roosevelt Room, and he ran through his agenda. . . . I think he knew that a good chunk of the success of his presidency hinged on us. So I think he wanted some sense of confidence that we knew what we were doing, who we were, our backgrounds, things like that. We never had any meeting like that with 41.

One positive lesson from the forty-first president was the possibility of bipartisan cooperation in Congress. Although George H. W. Bush took office with Democratic majorities in both chambers, he secured the passage of important laws, including the Americans with Disabilities Act and the Clean Air Act amendments of 1990. With a much stronger congressional GOP and a greater interest in domestic policy, George W. Bush could reasonably hope to accomplish a good deal on Capitol Hill.

His governorship reinforced that expectation. Texas would later gain a reputation as a deep-red state, but in 1995, when Bush took office in Austin, Democrats had controlled both chambers of the state legislature since Reconstruction. He developed a working relationship with the Democratic legislature, particularly on education reform. Texas elects its lieutenant governor independently of the governor and vests the office with significant power. As president of the state senate, the lieutenant governor appoints all the committee chairs and assigns bills to committees. Bush had to work with the much-feared Democratic lieutenant governor Bob Bullock. They eventually built such a strong rapport that Bullock endorsed Bush for president. Governor Bush's relationship with Bullock affected his approach to Congress. Karl Rove said, "I think it's an overstatement to say that he felt that everybody could be like Bullock. He was sophisticated enough to know that there would be different creatures in Washington, but on the other hand, it made him absolutely stubborn about the idea that he needed to try."

Apart from external influences, Bush's personality shaped his dealings with Congress. His Oval Office persona was different from his genial public persona. Speechwriter Matt Latimer wrote: "It was not a revelation to anyone that the president could be . . . well . . . a man with a generous supply of moods."[4] David Frum, another speechwriter, put it this way: "He was tart, not sweet."[5] Bolten explained that, despite Bush's hopes for bipartisanship, Congress's inefficiency and theatrics often exasperated him. Bush, he said, "did not approach his role with a great deal of respect for the quality of the work that was coming out of the Hill." According to Bolten, Bush lacked his Republican predecessors' tolerance of congressional inefficiency: George W. Bush "did not have that personality that suffered idiocy so comfortably as I think both [Ronald Reagan] and [George H. W. Bush] did."

Bush's relationship with Congress went through four distinct phases. In the beginning, his party led an evenly divided Senate and held only a narrow majority in the House. Having run on a platform of "compassionate conservatism," he concentrated on gathering bipartisan support for his domestic policy. The second phase began when Republican senator James Jeffords switched parties in mid-2001, which gave Democrats control of the Senate and complicated the Bush administration's legislative strategy. Despite the change in control, Bush's focus remained on domestic policy until the morning of September 11, 2001. When chief of staff Andrew Card told him that America was under attack, Bush became a wartime president with wartime prestige and a wartime legislative agenda. The 2002 midterm election started the third phase. In a break with the historical pattern of midterm losses for the president's party, the GOP picked up seats in the House and regained control of the Senate. Though he remained a wartime president, Bush pushed for significant domestic measures, with mixed results. The final phase started with the 2006 midterm election, when his party took what he called "a thumping." For the final two years of his presidency, Bush's posture on Capitol Hill was mostly defensive.

The Fifty-Fifty Senate

George W. Bush was the first Republican since Dwight Eisenhower to assume the presidency with GOP control of both chambers of Congress. But the party's grip on legislative power was tenuous. Republicans had unexpectedly won control of the House six years earlier, only to see their strength steadily ebb, from 230 seats after the 1994 midterms down to 221 after Bush's victory in 2000. The peculiar cycle of Senate elections also proved problematic. In 2000 the GOP lost several of the seats it had won in the 1994 sweep. At the start of the 107th Congress, the Senate's partisan makeup was exactly 50–50. The Constitution empowers the vice president to cast tie-breaking votes in the Senate, but it does not specify how this power affects party control. Democratic leader Tom Daschle of South Dakota and Republican leader Trent Lott of Mississippi negotiated an agreement to fill the constitutional lacuna.[6] The vice president's party—the Republicans—would count as the majority and hold all the committee chairs. The two parties would share committee staff budgets evenly, and Lott, as the majority leader, would refrain from "filling the amendment tree," a process by which the majority can block the minority's floor amendments to bills. The agreement also provided that control of committees would shift if either party attained a numerical majority during the 107th Congress.

By the second decade of the twenty-first century, the congressional parties were tightly sorted, with Democrats to the left, Republicans to the right, and few lawmakers from either party in the middle. The partisan sorting was already under way when Bush took office, but it was incomplete. Despite the ongoing realignment of the South from Democratic to Republican, Democrats still held nine of twenty-two Senate seats from the Confederacy: Blanche Lincoln (Arkansas), Bill Nelson and Bob Graham (Florida), Max Cleland and Zell Miller (Georgia), Mary Landrieu and John Breaux (Louisiana), John Edwards (North Carolina), and Ernest Hollings (South Carolina). Southern voters kept most of these senators from straying too far from the center. Said Nick Calio, assistant to the president for legislative affairs during the first two years of the Bush administration: "Breaux was great, he was our go-to guy. Particularly with the combination of Breaux and Lott we were able to get a lot of stuff done. Breaux had great influence over the other Democratic moderates." Some of those moderates were from outside the South, such as Ben Nelson of Nebraska. As Calio recalled, "It was a broad target list of people we could potentially work with on various issues. Knowing we couldn't get them on each issue, but it included Dianne Feinstein [D-CA] and Evan Bayh [D-IN]."

On the other side of Capitol Hill, Republican leaders worked hard to make the most of their thin majority. House Speaker J. Dennis Hastert (R-IL) became known for the informal but powerful "Hastert rule," the practice of allowing floor votes only on measures that had the support of "a majority of the majority"—that is, a majority of the Republican House conference. Hastert denied that it was an innovation:

The Hastert rule is kind of a misnomer. They asked me when we were doing immigration, "Why don't you just move this bill and get all the Democrat votes?" First of all, I'm not going to move anything when I don't have a majority of my own people, which is common sense. Every Speaker that ever was, if you start moving bills for which you don't have your own majority, you're not the leader anymore; someone else is the leader. So that was just kind of a common-sense thing that I said. Then they put that down as the Hastert rule.

House GOP whip Tom DeLay (R-TX) earned the nickname "The Hammer" for his hard-hitting manner, but he was effective because he catered to his partisan colleagues' political needs. His concierge services included help with vote schedules, pet projects, and campaign fund-raising events.[7] Unlike previous whips, he seldom worked across the aisle. Before the new administration took office, he reportedly told Bush that the chamber was no longer a place of bipartisanship. Calio, who had worked for President George H. W. Bush, noted the difference. "By the time I came back in 2001," he said, "the Republicans were very adept at passing bills solely with Republican votes in the House." Many Republicans did not care to work with Democrats, and the feeling was mutual. Said Karl Rove: "I was part of that Texas crowd that was sort of taken aback by how partisan it was. You had things like [George] Miller and [Edward M.] Kennedy willing to work on No Child Left Behind, but the vast preponderance of Democrats in the House were just hostile to Bush. He'd stolen the election." Nevertheless, the moderate Blue Dog Coalition of House Democrats had thirty-four members, potentially giving Bush an occasional cushion on close votes.[8]

Bush understood the importance of a high-performing legislative office within the White House. In addition to Calio, he enlisted veteran Capitol Hill aides David Hobbs, Jack Howard, and Ziad Ojakli. "Most of us came from [congressional] leadership offices," said Hobbs. "I know later when I was hiring people I always wanted people from leadership offices because they were used to saying no to people other than their own boss." Bush included them in key meetings, said Hobbs, which enabled them to push back on officials who claimed to be speaking for the White House. "And we'd say, 'No, the President wants this. I talked to him, he wants it, we're going to get this done.'"

The legislative staff worked closely with other administration officials, leveraging their connections with interest groups and members of Congress. "The dirty little secret," said Rove, "is that everybody who is a senior aide to the President gets deployed by the legislative shop. You're given your assignments." He explained that staff had to touch base and report their contacts with lawmakers: "You get a phone call from Harry Reid, you had to tell three people. If appropriate, the President, at the appropriate time the Chief of Staff, and always the legislative chief."

In this respect, Vice President Cheney's role was noteworthy. Other vice presidents had served as liaisons to the Senate, but as a former White House chief of staff and secretary of defense, Cheney brought extraordinary expertise and prestige to his new job. And as a former member of the House GOP leadership, he also had deep connections there. Before he abruptly left for the Pentagon in 1989, colleagues widely assumed that Cheney would become his party's top leader in the House. He wrote in his memoirs: "The relationships I had in both houses of Congress meant that I was often the first person in the White House to hear if there was a problem. I'd get a call from Speaker Denny Hastert or Senate Majority Leader Trent Lott, for example, giving me a heads-up if a piece of legislation was going off the rails."[9] Calio, however, emphasized that Cheney worked closely with the legislative staff: "Particularly if he was going to the Hill, like for policy lunches. He would report back on what was going on. It was very collaborative. We'd tell him what we needed, where we needed him—which we did a lot, particularly [during] that early part because we had to have him in the chair in the Senate on 50–50 votes." And members of Congress saw the vice president as a conduit to the White House. Judd Gregg, a Republican senator from New Hampshire, said Cheney "was there for Members to talk to and communicate with and express their angst, their anger, their disappointment, or their feelings of success relative to the administration's positions. I thought that was incredibly effective for the President, to have that happen."

In his memoirs, Rove recalled the assumptions that drove the administration's early months: "What really matters is the first 180 days, because voters look for real achievements by the August recess. Most pieces of legislation need to be well along by then if they are to pass in the president's first year."[10] Bush's first major initiative was a tax cut. During the 1990s, a harmonic convergence of steady economic growth, reduced defense spending thanks to the Cold War peace dividend, and tax increases (supported at high political cost by George H. W. Bush in 1990 and Bill Clinton in 1993) had produced budget surpluses. For the GOP, these surpluses represented an opportunity to reduce the tax burden rather than pay down the federal debt. As Bush explained in a radio address: "A surplus in tax revenue, after all, means that taxpayers have been overcharged. And usually when you've been overcharged, you expect to get something back."[11]

Bush insisted on tax reductions totaling $1.6 trillion. Said Calio: "It goes back to that first conversation I had with him in Austin where he leaned across the table and said, 'No, we're not going to argue with ourselves, we're not going to compromise. We're going to keep saying 1.6, 1.6.'" Bush, the Harvard MBA, may well have been applying the teachings of management guru Peter Drucker, to whom he would award the Presidential Medal of Freedom two years later. "The effective executive has to start out with what is 'right' rather than what is acceptable precisely because a compromise is always necessary in the end," Drucker wrote. But without a clear marker, the executive "cannot distinguish between the right compromise and the wrong compromise."[12]

The tax bill set a pattern: Bush gave the legislative staffers a clear goal, and he made sure the lines of authority within the administration were also clear. Said Calio: "The President appointed me and Mark Weinberg from Treasury as the two leads on the tax bill, which really rankled [Rep.] Bill Thomas because . . . he was now chairman of the Ways and Means Committee. Basically, we're two piddly staffers who are going to be negotiating the tax bill for the White House." There was no freelancing. From Cheney on down, everyone in the White House told lawmakers they had to go through the two aides.

For Bush, it made political sense to kick off with a big tax cut. Economic adviser Keith Hennessey noted that Bush had developed a detailed tax proposal during the presidential race. "They had something ready. . . . They just had to write it up and hand it to the House guys and to us and say, 'This is what we want to do.' It's not as if they had to do months of internal decision making." The idea united Republicans and won majority approval among the general public.[13] Alan Greenspan, then at the height of his bipartisan esteem as chair of the Federal Reserve, endorsed the idea in Senate testimony. "In today's context," he said, "where tax reduction appears required in any event over the next several years to assist in forestalling the accumulation of private assets, starting that process sooner rather than later likely would help smooth the transition to longer-term fiscal balance."[14] According to Mitch Daniels, who was OMB director at the time, a springtime economic downturn changed the terms of the debate in ways that bolstered the case for tax cuts: "So even by the time of the tax cut the rationale was beginning to shift to fighting recession. I always thought it was maybe the luckiest fiscal move that we've seen. Again, it was crafted for a different reason." And the proposal had a significant procedural advantage. Because the

Republicans used the budget reconciliation process to bring it to the floor, it was not subject to a Senate filibuster.

Final action on the measure took place in May 2001. The tax cut passed the House with the support of 211 Republicans and 28 Democrats. Voting against it were 153 Democrats and no Republicans. On the Senate side, only two Republicans voted no: Lincoln Chafee (Rhode Island) and John McCain (Arizona). A dozen Democratic senators supported it, including Feinstein. The final total was $1.35 trillion in cuts, less than Bush had originally demanded but more than he would have gotten if he had compromised too soon.

Bush's other first-year legislative priority was education reform, an issue he had stressed during the presidential campaign. Right after the Supreme Court decision that sealed his victory in the 2000 election, he told Rove that he wanted to call Sen. Edward Kennedy (D-MA), the ranking Democrat on the Health, Education, Labor and Pensions (HELP) Committee. "And he talks to Kennedy before he talks to [Republican leader] Trent Lott. We deliberately made George Miller, the ranking Democrat on Health, Education and Labor, the first House member that he met with." Unlike other issues, education reform had the potential to be more than nominally bipartisan. "That's why he started working with Kennedy," explained Jack Howard. "Some of us would say, 'Ted Kennedy is not quite Bob Bullock, but we get the idea.' There was a real conscious effort, up until 9/11, to try to find, who is that Democratic dealmaker out there that I can work with?"

Margaret Spellings, White House domestic policy adviser and, during Bush's second term, secretary of education, said that labeling of the bill was important. "In the first meeting with the principals, Kennedy was the one who raised this issue. He said, 'We're going to make this S1,' and then [House Education Committee chair John] Boehner said, 'We're going to make it HR1.' So in the very first conversation with Bush, it's number one. Bush always called it No Child Left Behind." Republicans were reluctant to expand the federal role in education and did not have the same policy priorities as Democrats. As Spellings put it: "Left to their own devices Republicans are not dialed in to closing the achievement gap. That's not where they live. It's not that they didn't get there, but it wasn't an accident. Absolutely it wasn't an accident." Conversely, Democrats were leery of Bush. George Miller observed that he and Kennedy "flew cover for this with the center-left crowd—and John Boehner flew a great deal of cover, [and] obviously

George Bush, with conservatives who saw this as a massive intrusion, with all of the testing, the reporting."[15]

By mid-June, both chambers had passed versions of the bill by large margins. Then came a complication that would affect everything on Bush's legislative agenda.

Power Shift, Agenda Shift

On May 24, 2001, Senator Jeffords of Vermont announced that he was becoming an independent and would caucus with the Democrats. The 50–50 GOP Senate was now effectively a 51–49 Democratic Senate. Daschle would set the chamber's agenda, under the terms of the bargain he had struck with Lott at the start of the session, and all committee chairs would shift from Republicans to Democrats.

Jeffords was among the last of the liberal Republicans, increasingly out of step in an increasingly conservative party. As the session wore on, Senate Democrats noticed his discomfort and started to make overtures. Chris Dodd of Connecticut told him, "Look, Jim, there's room for you over here."[16] Daschle then put party whip Harry Reid (D-NV) in charge of flipping Jeffords.

Republicans were late to catch on to the impending switch. Calio recalled that Jeffords had spoken up about his differences with the administration, including its failure to support full funding of the main federal law on special education. Bush staffers also had "pretty pointed" conversations with Jeffords about the details of the tax bill, which he eventually supported, albeit grudgingly. "But really we didn't have a clue until Olympia Snowe [R-ME] called Andy [Card, chief of staff] on that Monday and I think [Jeffords] defected on Thursday." President Bush invited Jeffords to the Oval Office, but the senator did not change his mind. Ziad Ojakli, deputy legislative assistant for the Senate, recalled that senior Republicans then met with Jeffords in the vice president's ceremonial office on the Senate side of the Capitol. "They were all doing their best—these were all the old bulls who were going to lose their committee chairmanships. . . . There were people in tears, they were very emotional. They did everything they could to try to get him to stand down and stay with the party, but there was no moving him."

Jeffords cared about the feelings of his Republican friends. Shortly after the switch, Reid told reporters about his conversations with Jeffords: "He said, 'This is hard for me, Senator Grassley wanted to be chairman of that committee [Finance] for a long time . . . I don't know if any of you know how hard it is to give up a committee.'"[17] Jeffords had chaired the HELP Committee. Reid, who was in line to chair the Environment and Public Works Committee, passed it up so Jeffords could take it. For a senator from environment-conscious Vermont, leading that committee was quite a prize.

Kennedy now led the HELP Committee, but because he was backing the president's education bill, his ascent posed no obstacle to its final passage. Nevertheless, the shift of Senate control knocked the Bush administration off its legislative stride. Said Spellings: "We'd gotten some things done and then by the time the August recess came things were sort of deteriorating. That's why Bush was in a school on 9/11. We were going to jumpstart the whole thing with the . . . back-to-school thing, and try to get it done. Obviously 9/11 blew all that temporarily."

The September 11 attacks shifted the administration's focus to national security, a constellation of issues on which presidents have an institutional advantage. As Alexander Hamilton wrote, "It is of the nature of war to increase the executive at the expense of the legislative authority."[18] The first legislative product of the new war on terror was a broadly worded resolution authorizing the president to "use all necessary and appropriate force against those nations, organizations, or persons he determines planned, authorized, committed, or aided the terrorist attacks that occurred on September 11, 2001."[19] Daschle was the primary sponsor of the measure, which passed both houses with only a single dissenting vote, from Rep. Barbara Lee (D-CA). A few weeks later, the USA Patriot Act also passed by wide margins.

The education bill did not disappear. Domestic Policy Council director John Bridgeland said the legislation had hit the doldrums by late summer. "Then 9/11 hits. As horrible as that was, it gave us another period of bipartisan cooperation. To this day I think No Child Left Behind got passed in part because that spirit continued a little bit afterward." Spellings elaborated: "In the aftermath of 9/11 there was incredible good will and patriotism on the Hill and a sense of we're going to pull together on everything. We're all Americans first. We can't do much but we can do this." In December the education bill passed 381–41 in the House and 87–10 in the Senate. Spellings noted that special circumstances were at work: "We were at the goal line though, and we had gone all the way to damn near the end. We just needed a little push over the top."

Another domestic proposal that moved in the wake of 9/11 was the bipartisan campaign finance reform bill. Among other things, the measure banned national party organizations from receiving "soft money"—unlimited contributions from individuals, unions, or corporations for "party building"—in federal elections. John McCain (R-AZ) and Russ Feingold (D-WI) had been promoting the bill for years, and the window for passage opened when Democrats took control of the Senate and corporate scandals increased public support for reform. Ojakli said: "That's when campaign finance reform starts moving and Daschle is back to driving the Senate's agenda and driving it in a way that fits what the Democrats want." In the House, the bill's supporters overcame opposition from the GOP leadership by getting a majority of members to sign a discharge petition to move it out of committee—the first successful use of that procedure since 1993. McCain-Feingold passed the House 240–189. The Senate approved it by a vote of 60–40, just clearing the filibuster threshold. Bush disliked the bill but ended up signing it. A veto would have looked bad to the general public, 76 percent of whom supported the soft-money ban.[20] Also important, said Bolten, was the need to appeal to congressional Democrats. "So I can't say that 9/11 made it more incumbent on the President to go along with campaign finance reform. I can say as a general proposition that if occasions for confrontation with Democrats could be avoided, the President was more likely to be inclined to do that in the aftermath of 9/11 because he had this higher priority, which had to trump all other issues in getting support."

The most important national security vote of 2002 was the one authorizing the use of military force against Iraq. Although the issue would later become contentious and divisive, the original vote was bipartisan. "No one ever questioned whether there were weapons of mass destruction [in Iraq], everybody assumed it," said Calio. "You have to look at the context in which many people were looking at it, which was in '89 and '90, '91, we were convinced there were no weapons of mass destruction and got there and found out that there were actually." Congressional Democrats, especially those with an interest in higher office, did not want to be on the wrong side of this issue, as they had been when Congress voted to support the highly successful first Iraq War in 1990. "For me," Calio said, "it was clear early on [that approving the use of force] was not a matter of if, it was a matter of when." Voting in favor in the House were 215 Republicans and 81 Democrats. Voting no were 126 Democrats and 6 Republicans. In the Senate, Democrats voted in favor of the resolution 29–22 (counting Jeffords as a Democrat). Among Republicans, only Chafee voted no.

Congress took the initiative in creating the Department of Homeland Security. "There was disagreement because some people on the Hill, notably Senator [Joseph] Lieberman [D-CT], believed that we needed a department to house Homeland Security and it should be a new function with a new focus," said Calio. "We originally did not want that, we wanted it operated out of the White House. As time went on, it was getting traction on the Hill and in the White House, but we wanted it on our terms." Despite a growing consensus about the need for such a department, protections for government workers were a sticking point with Democrats. Bush wanted flexibility to bypass civil service rules and waive collective bargaining if he deemed that national security was at stake. In the end, centrist Democrats John Breaux and Ben Nelson joined Republican Lincoln Chafee to craft a compromise that gave Bush most of what he wanted.

The squabble over collective bargaining was not the only indication that partisan polarization would soon reemerge. Legislative staffer Ojakli said: "The big problem we dealt with, and I think this was the beginning of partisanship, where the wheels started coming off, especially post-9/11, was judges. It was really—I won't even say the end of bipartisanship, but the beginning of the end." In mid-2001 Bush had nominated district court judge Charles Pickering of Mississippi for a seat on the US Court of Appeals for the Fifth Circuit. When Patrick Leahy (D-VT) took the chair of the Senate Judiciary Committee, he took his time with the Pickering nomination, citing the need for more documents. Civil rights groups organized opposition to Pickering, and his confirmation hearing was bumpy. Kennedy recalled: "He thought he was entitled to the nomination, but he was the one who got caught by cross burning. He called the Justice Department to get a reduction in a sentence for people who burn crosses on people's lawns, which wasn't a good idea. John Edwards is the one who did the questioning, and he did a very effective job."[21] Early in 2002 the committee rejected Pickering's nomination on a party-line vote. Lott was a friend of Pickering's, and the rejection angered him. "If we don't see marked progress, if we don't see an end to the character assassination," Lott said, "the Senate will not be the same for a long time."[22]

As the 2002 midterm elections loomed, staffers debated the appropriate role for the president. Some aides argued that he should continue to downplay partisanship so that he could sway congressional Democrats on roll-call votes and maintain an image of national unity. Rove disagreed: "I argued that any short-term goodwill from this above-the-fray behavior would be overwhelmed by the disadvantage of his party's losing ground in Congress," he wrote in his memoirs. "My argument, and mounting evidence that Democrats in Washington were obstructing Bush, carried the day."[23] Bush decided to play an unusually direct role in the 2002 midterm campaign, which was a risky decision. The party holding the White House had lost Senate seats in most midterms since the direct election of senators began in 1914. Nevertheless, Bush went all in. Said Rove:

> We went into it with eyes wide open. First of all, we would have to reduce primaries wherever we could, recruit the best candidate, reduce the likelihood of primaries, and then raise an ungodly amount of money for them, which meant that the President would have to commit himself to an extraordinary effort on behalf of these candidates. We also had people that we tried to help, that we tried to keep in the Congress. For example, we told Connie [Constance] Morella [R-MD] we'd do anything we can—Even though she was not a straight party vote, we said we'll do everything we can to keep you in. What can we do to help you? Senate was basically aimed at getting control. How many seats could we get to gain control and where could we get them, and then move heaven and earth to make it happen.

This active approach displeased the legislative staff. "If there was ever a disconnect between us and the Political Office, it was over that," said Calio. "We needed the votes. Usually the communication was pretty good but sometimes you'd just get whacked. You're working somebody on a vote and then we're running ads against them or we're doing a fundraiser for their opponent, which as a matter of timing was not very good."

Had the midterm gambit failed, the hostility of a still-Democratic Senate would have been an enormous obstacle for the rest of Bush's first term. But the GOP had a good election night. It gained seats in the House, only the second time an incumbent party had done so in a midterm election since 1934. In the Senate, Republicans lost a seat in Arkansas but defeated Democratic incumbents in Georgia and Missouri. When Senator Paul Wellstone of Minnesota, who was seeking reelection, died in a plane crash, the state Democratic Party nominated former vice president Walter Mondale to replace him. Initially, Mondale seemed likely to win. But shortly before the election, a televised memorial service for Wellstone devolved into a partisan pep rally at which Democrats booed Lott as he entered. The spectacle offended many Minnesota voters, and the resulting public backlash helped Republican Norm Coleman score an upset victory. The Republicans' net gain of two seats enabled them to recapture the majority in the Senate.

Unified Government

The 108th Congress did not start well for the GOP. Even before it took office, the past reached out and wounded the party. At a celebration of the hundredth birthday of retiring senator Strom Thurmond, Lott said: "I want to say this about my state: When Strom Thurmond ran for president, we voted for him. We're proud of it. And if the rest of the country had followed our lead, we wouldn't have had all these problems over all these years."[24] Thurmond's third-party campaign for president in 1948 had been explicitly segregationist. When news of Lott's remarks got out, the denunciations poured in. He apologized, explaining that he was just trying to praise an old man. But civil rights activists argued that the comment was part of a long pattern of racial insensitivity.

Lott's political support suddenly started to crumble, and his staff suspected that someone in the White House was trying to get rid of him. Bush himself spoke out during a speech in Philadelphia: "Recent comments by Senator Lott do not reflect the spirit of our country. He has apologized, and rightly so."[25] In his memoirs, Lott wrote that Bush "hammered away at those last three words in a tone that was booming and nasty. Watching from Florida, Tricia [Lott's wife] and I were totally flattened emotionally."[26] When CNN quoted an anonymous White House source stating that Bush would not oppose a challenge to Lott's leadership post, the senator knew the president was cutting him loose.[27] Lott stepped down as party leader but stayed in the Senate. According to Ojaki, Lott resented Bush. "He wasn't mad at me, but he said, 'The President is going to have to ask me for every single vote.'"

Lott's replacement as GOP leader was Bill Frist of Tennessee. Frist did not have Lott's racial baggage, and as a respected heart surgeon, he stood to burnish the party's public image. Although Frist was reportedly more willing to defer to the White House, he lacked Lott's legislative skills. Said Jack Howard, "Frist just didn't have the experience. I'm not passing judgment at all; you can't do on-the-job training in the job."

The Bush White House was happy that the GOP now had clear control of both chambers of Congress, but the joy did not last. "As the time passed," said Spellings, "it's sort of the honeymoon, the Republicans' 'We're going to follow you anywhere' kind of thing. That began to wane.... Needless to say, we had the opportunity to remind them of [Bush's campaign help] many, many times. Or Karl [Rove] did. But they're not always grateful."

In 2003 Bush's legislative priorities were another tax cut and an expansion of Medicare to cover prescription drugs. The vote on this tax cut was more polarized than it had been on the 2001 measure. In the House, only seven Democrats voted for it, and only one Republican voted against it. In the Senate, McCain and Chafee voted no, while Nelson voted yes, creating a tie that Vice President Cheney broke in the bill's favor.

Starting with President Ronald Reagan, it took little effort to get Republicans to vote for a tax cut. The prescription drug bill was different. Particularly in the House, conservative Republicans were cold to the idea of expanding the federal welfare state. "In its rush to pass something—anything," Rep. John Shadegg (R-AZ) wrote, "Congress is on the verge of imposing a staggering financial burden on our children and grandchildren, pushing Medicare closer to financial collapse and losing a once-in-a-lifetime opportunity for reform."[28] Democrats, conversely, thought the bill was inadequate and failed to meet the needs of senior citizens.

Bush's aides seldom resorted to direct political threats against lawmakers, believing such tactics could backfire in the long run. Given the opposition from both parties, however, they made an exception this time. When the bill came up for a final roll-call vote on the House floor, it was still short of passage when the normal time for voting had expired, so Hastert kept the vote open for hours. The move was technically within the rules, but it was a hardball departure from normal practice. Billy Tauzin, a former member from Louisiana who was then the top lobbyist for the drug industry, cryptically told CBS: "People were being talked to."[29] David Hobbs, who had succeeded Nick Calio as head of the White House legislative office, recalled that Karl Rove told one recalcitrant Republican: "You're dead to me if you don't vote with us." Rove reinforced the message with a call to the member's top fund-raiser. When Hobbs later asked the member how he would vote, he got an affirmative answer—along with a middle finger to express resentment of the hardball tactics. At four o'clock in the morning, Hastert said, the bill was still short of a majority when he and Hobbs arranged a call between Bush and two Republicans. "So they go out, change their vote to yes, and I get my two votes. When I get my two votes, we got 16 Democrats to come over and vote for it, so we pass it. . . . But the fact was, we didn't get it done until I got them in to the President to talk." "I've been in politics for 22 years," said Walter Jones (R-NC), "and it was the ugliest night I have ever seen in 22 years." Tauzin laughed off the comment: "Well, he's a young member. Had he been around for 25 years, he'd have seen some uglier nights."[30]

Passage in the Senate was less dramatic. Democratic leaders had reservations about the bill but did not want Bush's 2004 reelection campaign to paint them as obstructionists. They voted for cloture, which cleared the way for final approval by a vote of 54–44.

In the 2004 election Republicans maintained control of both chambers of Congress. They won some additional House seats, mostly because of an audacious gerrymander in Texas. On the Senate side, they scored a remarkable net gain of four seats. GOP candidates advanced the South's realignment by picking up open Democratic seats in Florida, Georgia, Louisiana, North Carolina, and South Carolina. In South Dakota, Republican John Thune defeated Democratic leader Tom Daschle. The GOP lost open seats in Colorado and Illinois, the latter to a young state lawmaker named Barack Obama. In the presidential race, Bush won 53 percent of the electoral vote and 50.7 percent of the popular vote. By historical standards, his margins were slim, but they were better than his showing in 2000. He claimed a mandate: "I earned capital in the campaign, political capital, and now I intend to spend it."[31]

It was an unfortunate boast. With more than 49 percent of the electorate voting against him, Bush did not have much political capital at all. Within a year, he would hemorrhage support as the situation in Iraq got worse and the purported weapons of mass destruction turned out not to exist. And whatever political capital Bush did have, he did not spend wisely. During the campaign, he had spoken of an "ownership society" in which Washington would help Americans build wealth instead of keeping them dependent on government programs.[32] Now he intended to revive an idea he had brought up in the 2000 campaign, only to put it on hold during his first term. Bush proposed that workers be allowed to put part of their Social Security contributions into individual investment accounts.

In 2005 public attitudes toward the Social Security proposal started out lukewarm and then turned frigid.[33] The idea might have been viable in the 1990s, when Newt Gingrich and Bill Clinton were engaged in private negotiations on entitlement reform.[34] But several things had changed since the turn of the century. Though not as deep as the crash that would take place in 2008, the bear market that followed the burst of the dot-com bubble reminded voters that stocks are risky investments. Confidence in the financial system also suffered from accounting scandals involving Worldcom, Tyco, and other companies. Most important, the Bush plan involved enormous transition costs, with billions of dollars going into personal accounts instead of the Social Security system. Between 2000 and 2005, the federal budget had already lurched from surplus to deficit. As Judd Gregg put it: "By that time, the ability to do Social Security reform the way he wanted to do it was lost. . . . You needed a huge pile of money for transition to that type of program. That pile of money didn't exist after the recession, driven by 9/11 and the bubble breaking, so you couldn't do that transition any longer."

Hastert recalled that internal polling indicated voting for Bush's proposal would hurt House Republicans. "The thing that would split our party and split our base would be Social Security. We all want to do Social Security reform, but to go into the private sector with Social Security, the populace wasn't there. It was an issue that the Democrats could demagogue." Hastert told Bush the idea was a nonstarter. "We weren't going to get it done. The numbers weren't there. We can't do it, not going to do it. The will isn't there to do it in the House, and certainly if the will is not in the House, the will is not in the Senate."

The plan never reached the floor of either chamber. Economic adviser Keith Hennessey explained what finally put the Social Security plan out of its misery: "When Katrina and Rita hit, that obviously changed the focus of the administration. It certainly stopped the public speeches on Social Security. So that became the ending point more by happenstance than anything."

Just as Bush's campaign to change Social Security was failing, he proposed an immigration reform bill that would set up a temporary-worker program and offer undocumented immigrants a path to legal status. Bush described his policy as a humane way of enforcing the law and bringing undocumented people into the mainstream economy. Politically, it was a way to appeal to Latino voters. Most Republican senators opposed the bill, but without a "Hastert rule" in that chamber, twenty-three of them joined thirty-eight Democrats and Jeffords to pass it by a filibuster-proof majority. The view from the House was different. Once again, Hastert had to pull the plug: "I had an early meeting with the President. I went down and told him we can't get this through committee; it's not going to happen. He was very upset. Sometimes you had to tell him the bad news."

Those setbacks were just two episodes in a long political horror show for Bush and the congressional GOP. Another was the case of Terri Schiavo, a brain-damaged Florida woman whose husband and parents clashed over her treatment: he sought to remove her feeding tube, and her parents wanted to keep her alive. Under pressure from religious conservatives, Congress passed a law that gave the parents another chance to plead their case in federal district court, and Bush signed it. Outside the GOP's base, this intervention was unpopular. Senator Frist blundered when he viewed a video of Schiavo and claimed he detected a response to stimuli, even though the physicians who examined her said otherwise. As a surgeon, Frist came under harsh criticism for opining on a case outside his specialty.[35] In the end, the parents' legal challenges failed, and Schiavo died after the feeding tube was removed. The case shook Republicans and mobilized Democrats. Rep. Debbie Wasserman Schultz (D-FL) said: "The Terri Schiavo case literally was the thing that, from that point forward, brought our caucus together and gave us the ability to become more unified."[36] White House communications director Dan Bartlett reflected: "It's hard, and I know every President deals with it, that pressure. It makes us do things that you look back on, like the Terri Schiavo deal, and you just think, *Really? We really did that?* You want to just pull your hair out over some of those decisions we made."

Apart from Bush, the congressional GOP had other problems. In the early 1990s Republicans liked to argue that years of uninterrupted control had made the Democrats arrogant and corrupt. A decade later, Republicans faced similar criticism. In 2005 a Texas grand jury indicted Tom DeLay for illegally using corporate money in state elections. Republican conference rules forced him to step down from the House leadership. (After he quit Congress, DeLay was convicted by a jury, but an appeals court eventually overturned the conviction.) House members Randy "Duke" Cunningham (R-CA) and Bob Ney (R-OH) pleaded guilty to bribery. (In 2021 Donald Trump pardoned Cunningham.) Ney's case was part of a much larger scandal involving GOP lobbyist Jack Abramoff, which cast a shadow on the many Republicans associated with him. Rep. Mark Foley (R-FL) resigned after news reports claimed he had sent sexually charged emails and text messages to House pages. Questions arose when it was revealed that House Republican leaders had disregarded earlier reports about Foley's conduct. Though it was not public knowledge at the time, Hastert himself would be accused of sexually abusing minors many years before, and much later he went to prison for illegally concealing hush-money payments.

In the 2006 midterm campaign, Democrats had a target-rich environ-

ment: the war in Iraq, the sluggish response to Hurricane Katrina, the Schiavo case, and the "culture of corruption" in Congress. Unified GOP control
of the executive and legislative branches had freed the Democrats from responsibility for governing and made it hard for Republicans to shift the
blame for bad news. On Election Day, voters ended the Republican reign
on Capitol Hill. In the Senate, Democrats scored a net gain of six seats to
win a fifty-one-seat majority (with independent Bernie Sanders included
in the party's caucus). House Democrats won a majority by netting thirty-
one seats. "If you look at race by race, it was close," said Bush at a press
conference. "The cumulative effect, however, was not too close; it was a
thumping."[37]

Ending on the Defensive

During the six years that Republicans controlled one or both chambers of
Congress, Bush issued many signing statements that limited the effect of
certain pieces of legislation, but he vetoed just one bill. The Stem Cell Research Enhancement Act of 2005 (H.R. 810 of the 109th Congress) would
have allowed federal funding of research using stem cells derived from dis-
carded human embryos created for in vitro fertilization. Bush vetoed it in
2006, saying that it would cross an ethical line by forcing taxpayers to fund
the destruction of human embryos. An attempted override fell short in the
House.

Rove explained: "The reason for the paucity of vetoes, is there was a
paucity of things that he felt necessary to veto. We had very strong support
among the House Members, which gave us leverage." Hobbs, however, said
there were times "when it would have been better politically, better for the
President, better for us, better for them if the President had vetoed it. Like
Reagan did. A water resources bill. He vetoed it and when it got overridden
410-to-something, it still created that perception that he was a fiscal conservative." Instead, libertarians and economic conservatives were accusing
Bush of doing nothing to stem the growth of big government.[38]

When Democrats controlled Congress during Bush's final two years in
office, he vetoed eleven more bills. Congress overrode four vetoes dealing
with domestic policy. The administration had some success on national security policy, notably when the House sustained the president's veto of a
bill that would have set a timetable for withdrawal from Iraq. Secretary of

defense Robert Gates explained how the administration fended off other Democratic initiatives: "What was critically important was that we were able to hold the Republican minority in the Senate to prevent an override of a veto or to allow something to go to a vote where a simple majority would be sufficient. There were some Republican defections. It became very dangerous in the summer of 2007; we hung by a whisker."

With Nancy Pelosi (D-CA) as Speaker of the House and Harry Reid (D-NV) as majority leader of the Senate, there was little chance to advance Republican priorities. When Hastert stepped down from the GOP leadership and John Boehner (R-OH) took his place, he found that minority status was just as unpleasant as it had been before 1994. "The Democrats have not made good on a single promise they made during 2006, especially when it comes to fostering a more open and deliberative House of Representatives," said Boehner, echoing complaints Democrats had been making for twelve years. "Instead of making the House more open and deliberative, they've gone in the opposite direction, doing things we never even contemplated during our time in the majority."[39] Senate Republicans were not any happier about Majority Leader Reid.

In September 2008 cranky and polarized lawmakers confronted the worst economic crisis since the Great Depression. Under chaotic conditions, the administration proposed a massive bailout of financial institutions. Bush's Troubled Asset Relief Program (TARP) came to the House floor and fell 13 votes short of the 218 needed to pass. Keith Hennessey said: "Before that first TARP vote there were lots of angry people calling from back home in the district, calling their members' offices saying, 'I don't care what's going on. Don't you dare bail out those greedy bastards on Wall Street, hell no.'" A few days later, the House reversed course. Rove credited Bush's lobbying for the turnaround: "This is where eight years of having cordial relations with the Congress and going out of his way to develop a personal relationship was so critical. . . . Whatever political credit he had left on Capitol Hill was exhausted by the time TARP passed. But thank God he'd built it up." Hennessey offered a different explanation, citing the drop in the Dow Jones average: "Then after the first TARP vote and after the market plummeted, the same angry people were calling their Congressman's office saying, 'I don't care what you have to do, you fix my 401(k).'"

The final vote for TARP was 74–25 in the Senate and 263–171 in the House. Treasury secretary Hank Paulson quoted a quip by Rep. Barney Frank (D-MA): "Sometimes when kids run away from home they have to get hungry before they come back." Looking back, Paulson said, "The TARP legislation is the last and the biggest and most important example of bipartisan Congressional action America has witnessed in a long time." That was the kind of legislative outcome Bush had contemplated years earlier when he promised to be a "uniter, not a divider." But the frightful circumstances he faced were not what he had hoped for.

Arithmetic and Circumstance

Throughout his tenure, Bush benefited from a competent legislative staff. Presidential success with Congress depends on other things as well, especially the composition of the two chambers, the state of public opinion, and the impact of external circumstances. Good staff support can make the most of a favorable political climate, but it cannot do much when the weather starts to get rough.

In the first phase of the Bush legislative presidency, Republicans held a wafer-thin majority in the House and controlled the 50–50 Senate only because of the vice president's tie-breaking vote. In this setting, Bush decided to make a tax cut his first major legislative priority. Whatever its long-term economic merits, the proposal was a shrewd political move. It reassured rank-and-file conservatives who worried that Bush was his father's son, and it was palatable to moderates of both parties. The budget surplus had eased concerns about the affordability of tax cuts, and a looming economic slowdown bolstered the case for economic stimulus. Because polarization had not yet reached the levels of future years, some Democratic lawmakers were willing to go along. And so, with some adroit lobbying by White House aides, Bush notched a big win.

Notwithstanding bipartisan support for measures such as education reform, the Jeffords switch and the resulting shift in Senate control threatened to hinder the Bush agenda. On September 11, 2001, that agenda changed. With national security at the forefront, Bush could count on the inherent advantages of the presidency in foreign affairs, as well as on the rally effect that often accompanies international crises. The authorization for the use of military force in the war on terror enjoyed near-unanimous support from congressional Democrats, with the exception of Rep. Barbara Lee (D-CA), who would later point with pride to her "no" vote. Similarly, many House Democrats and most Senate Democrats initially supported war in Iraq.

Republican gains in 2002 departed from the historical pattern of mid-term elections and gave Bush more leverage on Capitol Hill. Two years later, his reelection left him confident if not downright cocky. Thinking that he had abundant political capital, he pushed for the creation of private Social Security accounts. That proposal entailed titanic transition costs, which became all the more daunting because tax cuts and foreign wars had already plunged the federal budget back into the red. The public response went from tepid to negative, and the plan never made it to the floor of either chamber.

Around this time, progressive scholars fretted that Bush had built an unstoppable Republican machine. The electorate had other ideas. With a mounting death toll in Iraq and a witches' brew of domestic problems, voters ousted the GOP majorities in Congress in 2006, and the Bush administration ended on a defensive note.

Could Bush have avoided the congressional frustrations of 2005–2009? Tweaking legislative strategies and tactics would have made little difference. An alternative history of the second term would have required some fundamentally divergent policy decisions in the first term. If Bush had spent the budget surplus on Social Security reform instead of tax cuts, he might have been able to win congressional approval, but it would have been a tough sell. Vastly more important, if Bush had decided not to invade Iraq, the whole world would have been different. Without the loss of blood and treasure, he might have achieved far more legislative success and ushered in the era of GOP dominance that progressives feared. Then again, it is impossible to know what disasters might have stemmed from the survival of Saddam Hussein's regime.

When it came to the mechanics of legislative relations, the Bush White House did about as well as it could have. As for the big decisions, debates will persist for many years to come.

Notes

1. Donald F. Kettl, *Team Bush: Leadership Lessons from the Bush White House* (New York: McGraw-Hill, 2003), 18–19.

2. Unless otherwise indicated, all quotations in this chapter relating to the Bush presidency are from interviews conducted as part of the George W. Bush Oral History, available at the Miller Center's website: https://millercenter.org/the-presidency/presidential-oral-histories/george-w-bush.

3. George W. Bush, *Decision Points* (New York: Crown, 2010), 81–82.

4. Matthew Lattimer, *Speech-Less: Tales of a White House Survivor* (New York: Crown, 2009), 243.

5. David Frum, *The Right Man: An Inside Account of the Bush White House* (New York: Random House, 2005), 27.

6. "The Senate Powersharing Agreement of the 107th Congress (2001–2003): Key Features," Congressional Research Service, December 27, 2006, https://www.everycrs report.com/reports/RS20785.html.

7. Peter Perl, "Absolute Truth," *Washington Post*, May 13, 2001, https://www.wash ingtonpost.com/archive/lifestyle/magazine/2001/05/13/absolute-truth/a77055fc-17fd -4120-be8e-2ce8d4e3a23a.

8. Blue Dog Coalition, "Historic Blue Dog Coalition Rosters," February 13, 2020, https://medium.com/@BlueDogCoalition/historic-blue-dog-coalition-rosters-19bff -be8ce22.

9. Dick Cheney with Liz Cheney, *In My Time: A Personal and Political Memoir* (New York: Threshold Editions, 2011), 308.

10. Karl Rove, *Courage and Consequence: My Life as a Conservative in the Fight* (New York: Threshold Editions, 2010), 229.

11. George W. Bush, radio address, February 24, 2001, American Presidency Project, ed. Gerhard Peters and John T. Woolley, https://www.presidency.ucsb.edu/node/216845.

12. Peter F. Drucker, "The Effective Decision," *Harvard Business Review*, January 1967, https://hbr.org/1967/01/the-effective-decision.

13. Wendy W. Simmons, "Majority of Americans Continue to Support Bush's Tax Cut Plan," Gallup, March 9, 2001, https://news.gallup.com/poll/1924/majority-americans -continue-support-bushs-tax-cut-plan.aspx.

14. Testimony of Alan Greenspan, "Outlook for the Federal Budget and Implications for Fiscal Policy," Committee on the Budget, US Senate, January 25, 2001, https://www .federalreserve.gov/boarddocs/testimony/2001/20010125.

15. Interview with George Miller, October 13, 2009, Edward M. Kennedy Institute, https://www.emkinstitute.org/resources/george-miller-oral-history.

16. Douglas Waller, "How Jeffords Got Away," CNN, May 28, 2001, http://www.cnn .com/ALLPOLITICS/time/2001/06/04/jeffords.html.

17. Katharine Q. Seelye, "From a Miner's Shack to the Senate, Guided by a Light," *New York Times*, May 28, 2001, https://www.nytimes.com/2001/05/28/us/public-lives-from -a-miner-s-shack-to-the-senate-guided-by-a-light.html.

18. Alexander Hamilton, Federalist 8, https://avalon.law.yale.edu/18th_century/fed 08.asp.

19. Public Law 107-40, https://www.congress.gov/bill/107th-congress/senate-joint -resolution/23/text.

20. David W. Moore, "Widespread Public Support for Campaign Finance Reform," Gallup, March 20, 2001, https://news.gallup.com/poll/1885/widespread-public-support -campaign-finance-reform.aspx.

21. Interview with Edward M. Kennedy, February 12, 2007, Edward M. Kennedy Institute, https://www.emkinstitute.org/resources/george-miller-oral-history, https://miller center.org/the-presidency/presidential-oral-histories/edward-m-kennedy-oral-history -02122007.

22. "Judiciary Committee Rejects Federal Judge Nominee," CNN, March 15, 2002, https://www.cnn.com/2002/ALLPOLITICS/03/14/pickering.

23. Rove, *Courage and Consequence*, 313.

24. Sheryl Gay Stolberg, "Under Fire, Lott Apologizes for His Comments at Thurmond's Party," *New York Times*, December 10, 2002, https://www.nytimes.com/2002/12/10/us /under-fire-lott-apologizes-for-his-comments-at-thurmond-s-party.html.

25. George W. Bush, remarks at White House Conference on Faith-Based and Community Initiatives, Philadelphia, December 12, 2002, American Presidency Project, https://www.presidency.ucsb.edu/node/211782.

26. Trent Lott, *Herding Cats: A Life in Politics* (New York: ReganBooks, 2005), 259.

27. Lott, 272.

28. Quoted in Robin Toner and Robert Pear, "Bush Seeks Medicare Drug Bill that Conservatives Oppose," *New York Times*, June 24, 2003, https://www.nytimes.com/2003 /06/24/us/bush-seeks-medicare-drug-bill-that-conservatives-oppose.html.

29. Michelle Singer, "Under the Influence," CBS News, March 29, 2007, https://www .cbsnews.com/news/under-the-influence/.

30. Singer.

31. George W. Bush, news conference, November 4, 2004, American Presidency Project https://www.presidency.ucsb.edu/node/215110.

32. Office of the Press Secretary, "Fact Sheet: America's Ownership Society: Expanding Opportunities," August 9, 2004, https://georgewbush-whitehouse.archives.gov/news /releases/2004/08/20040809-9.html.

33. Lydia Saad, "Little for Bush to Savor in Latest Social Security Polling," Gallup, June 30, 2005, https://news.gallup.com/poll/17140/little-bush-savor-latest-social-secu rity-polling.aspx.

34. Steven M. Gillon, *The Pact: Bill Clinton, Newt Gingrich, and the Rivalry that Defined a Generation* (New York: Oxford University Press, 2008).

35. Charles Babington, "Frist Views Video, Disputes Schiavo Diagnosis," NBC News, March 19, 2005, https://www.nbcnews.com/id/wbna7235267.

36. Wes Allison and Anita Kumar, "What Terri's Law Cost the Republicans in Congress," *St. Petersburg (FL) Times*, December 18, 2005, https://www.gainesville.com/news /20051220/terri-schiavo-derails-social-agenda-of-christian-right.

37. George W. Bush, news conference, November 8, 2006, American Presidency Project, https://www.presidency.ucsb.edu/node/271486.

38. Michael D. Tanner, *Leviathan on the Right: How Big-Government Conservativism Brought Down the Republican Revolution* (Washington, DC: Cato Institute, 2007).

39. Patrick O'Connor, "Dems Bend Rules, Break Pledge," *Politico*, May 16, 2007, https://www.politico.com/story/2007/05/dems-bend-rules-break-pledge-004046.

CHAPTER SIX

George W. Bush's Supreme Court Nominations: From Oral History to Oral Argument

Barbara A. Perry

The surging crowd surrounding the US Supreme Court on December 1, 2000, testified to the ongoing constitutional crisis embroiling the nation in the aftermath of the presidential election's uncertain outcome. Republican partisans carried signs emblazoned with "Sore Loserman," a word play on the Al Gore–Joe Lieberman ticket. Another Al, the Reverend Al Sharpton, led a Democratic throng chanting "Count every vote!" through the clogged sidewalks around the "marble temple" that houses the country's highest tribunal. One protester was dressed as a ballot box, treating the impending oral argument in *Bush v. Palm Beach County Canvassing Board* like a Halloween party.[1] Inside the three hundred–person–capacity courtroom, the spectators who squeezed in represented a who's who of Washington elites—members of Congress, journalists, lawyers, scholars, and justices' family members.

Bush's counsel, renowned Supreme Court advocate Theodore Olson of the white-shoe Washington law firm Gibson, Dunn, took a moment to savor the scene before stepping to the podium. "Everybody in the world, it seemed like, was in that Court. I just looked out there and you could see the leading people from the two campaigns were there and people from the Senate and from the White House. . . . I thought I'd better remember this, because this is something that has never happened," Olson recalled thinking. Despite his jitters about arguing such a consequential case, he took time to reflect: "This is history that is happening and you had better just let thirty seconds of it sink in because you'll want to remember this or tell people about it at some point."[2]

Those fortunate enough to get a seat heard what would be the first of two oral arguments on whether the recount ordered by the Florida Supreme Court violated the US Constitution and federal law. The stakes could not have been higher. Stopping the recount would mean that Texas governor George W. Bush remained ahead by several hundred votes, thereby winning the state's 25 electoral votes and the presidency with the bare majority required in the Electoral College: 271.

The nine-member Supreme Court, led by Chief Justice William Rehnquist, had served together for six years, since 1994, when Stephen Breyer joined associate justices John Paul Stevens, Sandra Day O'Connor, Antonin Scalia, Anthony Kennedy, David Souter, Clarence Thomas, and Ruth Bader Ginsburg. Although seven of the justices had been appointed by Republican presidents Richard Nixon, Ronald Reagan, and George H. W. Bush and just two by Democratic president Bill Clinton, they sometimes split almost evenly on controversial issues. Rehnquist, Scalia, and Thomas were reliable conservatives; Stevens, Ginsburg, Souter, and Breyer often formed a liberal bloc. O'Connor and Kennedy played the role of swing voters, sometimes siding with the liberals and sometimes with the conservatives, thus determining the outcome of politically charged cases.

Ultimately, the Supreme Court's decision in the second case on the Florida vote-count controversy, *Bush v. Gore*, reflected these divisions. Rehnquist, Scalia, Thomas, Kennedy, and O'Connor ruled that continuing the Florida vote recount without clear standards would violate the equal protection clause of the US Constitution's Fourteenth Amendment. Souter and Breyer agreed with them about standardless recounts but argued that Florida still had time to implement procedures that passed constitutional muster. In full dissent, Stevens and Ginsburg maintained that the recount should continue.[3]

In addition to handing Bush the presidency, the decision's narrow margin indicated that the tribunal's balance might tip in a decidedly conservative direction if Bush had an opportunity to name future justices.[4] In 2000 the justices' average age was sixty-six, with Stevens (eighty), Rehnquist (seventy-six), O'Connor (seventy), Scalia (sixty-four), and Souter (sixty-four) near or beyond the traditional retirement age for the general public. Under Article III of the Constitution, however, federal judges serve for "good behavior," in effect, for life. Political scientist Henry J. Abraham often remarked, just slightly in jest, that Supreme Court justices' longevity is second only to that of symphony orchestra conductors.[5]

Republicans and the Supreme Court

The Republican Party's 2000 platform included five references to the nation's highest court, citing differences with its liberal decisions on issues such as voluntary prayer in public schools, use of public school premises by religious organizations, partial-birth abortion, and the exclusion of illegally gained evidence (which it condemned for letting "countless criminals get off on technicalities"), but agreeing with its conservative ruling to ban the "involuntary use of union dues for political purposes." The party platform took aim at "scores of judges with activist backgrounds in the hard-left [who] now have lifetime tenure" and promised that "Governor Bush is determined to name only judges who have demonstrated respect for the Constitution and the processes of our republic."[6]

Judicial restraint (as opposed to judicial activism) is the hallmark of conservative legal philosophy, which purports to interpret the Constitution based on the framers' "original intent" and to construe their language, and that of subsequent laws, using the "literal" definitions of words at the time the laws were written. Justice Scalia, a 1986 Reagan appointee, embodied this jurisprudence and became the avatar for Republican presidential candidates when referring to their future Supreme Court nominees.

Bush's acceptance speech at the 2000 Republican convention eschewed references to the third branch of government. He did, however, raise the legislative and judicial issue of partial-birth abortion, declaring that he would sign a bill to ban it.[7] As the leader of a party that had longed to reverse liberal jurisprudence since the 1960s, Bush was prepared to act if an opening arose on the Supreme Court. "We solicited thoughts early on in a very low-key way from Judiciary [Committee] members to say who should we be looking at. We even got suggestions from Democrats. [Joseph] Lieberman, for example, gave us some input about possible Supreme Court [nominees]," remembered Karl Rove, Bush's senior adviser and White House deputy chief of staff for policy. "We [were] just getting prepared. It was low key, but we were building internally our own roster of . . . people."

As Harriet E. Miers, Bush's staff secretary and then White House counsel, put it, "We had an evergreen process because . . . somebody could drop over unexpectedly. . . . Or retire unexpectedly, and so you had an evergreen process of from whom could you choose a replacement for a Supreme Court justice. When I arrived in the counsel's office or in preparation for arriving [in 2005], . . . there were a lot of materials that had been generated to analyze potential nominees. There had been a selection of people."

Alberto Gonzales, Bush's White House counsel and then attorney general, observed that "it was important that [Bush] not make the same mistake as his father did with [David] Souter. So we had the process in place to prevent that from happening." The second President Bush wanted to avoid naming a Supreme Court justice who was thought to be conservative only to witness his seeming conversion to liberalism once he took the bench, as Souter had done. Gonzales (whom Governor Bush had appointed to the Texas Supreme Court) also remembered that Bush "often commented about nominating the best person possible while avoiding a big confirmation fight."

Despite the justices' advancing age, none stepped down during Bush's first term. In 2004 the GOP platform once again assailed liberal jurists and promised "judges who uphold the law":

> Scores of judges with activist backgrounds in the hard-left now have lifetime tenure. Recent events have made it clear that these judges threaten America's dearest institutions and our very way of life. In some states, activist judges are redefining the institution of marriage. The Pledge of Allegiance has already been invalidated by the courts once, and the Supreme Court's ruling has left the Pledge in danger of being struck down again—not because the American people have rejected it and the values that it embodies, but because a handful of activist judges threaten to overturn common sense and tradition. And while the vast majority of Americans support a ban on partial birth abortion, this brutal and violent practice will likely continue by judicial fiat.

After focusing on specific issues before the nation's courts, the platform turned to the constitutional principles of separated powers and checks and balances among the three branches. "We believe that the self-proclaimed supremacy of these judicial activists is antithetical to the democratic ideals on which our nation was founded. President Bush has established a solid record of nominating only judges [to the lower federal courts] who have demonstrated respect for the Constitution and the democratic processes of our republic, and Republicans in the Senate have strongly supported those nominees." In contrast, Senate Democrats had filibustered Bush's nominees, which the platform labeled "obstructionist" as well as "unprecedented and highly irresponsible."[8]

When Bush rose to accept his party's renomination, he was nearly three years into a wartime presidency that had begun after the terrorist attacks on September 11, 2001. Most of his convention speech cited his successes against al Qaeda and the long road to victory in the global war on terror. But he also attacked the liberalism of his Democratic opponent, Massachusetts senator John Kerry, and played the cultural divide card: "Because the union of a man and woman deserves an honored place in our society, I support the protection of marriage against activist judges. And I will continue to appoint federal judges who know the difference between personal opinion and the strict interpretation of the law."[9]

A Supreme Court Vacancy

In October, barely two months after the GOP convention, the Supreme Court's public information officer announced that doctors had diagnosed Chief Justice Rehnquist with thyroid cancer, and he had undergone a tracheotomy. The court provided few specifics, other than to say that Rehnquist intended to return to his center chair on the bench. Although the chief justice insisted on presiding at Bush's swearing-in on January 20, 2005, Rehnquist, using a cane and looking frail, did not return to the court to hear oral arguments until March.

Miers recalled, "When it became more obvious that there might be really a need for a selection, we started this interviewing process that was quite elaborate. . . . I'm proud to say it was quite secretive and didn't get leaked." For each of the dozen or so potential nominees, all of whom were federal judges, researchers compiled a notebook containing their history and references to their judicial opinions. A vetting committee, led by Vice President Dick Cheney, included Miers, Rove, Gonzales, and Cheney aide I. Lewis "Scooter" Libby. They winnowed the candidates to a handful, interviewed them, and developed a short list for the president to consider if an opening occurred.

On the last day of the Supreme Court's term in June 2005, Rehnquist could barely speak as he announced the court's opinion upholding the display of the Ten Commandments on the grounds of the Texas capitol. A few weeks earlier, Justice O'Connor had informed the chief justice that she was considering retirement after one more term to care for her husband, who had Alzheimer's disease. She had thought Rehnquist might confide that he would be leaving after the current term. Instead, he said he intended to remain on the bench and noted that the court could ill afford two vacancies, should he need to step down in a year. O'Connor felt she had no choice but to retire immediately, a year earlier than anticipated.[10]

Just prior to the Independence Day weekend, O'Connor sent a letter to the White House announcing that she would retire "upon the nomination and confirmation of my successor." Miers received the missive and informed the president. Despite O'Connor's age (seventy-five) and previous treatment for breast cancer, she remained in robust health, and her announcement came as a surprise. The president's vetting team now had to pivot from planning to replace the conservative chief justice to selecting a successor to the Supreme Court's first female justice, who had become a swing voter—sometimes siding with the liberal bloc and sometimes with the conservative wing.[11] Miers noted that gender added "complexity" to the selection process. "We were still going to get whoever it was that the president wanted to nominate," she explained, "but that obviously was an additional factor that was going to be considered. It wasn't going to be the driving factor." Because "the president was going to nominate somebody whose philosophy was consistent with his," Miers recalled that O'Connor's swing-vote status did not shape discussions of her replacement.

It mattered, however, to conservative interest groups, which were still stinging from the Democratic Senate's rejection of Robert Bork for a swing seat on the Supreme Court (vacated by Lewis F. Powell Jr.) in 1987. Now that Republicans held the majority in the Senate, they and their supporters were elated over O'Connor's announcement. Finally, conservatives could glimpse the promised land, where her moderate jurisprudence would be replaced by a reliable conservative vote.[12]

Rove, too, considered the swing seat an important variable in the selection process. Fourth Circuit Court judge J. Harvie Wilkinson III interested Rove because Wilkinson "was part of the mountain valley Republicans that existed in the Shenandoah Valley [of Virginia] in the 1960s to 1980s. He ran for [office] as a very young man and represented mountain Republicanism: strong on roads and schools and moderate on race. I've always been intrigued by that weird strain of Southern Republicanism," said Rove. "So I was a fan of his. He'd written a couple of good books, and I followed him over the years. He was a possibility." Yet Wilkinson's perceived moderation

spooked Rove: "The more we looked into him, the more he might be another [Justice] Kennedy."

If friendship had guided Bush's decision—as it had influenced all four
of Harry Truman's appointments, JFK's nomination of Byron White, and
LBJ's pick of Abe Fortas—he would have chosen his new attorney general,
Alberto Gonzales, and created a "Hispanic seat" on the Supreme Court.[13]
Yet conservatives squawked that "'Gonzales' was Spanish for 'Souter'"—that
is, a presumed conservative who turned out to be liberal.[14] The Right did
not trust Gonzales on affirmative action and abortion, two issues on which
O'Connor's replacement could be useful to reverse precedents that conser-
vatives found objectionable.[15]

Miers called Gonzales to the White House as soon as word arrived of
O'Connor's decision. Miers, Gonzales, Card, Rove, and Cheney met with
Bush in the Oval Office to discuss the process for choosing a nominee.
"Then everyone leaves but the vice president and the president," Gonzales
remembered, "because the president wants to talk to me. . . . 'I'm not going
to put you on the Court,'" Bush told his Texas friend. "Not a problem," Gonzales graciously replied. "I like being attorney general. I will work hard to
get your nominee confirmed." The attorney general had already met at the
Justice Department with one of the front-runners: John Roberts of the US
Court of Appeals for the DC Circuit. "I asked him a number of questions,
and he was extremely thoughtful. He has a very warm, soothing personality, a very confident person." Gonzales said, "After that meeting I was convinced, 'This [is] the guy we ought to go with.'"

Ed Gillespie, former head of the Republican National Committee
(RNC), had been brought in to run the administration's effort on Capitol
Hill. He observed that Bush "clearly had learned from his father's experiences. Justice Souter was like the thing that's in everybody's mind that you
just have to avoid at all costs, and Justice Scalia is what you want to get at all
costs. That basically was the mentality."

Liberals and some conservatives, including First Lady Laura Bush, urged
the president to fill the O'Connor vacancy with a female judge to maintain
the "women's seat" established by Reagan in 1981. Several qualified conservative women serving on the federal appellate courts would have met the
criteria of ideology as well as gender. Gillespie remembered:

> There were women on the list and there was a propensity that if it were
> a woman that would be a good thing. So if it came down to a choice of

two 100 percent equally qualified people and one was a woman, you'd probably tilt toward the woman, which was understandable. But there was not a directive: find a woman. It was that it would be great if we were able to replace a woman with a woman.

In a public statement, Bush described his approach to the nomination: "I will let my legal experts deal with the ramifications of legal opinions. I will try to assess their character, their interests. I'll pick people who, one, can do the job, people who are honest, people who are bright, and people who will strictly interpret the Constitution and not use the bench to legislate from."[16] His last point, a reference to the conservative jurisprudential catechism and the GOP platform, was an attempt to calm conservatives who feared he would make the same mistake as his father. Souter had a sparse federal judicial record before ascending to the Supreme Court, where his predecessor, the liberal justice William Brennan, took him under his wing (Brennan maintained chambers at the court after his retirement).[17]

John G. Roberts Jr.

In Cheney's vetting committee interview with John Roberts, Rove appreciated the story of how the judge had discovered his conservatism:

> He did not grow up in a political household. He grows up in a middle-class Catholic household in northeastern Indiana. They don't talk politics around the kitchen table, and yet you have a sense of solidity about the guy, quiet solidity. I wondered where he became a conservative and why he became a conservative. When did he have a political awakening? So I asked him, and he said at Harvard, because in the inevitable bull sessions after hours he realized he didn't view the world the same way as his classmates did. He figured out that he was a conservative and they weren't. I thought it was very interesting that he came to his world view by his upbringing and didn't realize it until later.

Miers recalled that "there was a great deal of support for . . . Roberts among the people who were involved in the research and people in my office and people of the Justice Department who had worked with him or clerked for him. . . . But despite his stellar educational credentials and character, his interview with the vice-president's committee was somewhat disappointing." She preferred Third Circuit Court of Appeals judge Samuel A. Alito Jr., who possessed a lengthier judicial record—more than fifteen years on the federal bench—and whose written opinions impressed her in the way they addressed complex issues.

After two sets of interviews with potential candidates, all of which were conducted in absolute secrecy, Cheney's committee recommended a list of five to President Bush: Roberts, Alito, Wilkinson, and two other federal appellate judges, Michael Luttig and Edith Clement. Bush then interviewed each of them with Miers present. No matter how hard the president tried to put Alito at ease, the introverted judge could not mask his jitters. He literally quaked with nervousness. In contrast, Roberts "aced the interview," according to a White House adviser. Another aide explained that the president and Roberts "really clicked well. [Bush] relies on his intuition about people as well as his views on substantive issues. In this case, the stars aligned."[18]

With his conservative Catholicism (potentially indicating a pro-life vote on abortion cases), Harvard undergraduate and law degrees, Supreme Court clerkship for Rehnquist, stints in the Reagan Justice Department and White House, experience as a Supreme Court litigator in private practice, and brief tenure on the DC Circuit, Roberts seemed destined for a Supreme Court appointment by a Republican president. Like most presidents, Bush placed ideology at the top of his list of criteria. Roberts got the nod.

One of the first responses to Bush's choice came from the justice being replaced. The media tracked O'Connor down at an Idaho stream, where she was fly-fishing. Wading in the water, wearing a fishing vest decorated with red-feathered lures, she called over her shoulder when asked about Roberts, "He's good in every way, except he's not a woman."[19]

As for the "Sherpa" chosen to guide Roberts through the Senate confirmation hearings, Ed Gillespie could not have been more impressed: "Roberts is phenomenal, he's just phenomenal. He's instantly likable. He's just brilliant and a genuinely good person. When I met him at that point, I was really impressed. . . . He's just really good. It was great to work for him. He felt very guilty about people having to work through August, during the summer months, losing their summer vacation time." In terms of public imagery, Gillespie recalled that Bush's announcement of Roberts's nomination at the White House "was great with Jack [the judge's young son], dancing and everything. His wife is lovely. They're very down-to-earth people."

As Roberts began to make courtesy calls on senators, the Senate Judiciary Committee scheduled hearings on his nomination for just after Labor Day. "I went with him on the Republican visits; I did not go with him on the Democratic visits. I did not think that the Democratic members would want me sitting in on the visits," Gillespie recounted. He found the meetings with individual GOP senators "interesting. First of all, we hadn't had a Supreme Court nomination in a long time; I guess it was eleven years. . . . So there was electricity around it. It was really exciting." During those meetings, "Roberts was charming. He charmed the senators. . . . Roberts had these guys eating out of his hand," Gillespie crowed. "There was a scribe who took copious notes about the questions and the answers, the answers the judge gave. You knew whatever he said in those meetings he couldn't say anything different in the public hearing. There was no winking and nodding. He was very good. We had prepared for those as well, for the one-on-one meetings." After the meetings on Capitol Hill, "we'd come back and we'd sit in the Wardroom, which is right off the White House mess, and we would do a download from them. I would listen and I would probe the Democratic ones that I didn't go to. Then you kept a book so that you knew going into the hearings" what the questions might be.

The White House "legislative staff knew what the senators' interests were," Gillespie explained, "where they'd been on these issues and what they were likely to home in on." He noted that the committee members "pride themselves on being able to go deep on these things, but the truth is they can't go all that deep. They certainly couldn't go deeper than Roberts even before the prep. But you know, the Commerce Clause, *Griswold v. Connecticut*. You know the ones that they're laying traps for you on. Once you get past those, there was nothing we were worrying about in terms of Roberts's command of the facts and his ability to answer questions."

With a majority in the Senate, Republicans hoped for a speedy confirmation that would allow Roberts to settle into O'Connor's chair before the opening of the term in early October. Then, on September 3, Chief Justice Rehnquist succumbed to his cancer. Wasting no time, the president's vetting committee pivoted. "The immediate shift was to make Judge Roberts the nominee for chief justice," Miers explained. Gillespie thought it was slightly less "automatic" that Roberts would become the choice for chief. "There was discussion," he said. "But by that point everybody around the president and the president himself were pretty—'smitten' seems almost silly—but were pretty smitten by John Roberts. I mean, the guy is really something, really impressive. I'm told, I don't know this from the president himself, but I'm told the president felt almost immediately he could be the chief justice, we could make him chief." Gillespie observed that part of the discussion centered on whether one of the associate justices should be promoted instead. "But from what I now understand, the truth is that sometimes there's an argument to be made not to elevate but to drop somebody in fresh anyway for the dynamic of the Court."

"Roberts has these innate leadership qualities that the president felt would serve well as the chief justice," recalled Gillespie. "I think the president was there pretty quickly. I think there were others who were saying let's think, let's wait, but I think the president's instincts were almost immediately, let's just swap them." In fact, Gillespie thought it might be simpler to replace Rehnquist with another conservative rather than have a fight break out over O'Connor's swing seat. Gillespie and his colleagues worried about the "worst kind of Ted Kennedy rhetoric," referring to his 1987 attack on Bork, but when Roberts became the nominee for chief justice, they decided that "in some ways it would make it easier."

Roberts returned to the White House for the second time in two months, this time to be nominated to replace his mentor in the center chair. After the president's announcement, Roberts headed for the Supreme Court to serve as Rehnquist's pallbearer. The next week, he returned to the Hill for his Senate confirmation hearings. When asked what made Roberts appealing during the confirmation process, Gillespie responded:

> One, his demeanor; two, his story was a good one. I picked up right away that he had a union card, which I thought was good; he had a steelworkers' card. At one point he worked in his father's plant, and he had to join the union, and he had to carry the card. I shouldn't say "had to," he did. I liked that. Small school, football player, Catholic. There were a lot of things that were net-net positive. . . . Then we went to work to sell him. Not just to sell him, but prepare him as well, which was kind of interesting for me. I had a team.

Gillespie and his team—from the Department of Justice (DOJ); the White House legislative affairs, counsel, and press offices; and the vice president's representative—met every morning "about what needed to be done that day." According to Gillespie:

The prep work for the hearings was pretty grueling. One of the things I insisted on was, what time were the hearings? I made us go real time. So it's not just like he [Roberts] would do an hour and leave; he sat for three hours from 9:30 to 12:30. We broke for lunch, brought him back at 2:00, sat until 7:00. When you looked back at the history you knew that that was a possibility, which it turned out to be. That's what we ended up doing.

Gillespie took issue when the committee's ranking Democrat, Sen. Patrick Leahy, asked for a third day of hearings: "Roberts did not want to do the third-day hearings; he really didn't. He was tired of it. He had been great the whole time. There was high risk going back a third day, what's the point? It wasn't fair. I felt he was right." When Gillespie raised an objection with Arlen Specter, the committee's chair, the Pennsylvania Republican argued, "Why shut him down now, he's doing great. Don't give the Democrats a process argument." But Spector agreed to limit the third day's session to two hours. When Gillespie told Roberts, "he was not happy. I said, 'Two hours, lifetime appointment.' He kind of laughed. He did fine. [The Democrats] were all out of bullets. They were doing it because they can."

Roberts was worried that opponents might bring up the adoption of his two children, Josie and Jack. Gillespie recalled:

I do remember at one point there was some question about—I mean, there's ugly stuff. . . . I said to him, "Judge, honestly, you focus on other things; don't worry about this. I promise you I will not let them get near your family." And I wouldn't have. I would have gone ballistic if somebody had gone after the adoption. I don't think there was anything to go after. . . . It felt like he took some comfort. He'd like me to do something like that. I meant it. So I think they [nominees] understand it's a part of the process now.

Roberts was poised, prepared, genteel, fluent, and witty—and those characteristics, which had served him well as a litigator and a judge, carried him through the occasionally pointed questioning and assured his confirmation by the full Senate, 78–22, just in time to assume the chief justiceship when the Supreme Court began its 2005 term on October 3.

Harriet E. Miers

With Roberts's appointment settled, the president returned to the search for O'Connor's replacement. Miers continued to support Alito, but the president "wanted to nominate a woman," she recalled; "he wanted us to do a very thorough job of outreach." As Rove remembered, Miers's name "came to the president" as a possible nominee. "It may have come from two or three coincidental sources," he said, "but we should have stepped back and said, 'Wait a minute, let's hold on.' But he knew her. He knew how strong she was. He depended on her not only in the White House as general counsel and staff secretary, but, when he was governor of Texas, he sent her in to clean up a terrible scandal at the lottery commission, and she did so with enormous skill and ability."

As Rove elaborated, "Before Roberts was sworn in—I say that to be clear—*before* he was sworn in, he proactively sought out the president and said, 'I want to tell you how impressed I am with the cast of her [Miers's] mind and how capable she would be if she were on the bench.'" "As time passed, there was this sense that I was under consideration," Miers explained, "which came as quite a revelation, to say the least." She had never aspired to be a judge at any level, much less a justice of the nation's highest court for life. But when the president honored her with the nomination, Miers felt it would be inappropriate to refuse.

Gonzales, who liked Miers very much, was nevertheless stunned by the president's sudden decision. As a participant in the painstaking vetting process for Supreme Court appointments, Gonzales knew that Miers had "never appeared on that list [of potential nominees]. We had put this thorough process in place at the president's request to avoid a David Souter–like mistake." His staff at the Justice Department urged the attorney general "to go to the White House and tell the president, 'Don't do this.'" Gonzales pleaded with Bush to name Luttig or Alito, but he could tell the president had "already decided." Returning to the DOJ, the attorney general informed his staff, "OK, I told him, but it's done."

Gillespie worried that the second search for O'Connor's replacement was not broad enough. He compared it to the secrecy surrounding Bush's selection of Cheney as his running mate in 2000. According to Gillespie, who had been head of the RNC at the time, Cheney's addition to the ticket hurt the party. So when White House chief of staff Andy Card called Gillespie to report that the president had settled on a nominee and would name "her" the next day, Gillespie feared that Bush's choice was an insider, Harriet Miers, and that she would be a "hard sell" to the Senate. He "had worked very closely with Harriet through the Roberts nomination and liked her a lot," but he thought the Democrats would see it as cronyism.

Ultimately, "I underestimated the conservative backlash," Gillespie realized:

> I knew, having gone through the Roberts nomination, how important the paper trail was for the [nominee's previous] rulings. I knew we didn't have that here, and there was a little bit of a pig in a poke, and it was a Souter risk. But it was intense. I think because there had been eleven years [since the last nomination] and you had people like Luttig and Roberts and Alito and others who had had time on the court who were beacons and had strong records. For that matter [Fifth Circuit Court of Appeals judge Priscilla] Owen and others too. So it was not like, Oh, there are slim pickings here, so that's fine. It was kind of, wait a second.

Gillespie noted that mobilizing interest groups in favor of a nominee "has become a very important dynamic. It was flat. It just wasn't there like it was for Roberts. People were fired up [for him]. You could feel it. They wanted Roberts confirmed. Surrogates and people were talking to senators and all of that. It was just deafening silence out there when Harriet got announced."

In announcing Miers's nomination, Bush inexplicably overshadowed his successful appointment of Roberts. Just a few hours before the new chief justice took the oath of office and made the traditional walk down the Supreme Court's white marble steps with his most senior colleague, Justice John Paul Stevens, the president shocked the nation with his improbable choice of Miers to fill O'Connor's seat. Single and childless, Miers lacked the all-American family that had surrounded Roberts when Bush announced his nomination the previous July. She looked as stunned as she felt standing next to the president in the Oval Office.[20]

The *Washington Post*'s lead story on Miers's nomination foreshadowed the problems Bush's friend would face. Although she had overcome gender barriers in the "Texas legal world" and carved out a successful law career, rising to head the state bar association, the *Post* observed that she possessed "no judicial or constitutional background."[21] More than three decades had passed since nominees with no judicial experience—Powell and Rehnquist, both named by Nixon in 1972—had been confirmed for associate justiceships. Since the Reagan years, Republicans had preferred to appoint incumbent judges with track records, and other presidents had followed suit. In addition, most justices in the modern era had arrived at the pinnacle of their legal careers with degrees from the nation's most prestigious law schools and undergraduate institutions. Many had clerked for Supreme Court justices or well-respected appeals court judges. Miers had no such experience, and both her degrees were from Southern Methodist University.

"I think how unfair is this, that because she didn't go to Harvard or Yale or Princeton or Columbia that she is somehow unworthy of the high court," Rove reflected. "She was a major partner of a major Texas law firm, first bar president, brilliant lawyer, but having said all that, we should have considered the idea more thoughtfully."

The nomination careened downhill from the outset. Conservatives turned against Miers immediately, arguing that her lack of judicial background could lead to another Souter fiasco. As Gillespie explained, a nominee's prior judicial decisions had become crucial: "From a conservative perspective, they want somebody who they can look at the rulings and get a sense of what their judicial philosophy is." How could the president, "compassionate" though his conservativism might be, risk placing a "stealth nominee" in the high court's swing seat? Miers was being "Borked" by members of her own party. One item in her paper trail especially riled Republicans: she had contributed to Al Gore's 1988 presidential campaign and the Democratic National Committee! "We ill-served the president," Rove admitted. The nomination "caught our allies by surprise . . . ; we didn't have time to sell it to our natural outside allies," such as the conservative Federalist Society.

When Miers began to make her courtesy calls on senators, her candidacy continued its downward trajectory. "There wasn't a good vibe," Gillespie related. "Definitely not like Roberts. Harriet is reserved. She's very smart but she's quiet. There just wasn't a good vibe coming out of [the senators]." It wasn't easy for the senators either, "especially someone like [Arizona Senator] Jon Kyl, who liked the president. They all liked the president. There was no personal animus toward the president that I ever picked up anywhere with the Republican senators. They all liked him. So that also makes it kind of hard to say this ain't going to fly."

Miers had never imagined a Supreme Court nomination for herself; nor had she even contemplated a Washington career. Politics is a blood sport, and the political attacks that are part of life in the nation's capital shocked her. "Just objectively, to take somebody's career and try to demolish it is a mean thing," she observed. "It's just a mean thing, but we live in a mean society sometimes, and these particular activities are as mean as they get sometimes, so again, you have eyes open. I can't complain."

Miers had only a few weeks to prepare for her confirmation hearing, leaving her inadequate time to complete the lengthy questionnaires about her career and master all the constitutional law issues and cases needed to converse informedly with her Senate interlocutors. "I don't think anyone anticipated the complexity of trying to explain a life like mine," Miers concluded with the benefit of hindsight. "I don't think that was fully appreciated, and looking back, it's probably something that if I had been thinking, I would have raised, and it would have been a good reason why I should not have been chosen, because it's one thing to look back at ten cases that a judge had decided. It's another to re-create the [law] practice of someone for more than thirty years."

Miers would have liked to see someone with her practical litigation experience take a seat on the Supreme Court, but she acknowledged, "I know I didn't perform perfectly in every one of these meetings [with senators], but some expectations there and some behavior was just more than I could deal with." She also had the unfortunate experience of following on the heels of Roberts, who had easily displayed his deep familiarity with the law during his meetings with the senators. The last straw for Miers's collapsing nomination came when the Judiciary Committee requested documents related to her White House position. "The fact that you could seriously consider asking for the kinds of records that a White House counsel sees and deals with and opines on I don't think was fully appreciated," Miers reflected.

In general, Gillespie explained, "what happened was there was disappointment among the Federalist Society types and dispiritment there. The Democrats sensed it, and they hung back. They let Republican-on-Republican violence break out. It just got to the point where it was unsustainable." He could feel the confirmation slipping away and felt compelled to inform the president's chief of staff. "I told him—and I wasn't sure if it was my job. I mean, my job was just to sell but I felt like he needed to have a reality check. I said, 'This is going to be really, really hard. I'm going to keep doing it, don't get me wrong, but I feel I owe it to you and to the president to make sure you understand that it may not be doable.'"

"So it just got to the point where it was pretty clear that the right thing to do was to step down so we could get on to Plan B," said Miers. "I had knowledge that if I withdrew, I was going to continue on as counsel, so I decided and did. I called the president and told him I felt like it was time to step down." A little more than three weeks after announcing Miers's nomination, the Bush administration pulled the plug.

Rove concedes that the administration's failure to use its standard Supreme Court selection process led to the Miers miscalculation. "That proves why the idea of having a strong process in place by which you make decisions—by which you examine an issue, collect input, analyze data, and present it to the president—is important. Because the one instance where we didn't have that happen, it blew up in our face." He credits Miers for having the courage to call "a halt to the exercise." Rove believes the president was willing to try to push the nomination through the Senate, where the GOP held the majority. But too many Republican senators questioned Miers's ideology. According to Rove, Miers argued that the president could not "afford this kind of expenditure of political capital in a cause that may fail. The damage will be greater if we push it through and lose, and there will still be greater damage if we push it through and win, because we will have expended a precious commodity that is more difficult now in the second term to re-create, and there are other good choices."

On to plan B. Ironically, the president turned to Miers's first choice for O'Connor's replacement: Samuel Alito. The White House went back to the systematic process that had produced John Roberts, but without having to start from scratch. "At that juncture everything was prepared," said Miers. "[Bush] knew what his options were. It's kind of like once he's talked to someone, he's not going to call them back in and talk to them again. . . . He had available to him all the information that he needed to go in the direction that he went."

What was it like for Miers to go through such a searing experience and then stay on as White House counsel for another fourteen months before returning to Texas? Always gracious and loyal to her boss, Miers said, "I was not a victim at all. I had the ability to function in that job [of counsel]. I had all of the background. I know the president received unjust criticism by some for having 'subjected me' to the nomination. That's ridiculous. It's totally ridiculous. It worked well for everybody that I stayed, and I hope that that's the truth. I hope to high heaven."

"When she withdrew her nomination, I felt awful about it," Gillespie confessed. "Nobody felt good. I think it was the next day, Alito was there in the White House, and she was there with him. . . . I know this, after she stepped aside, she was right back at the job for the president of the United States as his counsel and doing everything she could to confirm Justice Alito."

Samuel A. Alito Jr.

On top of the Miers misstep, Bush had to contend with the defeat of his Social Security reform initiative at the hands of Republican House members and the blowback against his failure to address Hurricane Katrina's devastation along the Gulf coast in August 2005, especially the tragic flooding of New Orleans. Further complicating the Alito nomination was the jurist's demonstrated conservatism as an appeals court judge for more than fifteen years. "It's why Alito's nomination was more contentious [than Roberts's] even though it was for an associate justice slot. We were replacing a moderate justice [O'Connor] with a conservative justice," remarked Gillespie.

Yet Alito's obvious credentials (Princeton, Yale Law School, federal appellate court clerkship), his voluminous conservative record in the Reagan Justice Department and as a US attorney, and his restraintist judicial opinions after President George H. W. Bush named him to the Third Circuit Court of Appeals clearly trumped gender considerations when Bush chose him to replace the first woman justice. Alito's clear ideology (he was sometimes called "Scalito" for his similarities to Justice Scalia) and stellar credentials immediately distinguished him from Miers. "Judge Alito is one of the most accomplished and respected judges in America, and his long career in public service has given him an extraordinary breadth of experience," remarked the president in announcing his third nominee for O'Connor's seat. He added that the duration of Alito's tenure on the appellate bench surpassed that of all Supreme Court appointees over the past seven decades.[22]

At Bush's announcement of Alito's nomination, the judge graciously mentioned the woman he hoped to replace. As an assistant solicitor general in the Reagan administration, Alito had made his first argument before the Supreme Court in 1982. Justice O'Connor, who had been on the bench for barely a year, posed the initial query and pitched him a "kind" question, "sensing, I think, that I was a rookie," recalled Alito. "I was grateful to her on that happy occasion, and I am particularly honored to be nominated for her seat."[23]

Senate majority leader Bill Frist pronounced Alito "outstanding," but his counterpart, minority leader Harry Reid, criticized Bush for nominating someone "likely to divide America, instead of choosing a nominee in the mold of Sandra Day O'Connor." Senate Judiciary Committee member Charles Schumer (D-NY) accused Bush of making the Supreme Court look "less like America and more like an old boys club," with Justice Ginsburg now being the only female justice. The committee's moderate Republican chair, Arlen Specter, expressed concern about Alito's opposition to *Roe v. Wade*.[24]

With Chief Justice Roberts newly installed as the latest conservative on the Supreme Court (joining Scalia, Thomas, and sometimes Kennedy), the tribunal had four liberals: Stevens, Souter, Ginsburg, and Breyer. This even division meant that, especially in highly controversial political cases, Alito would likely move the court in a more conservative direction. In his courtesy calls with liberal senators, the judge attempted to allay Democrats' fears by distinguishing between his personal views and the law-based decisions issued by a court. The battle over O'Connor's swing seat continued in the two months between the nomination and the start of hearings in early January 2006, with interest groups on the left and right running ads opposing or supporting the nomination. Liberals' television spots declared, "The right wing has taken over the West Wing. Don't let them take over your Supreme Court."[25] Conservative groups borrowed a page from the GOP platform, arguing that Alito's opponents had a "clear agenda . . . to take God out of the Pledge of Allegiance . . . [and] redefine traditional marriage. They support partial-birth abortion [and] sanction the burning of the American flag."[26]

For the third time in six months, Ed Gillespie returned to the Hill to guide a Supreme Court nominee through the Senate confirmation process for President Bush. They started with the same advantage Roberts had: a majority consisting of fifty-five Republican senators. As a federal judge for a decade and a half, Alito was even more experienced than Roberts. His natural introversion, however, was closer to Miers's personality. Gillespie shared his impressions:

[At first I] thought he was kind of cold and—I don't know how to say it—arrogant maybe, I guess. He's not at all. He's humble and he's reserved. Shy sounds too pejorative. He's reserved. He was not Roberts. Roberts kind of enjoyed the give-and-take and the jousting with these senators who could go maybe two questions deep, but not much more.

I think Justice Alito didn't enjoy that as much as Chief Justice Roberts did. But he was good; he was just so good. The legal people around, the lawyers and the DOJ folks, they were really blown away by him, his depth of knowledge, his grasp. He'd served on the bench longer than the [new] chief.

Roberts, who had served on the DC Circuit Court of Appeals for only about two years, sometimes needed a "refresher" on topics, according to Gillespie:

Alito didn't need any of that. Somebody would maybe parry with him a little bit and he would say, "Well, that's true." But he never said, "Remind me about that again." He had command of virtually everything under the sun. So it was a different dynamic. But all those groups, the outside folks, there was a lot of energy again. The senators liked the jousting with him even though he didn't necessarily like it with them. He understood it; he never complained or grumbled or anything, but it was just a different dynamic.

Once hearings finally commenced, Democratic members of the Judiciary Committee, led by Senator Kennedy, came out swinging, just as they had when opposing Robert Bork nearly two decades earlier. Kennedy acknowledged that his strategy was to fire the first salvo in a nomination fight. "Otherwise," he said, "the rhythm of these battles flows in favor of the nominees quite strenuously, and it makes it more and more difficult [to defeat them].[27]

But Gillespie noted that times had changed since Bork's failed nomination. "There are no sneak attacks now," he commented:

You're prepared for all of that, and you don't let it go unanswered, and you parry, and you jump right in. To a certain extent it's sad, but this is where it is. The process has been so denigrated that a lot of it becomes noise anyway. Ted Kennedy giving the "Robert Bork's America" speech, you can only give that once. You're not going to get away with that a second and third time. People start to discount it.

The main difference between 1987 and 2006 was the majority party in the Senate: Republicans held the majority when Alito's nomination came before it. Nevertheless, Democrats on the Judiciary Committee sparred with the nominee over abortion, presidential authority, judicial precedents, race, gender, federal power, states' rights, terrorism, and the death penalty. "He did very well in the hearings, too. The left, particularly Kennedy on the committee and to a lesser extent [Illinois senator Richard] Durbin, they kind of swung a little wildly because they were frustrated. They couldn't touch him intellectually. There was no one on the committee who was anywhere even in his area code," Gillespie boasted.

On day three of the taut spectacle, Senator Kennedy speculated that Alito might be a racist because he had joined an undergraduate club at Princeton that had no black members, and Sen. Lindsey Graham (R-SC) defended the nominee. At that point, Mrs. Alito left the hearing room in tears. Later reports indicated that she also suffered a migraine. Recalling the painful incident, Gillespie commented that the attack on Judge Alito "was pretty reprehensible. . . . At a certain point he's not the nominee for the Supreme Court, it's her husband getting slimed and she just couldn't take it anymore." At the time, Gillespie wondered how the public would respond to the racism charge and Mrs. Alito's reaction:

> You never know. It played out . . . [as] people going, "No wonder. Why would anybody even subject themselves to this crap? How are we ever going to get good people to serve on the Supreme Court if this is what you're going to get put through? God bless her, I feel sorry for her." . . . It was really like one of those truly human moments where I just felt so bad for her as a spouse to have to see her husband put through—I thought it was unseemly and reprehensible, but you put your armor on and you go through it, but she doesn't have armor.

After four days of hearings, the committee voted 10–8 along partisan lines to send the nomination to the full Senate. The two Democratic senators from Massachusetts, Kennedy and John Kerry, made a last-ditch attempt at a filibuster to block a confirmation vote. To succeed, they needed the support of at least forty-one Democrats, but seven moderate members of their party had already agreed with a like number of Republicans to eschew filibusters for Supreme Court nominations except in "extraordinary circumstances."[28]

A dozen more Democrats joined this "Gang of 14," along with another forty-six Republicans, to end the debate and call for a vote on Alito's nomination. The Senate voted 52–48 to confirm on January 31, 2006. Alito took the oath from Chief Justice Roberts the same day, just in time to don his judicial robe and attend Bush's State of the Union address. For the first time in its history, the Supreme Court consisted of all members from non-Protestant denominations: six Catholics and three Jews. "There was some talk about it; there wasn't any consideration of it in terms of the nomination or anything, but it became apparent—I remember somebody saying the Supreme Court is going to be [a] majority of Catholics," Gillespie observed.

The "Bush Twins"?

Have President George W. Bush's two appointees to the nation's highest court wrought the judicial revolution he anticipated and Republicans have advocated for decades? Rove had shied away from recommending Fourth Circuit Court of Appeals judge J. Harvie Wilkinson III as a nominee for fear that he was too moderate, but then, he quipped, "we appointed Roberts, and we got the Obamacare decision." Rove was referring to the 2012 decision in which the chief justice cast the deciding vote, joining the court's four liberals, to uphold the provision of the Affordable Care Act (ACA) requiring all Americans to carry health insurance. The chief justice typically writes the court's opinion when he is in the majority on landmark cases. For conservatives, Roberts added insult to injury by not only voting in the majority but also arguing in his opinion, which has the force of law, that Congress could impose the so-called individual mandate under its taxing power. Americans who chose not to purchase health insurance would have to pay a penalty to the IRS.[29]

Three years later, against another conservative challenge to the ACA, Roberts again voted with the majority, as did his moderate colleague Justice Kennedy, in a 6–3 decision that upheld the law's tax-credit policy for those who purchased health insurance through the government exchanges. "Our role is confined—to say what the law is," wrote the chief justice, using conservative restraintist theory to sustain a liberal law.[30] Congress eliminated the individual mandate in 2017 and asserted that the entire ACA should fall. When two states brought a case to the Supreme Court to test that assertion in 2021, the justices dismissed the litigation for failure to show a remediable harm. Roberts joined the seven-justice majority but assigned the opinion to Justice Breyer. The Supreme Court's third case involving Obamacare was not the charm for conservatives; in a scathing dissent, Justice Alito accused his colleagues of mistakenly saving the ACA from the constitutional ash heap once again.[31]

Despite his devout Catholicism, Roberts also disquieted conservatives by dissenting from the Supreme Court's procedural ruling not to enjoin Texas's controversial 2021 abortion law, which virtually banned abortion after six weeks of pregnancy and allowed private citizens to enforce the edict through lawsuits.[32]

When Roberts has strayed from the conservative fold, it has most often been in the service of his institutional regard for the Supreme Court and his effort to maintain its legitimacy in the eyes of the American people. In the summer after his first term at the court's helm, Roberts sat for an interview with George Washington University law professor Jeffrey Rosen and stated that his goal was to increase collegiality and unanimity among the nine justices because unanimous decisions are difficult to overturn. More stability in the law can then produce more public respect for the court, Roberts asserted.[33] His protective stance toward the Supreme Court's image and authority—which, as Alexander Hamilton argued, cannot draw on the powers of the "purse" or the "sword"[34]—included countering Donald Trump's 2018 partisan attack on an "Obama judge" in the Ninth Circuit who had ruled against his immigration policy. "We do not have Obama judges or Trump judges, Bush judges or Clinton judges," Roberts declared. "What we have is an extraordinary group of dedicated judges doing their level best to do equal right to those appearing before them."[35] Roberts clearly disdained Trump's politicization of the judiciary. Yet he wrote the court's majority opinion in *Trump v. Hawaii*, which upheld the president's travel ban on visitors from several Muslim countries suspected of exporting terrorism.[36]

Bush and his conservative allies had reason to be pleased with Roberts's leadership and Alito's vote in voiding campaign finance regulations, limiting the Voting Rights Act, and expanding the free exercise of religion.[37] According to political scientists Lee Epstein, Andrew D. Martin, and Kevin Quinn, Roberts was just to the right of center in his jurisprudence, while Alito hewed to a more reliable conservatism.[38]

One case is especially illustrative of the two Bush appointees' evolving judicial differences. In 2020's landmark *Bostock v. Clayton County, Georgia*, Roberts supported the 6–3 decision, delivered by Trump appointee Neil Gorsuch, that the 1964 Civil Rights Act's employment protections extend to gender identity and sexual orientation. Alito penned a stinging dissent, noting that the law as written did not encompass LGBT categories.[39] In 2007, early in his tenure on the court, Alito also applied a narrow reading to the 1964 Civil Rights Act, arguing for the conservative majority in *Ledbetter v. Goodyear Tire & Rubber* that a woman who alleged gender-based pay discrimination had to file suit within the statute's mandated 180 days, even if she didn't know about the salary discrepancy until she retired. Justice Ginsburg's heated dissent urged Congress to amend the law.[40] Led by Sen. Hillary Clinton (D-NY), Congress passed the Lilly Ledbetter Fair Pay Act, the first bill signed into law by President Barack Obama.

In that same term, Alito handed President Bush a particularly welcome victory. Writing for a 5–4 majority in *Hein v. Freedom from Religion Foundation, Inc.*, he ruled that taxpayers lacked standing to bring lawsuits challenging expenditures by the Bush administration's Office of Faith-Based and Community Initiatives.[41] Bush and his supporters believed that religious institutions could receive federal funds to implement social programs without violating the First Amendment's ban on government establishment of religion. In 2014, again displaying support for the accommodation of religious beliefs, Alito led another five-justice majority in *Burwell v. Hobby Lobby* to exempt family-owned businesses from the Affordable Care Act's requirement that companies that provide health insurance must include coverage for contraception.[42]

In *District of Columbia v. Heller*, pro-gun Republicans were gratified in 2008 when Roberts and Alito rounded out the court's conservative wing to assert that the Second Amendment protects an individual's right to possess firearms.[43] Two years later, Alito, writing for the majority in *McDonald v. City of Chicago*, applied the precedent to states and cities.[44]

Departing from his predecessor's pro-choice posture and support of affirmative action, Alito has flipped O'Connor's swing seat to a steadfastly conservative vote, just as Bush and his advisers had hoped. One of Alito's favorite descriptions of the Supreme Court's role was offered by Justice John Marshall Harlan II, who wrote in 1964 that the tribunal should not be thought of as "as [a] general haven for reform movements. This Court . . . does not serve its high purpose when it exceeds its authority, even to satisfy justified impatience with the political process."[45] Alito has embraced this restraintist view of judicial interpretation more tightly than the chief justice has. They were labeled "judicial twins" in their earliest terms on the court, when they voted together more than 90 percent of the time,[46] but Roberts's conception of his leadership role and the tribunal's place in the constitutional cosmos has taken him in a different direction. He now sides with Alito in only about 60 percent of cases. As Epstein observed about the chief justice at the end of the 2019–2020 term, "He is drifting left at a statistically significant rate—and at a rate roughly resembling Souter's liberal turn in the 1990s."[47] That surprising result was the last outcome the Bush team wanted or predicted after their careful selection of John Roberts in 2005.

Bush's Judicial Legacy

Despite Roberts's unanticipated departure from a consistent conservative posture, his generally right-of-center jurisprudence in religion, affirmative action, abortion, voting rights, and campaign finance cases has achieved the Republican Party's long-awaited reversal of liberal Supreme Court precedents. John Roberts impressed George Bush in their prenomination interview with his keen intellect and affable persona. The chief justice has represented the Supreme Court with a scholarly dignity of which his appointing president can be proud.

Conversely, Samuel Alito has embraced the late Antonin Scalia's role of loading predictably conservative opinions and public speeches with pointed barbs at his opponents on the bench and in the media. Although Bush tried to embody compassionate conservatism, he cannot be disappointed by Alito's votes, even if his style grates. Combined with Trump's troika of conservative justices, Bush's appointments to the nation's highest court may contribute to a five- or six-justice majority that could turn the court in a rightward direction for years to come.

This restructuring of the tribunal's ideology and decisions is a result of the careful process George Bush and his advisers applied to the Roberts and Alito selections. Departing from this vetting process by prioritizing gender and naming his friend Harriet Miers to fill the O'Connor seat nearly cost Bush the outcome he and his party desired. The lesson from this experience is that friendship and social characteristics should not be the primary criteria for lifetime appointments. Most presidents prioritize ideology in choosing Supreme Court justices, but merit should place a close second. As Alberto Gonzales explained about the forty-third president, "He sometimes followed his gut. But more often he followed a process in place so you minimize mistakes. I like to cite an example of where he didn't follow that model to results that weren't ideal. That was the nomination of Harriet Miers for the Supreme Court."

Notes

1. *Bush v. Palm Beach County Canvassing Board*, 531 U.S. 70 (2000).

2. All quotations in this chapter relating to the Bush presidency are from the Miller Center's George W. Bush Oral History, unless otherwise noted. The interviews are available at https://millercenter.org/the-presidency/presidential-oral-histories/george-w-bush.

3. *Bush v. Gore*, 531 U.S. 98 (2000); Stephen G. Bragaw and Barbara A. Perry, "The 'Brooding Omnipresence' in *Bush v. Gore*: Anthony Kennedy, the Equality Principle, and Judicial Supremacy," *Stanford Law and Policy Review* 13, 1 (2002): 19–32.

4. Subsequent media tallies confirmed that Bush would have won the determinative Florida vote by three hundred to five hundred ballots, even if the recount had continued.

5. Abraham frequently made this remark in conversations about the lengthy service of Supreme Court justices. See Henry J. Abraham, *Justices, Presidents, and Senators: A History of the U.S. Supreme Court Appointments from Washington to Bush II*, 5th ed. (Lanham, MD: Rowman & Littlefield, 2007), which, starting with its initial publication in the 1960s, pioneered the systematic study of Supreme Court appointments.

6. "The 2000 Republican Party Platform," American Presidency Project, University of California–Santa Barbara, https://www.presidency.ucsb.edu/documents/2000-republican-party-platform.

7. "Full Text of Bush's Acceptance Speech," *New York Times*, August 4, 2000, https://movies2.nytimes.com/library/politics/camp/080400wh-bush-speech.html.

8. "The 2004 Republican Party Platform," American Presidency Project, https://www.presidency.ucsb.edu/documents/2004-republican-party-platform.

9. "George W. Bush: 2004 Republican National Convention Address," American Rhetoric, September 2, 2004, https://www.americanrhetoric.com/speeches/convention2004/georgewbush2004rnc.htm.

10. Barbara A. Perry, *The Supremes: An Introduction to the U.S. Supreme Court Justices*, 2nd ed. (New York: Peter Lang, 2009), 14. Journalist Joan Biskupic relates this same story in her book *The Chief: The Life and Turbulent Times of Chief Justice John Roberts* (New York: Basic Books, 2019), 148–149. Biographer Evan Thomas, however, reports that Chief Justice Rehnquist indicated his intention to remain on the court at a June 23, 2005, bridge game with O'Connor. Evan Thomas, *First: Sandra Day O'Connor* (New York: Random House, 2019), 376–377.

11. Barbara A. Perry, *A "Representative" Supreme Court? The Impact of Race, Religion, and Gender on Appointments* (New York: Greenwood Press, 1991), chap. 5.

12. Perry, *Supremes*, 15.

13. Barbara A. Perry and Henry J. Abraham, "From Oral History to Oral Argument: George Bush's Supreme Court Appointments," in *41: Inside the Presidency of George H. W. Bush*, ed. Michael Nelson, Russell L. Riley, and Barbara A. Perry (Ithaca, NY: Cornell University Press, 2014), 179–182.

14. Abraham, *Justices, Presidents, and Senators*, 3.

15. Perry, *Supremes*, 15.

16. Quoted in Jim Vandehei and Peter Baker, "Bush Answers Gonzales Critics," *Washington Post*, July 7, 2005, A1.

17. Perry, *Supremes*, 81–82.

18. Quoted in Peter Baker, "Unraveling the Twists and Turns of the Path to Roberts," *Washington Post*, July 25, 2005, A3.

19. Quoted in Dan Balz and Darryl Fears, "Some Disappointed Nominee Won't Add Diversity to Court," *Washington Post*, July 21, 2005, A15.

20. Perry, *Supremes*, 130.

21. Michael A. Fletcher, "White House Counsel Miers Chosen for Court: Longtime Aide to Bush, but Never a Judge," *Washington Post*, October 4, 2005, A1.

22. Perry, *Supremes*, 135.

23. Quoted in Perry, 135.

24. Perry, 135.

25. Quoted in Jo Becker, "Television Ad War on Alito Begins: Liberals Try to Paint High Court Nominee as Right-Wing Tool," *Washington Post*, November 18, 2005, A3.

26. Quoted in Becker. Ironically, even conservative Justice Scalia had voted to uphold flag burning as a form of political protest protected under the First Amendment's free speech clause in the 1986 case *Texas v. Johnson*.

27. As quoted in Barbara A. Perry, *Edward M. Kennedy: An Oral History* (New York: Oxford University Press, 2018), 256.

28. Abraham, *Justices, Presidents, and Senators*, 321.

29. *National Federation of Independent Business, et al. v. Sebelius*, 567 U.S. 519 (2012). For a detailed description of how Roberts shocked conservatives by joining the court's liberals to uphold Obamacare, see Biskupic, *Chief*, 10, chap. 9.

30. *King v. Burwell*, 576 U.S. 473 (2015); Biskupic, *Chief*, 289–291.

31. *California v. Texas*, 593 U.S. ___ (2021); Adam Liptak, "Affordable Care Act Survives Latest Supreme Court Challenge," *New York Times*, June 18, 2021, https://www.nytimes.com/2021/06/17/us/obamacare-supreme-court.html.

32. *Whole Women's Health v. Austin Reeve Jackson*, 594 U.S. ___ (2021).

33. Jeffrey Rosen, "Roberts' Rules," *Atlantic Monthly*, January–February 2007, https://www.theatlantic.com/magazine/archive/2007/01/robertss-rules/305559/.

34. Alexander Hamilton, Federalist 78, https://founders.archives.gov/documents/Hamilton/01-04-02-0241.

35. Pete Williams and Associated Press, "In Rare Rebuke, Chief Justice Roberts Slams Trump for Comment about 'Obama Judge,'" NBC News, November 21, 2018, https://www.nbcnews.com/politics/supreme-court/rare-rebuke-chief-justice-roberts-slams-trump-comment-about-obama-n939016.

36. *Trump v. Hawaii*, 585 U.S. ___ (2018).

37. Biskupic, *Chief*, 9. The campaign finance and voting rights cases are *Citizens United v. Federal Election Commission*, 558 U.S. 310 (2010); *Shelby County v. Holder*, 570 U.S. 529 (2013); and *Brnovich v. Democratic National Committee*, 594 U.S. ___ (2021). For an explanation of the Roberts Court's expansion of religious freedom, see Richard Garnett, "Symposium: Religious Freedom and the Roberts Court's Doctrinal Clean-up,"

SCOTUSblog, August 7, 2020, https://www.scotusblog.com/2020/08/symposium-reli
gious-freedom-and-the-roberts-courts-doctrinal-clean-up/.

38. See Lee Epstein, Andrew D. Martin, and Kevin Quinn, research page, Washington
University, http://epstein.wustl.edu/research/PossibleTrumpJustices.html.

39. *Bostock v. Clayton County, Georgia*, 590 U.S. ___ (2020).

40. *Ledbetter v. Goodyear Tire & Rubber*, 550 U.S. 618 (2007).

41. *Hein v. Freedom from Religion Foundation, Inc.*, 551 U.S. 587 (2007).

42. *Burwell v. Hobby Lobby*, 573 U.S. 682 (2014).

43. *District of Columbia v. Heller*, 554 U.S. 570 (2008).

44. *McDonald v. City of Chicago*, 561 U.S. 742 (2010).

45. Dale Russakoff and Jo Becker, "A Search for Order, an Answer in the Law," *Washington Post*, January 9, 2006, A1.

46. Barbara A. Perry, "The 'Bush Twins'? Roberts, Alito, and the Conservative
Agenda," *Judicature* 92, 6 (May–June 2009): 309.

47. As quoted in Adam Liptak, "In a Term Full of Major Cases, the Supreme Court
Tacked to the Center," *New York Times*, July 10, 2020, https://www.nytimes.com/2020/07
/10/us/supreme-court-term.html/. Epstein, Martin, and Quinn's extensive database on
Supreme Court justices and their votes indicates that conservative justices are more
likely to move left over the course of their careers than liberal justices are to shift right.
See Oliver Roeder, "Supreme Court Justices Get More Liberal as They Get Older," Five
ThirtyEight, October 5, 2015, https://fivethirtyeight.com/features/supreme-court-jus
tices-get-more-liberal-as-they-get-older/.

CHAPTER SEVEN

George W. Bush's Vice President: A New Look at Dick Cheney

Joel K. Goldstein

Events often come into clearer focus as they recede into the past. The passage of time compensates for the loss of individuals' memories by furnishing researchers with other sources. Participants share previously undisclosed information and insights. Protected documents become accessible. As events become more distant and protagonists leave the stage, passions subside, and events appear in a wider and less charged context.

And so the historical process goes forward in the study of presidencies as it does with other events. We learn, we reconsider, we revise, we make another attempt to identify and understand the past and to extract its lessons—recognizing, especially early in that process, that subsequently released information may necessitate further reconsideration.

More than twenty years after George W. Bush's presidency began and several presidential terms after its end, the role of Vice President Dick Cheney in the Bush administration looks quite different from the way it has commonly been portrayed. Cheney's vice presidency was distinctive in so many ways that some distortion was inevitable as observers tried to arrange the seemingly anomalous pieces into a portrait that was both coherent and correct. After all, Cheney chaired the vice-presidential search that ended in his own selection. His impressive record of high-level government service contrasted with Bush's modest resumé, especially with regard to Washington and national security experience. Alone among recent vice presidents, Cheney disclaimed presidential ambitions, an unorthodox attitude, given the second office's record of serving as a coveted presidential springboard. Bush placed Cheney in charge of the abbreviated 2000–2001 presidential transition. And when America was attacked on September 11, 2001, during the administration's first year, Cheney not only assumed immediate control in the Presidential Emergency Operations Center (PEOC) during Bush's absence but also urged a reluctant Bush to stay away from Washington due to concerns about the continuity of government, and he issued an order that America's fighter planes should shoot down any unresponsive civilian aircraft. Both he and Bush characterized Cheney's action as conveying the president's order, but the images of that day placed Cheney in the government's center chair.

These frames from Cheney's early vice-presidential tenure encouraged the perception of a uniquely powerful vice president serving a diminished president. Cheney appeared to be the power behind the Oval Office, a co-president,[1] or at least history's most influential vice president.[2] Many of these robust portrayals of Cheney's role rested somewhat on the widespread perception that Bush was in over his head.

Cheney was certainly a significant figure in the George W. Bush presidency, but recent evidence confirms that conventional understandings have exaggerated and distorted his role and influence. America's forty-third presidency belonged not to Cheney or to Bush-Cheney. Bush was in charge, the decider (as he famously proclaimed), more conspicuously in the second term but also in the first. Cheney was a significant presidential adviser and occasionally an operator, but above all, he was a presidential subordinate whose role varied, depending on the issue and the time. Although invited to participate generally in the Bush administration, Cheney focused his office's resources on his own priorities rather than reflecting all of Bush's. He played an important role in shaping and defending Bush administration policies regarding the war on terror and the Iraq War, among other areas. Although Cheney's strategic approach involved him in some of the transcendent problems facing the Bush administration, it removed him from, or diminished his role in, other areas, including some that Bush regarded as signature achievements. And even when Cheney was engaged in decision making, Bush was not the vice president's puppet. Bush often followed Cheney's advice, but not always—not even during his first term or on national security matters.

This chapter corrects some common misperceptions of Cheney's role in Bush's presidency by drawing from forty-four richly rewarding oral history interviews conducted by the Miller Center, as well as other materials.[3] Chou En-lai reportedly claimed that 1972 was too soon to assess the consequences of the French Revolution.[4] Without accepting the spirit of this wonderful but apparently apocryphal story, it must be recognized that impressions of the Bush presidency and the Cheney vice presidency are necessarily subject to further rounds of revision to accommodate additional information as it becomes available.

Before the White House

The process of conducting the vice-presidential search is instructive regarding Bush's leadership style and the Bush-Cheney relationship. Cheney's selection as Bush's running mate was unique. Never before (nor since) had the person in charge of the vice-presidential search become the person chosen as the running mate.

Finding a Running Mate

Neither the vice presidency nor Cheney were novel subjects for Bush as he began to consider his selection of a running mate. His father, George H. W. Bush, had been vice president for eight years before making the controversial decision to add Sen. Dan Quayle to the ticket when he ran for president in 1988. Bush had suggested that his father replace Quayle in 1992 with Cheney, the secretary of defense and a star of the administration.[5] The younger Bush later asked Cheney to head his own presidential campaign, but Cheney declined. In spring 2000 Bush sent aide Joe Allbaugh to ask Cheney whether he was willing to consider joining the ticket, but Cheney rejected the idea for multiple reasons, including his happiness as Halliburton's CEO and his history of heart problems. In response to a subsequent request, Cheney agreed in April to head the search for a running mate.[6] Three months later, Bush announced Cheney as his vice-presidential pick.

The Cheney-led search began conventionally.[7] Cheney assembled associates to assist him,[8] and more than thirty prospective candidates were identified.[9] Cheney contacted some of them, and an intrusive vetting process began with a demanding questionnaire and a request for documents. Bush initially may have hoped to choose a running mate who would help him carry a swing state, but the prospect who best fit that criterion, Sen. Connie Mack of Florida, unequivocally removed himself from consideration in private conversations,[10] as did Gen. Colin Powell and Sen. John McCain publicly.[11] Cheney pursued his close friend Donald Rumsfeld, whose resumé—member of the House of Representatives, Gerald R. Ford's chief of staff, secretary of defense, and corporate executive—resembled Cheney's. But Rumsfeld was a past political adversary of Bush's father, and although Rumsfeld endorsed him early on, Bush declined to consider Rumsfeld.[12]

Bush's finalists included four past or present governors (Lamar Alexander, John Engler, Frank Keating, and Tom Ridge) and five past or present senators (John Danforth, John Kyl, Chuck Hagel, Bill Frist, and Fred Thompson).[13] Bush met with senior staffers to solicit ideas as he was "getting near a decision," but no one mentioned Cheney or even knew he was a possibility. Policy aide Josh Bolten favored Danforth or Hagel; his associate Kristen Silverberg remembers Bolten suggesting Joe Lieberman, who became Al Gore's running mate, as an outside-the-box idea.[14]

Convention dictated that someone with Bush's political profile would choose a running mate with the Washington and national security experience he lacked—in other words, someone like Cheney.[15] The pool of candidates offered few appealing options. The governors lacked national security experience, and Frist, Thompson, Hagel, and Kyl were fairly new to the Senate. Only Danforth, who had served three terms in the Senate, seemed a plausible choice. Bush and Cheney discussed the search "numerous" times, with Bush saying more than once that Cheney was the solution to his "problem."[16] By late June, Bush began to regard Cheney as his best bet.[17] When Bush discussed options with his father and mentioned Cheney, the former president assessed his longtime associate as "a great choice."[18]

After Cheney concluded his "final report" to Bush on July 3, 2000, Bush came right out and stated that he thought Cheney was his best choice.[19] Whether Bush "noticed something different" in Cheney's "body language" that triggered the comment, as Bush's friend Clay Johnson stated, or whether Bush had already decided "to make another run" at Cheney, as Bush recalled, Cheney was becoming open to the possibility.[20] Although he had never seen a happy vice president, discussing the office with Bush awakened Cheney to its potential.[21] He apparently told Bush that he had suffered three heart attacks, was happy in his current circumstances, and would need to speak to his wife, and he revealed that his daughter Mary was gay—none of which bothered Bush. Cheney agreed to explore the steps necessary to become a viable candidate, such as changing his state of residence (from Texas back to his home state of Wyoming) and extricating himself from Halliburton.[22]

The revelation that Cheney was under consideration stunned Bush insiders.[23] Chief strategist Karl Rove, who favored Danforth, was opposed,[24] as was communications adviser Karen Hughes, who preferred Ridge.[25] During the first part of July, Cheney advised Halliburton officials that he might become Bush's running mate, and he underwent a physical and cardiac examination to allay health concerns.

Bush convened a meeting with Cheney, Rove, and perhaps other aides at the Texas governor's mansion. Although accounts of that meeting vary somewhat, they agree that Rove argued against Cheney's selection and that Cheney found some of Rove's arguments persuasive,[26] including two arrests for driving under the influence in his twenties, being kicked out of Yale twice, heart problems that could disrupt the campaign by requiring hospitalization, his association with the oil business, his residency in Texas (which, under the Twelfth Amendment to the Constitution, would preclude Texas electors from supporting both him and Bush), and his "deeply conservative" voting record. Cheney made those same arguments to Bush.[27] In addition, Cheney's selection would not increase Bush's electoral votes because Wyoming's were already securely Republican.[28] When Danforth met with Bush on July 18 for a vice-presidential interview, Cheney attended the first part of it. Danforth impressed Bush, but he had already decided on Cheney.[29] Cheney changed his voter registration back to Wyoming on July 21, triggering media speculation that he was Bush's choice. Bush made the formal offer on July 25 and announced it that day.[30]

Although a vice-presidential selection process that ended with the searcher becoming the selectee was unprecedented, its unorthodox character does not mean that Cheney manipulated the process in his own favor or that Bush made the wrong decision. Historically, Cheney was the only head of a vice-presidential search team who was a plausible pick. His initial reluctance is credible, given the vice-presidential history he had witnessed and the rewards of his life at the time.[31] Other modern vice presidents, such as Walter F. Mondale and Joe Biden, changed their minds and considered the possibility after overcoming misgivings, as did Danforth in 2000. Perhaps the vice presidency became more appealing to Cheney the more he worked with Bush, imagined the possibilities of the office, and acknowledged the limited options available to Bush. Dan Bartlett, a Bush aide who was often critical of Cheney, dismissed the suggestion that Cheney engineered his own selection or that he expected to be selected until relatively late in the process.

Of course, the process was imperfect. Bolten wondered who had vetted Cheney: his daughter Liz?[32] No one had, at least not in the usual manner modern vice-presidential candidates are screened. Accordingly, Bush was unprepared to answer the Gore campaign's early attacks on Cheney's voting record in Congress, forcing aides to scramble to learn about it. Cheney's presence at the beginning of the Danforth meeting was odd, and the overall search process left some participants feeling bruised or misused amid indications that they had never been seriously considered, notwithstanding the considerable time and expense they devoted to the process.[33] In some respects, the process appeared "sloppy" in hindsight, recalled Bartlett.

Yet the odd process did not prevent Bush from making an educated choice. Cheney was highly regarded, based on his experience, and he had been confirmed to a sensitive cabinet position in 1989. Working closely with Cheney for months on the selection process gave Bush insights into his running mate that few presidential candidates are privy to. Bush sought his father's opinion, based on his close association with Cheney in various contexts. Bush also discussed the choice with top aides and considered counterarguments from both Rove and Cheney himself. The finalists, Cheney and Danforth, were clearly the most eminent candidates, and they fit the profile that someone with Bush's background would prudently select. Perhaps Danforth would have been a better choice, with different inclinations to inform decision making, but Cheney's range of public service made his resumé compelling. Bush's selection of the more conservative Cheney may have signaled the tendencies that would have shaped his conduct in any event. Nor is it clear that any selection process would have revealed weaknesses in Cheney that appeared later. Cheney did not bring a big home-state electoral dowry, but the idea that candidates focus on that criterion is a relic of earlier American history.[34] Modern running mates must be presidential, and they are chosen to send favorable messages about the presidential candidate. Not surprisingly, Bush concluded that his choice must send the message that he would surround himself with able associates to compensate for the experience he lacked. Choosing either Cheney or Danforth would have sent that signal.[35] Bush's ultimate choice was widely praised. Sen. Mitch McConnell described Cheney as a "big leaguer" who could be president.[36] Sen. Trent Lott thought Cheney was Bush's best choice, and McCain lauded his "leadership skills" and "incredibly impressive resume."[37] Sen. Judd Gregg called Cheney a "huge talent."

Bush's unconventional process was successful though unorthodox.

Bush never eliminated Cheney from consideration, despite Cheney's initial reluctance. As most other options appeared implausible, Bush became convinced that Cheney was his best alternative, and Cheney's position eventually changed. Rejecting the claim that he had "manipulated the process," Cheney later suggested that he "was the one who was manipulated by the process."[38] Perhaps he was right and Bush, not Cheney, was the manipulator.

Bush's vice-presidential selection process signaled aspects of his approach to decision making that Cheney somewhat reinforced. Bush focused on the big picture, on reaching the destination even if it meant following an unusual path. Perhaps because he recognized that all decisions have costs, and perhaps because he valued ends over means, Bush accepted the risks of an unconventional selection process to achieve a preferred outcome. Cheney, too, seemed willing to bend the process once he concluded that Bush had made the right choice. That said, as president, Bush sometimes paid a price for skipping steps in normal procedures, sometimes at Cheney's encouragement.

Campaign 2000 and Transition 2000–2001

Although Cheney was not an electrifying campaigner, he probably contributed to the ticket's success. His acceptance speech effectively linked Al Gore to Bill Clinton's unethical behavior. Appropriating a line from Gore's 1992 acceptance speech, Cheney declared, "It is time for them to go." Gore would try to separate himself from Clinton, but "somehow we will never see one without thinking of the other. . . . They came in together. Now let us see them off together."[39] Cheney won the vice-presidential debate against Sen. Joe Lieberman. And the selection of Cheney reassured voters that Bush would appoint qualified advisers. In an election decided by a few hundred votes in Florida, Cheney's help in improving Bush's image cannot be discounted.

Cheney's influence appeared in the period preceding the inauguration. Seeing Cheney "as an experienced partner in the creation of government," Bush dispatched him to Washington for the abbreviated transition.[40] Cheney worked with Bush's longtime friend Clayton Johnson, chief of staff–designee Andrew Card, and others. Cheney influenced the cabinet appointments of Paul O'Neill as secretary of the treasury and Donald Rumsfeld as secretary of defense, although Condoleezza Rice also may have suggested Rumsfeld for Defense rather than CIA director after others had been eliminated.[41] Cheney's preferred candidates were not always selected, according to Johnson and Bush aide Margaret Spellings. Former Cheney associates Paul Wolfowitz and Steve Hadley landed significant positions at the Pentagon and the National Security Council (NSC), respectively, probably to reward their service as Bush campaign foreign policy advisers under Rice and not because they were Cheney associates.[42] Cheney helped place some like-minded people in important positions, including John Bolton as undersecretary of state, Sean O'Keefe as deputy director of the Office of Management and Budget (OMB), and Zal Khalilzad at the NSC.[43]

Cheney's actions during the transition signaled his political orientation. Shortly after the Supreme Court's decision in *Bush v. Gore* stopped the Florida recount, awarding the victory to Bush and Cheney by the narrowest Electoral College margin since 1876–1877, Cheney surprised his hosts at a Capitol Hill lunch—five moderate Republican senators—by insisting that the close presidential vote and 50–50 Senate division would not prompt the Bush administration to retreat from its conservative platform.[44] Cheney articulated this message publicly, too.[45]

The First Term

As vice president, Cheney functioned as an important presidential adviser who sometimes performed operational assignments. He was "truly a counselor to the President," said Bolten.[46] Elliott Abrams, an NSC staffer and Cheney associate, echoed this description, calling Cheney "a real counselor and adviser" to Bush. Cheney differed from Bush's other advisers. He was an elected constitutional officer, a heartbeat away from the presidency; he lacked a departmental affiliation that tied him to a bureaucracy he had to manage or a policy area on which he had to concentrate. Cheney's role varied, depending on the subject, and it fluctuated during the two terms. He exercised major influence in national security matters and a few other areas, especially during the first term; he was less significant in other areas, including some of Bush's priorities. Even in national security matters, Cheney did not always prevail, and he did so less frequently in the second term. Whether "the apex of [Cheney's] power and influence was in the transition and the first few months of the Presidency," as Bolten thought,[47] or whether it grew after 9/11 elevated national security issues, Cheney eventually became less influential.[48]

Cheney's Vice-Presidential Assets

The context on January 20, 2001, supported a consequential vice presidency. The office had been dramatically changed after Cheney left the Ford White House in 1977 and President Jimmy Carter and Vice President Walter F. Mondale imagined and implemented a new model of the vice president as an adviser and a troubleshooter with sufficient resources to perform those roles. Their successors imitated that model, entrenching it.[49] Cheney's reputation and relationship with Bush enhanced his position. The Bush-Cheney relationship was professional but "very close," and Bush had "a lot of confidence" in Cheney (Colin Powell) and "a great deal of regard" for Cheney's opinions (Harriet Miers). Cheney had extensive access to Bush; he was included in all briefings and, along with his staff, was part of White House operations. The understanding that Cheney had abandoned any presidential ambitions was seen as a "virtue" (Bartlett) and encouraged the perception of a common agenda and camaraderie (Bolten).[50]

Cheney brought important assets to the job. Few Bush insiders had held senior White House positions, but Cheney had been Ford's chief of staff. From his service in the White House, in the House of Representatives, and as secretary of defense, Cheney had friends in high places all over town, people who shared information and trusted his judgment. And Cheney knew how to operate. As Treasury Secretary John Snow put it, Cheney was "a very talented guy" who was "a pro at government." As Ford's chief of staff, Cheney had marginalized Vice President Nelson A. Rockefeller, but as Bush's vice president, he developed a "very close" relationship with Bush's chief of staff Card, which facilitated his own involvement. Key figures in the Office of the Vice President (OVP), including Lewis "Scooter" Libby, Mary Matalin, and speechwriter John McConnell, doubled as members of Bush's staff.[51] Libby was especially important, serving as Cheney's chief of staff and national security assistant as well as assistant to Bush. Cheney's counsel David Addington had government experience in national security law that became valuable to White House counsel Alberto Gonzales in the aftermath of 9/11, and his long relationship with Cheney and aggressive style augmented his clout.[52] Cheney's personal and professional relationship with Rumsfeld strengthened his position in national security discussions, and his inclusion on various White House domestic, economic, and security councils fostered his broader participation. Many Bush officials spoke positively about their interactions with Cheney, although a number were critical of some others in the OVP.

Cheney brought talent as well as experience to the job. Colleagues described him as "very smart" (John Bridgeland), with an "incredibly photographic memory" that allowed him to "absorb everything" from briefings and then "to sort of disaggregate everything that he had been told and then put it back together in a way that was particularly compelling" (Eric Edelman).[53] According to Gen. Peter Pace, Cheney spoke infrequently in briefings, intervening occasionally to raise a question. Yet these rare interjections added value. Gen. George Casey observed, "You know, when you're in the meeting and there's one guy in the back who is really smart, and you know he always asks one really great question that nobody else has thought about? That was Cheney."

Cheney skillfully used his extensive access to Bush. The opportunity for private presidential audiences allowed him to advise Bush without having others contest the information or the arguments he offered.[54] Cheney could withhold comment in briefings, assuming the posture of a recipient of information and counsel (like Bush), whereas other advisers were there as presenters trying to persuade (Keith Hennessey). He often remained in the Oval Office after a briefing had ended to share his thoughts with Bush (Pace, Jay Lefkowitz). Cheney gave Bush candid advice, but it was generally during private conversations that he would "make his case" (Bartlett).[55] Cheney's "proximity" to Bush and the fact that he was often "the last person to see" Bush contributed to his influence (Powell).

Bush, the Decider

Cheney's role was not unlimited. During the transition, Addington returned a draft, signed by Cheney (Philip Zelikow), that proposed to enhance the OVP's role in NSC operations and make Cheney chair of the principals' committee, which consisted of the secretaries of state and defense, the vice president, and the national security adviser. The committee would presumably meet regularly to discuss, refine, and narrow the issues for subsequent presidential decision. Previous vice presidents had not always joined the principals' committee, and chairing the group was normally part of the NSC adviser's coordinating role. Rice secured Bush's opposition to this proposal, Hadley apparently spoke independently to Cheney or Libby, and the OVP withdrew the suggestion.[56]

The effort to make Cheney chair of the committee may have been a mistake, a case of staff overreach, as some have suggested. Yet the episode reveals something about decision making in the Bush White House. Bush's support of Rice as principals' committee chair was decisive. Bush, not Cheney, was the president. Indeed, the insistence that Bush, not Cheney, was in charge is a recurring theme in the Miller Center's oral histories. Nicholas Calio, who worked closely with both men as legislative liaison, said the idea that Cheney ran things was "totally out of sync with the facts." Rove said it was "ridiculous," and Miers thought the suggestion reflected an "underestimation" of Bush. Bartlett described Cheney as "very deferential" to Bush in all settings. Such perspectives of the Bush-Cheney dynamic might be discounted if expressed only by longtime Bush associates, but others with less reason to safeguard Bush's reputation are equally insistent that Bush dominated the relationship. Gen. Tommy Franks rejected the idea that Cheney was pulling the strings, as did Treasury Secretary Snow, who described Bush as the "brains of the operation" and the "decider." Michael Chertoff, who saw Bush and Cheney frequently during the second term, said that "the President was the President, and everybody else was at a different level," including Cheney. Rumsfeld dismissed the idea that Cheney made the decisions as "utter nonsense."[57] As will be shown later, Bush and Cheney operated consistent with this understanding, even though Bush valued Cheney's contributions.

Cheney's Self-Imposed Structural Limits

Cheney imposed boundaries on himself based on his use of OVP resources. He sometimes claimed that because he was unencumbered by the presidency's ceremonial duties, he could focus on intelligence and other matters that interested him. Yet Cheney's choices about what to work on were not simply an artifact of not having to pardon turkeys before Thanksgiving or welcome championship sports teams.[58] Instead, Cheney structured his vice presidency to emphasize certain matters while minimizing or even excluding others.[59] Though he was formally a generalist, Cheney ignored many domestic and some diplomatic matters, narrowing his areas of influence and preserving resources for issues that mattered to him.

With some exceptions, Cheney focused heavily on national security issues. Indeed, Powell complained that the vice president created a second NSC in the OVP that adversely affected the "information flow" and caused "a great deal of confusion" in foreign policy. Cheney visited America's intelligence agencies during his first weeks in office and met with their leaders.[60] He had a voracious appetite for intelligence (John Negroponte, Michael Hayden), and Edelman called him "the closest student of intelligence of anybody in the administration."[61] He studied raw intelligence, scheduled special briefings, and solicited supplemental information.[62] Cheney, along with Libby, received the presidential daily briefing early every morning at his official residence at the Naval Observatory, supplemented by "behind the tab" items responding to Cheney's earlier inquiries. He then attended Bush's briefing in the Oval Office. Sometimes Cheney asked that Bush be briefed on "behind the tab" material,[63] or he raised questions during the silence while Bush read.

Cheney was welcome to participate when Bush met foreign leaders, but his foreign policy interests were "particular." They included the Middle East, Iraq, Russia, Europe, and Asia but not Latin America.[64] "I didn't spend a lot of time on Cuba," Cheney observed, even though many others had shown interest in that nation.[65] Bush's creation of the Millennium Challenge Corporation (MCC) and the President's Emergency Plan for AIDS Relief (PEPFAR) allowed the president to incorporate moral teachings to address humanitarian problems in Africa,[66] but Cheney played no apparent role in those initiatives (Mark Dybul),[67] which were sufficiently important to merit almost an entire chapter in Bush's memoir.[68]

In addition to advising the president, Cheney assumed some operational assignments. For instance, Bush assigned Cheney to chair an energy policy task force, and the vice president defended its proposed energy strategy in some high-profile speeches.[69] Cheney also attended weekly Senate Republican policy lunches, where he rarely spoke;[70] however, his presence gave his fellow Republicans "direct access" (Gregg). He worked to secure votes to pass Bush's 2001 tax cut, even speaking on Rhode Island radio to pressure moderate Republican Lincoln Chafee to support it. Cheney's tactics may have played a role in the Republicans' loss of the Senate when Vermont moderate Jim Jeffords switched parties in May 2001.[71] That spring, Bush assigned Cheney to analyze America's homeland security.[72] Later, Cheney helped broker the compromise between House and Senate Republicans that produced the 2003 tax cut.[73]

At times, Cheney exploited his access to Bush "to short-circuit the system."[74] After Environmental Protection Agency administrator Christine Todd Whitman announced that the United States would address climate change by reducing carbon dioxide emissions in ways consistent with a Bush campaign position, four Republican senators sought clarification from the president. Cheney's staffers submitted a memo recommending that Bush moderate his policy because the science on global warming was allegedly inconclusive. Before Whitman's meeting with Bush on March 13, Cheney obtained Bush's signature on a letter to the four senators denying that "the government should impose on power plants mandatory emissions reductions for carbon dioxide, which is not a 'pollutant' under the Clean Air Act."[75] When Rice belatedly learned of the letter, she asked Bush to include language to mollify allied nations, only to learn that Bush had already signed off on it. Whitman arrived as Cheney was departing to hand-deliver the letter. Responding to Rice's call, Powell raced to the White House, but he arrived too late to try to reverse Bush's decision. The letter provoked American allies, who read it as a disavowal of the Kyoto Protocols,[76] and Powell lamented Bush's failure to lay the necessary groundwork. Bolten characterized Cheney's ability to persuade Bush to shift his position without input from Powell or Whitman as "a rare policy process foul up" on the domestic side,[77] whereas Powell regarded it as one of several instances in which the OVP hijacked foreign policy.

Cheney's intervention was related to his leadership of Bush's energy task force, whose recommendations emphasized fossil fuels. This focus generated litigation based on the perception that Cheney's group engaged with energy producers but not with environmentalists.[78] The task force gave Cheney a forum to assert an executive branch prerogative to operate without disclosing the groups with which it met. Bush backed Cheney, notwithstanding pressure from within the West Wing to surrender the information.[79] Some Bush aides, including Bartlett, thought the political cost exceeded the claimed legal benefit.

Yet Cheney rarely weighed in on domestic policy issues (Bolten, Bridgeland). Neither Bush's memoir nor Cheney's suggests that the vice president had any role in No Child Left Behind, an issue that was important to Bush.[80] Margaret Spellings, Bush's domestic adviser, confirms that Cheney was not involved. In fact, former Speaker of the House John Boehner reveals that Cheney favored a conservative amendment to empower the states that would have been a poison pill for Senate Democrats. Cheney was visibly unhappy when Bush accepted Boehner's recommendation that he oppose the amendment to enhance the chance of Congress passing the measure.[81] On another issue, Bush devoted substantial time to deciding whether federal funds should support research on the use of embryonic stem cells for the treatment of certain diseases. It was "a big, big decision" for Bush, but Cheney "didn't have any role in the decision. I didn't work on that problem," he said.[82] Neither Bush's memoirs, Cheney's memoirs, nor the oral histories suggest that Cheney was significantly involved with the Medicare reform proposal that created a prescription drug benefit.[83] In 2005 Cheney deflected Bush's request that he lead a task force dealing with Hurricane Katrina, which the vice president viewed as a symbolic assignment, and he limited his involvement to a short visit to the affected area.[84]

When the vice president did engage in domestic issues, Bush sometimes rejected his advice. The Supreme Court was deliberating whether state universities could consider race in admissions decisions, and Cheney favored arguing against the constitutionality of affirmative action because racial diversity was not a compelling state interest. Bush rejected this position (Theodore Olson), asserting instead that the plans under review were too broad to be constitutional. Cheney and the OVP were hostile to the faith-based initiative (James Towey), another issue that was important to Bush.[85] And although Bush's criticism of Senate minority leader Trent Lott's racially insensitive tribute to Sen. Strom Thurmond led to Lott's replacement by Frist, Cheney disagreed with the administration's apparent abandonment of his friend Lott.[86]

National security issues interested Cheney most. Upon taking office, he requested an intelligence memo regarding Iraqi dictator Saddam Hussein's support of terror and his connection to the George H. W. Bush assassination plot and the 1993 World Trade Center attack.[87] Bush's first foreign visit, to Mexico, was disrupted by news that American planes enforcing no-fly zones had triggered Iraq's air-raid defenses, leading to a US bombing response that allegedly killed and wounded Iraqi civilians, setting off international criticism. Rice, when briefed on the incident, had failed to ask questions that might have alerted her to the possibility of the mission disrupting Bush's visit. Cheney, however, was pleased that the administration had sent an early warning to Saddam Hussein.[88] On another issue, Cheney, unlike Powell, expressed strong misgivings about engaging with North Korea. When Powell sent assistant secretary of state James Kelly to North Korea in February 2004 with approved instructions, Cheney used his access to Bush to have those instructions changed without timely advice from the State Department.[89] "Cheney had the ability to go in and see the President on many occasions and suddenly something happens," Powell later complained.

Yet Cheney did not always prevail in early national security debates. A midair collision between a navy reconnaissance plane and a Chinese fighter in late March 2001 provoked an international incident when the American crew made an emergency landing in China and the Chinese pilot was killed. Bush approved the conciliatory statements recommended by Powell and Rice, but Cheney thought them too accommodating.[90] Then, Bush kept a peacekeeping force in Bosnia, despite Cheney's and Rumsfeld's recommendations to remove it.[91] Later in August 2003 Cheney and Rumsfeld opposed US intervention in Liberia to encourage its tyrannical leader, Charles Taylor, to resign.[92] When Bush decided to give a speech to the UN General Assembly calling for the creation of a Palestinian state, Cheney's office "grumbled."[93] Cheney opposed Bush's decision to reaffirm his support for a Palestinian state in his June 24, 2002, Rose Garden speech, although he strongly supported Bush's call for Palestinian leader Yasir Arafat's replacement by elected "new leaders, not compromised by terror."[94]

September 11, 2001

Shortly after a hijacked plane struck the second tower of the World Trade Center, a Secret Service agent forcibly moved Cheney from his West Wing office to the PEOC. As Rice, Bolten, and other officials assembled there, Bolten recalled that Cheney "took the center seat, took charge," and was on the phone multiple times with Bush, who had started the day promoting his education bill at a Florida elementary school. Cheney refused to move to a safer location, preferring to stay where he was and preserve communication with Bush. Cheney advised Bush against returning to the capital during their early calls.[95] When another hijacked plane was reported to be headed to Washington, a military aide asked Cheney for permission to shoot or force it down, which Cheney calmly gave. The military aide asked again, a repetition Bolten attributed either to protocol or to Cheney's calm response. Not knowing whether Bush had authorized such an order, Bolten urged Cheney to alert Bush, which he did. Rove claims Bush previously authorized such an order and later reconfirmed it.[96] The 9/11 Commission was unclear when Bush actually authorized the shoot-down order. Throughout the day, Edelman recalled, Cheney was "incredibly focused," calm, and "several steps ahead of everybody else in the room."[97]

September 11 transformed Bush's presidency and Cheney's vice presidency. Tellingly, Cheney began his memoir with a ten-page prologue entitled "September 11, 2001." High-level decision makers wondered whether they could have anticipated 9/11 and sought to prevent a reoccurrence. Cheney's continuity-of-government concerns caused him to frequent "undisclosed locations," which often made him a virtual participant, removed him from normal West Wing interactions, and generated media caricatures.[98] Yet the new priority of national and homeland security increased the perceived value of Cheney's experience, especially his past service as secretary of defense. The war on terror became "omnipresent," said Bush adviser Joel Kaplan. "It was the purpose of the administration, protecting the country. It infused everything we did."

That new focus dominated Cheney's activities for the remaining seven years of the Bush administration. Cheney played a leading role in formulating and advocating administration policies related to the war on terror. Significantly, when Bush met with his national security advisers at Camp David on the weekend after 9/11, it was Cheney who placed the events in context for a national and international audience during a riveting Sunday morning interview on *Meet the Press*, providing a window into his thinking. People needed to understand, Cheney said, that "things have changed," that the "world shifted in some respects" due to circumstances that were "qualitatively different" from prior acts of terrorism. The United States was now confronted, Cheney said, with "a long-term proposition" that would require years of work to dismantle global terrorist networks. Cheney had "no doubt" that Osama bin Laden and al Qaeda had "played a significant role" in 9/11. Terrorists and those who harbored them would face "the full wrath of the United States" as America used a range of resources, including working through "the dark side . . . to spend time in the shadows of the intelligence world."[99]

Whether 9/11 changed Cheney or simply brought latent attitudes to the surface, he acknowledged that he became more "aggressive," "hard-nosed," and "iron assed."[100] Fear of subsequent attacks gripped decision makers. Five years later, when Robert Gates returned to government, he told Edelman how struck he was by the degree to which people in the administration had been "traumatized by 9/11 and the concern that . . . we can't let this happen again on our watch."[101] One humorous moment revealed that anxiety: While receiving a CIA briefing at the Naval Observatory, Cheney admonished his dog, Dave, to get off the furniture. On hearing Cheney's command, "Dave, get down," Cheney's CIA briefer, who was also named Dave, hit the floor.[102]

Cheney became preoccupied with the possibility of terrorists using nuclear, biological, or chemical weapons against the United States.[103] He embraced the so-called 1 percent doctrine—that is, "we had to bend the efforts of government" to prevent even low-probability attacks because the consequences would be so grave.[104] Cheney pushed for the production of vaccines against smallpox, anthrax, and other agents.[105] He helped create the Homeland Security Council in the White House and recommended Pennsylvania governor Tom Ridge to head it.[106] Addington was heavily involved in the legal aspects of national security issues, especially those relating to the war on terror, and he functioned as "a deputy White House counsel, who in some respects was more important than the White House counsel" (Zelikow).

At times, Cheney circumvented interagency processes and went straight to Bush for authorization of measures related to the war on terror. For instance, the Terrorist Surveillance Program (TSP) emerged after Cheney asked intelligence officials whether additional presidential authority would allow the National Security Agency (NSA) to obtain valuable intelligence. NSA leader Michael Hayden suggested some possibilities, and Cheney took Hayden to see Bush, who approved a program that included certain safeguards, such as a periodic reapproval requirement. The program was initiated without an interdepartmental review, and few people knew of its existence. In view of Cheney's intelligence background and Bush's confidence in him, Bush followed Cheney's advice in establishing the program and relied on him to implement it.[107]

In November 2001 Cheney's office played a major role in creating a system of military commissions under the Pentagon to handle unlawful combatants accused of committing war crimes. Because Cheney and some others were unhappy about the pace of interagency deliberations to address the subject, the OVP participated in an alternative process of drafting an order that excluded the Department of State, the NSC, and military officers. Attorney General John Ashcroft was upset that the proposed system did not rely on federal courts and the Department of Justice, and he was disturbed that personnel in his own department's Office of Legal Counsel had helped formulate the proposal. Cheney secured Bush's signature on a four-page order for military commissions at their weekly lunch. Neither Powell nor Rice nor other interested parties were aware of the document's existence or its signing, much less having an opportunity to express their opinions.[108] The arrangements were apparently made during conversations between Bush and Cheney, with the legal documents prepared by Addington in consulta-tion with White House counsel Gonzales's office.[109] Rice told Bush that the OVP and the White House counsel had done him a disservice and that a repeat performance would prompt her resignation. Bush acknowledged the mistake and said he thought the order had been circulated.[110] Rice viewed this episode as one of several in which Addington's skill at "bureaucratic warfare" distorted the process.[111]

After 9/11, Cheney was a prominent proponent of the view that mem-bers of al Qaeda and the Taliban were not entitled to the protections af-forded prisoners of war under the Geneva Conventions. He and the OVP participated in efforts to justify the use of enhanced interrogation tech-niques to elicit information from suspected terrorists.[112]

Cheney and Iraq Post-9/11

Cheney came to see military action against Iraq as part of a strategy to pro-tect America from terrorism. Initially, during discussions at Camp David a few days after 9/11, Cheney pushed back against Paul Wolfowitz's call for a war against Iraq, joining others in rejecting such action and support-ing a focus on Afghanistan and al Qaeda.[113] Yet Cheney was concerned that a terrorist attack on the United States using weapons of mass destruc-tion (WMD) might occur,[114] and he identified Iraq as a likely supplier of such weapons. Cheney aggressively pursued intelligence connecting Sad-dam Hussein and al Qaeda,[115] and he and allies in the Defense Department emphasized that connection,[116] despite CIA skepticism.[117] Cheney advised Bush to make certain that the Pentagon prioritized the preparation of plans for a possible military attack on Iraq and suggested that such planning be done at the Central Command Headquarters in Florida, where it would be less likely to leak than in Washington.[118]

In mid-March 2002 Cheney traveled to the Middle East for discussions with Arab leaders on various issues, including, as Edelman put it, "what do we do beyond Afghanistan and how do we deal with Iraq." Some of these leaders expressed misgivings about such a war, but Cheney assured them that Bush would not act precipitously and discussed logistical requests.[119]

By summer 2002, the NSC's discussions, under Cheney's influence, were focused on how, not whether, to attack Iraq. Powell and others in the State Department, however, voiced the concern that war with Iraq would dominate the Bush presidency, and Powell urged Bush to persuade the United Nations to return weapons inspectors to Iraq. As Bush considered his options in August 2002, Brent Scowcroft and James Baker, national security adviser and secretary of state, respectively, in the George H. W. Bush administration (and the former president's close friends), published separate opinion pieces counseling against aggressive action toward Iraq.[120] Cheney then spoke to the Veterans of Foreign Wars in Nashville on August 26, 2002, asserting that Saddam was amassing WMD to use against America and its allies and that returning inspectors to Iraq was pointless and dangerous.[121] Cheney's speech blindsided others in the administration, and Bush instructed Rice to tell Cheney that he was considering the very course of action Cheney had disparaged. Cheney denied any intent to limit Bush's options and, in a second speech, read language he had requested from Rice. At the NSC meeting on September 7, Cheney and Rumsfeld recommended that Saddam be directed to disarm quickly or face war. Powell urged another UN resolution. Visiting British prime minister Tony Blair favored that course, too. Bush accepted the Powell-Blair approach, and at the UN Bush declared that if Saddam did not reveal his weapons program in accordance with the UN resolution, he would face war.[122]

Cheney became impatient with Bush during the winter of 2002–2003. "Are you going to take care of this guy, or not?" Cheney challenged Bush at one of their weekly lunches. Bush replied that he was not yet ready to move against Saddam.[123] This anecdote reveals not only Cheney's commitment to military action against Saddam but also the hierarchical nature of the Bush-Cheney relationship, even on overriding matters of national security. Cheney was an adviser—sometimes a blunt and forceful one—but Bush made the decisions when he was ready to do so.

Bush ordered an attack against Iraq on March 19, 2003, after Saddam's response to inspectors was deemed insufficient. Bush's decision was consistent with Cheney's counsel, although none of the president's principal advisers argued against it. When late-arriving (and ultimately incorrect) intelligence regarding Saddam's whereabouts seemed to present an opportunity to eliminate him at the war's outset, Bush summoned his national security advisers to consider whether to modify the war plan and attack that location first. After Bush's other advisers endorsed the change, Bush excused everyone except Cheney, and only after receiving the vice president's agreement did he order the modification.[124]

The fact that Bush valued Cheney's counsel on Iraq did not mean he always followed it. He rejected Cheney's advice on some important matters even as he moved closer to war with Iraq. After evidence developed in July 2002 that chemical weapons were being produced in northern Iraq near Iran, Cheney and some other advisers favored a missile strike followed by a military investigation. Bush declined to act because Powell and Rice warned that doing so would complicate the effort to build a war coalition.[125] Later that summer, Bush sided with Blair and Powell in seeking a UN resolution and other diplomatic measures that Cheney opposed.[126] Cheney reportedly argued that Bush did not need congressional authorization to use military force in Iraq, but Bush sought and received it anyway.[127] And Bush was more deliberative in deciding to move against Iraq than Cheney thought prudent. Ari Fleischer, Bush's first White House press secretary, later observed that Bush generally sided with Cheney regarding "the objective" in Iraq but often not the means of achieving it.

The 9/11 Commission's interview with Bush and Cheney in late April 2004 provided another window into the dynamic between them. Zelikow, executive director of the commission, recalled that, based on "the very common supposition back then" of Bush as a "figurehead," many members anticipated that Cheney would carry the burden of the discussion. The session "surprised all of them because Bush utterly dominated the conversation, did 95 percent of the talking without notes, and was clearly in command of the subject."

First-Term Rough Spots

Although American troops reached Baghdad in early April 2003 and Saddam was eventually captured, a stream of adverse developments followed that damaged Cheney's reputation and influence. WMD were not found and the situation in Iraq turned chaotic, preventing an early withdrawal of American troops. The Iraq engagement proved to be more complicated, protracted, and costly than anticipated, which necessarily impacted the credibility of its primary administration advocates, including Cheney.

In ways that were not foreseen initially, Cheney was affected by news reports that a former ambassador (later identified as Joseph Wilson) had gone to Niger at the OVP's request to investigate allegations of Iraq's attempt to purchase uranium. Wilson concluded that these reports were false, but the allegation had already appeared as part of the administration's argument that Iraq was developing WMD. Although the OVP had not dispatched Wilson or received reports of his findings, Libby's efforts to discredit the story ultimately resulted in his indictment, trial, and conviction of perjury during Bush's second term. These events focused unwanted scrutiny on the OVP, created tension within the West Wing, and ultimately cost Cheney a crucial associate. Later, despite Cheney's disagreement, Bush and Rice decided to admit that the president should not have relied on the uranium claim.[128]

In early March 2004 new Justice Department personnel concluded that an earlier legal analysis regarding part of the NSA's warrantless surveillance program (the TSP) was flawed and declined to reauthorize it, which was required for it to continue. In short order, the situation spun out of control. Cheney claimed that Bush might reauthorize the program without the attorney general's approval; then, high White House officials attempted unsuccessfully to obtain that approval late one night in Ashcroft's hospital room (where he was recovering from gallbladder surgery). Multiple high-ranking Justice Department officials threatened to resign. When Bush belatedly learned of the pending debacle, he accommodated the lawyers' objections without speaking to Cheney,[129] saving the program and averting an election year disaster that probably would have compromised his reelection.[130] Bush felt "blindsided" and attributed the situation to "bad judgment."[131] Because Cheney had handled the situation, presumably he was to blame.

Cheney volunteered to remove himself from the 2004 ticket.[132] Bush discussed the offer with Card, Rove, Bartlett, and others and weighed alternative selections, including Frist and Rice (Bartlett). The vice president had become a target of criticism, and replacing him would address the widespread perception that Cheney, not Bush, was in charge. Ultimately, Bush decided that Cheney should stay. Years later, Bush noted that he had not chosen Cheney as a "political asset," and he appreciated that Cheney accepted "any assignment" Bush gave him, provided "his unvarnished opinions," and recognized that Bush "made the final decisions."[133] They were reelected in 2004, this time with a popular vote majority (50.7 percent) and by 286–251 in the Electoral College.

The Second Term

Cheney was a less imposing figure during Bush's second term. The formal arrangements regarding access to the president remained, yet he often found himself on the losing side of important issues. Cheney attributed the new reality to Bush's greater experience and comfort as president.[134] Surely that played a part. Bush was, as Rice observed, "a different President in 2006 than he was in 2003." Bush was more secure, and experience had tempered him ideologically and tactically, so he was less receptive to some of Cheney's hard-line advice. And Bush had seen limits to Cheney's sagacity, such as when the war in Iraq followed a much worse trajectory than he (and others) had predicted and when Cheney mishandled the TSP reauthorization. With Rice replacing Powell at the State Department, Bush was prepared to try diplomatic approaches in areas where Cheney had misgivings. Rice's relationship with Bush made her a more formidable adversary for Cheney than Powell had been. Cheney and Rice had intense arguments during the second term,[135] including occasions when they "argued vehemently head to head in front of" Bush, according to Zelikow. Bolten estimated that Bush sided with Rice 70 percent of the time during the three years Bolten was chief of staff (2006–2009).[136] Rice was "in the catbird seat" during Bush's second term, observed John Negroponte, director of national intelligence and deputy secretary of state, whereas Cheney was "disengaging somewhat or getting more tired" and was not as "proactive" as Negroponte expected. Elliott Abrams rated Cheney among the three most influential people in Bush's presidency during the first term but not the second.

Libby's indictment and resignation in late October 2005 cost Cheney a valued aide and weakened the OVP. Abrams thought Cheney had a "terrifically effective staff until [Libby] left," and his departure "diminished Cheney's effectiveness."

A few months later, in February 2006, Cheney's obtuse response compounded the public relations fallout after he accidentally shot a fellow hunter, Harry Whittington, while quail hunting in Texas. Cheney decided that the local Corpus Christi newspaper should be notified first rather than communicating with the White House press office and alerting the national media. Disclosure of the incident was therefore delayed, feeding unflattering perceptions of Cheney as secretive. Cheney "shut down all internal communication" with Bush's public relations staff following the event (Bartlett). The White House staff was prevented from "say[ing] what they wanted to say" publicly about Cheney's mishandling of the situation, but Bush's former press secretary did (Fleischer). Ultimately, Bush interceded, and Cheney gave an interview to Fox News.[137]

Cheney battled to preserve aspects of the war on terror. He failed to dissuade Sen. John McCain from proposing a bill to ban torture during the interrogation of detainees, and Bush ultimately dispatched Hadley, not Cheney, to negotiate with Congress. With veto-proof majorities supporting the legislation, Bush signed it, but Addington inserted language in the signing statement to preserve some flexibility.[138] In June 2006 the Supreme Court held in *Hamdan v. Rumsfeld* that Common Article 3 of the Geneva Conventions protected detainees against "humiliating and degrading" behavior and "outrages upon personal dignity." Cheney and Addington wanted to attack the court's decision and deprive it of jurisdiction legislatively, but Bush decided to pursue legislation consistent with the decision, and Hadley was again sent to negotiate with Congress.[139] In August 2006 Rice argued that Bush should publicly acknowledge the CIA's interrogation and detention practices and transfer any remaining detainees from CIA sites to Guantánamo Bay for trial. Cheney favored having the CIA retain custody of the detainees. Bush accepted Rice's arguments, and his speech the following month announced the transfers, although he defended the interrogation program and stated that information it produced had helped prevent attacks and save lives.[140]

Cheney, along with other members of Bush's national security team, recognized that the situation in Iraq was deteriorating in 2006, and they began to question the Pentagon's strategy. Cheney did not initiate the review process that ensued, but he fully supported Bush's decision to send additional troops to Iraq to address the counterinsurgency. Cheney regularly listened to advisers from outside the current Pentagon hierarchy, and these briefings helped shape his conclusion that the mission in Iraq needed redefinition.[141] After Cheney met with Gen. David Petraeus at Fort Leavenworth in January 2006, his office used its relationship with former OVP staffer and then undersecretary of defense Edelman to obtain a "back-channel" draft of the army manual on counterinsurgency, which Petraeus was revising, so Cheney could read it.[142] Cheney also listened to retired four-star general Jack Keane, a surge advocate, whose views had "an important impact" on Cheney's level of confidence that the surge was both "necessary" and "doable" (John Hannah, Cheney's national security adviser). The OVP's Iraq reassessment occurred alongside studies at the NSC, the Pentagon, and elsewhere.[143] Cheney was perhaps content to take a less visible role in the process because Bush's surge strategy altered the approach of Cheney's friend and mentor Rumsfeld. Hadley recalled that Cheney was a "closet supporter" of the surge but was not "particularly vocal" out of deference to his old friend.[144]

After considering Rumsfeld's removal several times, Bush replaced him with Robert Gates in late 2006, shortly before deciding to launch the surge. Knowing that Cheney was "always a strong defender" of Rumsfeld and would oppose replacing him, Bush advised the vice president of his decision without asking his counsel.[145] "At that point, he wasn't seeking my advice. He knew what my advice would be. He just wanted to let me know," Cheney recalled.[146] Cheney soon became the "outlier" in Bush's national security team, as Bush, Rice, Gates, and Hadley agreed on most important matters.[147]

By late 2006, Cheney was focused on certain "unfinished business" of the Bush administration, especially with regard to Iran, because he feared the next administration would be unwilling to take the steps he thought necessary.[148] Cheney spoke of military action against Iran, which Bush and Gates opposed.[149] In particular, Gates opposed acceding to Israeli requests for military equipment that would facilitate its ability to attack Iran, and Cheney favored granting those requests and allowing Israel to attack Iran if the United States would not. Bush refused Israel's requests for military aid but agreed to greater collaboration with Israel on intelligence and other measures to curtail Iran's nuclear program.[150]

After learning that North Korea had built a nuclear reactor for Syria, Cheney urged Bush during a June 17, 2007, NSC meeting at the White House to bomb the reactor, but there was no support for his position. Later that month, Cheney again pushed for destruction of the reactor, but when Bush asked whether anyone else present at the NSC meeting agreed with Cheney, no one did—nor did Bush. Although Bush preferred diplomacy, Israel rejected that course and ultimately destroyed the reactor.[151]

Cheney was also unhappy with US efforts to address North Korea's nuclear threat, believing the State Department was overly optimistic that the country was moving toward denuclearization.[152] Cheney frequently phoned Hadley because he was "really exercised" over Bush's North Korea policy, although Cheney emphasized that he was simply expressing his views.[153] Cheney disagreed with Bush's decision to remove North Korea from the list of state sponsors of terrorism.[154]

Cheney's decline in clout cost the OVP influence, as did other events. In addition to the loss of Cheney's allies Libby and Rumsfeld, Bolten was a stronger counterweight than Card had been. Moreover, although earlier White House counsels Gonzales and Miers had deferred to Addington regarding national security matters, Fred Fielding did not when he assumed that role during Bush's last two years. Cheney's second-term national security staffers "picked their spots" and operated in just a few areas of high interest (Zelikow, counselor to Rice). Abrams, too, found that during the second term Cheney did not engage in some national security debates; instead, he focused his influence with Bush on a few matters that were most important to him. Even so, the OVP remained more active in national security than in domestic policy during the second term. By the time Karl Zinsmeister became director of the Domestic Policy Council in May 2006, it often seemed that "the Vice President's office had given up on actually trying to make a difference and changing anything on the domestic policy side."

Cheney disagreed with the Justice Department's position in *District of Columbia v. Heller*, believing that it did not go far enough to invalidate federal gun regulations.[155] The vice president signed an amicus brief that members of the Senate and House submitted on the Second Amendment. With Bush's permission, Bolten admonished Cheney and Addington regarding the "process foul" Cheney had committed by signing a brief at odds with the administration's position.[156] When Cheney justified his action as being grounded in his role as president of the Senate, Bolten reminded him that he was Bush's vice president and told Addington that any repetition would result in the OVP being moved to the Senate end of Pennsylvania Avenue. The conversations occurred in good humor, but they signaled that the OVP was not prevailing in the West Wing as it once had.[157]

Yet Cheney remained a forceful public voice defending the policies of the Bush administration, especially those related to the war on terror and Iraq, which he had helped design. He attributed the absence of a mass casualty attack on American soil after 9/11 to the TSP, enhanced interrogation, and other programs the Bush administration had put in place, and he insisted that the war in Iraq had left the United States and the world better off.[158]

In their closing days, Cheney pushed for Libby to receive a presidential pardon (Bush had already commuted his sentence), but the president's lawyers did not support this move.[159] When Bush decided against the pardon, Cheney accused him of "leaving a good man wounded on the field of battle" and was "deeply disappointed." Cheney called Bush's decision a "grave error," and he criticized the president for not making a "courageous" decision, implying that Bush had elevated his historical image over principle.[160] Bush feared his relationship with Cheney was ruptured.[161]

The Cheney vice presidency was an important part of the Bush presidency. Bush, Cheney, and others in the administration understood what many on the outside did not: Cheney acted as Bush's subordinate. Cheney served as a valued adviser to and operator for Bush. Although Cheney undertook some important specific assignments, advising the president was his principal role. That role reflected a hierarchy in which Cheney's function was to inform, persuade, and serve the "decider."

Cheney focused his attention primarily on national security matters and certain selected domestic issues. He was heavily engaged in important issues of the Bush presidency, including the war on terror and Iraq, but his relatively passive role in many other policy discussions meant that his tenure lacked the breadth of some other vice presidents. His decision to absent himself from various international and domestic issues may have reflected Cheney's own lack of interest in those areas, a necessary prioritization of his time and resources, a strategic decision not to try to shape decisions in which Bush was personally invested, or some combination of these considerations.

At times, Cheney circumvented normal processes to obtain action from Bush. These occasions do not detract from Cheney's recognition of Bush's authority. On the contrary, the fact that Cheney needed Bush's approval to shape policy confirms the hierarchy of the Bush-Cheney relationship. Although Cheney often contributed to the policy process with his comments and questions, his commitment to certain ends sometimes spurred him to take advantage of his access to Bush without allowing other voices to be heard. On those occasions, Bush could have insisted on hearing the views of others before acting. Bush's failure to do so suggests that he agreed with Cheney or did not want to engage in more discussion. An unorthodox process produced the vice president Bush wanted, but it did not always yield the best policy when incomplete deliberation left problems unexposed until it was too late.

Cheney entered the vice presidency with some advantages relative to many other recent vice presidents, especially during the first term. His prior service in a range of governmental offices strengthened his position, especially given Bush's more limited background. Cheney's work with Bush on the vice-presidential selection process and the 2000–2001 transition gave him valuable experience and rapport with Bush before taking office. His lack of presidential ambitions removed a distraction, encouraged the perception of a common agenda, and contributed to Cheney's ability to focus on issues of importance to him, although there were costs that became apparent later in the administration.

The OVP's heavy focus on national security issues may have caused some confusion and dysfunction within the administration, especially during the first term, when Cheney would occasionally short-circuit normal interdepartmental decision-making processes and present such matters directly to Bush for action. That experience should serve as a cautionary tale for future presidents. Over time, Bush became more confident and knowledgeable, and he was largely responsible for making Cheney's second term less consequential than the first. Cheney remained a player with a seat at the table and a respected voice in discussions, but Bush increasingly chose not to follow his advice. Cheney's eight years as vice president remind us that political relationships, like others, are dynamic, and the political influence of vice presidents and other presidential advisers and operatives is not constant. It varies over time and space and depends on a range of factors, including performance and a president's perception of to what extent a subordinate can help him or her shape and achieve administration goals as they evolve.

Notes

1. Shirley Anne Warshaw, *The Co-Presidency of Bush and Cheney* (Stanford, CA: Stanford University Press, 2009), 1, 2, 9, 240.

2. See, e.g., Stephen F. Hayes, *Cheney: The Untold Story of America's Most Powerful and Controversial Vice President* (New York: HarperCollins, 2007); David Nather, "A Power Surge under Scrutiny," *CQ Weekly*, June 11, 2007, 1734.

3. Unless otherwise noted, quotations and attributions in this chapter (individual sources are sometimes identified parenthetically) are from either the Miller Center's George W. Bush Oral History or Southern Methodist University's Center for Presidential History's Elections of 2004 or "The Last Card in the Deck": The Surge in Iraq series. All forty-four of the originally published Miller Center interviews were reviewed (others have not yet been released), but those quoted or cited for specific information in this chapter were those of Elliott Abrams, Daniel J. Bartlett, Joshua Bolten (including comments of Joel Kaplan and Kristen Silverberg), John Bridgeland, Nicholas E. Calio, George Casey, Michael Chertoff, Mark R. Dybul, Eric Edelman, Fred Fielding, Ari Fleischer, Tommy Franks, Robert Gates, Judd Gregg, Stephen J. Hadley, Michael Hayden, Keith Hennessey, Clay Johnson, Jay Lefkowitz, Harriet Miers, John Negroponte, Theodore B. Olson, Peter Pace, Colin L. Powell and Richard L. Armitage, Karl Rove, John Snow, Margaret Spellings, James Towey, Philip Zelikow, and Karl Zinsmeister. The only interview quoted from the Elections of 2004 series was Dick Cheney's. Interviews used

from the Surge in Iraq series were those of Josh Bolten, Dick Cheney, Eric Edelman, Robert Gates, Stephen J. Hadley, John P. Hannah, and Condoleezza Rice. Because Bolten, Cheney, Edelman, Gates, and Hadley are quoted from both sources, notes identify which series the quotes came from.

4. David Rothkopf, "Why It's Too Early to Tell How History Will Judge the Iran and Greece Deals," *Foreign Policy*, July 14, 2015, https://foreignpolicy.com/2015/07/14/why -its-too-early-to-tell-how-history-will-judge-the-iran-and-greece-deals/. For an insightful discussion of revisionism, see James M. Banner Jr., *The Ever-Changing Past: Why All History Is Revisionist History* (New Haven, CT: Yale University Press, 2021).

5. Peter Baker, *Days of Fire: Bush and Cheney in the White House* (New York: Doubleday, 2013), 42; Richard B. Cheney, Edwin Meese III, and Douglas W. Kmiec, "The Vice President—More than an Afterthought?" *Pepperdine Law Review* 44, 3 (2017): 535, 543.

6. George W. Bush, *Decision Points* (New York: Broadway, 2010), 65; Dick Cheney with Liz Cheney, *In My Time: A Personal and Political Memoir* (New York: Threshold, 2011), 254–255. Bush states that the request to run the search came in the initial conversation, whereas Cheney places it a few weeks later.

7. Joel K. Goldstein, *The White House Vice Presidency: The Path to Significance, Mondale to Biden* (Lawrence: University Press of Kansas, 2016), 190–192.

8. Cheney, *In My Time*, 255–256.

9. Karl Rove, *Courage and Consequence: My Life as a Conservative in the Fight* (New York: Threshold, 2010), 167.

10. Cheney, *In My Time*, 256; Rove, *Courage and Consequence*, 167.

11. James Rosen, *Cheney One on One: A Candid Conversation with America's Most Controversial Statesman* (Washington, DC: Regnery, 2015), 229.

12. Cheney, *In My Time*, 257–258.

13. Bush, *Decision Points*, 67; Rove, *Courage and Consequence*, 167–168.

14. Bolten and Silverberg, Miller Center Oral History, I:77–78.

15. Goldstein, *White House Vice Presidency*, 210–211.

16. Cheney, *In My Time*, 258.

17. Rove, *Courage and Consequence*, 168, 169.

18. Bush, *Decision Points*, 68.

19. Bush, 68; Cheney, *In My Time*, 259.

20. Bush, *Decision Points*, 68; Cheney, *In My Time*, 259.

21. Rosen, *Cheney One on One*, 104–105, 117; Cheney et al., "Vice President," 541.

22. Bush, *Decision Points*, 69; Cheney, *In My Time*, 259.

23. Bush, *Decision Points*, 69; Rove, *Courage and Consequence*, 168, 169; Baker, *Days of Fire*, 57.

24. Bush, *Decision Points*, 69; Rove, *Courage and Consequence*, 168, 169.

25. Baker, *Days of Fire*, 57.

26. Cheney, *In My Time*, 262–264; Rove, *Courage and Consequence*, 170–171; Bush, *Decision Points*, 69.

27. Cheney, *In My Time*, 263–264.

28. Rove, *Courage and Consequence*, 169–170; Bush, *Decision Points*, 69.

29. Bush, *Decision Points*, 70.

30. Bush, 70; Cheney, *In My Time*, 265.

31. Cheney et al., "Vice President," 541; Cheney, *In My Time*, 254–255.

32. Bolten, Miller Center Oral History, I:78.

33. Barton Gellman, *Angler: The Cheney Vice Presidency* (New York: Penguin, 2008), 4–6.

34. Goldstein, *White House Vice Presidency*, 218–219.

35. Goldstein, 199–201, 217–218.

36. Richard L. Berke, "Bush Is Seeking Safe and Solid Running Mate," *New York Times*, July 23, 2000, 1, 18.

37. Frank Bruni, "Bush Names Cheney, Citing 'Integrity' and 'Experience,'" *New York Times*, July 26, 2000, A1, A18.

38. Cheney, Center for Presidential History, Election of 2004.

39. Text of Dick Cheney's speech, August 2, 2000, https://www.cbsnews.com/news/text-of-dick-cheneys-speech/.

40. Bolten, Miller Center Oral History, I:119.

41. Condoleezza Rice, *No Higher Honor: A Memoir of My Years in Washington* (New York: Crown, 2011), 18; Rove, *Courage and Consequence*, 220.

42. Rice, *No Higher Honor*, 10 (describing Hadley's selection as NSC deputy).

43. Robert Draper, *To Start a War: How the Bush Administration Took America into Iraq* (New York: Penguin, 2020), 98.

44. Cheney, *In My Time*, 298.

45. Gellman, *Angler*, 61–67.

46. See generally Goldstein, *White House Vice Presidency*, 129–141, 147–148.

47. Bolten, Miller Center Oral History, I:119.

48. Goldstein, *White House Vice Presidency*, 164.

49. See generally Goldstein.

50. Bolten, Miller Center Oral History, I:129.

51. Rosen, *Cheney One on One*, 117–118.

52. Jack Goldsmith, *The Terror Presidency: Law and Judgment inside the Bush Administration* (New York: W. W. Norton, 2007), 77–78.

53. Edelman, Miller Center Oral History, 27.

54. Rice, *No Higher Honor*, 17.

55. Donald Rumsfeld, *Known and Unknown: A Memoir* (New York: Sentinel, 2011), 320.

56. Rice, *No Higher Honor*, 17; Draper, *To Start a War*, 98; Baker, *Days of Fire*, 87–88.

57. Rumsfeld, *Known and Unknown*, 320.

58. Rosen, *Cheney One on One*, 113.

59. Baker, *Days of Fire*, 110 (quoting Cheney aide Dean McGrath, stating that Cheney did not engage in all areas).

60. Rosen, *Cheney One on One*, 105–106.

61. Edelman, Miller Center Oral History, 39.

62. Cheney, *In My Time*, 314–315, 413.

63. Rosen, *Cheney One on One*, 113–116.

64. Edelman, Miller Center Oral History, 26.

65. Cheney, Center for Presidential History, Surge in Iraq, 31.

66. Bolten and Silverberg, Miller Center Oral History, I:81–88.

67. Rice, *No Higher Honor*, 225–229.

68. Bush, *Decision Points*, 333–354.

69. Remarks by the vice president at the annual meeting of the Associated Press, April 30, 2001; remarks by the vice president to the Nuclear Energy Institute's 2001 Nuclear Energy Assembly, May 22, 2001; remarks by the vice president at the US Chamber of Commerce rally supporting the Bush administration's energy plan, May 25, 2001; all at https://georgewbush-whitehouse.archives.gov/vicepresident/news-speeches/index.html.

70. Cheney, *In My Time*, 307–308.

71. Gellman, *Angler*, 74–78.

72. Statement by the president on domestic preparedness against weapons of mass destruction, May 8, 2001, https://georgewbush-whitehouse.archives.gov/news/releases/2001/05/20010508.html.

73. Cheney, *In My Time*, 310–313.

74. Rosen, *Cheney One on One*, 234.

75. Letter from the president to Senators Hagel, Helms, Craig, and Roberts, March 13, 2001, https://georgewbush-whitehouse.archives.gov/news/releases/2001/03/20010314.html.

76. Rosen, *Cheney One on One*, 121–123; Rice, *No Higher Honor*, 41–42; Baker, *Days of Fire*, 95–97; Gellman, *Angler*, 82–90; Richard J. Lazarus, *The Rule of Five: Making Climate History at the Supreme Court* (Cambridge, MA: Belknap Press, 2020), 30–35; Douglas Jehl with Andrew C. Revkin, "Bush, in Reversal, Won't Seek Cut in Emissions of Carbon Dioxide," *New York Times*, March 14, 2001, A1.

77. Bolten, Miller Center Oral History, I:54.

78. Goldstein, *White House Vice Presidency*, 135.

79. Cheney, *In My Time*, 317–318; Joel K. Goldstein, "Cheney, Vice Presidential Power, and the War on Terror," *Presidential Studies Quarterly* 40, 1 (2010): 102, 113–114.

80. Bush, *Decision Points*, 272–277.

81. John Boehner, *On the House: A Washington Memoir* (New York: St. Martin's Press, 2021), 124–128.

82. Cheney, Center for Presidential History, Surge in Iraq, 31–32. Regarding Bush's focus on the issue, see Baker, *Days of Fire*, 110–112; Bush, *Decision Points*, 106–121.

83. See Bush, *Decision Points*, 281–284, where he does not mention Cheney in his discussion of Medicare reforms or list him as a member of his "Medicare team."

84. Cheney, *In My Time*, 429–432.

85. Bush, *Decision Points*, 279–281.

86. Baker, *Days of Fire*, 237–238.

87. Draper, *To Start a War*, 99–100.

88. Draper, 39; Rice, *No Higher Honor*, 28–29.

89. Baker, *Days of Fire*, 313–314.

90. Baker, 99–100.

91. Robert Draper, *Dead Certain: The Presidency of George W. Bush* (New York: Free Press, 2007), 281.

92. Rice, *No Higher Honor*, 229–233.

93. Rice, 132–134.

94. Baker, *Days of Fire*, 202–204; Rice, *No Higher Honor*, 143–147; Cheney, *In My Time*, 383–384.

95. Bolten, Miller Center Oral History, II:25; Rosen, *Cheney One on One*, 208; Cheney, *In My Time*, 2.

96. Bolten, Miller Center Oral History, II:27–28; Rove, *Courage and Consequence*, 253–254.

97. Edelman, Miller Center Oral History, 50–52.

98. Cheney, *In My Time*, 337–338.

99. Vice president appears on *Meet the Press* with Tim Russert, September 16, 2001, https://georgewbush-whitehouse.archives.gov/vicepresident/news-speeches/speeches/vp20010916.html.

100. Cheney et al., "Vice Presidency," 554–555.

101. Edelman, Miller Center Oral History, 57.

102. Edelman, 63–64; Draper, *To Start a War*, 101–102.

103. Rice, *No Higher Honor*, 98–102; Cheney, *In My Time*, 341–344, 384–386.

104. Edelman, Miller Center Oral History, 64.

105. Cheney, *In My Time*, 384–386.

106. Bolten, Miller Center Oral History I:93.

107. Rosen, *Cheney One on One*, 119–121; Cheney, *In My Time*, 348–350; Baker, *Days of Fire*, 163–165; Goldstein, "Cheney, Vice Presidential Power, and the War on Terror," 116–118.

108. Rosen, *Cheney One on One*, 233–234; Baker, *Days of Fire*, 173–175; Goldstein, "Cheney, Vice Presidential Power, and the War on Terror," 118–120.

109. Edelman, Miller Center Oral History, 64–66.

110. Hadley, Miller Center Oral History, 21–22.

111. Rice, *No Higher Honor*, 104–106.

112. Cheney, *In My Time*, 157–162; Gellman, *Angler*, 168–179; Baker, *Days of Fire*, 193–195; Goldstein, "Cheney, Vice Presidential Power, and the War on Terror," 120–121.

113. Rice, *No Higher Honor*, 87; Baker, *Days of Fire*, 143–145; Cheney, *In My Time*, 334.

114. Vice president appears on NBC's *Meet the Press*, December 9, 2001; interview of the vice president by Jim Angle of Fox TV News, December 11, 2001; remarks by the vice president to the Council of Foreign Relations, February 15, 2002; vice president appears on *Meet the Press* (NBC), March 24, 2002; all at https://georgewbush-whitehouse.archives.gov/vicepresident/news-speeches/index.html; Cheney, *In My Time*, 368–369.

115. Rosen, *Cheney One on One*, 252–255; Draper, *To Start a War*, 100–101, 134–135, 138.

116. Draper, *To Start a War*, 138–139.

117. Draper, 148–149, 153–155.

118. Cheney, *In My Time*, 369.

119. Cheney, 371–380; Draper, *To Start a War*, 94–95; Edelman, Miller Center Oral History, 60.

120. Baker, *Days of Fire*, 207–210.

121. Vice president speaks at VFW 103rd National Convention, Nashville, August 26,

2002, https://georgewbush-whitehouse.archives.gov/news/releases/2002/08/20020826
.html.

122. Rice, *No Higher Honor*, 179–181; Cheney, *In My Time*, 388–391; Bush, *Decision Points*, 237–240; Baker, *Days of Fire*, 207–212, 215–218.

123. Bush, *Decision Points*, 251.

124. Bush, 223–224, 253–254: Cheney, *In My Time*, 398–399; Baker, *Days of Fire*, 257–260.

125. Draper, *To Start a War*, 186–187; Rice, *No Higher Honor*, 177–178; Baker, *Days of Fire*, 204–205.

126. Bush, *Decision* Points, 238–239; Cheney, *In My Time*, 390–391.

127. Draper, *To Start a War*, 221–222; Baker, *Days of Fire*, 226.

128. Rice, *No Higher Honor*, 222–223.

129. Rosen, *Cheney One on One*, 244.

130. Baker, *Days of Fire*, 314–319; Goldstein, "Cheney, Vice Presidential Power, and the War on Terror," 116–118.

131. Bush, *Decision Points*, 172–174; Rice, *No Higher Honor*, 115–116.

132. Cheney, *In My Time*, 417–418; Bush, *Decision Points*, 86–87.

133. Bush, *Decision Points*, 86–87.

134. Rosen, *Cheney One on One*, 123, 124.

135. Rice, *No Higher Honor*, 17.

136. Bolten, Miller Center Oral History, I:130.

137. Baker, *Days of Fire*, 441–446.

138. President discusses creation of military commissions to try suspected terrorists, September 6, 2006, https://georgewbush-whitehouse.archives.gov/news/releases/2006/09/20060906-3.html. See Baker, *Days of Fire*, 428–429, 435–436; Cheney, *In My Time*, 359–360; Bush, *Decision Points*, 177–179; Goldstein, "Cheney, Vice Presidential Power, and the War on Terror," 120–121.

139. Baker, *Days of Fire*, 468–469.

140. Rice, *No Higher Honor*, 501–503; Baker, *Days of Fire*, 483–486.

141. Cheney, Center for Presidential History, Surge in Iraq, 35; Gates, Center for Presidential History, Surge in Iraq, 31–32.

142. Edelman, Center for Presidential History, Surge in Iraq, 11; Cheney, *In My Time*, 441.

143. Cheney, *In My Time*, 438–442.

144. Hadley, Center for Presidential History, Surge in Iraq, 64–65.

145. Bolten, Center for Presidential History, Surge in Iraq, 18, 35; Rosen, *Cheney One on One*, 130–131; Cheney, *In My Time*, 442–444.

146. Cheney, Center for Presidential History, Surge in Iraq, 46.

147. Robert M. Gates, *Duty: Memoirs of a Secretary at War* (New York: Alfred A. Knopf, 2014), 98, 584.

148. Gates, 97–98.

149. Gates, 182.

150. Gates, 191–192; Rice, *No Higher Honor*, 708.

151. Rosen, *Cheney One on One*, 123–130; Cheney, *In My Time*, 465–473.

152. Cheney, *In My Time*, 473–477, 481–490.

153. Hadley, Miller Center Oral History, 24.

154. Cheney, *In My Time*, 486; Rice, *No Higher Honor*, 707–708, 710–711.

155. *District of Columbia v. Heller*, 554 U.S. 570 (2008).

156. Bolten, Miller Center Oral History, III:58–59.

157. Cheney, *In My Time*, 494–495.

158. See, e.g., interview of the vice president by Wolf Blitzer, late edition, January 11, 2009; interview of the vice president by Jim Lehrer, *The News Hour with Jim Lehrer*, January 14, 2009; and other speeches and interviews at https://georgewbush-whitehouse.archives.gov/vicepresident/news-speeches/index.html.

159. Bush, *Decision Points*, 104.

160. Cheney, *In My Time*, 410; Baker, *Days of Fire*, 1–4, 7–8, 11.

161. Bush, *Decision Points*, 105.

CHAPTER EIGHT

The Iraq War: Democracy Promotion and the Struggle for Strategic Solvency, 2002–2008

Spencer D. Bakich

George W. Bush took office with an agenda focused largely on domestic policy. A neophyte in international affairs, he selected a seasoned and widely respected foreign policy team, assuring that American statecraft would be conducted competently and effectively.[1] Initially, Bush's foreign policy sought to rectify the Clinton administration's alleged mistakes. No longer would the American military be focused on nation building and humanitarian interventions in regions of the world that had no bearing on US national interests.[2] Under Bush, the United States would instead attend principally to its relations with the great powers, invest in a military designed to deter aggression and prevail in war, and pursue security and prosperity unencumbered by liberal idealism and naïve attachments to international institutions.[3]

The terrorist attacks on September 11, 2001, upended this agenda almost completely. The global war on terror became the orienting framework of American foreign policy. Relations with other states, both large and small, now depended on whether and to what extent they supported the United States' campaign to destroy terrorist organizations. The mission of the US military expanded as the administration came to appreciate the connections among domestic governance, ideology, and radicalization. No region could be written off as inconsequential to US national interests because terrorist organizations could find sanctuary in countries with weak and failed governments anywhere around the globe; indeed, rogue states might augment terrorists' strength by providing them with weapons of mass destruction (WMD). What remained of Bush's pre-9/11 foreign policy agenda was a reticence to embrace multilateral solutions,[4] even if terrorism was seen as a scourge affecting all states, and a confidence that the president and his supremely talented foreign policy team would guide the United States through this dark hour.

The 9/11 terrorist attacks were also the predicate for America's invasion of Iraq.[5] Intent on preventing future deadly attacks, and confident after the seemingly easy victory against the Taliban regime in Afghanistan in late 2001, Bush launched the war against Saddam Hussein in early 2003, fully expecting that the Baathist regime would fall quickly, Iraqi citizens would revel in their newfound freedom, and a stable and democratic Iraq would take shape in short order.[6] Belying those expectations, the situation in Iraq quickly descended into chaos. American forces found themselves facing two foes: an insurgency of mostly Sunni former Iraqi army personnel and al Qaeda–affiliated foreign fighters, and a host of Shia militias, some with extensive ties to government ministries and all determined to secure exclusive control of the state. A sectarian civil war emerged by mid-2005, pitting these groups against each other and the occupying US military.

By fall 2006, Bush realized that America's approach to the war had to change, and in January 2007 he announced that the United States would increase its troop commitment in Iraq by roughly twenty-four thousand and adopt a counterinsurgency strategy to quell the violence. With this decision, the US-dominated coalition forces assumed responsibility for providing security to Iraq's population. The logic of the new approach was that the reduction in violence would provide time and space for meaningful political reforms.[7] Bush's "surge" bore fruit. By early 2008, the most violent places in the country had been pacified. The political environment in Iraq improved too, but these gains were tenuous.[8] In 2009 Bush bequeathed to his successor, Barack Obama, a war effort that had risen from its nadir in 2006 but was still far from achieving the administration's lofty goals. The war, moreover, had cost the United States dearly in terms of lives lost, money spent, and prestige squandered.

As the political scientist Richard Betts observes, *strategic solvency* is "the craft of balancing commitments and resources responsibly," a critical alignment between means and ends that sustains a nation's effort over the long haul.[9] Achieving strategic solvency is always difficult because a state's resources are finite, even though its objectives have no natural limitation.[10] Alignment between means and ends occurs only when leaders discipline themselves through honest assessments of what it is possible to achieve at acceptable levels of cost, risk, and time. The Bush administration faced the consequences of its early mismanagement of the war in Iraq and undertook the difficult steps required to salvage something from the wreckage. Strategic solvency, however, proved elusive because of the wide gulf between the administration's aspirations for a post-Saddam Iraq and the reality of what American power could deliver.

Origins and Aims of War

The terrorist attacks of September 11, 2001, altered the Bush administration's priorities, threat assessments, and risk tolerance. The post-9/11 milieu in Washington was an admixture of fear, anxiety, guilt, and, most important, determination to prevent another terrorist attack.[11] Because of the United States' open society and porous borders, playing defense against determined terrorists was believed to be ineffective. The United States would have to go on the offensive, taking the fight to al Qaeda wherever it could be found. On October 7 Bush launched Operation Enduring Freedom. Forces from the CIA and the American military, partnering with the indigenous Northern Alliance in Afghanistan, destroyed al Qaeda's base of operations and drove the Taliban-controlled government from power. Speed and improvisation were critical to the military successes in the initial phase of the Afghanistan War.[12] On December 7 Hamid Karzai assumed the position of interim leader of Afghanistan.

Early success in Afghanistan did much to restore confidence in US resiliency and power. Yet administration officials were determined to quickly expand the war on terror to other fronts. Bush's nightmare scenario entailed a foreign state providing terrorists with WMD.[13] With the stakes so high, Bush was willing to assume significant risk to avoid being surprised again.[14] "The prospect of an attack with either chemical, nuclear, or biological [weapons] might be a low probability event, but it was very high impact," Vice President Dick Cheney's deputy national security adviser Eric Edelman recalled. "Therefore, if there was even a slim probability, we had to bend the efforts of government to make sure it didn't happen."[15]

Officials in Washington believed that Saddam Hussein was the state actor most likely to collaborate with al Qaeda against the United States. Explaining his reasoning, Bush wrote, "There were state sponsors of terror. There were sworn enemies of America. There were hostile governments that threatened their neighbors. There were nations that violated international demands. There were dictators who repressed their people. And there were regimes that pursued WMD. Iraq combined all those threats."[16]

Although Saddam had been viewed as a threat to American security interests for years,[17] the perceived magnitude of that threat grew after 9/11. Intelligence agencies around the world assessed that Iraq either had or would soon have WMD, but the Bush administration was not primarily concerned about Saddam's current capabilities. Rather, it was American officials' perceptions of Saddam's intentions, and the possibility of future Iraq–al Qaeda cooperation, that drove the Bush administration, supported by Congress, to war. In his State of the Union address on January 29, 2002, Bush laid out this connection. Grouping Iraq with North Korea and Iran, the president declared, "States like these, and their terrorist allies, constitute an axis of evil, aiming to threaten the peace of the world."[18]

Perceived threats drove the United States to war with Iraq, but its war aims went beyond these security concerns. Whether the United States should explicitly seek to promote democracy in Iraq was the subject of debate. For some, the threats posed by Saddam were enough to justify war; questions pertaining to a post-Saddam Iraq were less compelling. Secretary of Defense Donald Rumsfeld, for example, maintained that chances were slim that democracy could be implanted in Iraq, given its "deep sectarian and ethnic divisions."[19] Rumsfeld advocated a quick handover of power to a cohort that could govern effectively. Cheney demurred, arguing, "If the United States took military action and removed Saddam from power, we had an obligation to ensure that what followed reflected our values and beliefs in freedom and democracy."[20] For Bush, promoting democracy in Iraq was both a moral and a strategic matter. "The transformation [from tyranny to democracy in Iraq] would have an impact beyond Iraq's borders," Bush maintained:

> The Middle East was the center of a global ideological struggle. On one side were decent people who wanted to live in dignity and peace. On the other were extremists who sought to impose their radical views through violence and intimidation. They exploited conditions of hopelessness and repression to recruit and spread their ideology. The best way to protect our countries in the long run was to counter their dark vision with a more compelling alternative. The alternative was freedom.[21]

Bush had come to these views over time, influenced by his own efforts to make sense of America's place in a changed international system and by his many meetings with democracy advocates. Bush met "these people and Jesus, you meet the Dalai Lama and you meet [Natan] Sharansky," National Security Council (NSC) staffer Elliott Abrams recalled, "all those years in prison and you meet Ellen Johnson Sirleaf, and how can you not be deeply impressed?" To Bush, standing up for and promoting democracy was central to the war on terror. His was an "authentic" vision of freedom and democracy, NSC staff member Peter Feaver added, one that Bush believed "resonates in the hearts of other people."

Although the perceived threat from Iraq's WMD program motivated the administration to go to war, for Bush, promoting democracy was a core strategic objective from the outset.[22] And it was this objective that would all but guarantee America's strategic insolvency in the Iraq War.

Planning for War

Many administration officials believed that the growing threat posed by Saddam required a military response, yet Bush was willing to try to redress the problem of Iraq's supposed WMD program through diplomacy. At the urging of Secretary of State Colin Powell and British prime minister Tony Blair, Bush agreed to take the case to the United Nations. Throughout 2002, Powell had grown increasingly alarmed by the administration's determination to confront Saddam militarily. Though he never invoked by name the so-called Pottery Barn rule, Powell did warn Bush, "if you break it you're going to own it." Powell argued that confronting Iraq through the United Nations, which was "the offended party," would bolster the international legitimacy of US policy and put the burden of avoiding war on Baghdad. On September 12, 2002, the president delivered a blistering speech at the United Nations condemning Iraq not only for its alleged WMD programs but also for its human rights violations and sponsorship of terrorism.[23] On November 8 the UN Security Council passed Resolution 1441, demanding that Iraq readmit weapons inspectors and give a full accounting of its WMD programs.[24] Saddam's use of chemical weapons on his own population and his years-long record of obstructing international weapons inspections led Bush to believe that war was very likely, if not inevitable. On December 7

Iraq submitted to the United Nations a twelve thousand–page document that failed to disclose any prohibited WMD or associated programs, a dossier the White House deemed insulting.[25] America's coercive diplomacy campaign ended in failure.

Achieving the president's objective of putting Iraq on the path to democracy would require a substantial commitment of resources. Military, diplomatic, intelligence, and economic assets would be needed to provide security for Iraq's citizens and to guide the country's political processes toward stability and democracy after the Baathist regime's downfall. Additionally, the United States needed to have capacities in place to rebuild and reform critical institutions (including the Iraqi army), promote the rule of law, and foster a civil society capable of sustaining representative self-governance. Crucially, the United States and its international partners could not allow the toppling of the Saddam Hussein regime to result in an environment of de facto anarchy in which tribal and sectarian identities forestalled the development of an Iraqi national identity. These were the conclusions of the State Department's "Future of Iraq" survey, a wide-ranging project that convened Iraqi exiles, academics, and other experts in the spring and summer of 2002 to forecast problems the United States would face in the event of war.[26] Richard Haass, the State Department's director of policy planning; the National Intelligence Council; and the Strategic Studies Institute at the US Army War College produced similar assessments in fall 2002 and winter 2003. The consensus among all these analyses was that the US military had to prioritize postcombat security for the Iraqi population and that the US government needed to commit fully and immediately to a postwar reconstruction mission in Iraq.[27]

Few of these warnings were heeded in the war plan constructed by Gen. Tommy Franks, commander of US Central Command (CENTCOM). Neither he nor Rumsfeld accepted any advice from outside the military chain of command during the war planning process. Referring to the "Future of Iraq" project, for example, deputy assistant secretary of state for Near Eastern affairs Ryan Crocker maintains that "OSD [Office of the Secretary of Defense] in particular saw it as a distraction and an effort of minimal value. . . . If not obstructionist, they certainly were not helpful in the process. And not too far into this I began to develop the concern that if and when the decision was made to go into Iraq this project would not have operational traction."

Rather than adopting a holistic view of the strategic challenges confronting the United States, Franks and Rumsfeld focused exclusively on the narrow task of defeating the Iraqi army in a conventional battle. Their underlying assumption was that the so-called revolution in military affairs that Rumsfeld had pursued as secretary of defense would enable the US military to leverage its technological advantages to such an extent that the invading force could be relatively small and still achieve a lopsided victory.[28] Franks believed the United States need only defeat the enemy "at points of decision," an operational concept that did not require an overwhelming force overall. This "light footprint" war plan appealed to many civilian defense officials and uniformed officers because it promised a quick war and a short occupation. Franks's planning assumed that of the 145,000 American troops deployed to Iraq by March, only a small residual force would remain by September.[29] The responsibility for postwar reconstruction, Franks insisted, belonged to others. "While we at CENTCOM were executing the war plan," Franks later recalled, "Washington should [have been] focus[ing] on 'policy-level issues.'" His message to the service chiefs and Pentagon bureaucracy was, "*You pay attention to the day* after and *I'll pay attention to the day* of."[30] Planning of the mission was undeniably the responsibility of CENTCOM, yet Franks and his staff evinced little enthusiasm for postcombat stability operations, a failure that resulted in widespread looting and violence immediately after the fall of Baghdad.[31]

Rumsfeld and undersecretary of defense for policy Douglas Feith were also opposed to a lengthy occupation. In part, this was a function of the common assumption that American forces would be operating in a benign environment after Saddam fell. OSD officials believed that, reminiscent of post–World War II France, US troops would be greeted as liberators and would find the Iraqis capable and cooperative.[32] The France analogy went even further, influencing the OSD's preferences for postwar governance. Rumsfeld, Feith, and deputy secretary of defense Paul Wolfowitz all favored a scheme by which control of Iraq would quickly be turned over to a core group of "externals"—Iraqi exiles who would return to their country to fill key leadership and institutional roles.[33] This governance model was appealing for three reasons. First, it comported with the gratifying notion that, as in World War II, the United States would be viewed as a liberating force. Second, it seemed to have a demonstrated track record. As Feith noted, "One could have called Charles de Gaulle an external, after all." And third, quickly handing over the responsibility for postwar reconstruction and governance to Iraqi externals obviated the need for the US military to engage in extensive and costly nation-building efforts.[34]

Bush, too, evinced little concern over the absence of a comprehensive postwar plan. As Powell remembered, the president "believed that suddenly a government would snap back in place and democracy would break out . . . that this was the beginning of a sweep throughout the entire Middle East of democracy." The inherent human impulse for freedom led Bush to anticipate a relatively easy transition in Iraq after major combat operations. As a result, American strategy was focused exclusively on conventional war fighting. Planning and preparation to consolidate the outcomes of the war were largely ignored, despite warnings emanating from other quarters of the US government.

The widening gap between the strategic means and ends was disconcerting to Lt. Gen. John Abizaid, director of the Joint Staff at the Pentagon. In August 2002 Abizaid tapped the director of strategic plans and policy, Lt. Gen. George Casey, to fill the void between the military and political components of the emerging strategy and to force senior officials to address the sizable postwar challenges that would confront the United States in Iraq. The result was the Iraq Political-Military Cell (IPMC), a small group of military and civilian officials that became, Casey recalled, "the place where people could go and talk about Iraq outside the war plan, about what was going to happen afterward and what we needed to do from a political-military standpoint." Casey, who had extensive experience operating in postwar environments in the Balkans, thought it likely that American forces in Iraq "would be a magnet" to terrorists who "would come to Iraq to fight us." He also anticipated the outbreak of sectarian violence in Iraq and believed it would take an entire army corps at least five years to stabilize the country. When he briefed the NSC on postwar planning requirements in October 2002, Casey recalled that he got some "knowing glances . . . and I realized from the questions [deputy national security adviser Steve Hadley] was asking how little they really understood about what I had been telling them. It was because this was fundamentally new to them."

The Iraq War commenced on March 19, 2003, two days after Bush's ultimatum that Saddam either abdicate or suffer the consequences of an all-out invasion. For the next twenty-one days, US-led coalition forces advanced from Kuwait to Baghdad. Unlike the 1991 Persian Gulf War, which featured sequential bombing and ground campaigns, Operation Iraqi Freedom entailed simultaneous air and land battles. On the ground, the US Army's V Corps and I US Marines Expeditionary Force moved quickly through southern Iraq, driving straight into the Iraqi military's vulnerable rear positions. Tactical penetrations into Baghdad itself, so-called thunder runs, were conducted on April 5, resulting in collapse of the city's defenses. Making these operations possible was the rapid attrition of Iraqi armor and artillery produced by coalition airpower.[35] By April 8, the number of Iraq's tanks had been reduced from 850 to 19; its field artillery pieces had declined from 550 to 40.[36] On May 1 Bush announced that major combat operations were over. From the deck of the carrier USS *Abraham Lincoln*, under a large banner declaring "Mission Accomplished," Bush delivered his remarks at roughly the moment when, perversely, violence and looting gripped Iraq's capital city. Major combat operations may have ended, but the war was far from over.

Although Bush decided in October 2002 to assign responsibility for postwar planning to the Department of Defense, it wasn't until January 20, 2003, that he made it official in National Security Presidential Directive 24. Led by retired lieutenant general Jay Garner, the Office of Reconstruction and Humanitarian Assistance (ORHA) was understaffed, underresourced, and unprepared for the monumental tasks confronting it. The delay in ORHA's formation, moreover, meant that Garner was unable to coordinate with his military counterpart, Gen. David McKiernan, before the war. In fact, no one was expecting Garner and his team when they deployed to Iraq in mid-March. Within days of Garner's arrival in Baghdad, Bush decided to disband ORHA and replace it with a new organization, the Coalition Provisional Authority (CPA).[37]

L. Paul Bremer, presidential envoy and head of the CPA, arrived in Baghdad in May and found the city ablaze. On May 23 Bremer issued two decrees that proved debilitating to American postwar aims. CPA Order 1 called for the removal of thousands of Baath Party members from Iraqi state institutions, and CPA Order 2 disbanded the Iraqi army in its entirety. The de-Baathification scheme alienated many Iraqi civil servants who, though Sunnis, were not Saddam loyalists, and it was used to fulfill the sectarian agenda of the Iraqi "external" Ahmed Chalabi. The dissolution of the army was even more damaging to American objectives because it effectively catalyzed a Sunni insurgency. The combination of the two orders was an affront to many Iraqi Sunnis and a direct challenge to their identity as leaders of the Iraqi state.[38]

The two CPA orders were drafted and implemented without extensive interagency deliberation and debate and over the objections of US military officers in Iraq. With respect to de-Baathification, in a March 10 meeting with Cheney, Rumsfeld, Powell, and national security adviser Condoleezza Rice, Bush approved a plan that would oust around 6,000 senior party members from their positions in government.[39] As drawn up by Feith's office on May 9, however, Bremer's plan included a far more expansive de-Baathification program. Although Bremer anticipated that the order would affect 20,000 party members, between 85,000 and 100,000 were ultimately driven from their jobs, including roughly 40,000 schoolteachers.[40] The decree disbanding the army was drafted by CPA adviser Walter Slocombe prior to Bremer's appointment. It contravened the widespread consensus that demobilization of the army must be undertaken slowly and carefully. US military and ORHA personnel were planning to use elements of the Iraqi army to assist in critical postwar stabilization efforts, given the small number of US forces available. Describing the decision-making process, NSC staffer Franklin Miller noted that "the most portentous decision of the occupation, disbanding the Iraqi army, was carried out stealthily and without giving the president's principal advisors an opportunity to consider it and give the president their views."[41] In short order, thousands of armed, organized, disenfranchised, and unemployed former military personnel formed the nucleus of an insurgency dedicated to defeating US objectives in Iraq.

Notwithstanding the rapid deterioration of security throughout Iraq during the summer of 2003, American troop strength decreased and Franks's theater command was withdrawn. His replacement, the newly promoted Lt. Gen. Ricardo Sanchez, assumed command of a much slimmer corps-level structure called Combined Joint Task Force 7. As Sanchez understood it, his mission was to facilitate the reduction of US troop strength while fulfilling the postconflict stabilization responsibilities assigned by CENTCOM.[42] Yet Bush and Bremer were now fully committed to a lengthy occupation to meet the president's goal of ensuring the emergence of a viable democracy in post-Saddam Iraq. American policy was thus caught between two competing impulses: to build the political institutions required to sustain representative self-governance, and to reduce the American military presence to reinforce the United States' image as liberator rather than occupier.[43] This tension remained unresolved as late as 2006 because no single decision maker in Iraq was authorized to reconcile the political and military components of American policy. Instead, two chains of command had been created, both originating in the OSD, and they proved unable or unwilling to act quickly and decisively. "The Pentagon was for a while like a black hole," Powell lamented, "nothing was resolved, nothing came out." Despite being given responsibility for postwar Iraq by the president, Rumsfeld informed Rice, Powell, and Cheney that Bremer "doesn't work for me anymore." Powell and Rice concurred that the secretary of defense had "abandoned his post."

The president's war aim of promoting democracy foundered as lawlessness and violence gripped many Iraqi cities, creating an atmosphere conducive to both an indigenous insurgency and an influx of al Qaeda–affiliated terrorists. Many of the assumptions underlying the Americans' light-footprint war plan were soon shown to be erroneous, caused in part by faulty intelligence. Recounting his frustration, Edelman noted:

> They [the intelligence community] told us . . . that all the generals were going to turn their turrets around and not contest the military when we came in. That was all wrong . . . nobody told us that Saddam was not going to actually try and fight with a conventional force but use the Fedayeen Saddam to fight an unconventional war. They told us that the police would be reliable once the senior Ba'athist leadership was removed and that they could provide security behind the lines as our lines move[d] forward. The police turned out to be a completely corrupt and hollow institution. We didn't know anything about Iraq. . . . What they didn't tell us was that Saddam had so totally atomized Iraqi society that there were no leaders inside who could amount to anything.[44]

Yet many in the US government never held the rosy assumptions prevalent in the OSD and the Office of the Vice President (OVP) and were concerned from the beginning about both the light-footprint approach and the shallowness of postwar planning efforts. Key officials from the Department of State, the Joint Staff, and the National Intelligence Council warned repeatedly that if the United States were to have any chance of moving Iraq in the direction of democracy, a "whole of government" strategy would be required, one that featured extensive coordination across departments and agencies and that focused as much on postwar stabilization and reconstruction as it did on major combat operations.

The ideal mechanism to facilitate such a strategy was the National Security Council staff system. Yet in his first term, Bush's NSC was dysfunctional, divided by personal and bureaucratic rivalries that its senior managers, Rice and Hadley, could not bridge.[45] Participants in the process attest to its failings, but there is little agreement as to why it functioned so poorly.

State Department officials blame the Defense Department's obstructionism, while Defense officials counter that State was inefficient and mismanaged.[46] Powell and Rice charge that Cheney created a shadow NSC staff that engaged in bureaucratic manipulation to get the upper hand in policy disputes.[47] Edelman disputes this, noting that Rice approved the arrangement between the NSC staff and the OVP. "By agreement with Condi [Rice], we [OVP officials] were all on the NSC email system. So we were included on all their emails and we got to see the briefing memos before we did our briefing memos for the Vice President. . . . But that was by design, not by some nefarious plan."

Finally, Rice is accused of failing to manage the "600-pound gorillas"—Cheney, Powell, and Rumsfeld. Feith and Rumsfeld allege that rather than identify and debate disagreements among officials, Rice papered them over with "bridging proposals, taking a little piece out of each agency's idea so everybody could say they were a winner, which we found very unsatisfying." The problem with this approach was that it bred "discontent, since fundamental differences remained unaddressed and unresolved by the President."[48] Yet Hadley denies that this was Rice's (or his) modus operandi: "That's not how the President remembers his first term. That's not how Condi remembers his first term. I can tell you it's not what we did in the second term. We brought them [disagreements] to the President for decision."

The participants do agree on two important points. First, the divisions among the principals were personal and vitriolic. "The worse it got," Hadley recalled, "the more it began to impair the decision-making process." Second, Bush is ultimately to blame for the poor performance of his interagency system. "I don't think that it is fair to say that it was just Condi, because when Condi moved over to the State Department and Steve Hadley became National Security Advisor, the practice basically continued," Feith recalled. "So it seems to me the only reasonable inference . . . is that is the way the President wanted it." Former deputy secretary of state Richard Armitage is even blunter in his assessment of Bush's performance—specifically, his unwillingness to wade into the disputatious process and force clear decisions: "at the end of the day he didn't have the courage to stand up to a good fight; he wouldn't do it."

In this decision-making system, the Defense Department had a preponderance of influence over how the United States went to war in Iraq. Rumsfeld enshrined the OSD's policy preferences for a relatively light deployment of forces aimed exclusively at overthrowing Saddam's regime and prevented information about likely postwar challenges from influencing the war plan. Over the course of the roughly fifteen months from November 2001 to March 2003, the war plan went through multiple iterations, receiving presidential approval along the way.[49] The result was a campaign plan that, when implemented, destroyed much of the Iraqi army and quickly overthrew the Iraqi government. But the postconflict phase that so concerned Abizaid and Casey went unaddressed in Franks's plan—an unbridged chasm between military operations and the ultimate strategic objective of creating a viable democratic state in the aftermath of war.[50]

American strategy in Iraq was, thus, fundamentally insolvent. Rumsfeld let Franks and his planning team focus exclusively on conventional combat operations and draft a war plan unencumbered by the explicit mission of translating military gains into the president's desired political outcome. Rumsfeld succeeded because Bush, Rice, and Hadley failed to manage the foreign policy process in a way that exposed the most likely trade-offs among different courses of action, fostered transparency and collaboration among the various departments, and knitted means and ends into a coherent strategy.

Stand Up, Stand Down

By December 2003, the Bush administration's optimism gave way to frustration as many of its expectations about postwar Iraq were dashed. Questions mounted about the administration's principal rationale for the war: Iraq's possession of banned WMD. In the run-up to war, Colin Powell argued in a February 2003 speech at the United Nations that Iraq possessed a sizable stockpile of chemical weapons and had the ability to produce biological weapons in mobile laboratories. Widely viewed as the most credible of American officials, Powell based his claims on a deeply flawed October 2002 National Intelligence Estimate.[51] Although the world didn't learn until January 2004 that Iraq did not in fact possess WMD, Powell soon realized that key components of his case were crumbling. When Powell's staff received photos of one of the suspected mobile labs in the weeks after the invasion, he declared, "That's no biological van, it looks like a mess truck or a shop van." The secretary's staffers concurred, replying, "Right. Don't ever say it is that again."

Security in Iraq continued to deteriorate as a Sunni insurgency formed in and around Baghdad during the summer of 2003, targeting American forces with increasing effectiveness. White House envoy to Iraq Robert Blackwill noted in November 2003 that the CPA was "an embattled island in a hostile city," with little understanding of the operating environment throughout the country. On the political front, the CPA's initial plan to draft a constitution for post-Saddam Iraq was in a state of flux as new political power brokers emerged, most importantly Grand Ayatollah Ali al-Sistani and the firebrand Moqtada al-Sadr, both Shia. Iraqi politics and society became factionalized because of the security deficit in key regions of the country, confirming the warnings of the "Future of Iraq" project the previous summer. The one bright spot for American officials came on December 13, 2003, when US forces captured Saddam in a cramped hole in the ground near the town of Dawr.[52]

On June 1, 2004, Gen. George Casey replaced Sanchez as the commander of coalition forces in Iraq. Rectifying the structural problems of Sanchez's corps-level command, Casey led a much larger headquarters called Multi-National Force–Iraq (MNF-I). MNF-I was responsible for setting the overall strategy, while combat operations were conducted by the subordinate Multi-National Corp–Iraq (MNC-I). Also under MNF-I was Multi-National Security Transition Command–Iraq (MNSTC-I), led by Lt. Gen. David Petraeus. Casey's mission, which he gleaned from Bush's May 24 speech at the Army War College and from UN Security Council Resolution 1546, boiled down to three essentials: help the Iraqis transition to a representative government, build security forces that could maintain order, and prevent terrorists from entering Iraq. This definition of the mission aligned with Casey's strategic preference, derived from his experiences in the Balkans, of empowering the Iraqis to assume responsibility for their own security. As Casey explained:

> The men and women of the American military, when you put them on the ground in a deployed environment, they're going to work 24/7 to get the job done. Well, we were in Bosnia nine years because we never let the Bosniaks and the Serbs do anything, or do very little. We did it all for them, and they used us and they pitted us against each other. So I had that in my mind too as I went into Iraq, and that influenced me significantly.

For Casey, building the capacity of the Iraqi Security Forces (ISF) was crucial to sustainable success.

Unlike many in the OSD, Casey understood that American forces confronted a hardened, dangerous insurgency in Iraq. Yet Casey's campaign plan has been criticized for failing to meet the standards of true counterinsurgency (COIN) strategy.[53] Part of the problem was that the American military was a thoroughly conventional force, ill equipped to think and act in unconventional ways. As a stopgap measure, Casey instituted a five-day COIN academy in late 2005 that introduced newly deployed commanders to the principles of counterinsurgency warfare.[54] But the military's doctrinal and organizational deficiencies were deep, precluding the early adoption of a classic COIN approach that focused on the hearts, minds, and above all safety of the Iraqi people. "I was leery of directing a force with a conventional mindset to deliver the Iraqi people," Casey explained. "They would have tied them up and delivered them." Rather than focusing on the allegiance of the Iraqi people, Casey's strategy was to develop the capacities of the Iraqi government. "My view was that the Iraqi government was more likely to deliver the Iraqi people than we, a foreign armed forces [were]," Casey noted. Throughout his thirty-one months in command, from June 2004 to February 2007, Casey strived to build the legitimacy of the Iraqi government and the capabilities of the ISF, an approach Bush summarized in June 2005: "as the Iraqis stand up, we will stand down."[55]

The critical component of Casey's strategy was development of the ISF. When Petraeus left MNSTC-I in September 2005, progress had been made in the overall size and quality of the Iraqi security sector. With 200,000 personnel, ISF ranks had doubled in eleven months, and some Iraqi army units were able to take a more prominent role in providing security.[56] Other units, however, were composed largely of militia members with a Shia sectarian agenda. The situation involving the Iraqi police was far worse. Violence in Iraqi cities outpaced the recruitment capacity of the Ministry of the Interior. Then, in 2005, the ministry fell under the control of Bayan Jabr, former leader of the Shia Badr organization, who filled the ranks of the police with militia members.[57] Newly empowered with state resources, Shia violence against the Sunni population grew. In fall 2005 US officials learned of a secret prison run by the Ministry of the Interior that held Sunnis captive under gruesome conditions.[58] By the end of 2005, Casey's strategy was undermined by a faltering ISF. Casey nevertheless persisted in his belief that the US military could do only so much for the Iraqis. Doing more would foster dependencies and thus jeopardize the mission of turning responsibility over to the host nation.

On the governance front, many American officials saw 2005 as a potential inflection point. The Sunni boycott of the January elections for the National Assembly weakened American hopes that a truly representative body would craft the new Iraqi constitution. Still, through deft diplomacy, US ambassador Zalmay Khalilzad was able to convince key Sunni parties to support the draft constitution, and on October 15 the document was ratified in a national referendum. On December 15 elections were held to fill a permanent Iraqi Council of Representatives. Voter turnout was high, due in large measure to the massive security presence provided by American forces. The result was a victory for the Islamic Dawa Party and its leader Nouri al-Maliki, who became prime minister in May 2006.[59] "Things were starting to look fairly good," NSC staffer J. D. Crouch remembered. "We got through the constitution, we got through a great election in the end of '05. I think there was a lot of sense coming from the field that we're turning the corner." However briefly, Casey's strategy appeared to be working.

This optimism was shattered on February 22, 2006, by a string of bombings carried out by al Qaeda in Iraq (AQI) in Samarra. The goal of Abu Musab al-Zarqawi, AQI's leader, was to consolidate his group's position in the broader Sunni resistance by igniting a full-scale sectarian civil war with Iraq's Shia population. That conflict had been under way for months, as the incidence of AQI suicide bombings, abuses by the Shia-dominated ISF, and Mahdi Army violence steadily rose. Even so, destruction of the Al-Askari Shrine elevated the sectarian bloodletting to new heights.[60] For the chairman of the Joint Chiefs of Staff, Gen. Peter Pace, the Samarra bombing offered a moment of clarity in this complex war. "Uh-oh, all this is a veneer of a representative government . . . Sunnis and Shi'as being treated equally," Pace realized. For Casey, too, the Samarra bombing provided new insights into the war he was fighting. "[It] struck me all of a sudden that this wasn't about an insurgency directed against us. The greatest threat to the accomplishment of our mission was this sectarian struggle that had the lid blown off it by the bombing of the mosque. And what I realized was that this was now an Iraqi struggle."

Despite the dramatic rise in violence on the streets of Iraq's cities, Casey was unwilling to abandon his strategy of bolstering Iraqi institutions, especially the ISF. Putting the Iraqis in the lead, irrespective of the government's sectarian Shia agenda, was critical to achieving success. To fully integrate the ISF into the coalition's war-fighting effort, MNF-I sponsored two operations in July and August 2006 aimed at the insurgency in Baghdad. Yet only two of the six intended Iraqi battalions participated in Operation Together Forward, and the coalition was unable to prevent the insurgents' return to temporarily scoured areas. A similar fate befell Operation Together Forward II, which showed that the coalition was incapable of holding and rebuilding the areas it had cleared.[61] By the end of the summer, it was clear that sectarian violence was raging and American strategy was failing.

The Surge

Though it carried the patina of democracy, by the summer of 2006 Iraq had a deeply corrupt government that was intent on securing Shia dominance at the expense of the Sunni population. In addition, the Sunni insurgency had been hijacked by AQI and was waging a brutal campaign of intimidation and terror in Baghdad and surrounding provinces, most notably in Anbar. In 2002 Casey warned that the US presence in Iraq would be a magnet for terrorists and that without Saddam's dictatorial rule, sectarian violence would likely erupt. Yet neither he nor Rumsfeld was willing to push for an alternative strategy to bolster Iraq's political and security institutions. To keep America's commitment limited, Rumsfeld argued repeatedly that the administration needed "to take our hands off the bicycle seat" and let the Iraqis take the lead in governing and securing their own country. Casey's Balkan experiences dovetailed with Rumsfeld's view, insofar as he believed that sustainable success would be achieved only when the United States transferred security operations to the Iraqis. The critical flaw in this approach was that it incentivized precisely the wrong behavior by the Iraqi government and permitted the growth of both the insurgency and AQI. In the fall and winter of 2006 officials in Washington grappled with the insolvency of US strategy. In January 2007 Bush announced a revamped course that narrowed the gap between means and ends and reversed the trend of escalating sectarian violence.

Throughout the spring and summer of 2006 Bush grew increasingly worried about the deteriorating conditions in Iraq. The reports the president read every morning showed an unacceptable level of casualties and a lack of demonstrable progress on the diplomatic, political, and security fronts. One day in May Bush said to his national security adviser, "Hadley, we need a new strategy." At the president's behest, Hadley initiated what would become a lengthy strategic review process. The central question was whether the existing strategy was irredeemably flawed and needed to be replaced, or whether it was sound and needed better resourcing. Asking foundational questions about a failing war is never an easy task. To make headway, NSC staffers Peter Feaver and Meghan O'Sullivan recommended a "debate among outside experts, in front of the President" and his entire national security team. The idea was to expose Bush to alternative perspectives that had not been well aired up to that point. The first day of the retreat at Camp David in June 2006 went well, allowing the principals to discuss different proposals in a structured manner. Feaver hoped this would be the beginning of a months-long, thoroughgoing strategic review that would produce a sounder approach to the war. "Instead the President sneaks off to Baghdad that very night, which Meghan and I did not know about," Feaver recalled. "Instead of launching a strategy review, it relaunches the original strategy." Bush felt it necessary to show his complete support for Maliki with a surprise visit. His NSC staffers, however, knew that American strategy needed to change, and they promptly went back to the drawing board.

Hadley understood that an NSC staff–driven review would get nowhere if the Defense Department stonewalled the effort. Without a clear directive from the president, the best Hadley could do was coax the secretary of defense into supporting a fresh look at the strategy. In July the national security adviser agreed to pose a lengthy set of difficult questions to Rumsfeld, Casey, and Khalilzad about the war's progress and America's approach to it. The results were dispiriting to Hadley and his staff and insulting to Casey and Khalilzad. The NSC staff felt it was their responsibility to highlight fundamental problems with US strategy, but Casey and Khalilzad chafed under what they viewed as micromanagement from Washington[62]—or, as Casey put it, being on the receiving end of the "8,000-mile screwdriver." Bush found his team's answers unconvincing, going so far as to challenge Rumsfeld on his favored metaphorical grounds. "OK, Don," Hadley remembers Bush saying, "I'm prepared to take my hands off the seat of the bicycle, but if the bicycle starts to fall you've got to grab it because we can't afford for the bicycle to fall and for us to start over again."

With or without interagency buy-in at the start, Bush and Hadley believed the review process had to begin immediately. Three reviews were conducted in parallel by the NSC staff, the Joint Staff, and the State Department. Hadley also consulted experts outside the government for advice. An independent strategic review directed by retired general Jack Keane and

Fred Kagan at the American Enterprise Institute (AEI) proved particularly useful as an "external validation of ideas, concepts, and conclusions reached independently by the internal reviews."[63]

The NSC staff evaluated a number of different courses American strategy could take. The review team judged that the option eventually known as "the surge" stood the best chance of changing the course of the war. This recommendation squared with the analysis of the Keane and Kagan team at the AEI, which found that the United States should increase its force in Iraq by five army brigades and two marine regiments (totaling roughly twenty-four thousand troops).[64] Because the reviews were conducted in parallel, the State Department's position reflected only what the military said was possible. State Department counselor Philip Zelikow recalls being told by the Joint Staff's director of operations, Gen. Doug Lute, "We're out of Schlitz. If you want to do Baghdad, that's going to take six to eight additional brigades. We just don't have six to eight additional brigades." Rather than advocate a strategy of pacifying Baghdad, the State Department recommended an approach tailored to the different types of conflicts occurring throughout Iraq. With respect to Baghdad itself, the idea was to control the capital's access routes and attempt to "contain the sectarian violence from turning into a full interethnic genocide and manage it and hope it turns."

The review process was formalized in November. Hadley's deputy, J. D. Crouch, was charged with pulling together the various recommendations and presenting the president with a full range of strategic options. After meeting with Rice and Zelikow from the State Department and John Hannah from the OVP, it was clear to Hadley and most of his staff that the surge option had the highest probability of tamping down the sectarian violence and creating conditions for political reconciliation among Iraq's warring factions. The problem was that the military was opposed to sending an additional five brigades to Iraq; at most, Abizaid and Casey were willing to send two brigades. According to Pace, sending more than two "would send the wrong message to the Iraqi government that we didn't trust them to do their job." Within the Pentagon, the service chiefs had other concerns about the AEI's five-brigade recommendation. Summarizing the chiefs' views, Pace noted, "if we in fact went to five [army] brigades after five-plus years of war and this being an all-volunteer force and guys being on their third and fourth deployments already, . . . we would break the force."

Caught between a highly influential retired general advocating a sizable increase in troops and the Joint Chiefs of Staff, CENTCOM commander, and theater commander recommending at most a modest bump in forces, Pace decided to play a finesse game:

> The wording we finally came up with was "up to five brigades." So George Casey and John Abizaid could say, "Aha, up to five. We only need two," but it gave me the ability and the service Chiefs the ability to plan to up to five. We'll have them one month at a time. Five months in a row, another brigade will go over. If we're successful we can turn it off and look like heroes. If we're not successful we're executing our plan and we're not falling further and further—this is not Vietnam, just another 10,000 guys. Just another 10,000 guys.

Even so, Pace took the chiefs' concerns seriously. Before briefing the president on the military's surge recommendations, Pace informed Bush that the military would ask him to do three things: (1) pressure the Maliki government to fully commit to the new strategy, (2) have a "civilian surge" accompany the military surge, and (3) ask Congress to increase the size of the US Army and Marine Corps. Reflecting on this critical episode in civil-military relations, Pace noted that although the president heard how hard the army and marines were driving their forces, Bush had "the knowledge going in the door that at the end of the day after he listens to all that, the recommendation from his Joint Chiefs is going to be up to five brigades. We can do that."

Important personnel changes occurred while the administration was rethinking its strategy. In the wake of the Republicans' November 2006 midterm defeat in Congress, Bush replaced Rumsfeld with Robert Gates as secretary of defense. Unlike Rumsfeld, Gates supported the surge and was viewed by many in the Pentagon as someone who could repair the damage done by Rumsfeld's abrasiveness and recalcitrance. More consequential for the course of the war, however, was the change in country team leadership: veteran diplomat Ryan Crocker replaced Khalilzad as ambassador, and Gen. David Petraeus replaced Casey as MNF-I commander. Petraeus requested all the brigade-equivalents the Pentagon identified as potentially available for the surge. Bush approved the request and, in a televised address on January 10, 2007, explained America's new course in the Iraq War.[65]

The decision to tap Petraeus was significant because it heralded a fundamental change in the way American power would be used. Petraeus's previous command posting had been at the Combined Arms Center at Fort

Leavenworth, where he oversaw the development of a new counterinsurgency manual for the US Army and Marine Corps.[66] Aligned with classic COIN principles, the new doctrine held that securing the population and fostering the rule of law were prerequisites for legitimate governance.[67] The United States would thus be responsible for fighting insurgents, providing security for the Iraqi population, and pressuring the Malaki administration to respect "preexisting and impersonal legal rules," functions viewed as necessary to create "widespread, enduring societal support" for the government.[68] The surge, in sum, entailed an augmentation of military resources and a change in the way US power was exercised in Iraq. Critically, America's strategic objectives went unchanged. The goal of the surge was to win, "and the definition of win," Bush explained, was for Iraq to be "an ally in the war on terror and a functioning democracy."[69]

In executing their mission, Petraeus and Crocker forged a remarkable partnership that enabled a tight alignment of the diplomatic and military components of the campaign, a crucial element that did much to ensure—for a time—that Maliki refrained from imposing sectarian restrictions on the surge's implementation.[70] As Crocker recalled, he and Petraeus

> were co-located, one waiting room separated our two offices. Our two staffs were basically locked together. There was no guidebook for it, we just intuitively sorted it out. Then we did everything together. Once a week we would go together to see the Prime Minister. I might have separate meetings, but that weekly meeting it was going to be both of us. That meant that each of us had to be thoroughly familiar with the other's issues, had to know how to react on the spot, reinforce each other as the conversation twisted and turned and, equally important, signaling to the Prime Minister, "Don't think you can game us. There just isn't going to be any daylight." We made sure that whenever there was an issue—and there were almost none in two pretty tumultuous years—if we had a difference of views, we sorted it out. That was never visible to Washington, to the Iraqis, or even within our own structure.

Although Bush made the critical decisions to scale up American force levels and bring in a new leadership team, much of what would constitute the surge was yet to be determined in January. Bush and Petraeus understood that securing Baghdad would be the top priority, but translating their focus into an operational scheme would take time. Among the most significant decisions made by the new MNC-I commander, Lt. Gen. Ray Odierno, was to concentrate on defeating the insurgency not only in Baghdad but also in its surrounding rural support zones, or "belts."[71] Upon arriving in Baghdad, Petraeus learned that marines in Anbar province were forming fledgling partnerships with former insurgents who, after getting a taste of AQI's brutal method of governing, had turned against it. The possibility of expanding the partnership with the so-called Sunni awakening had not been considered in any of the strategic reviews, nor did it feature prominently in the new counterinsurgency manual. Petraeus nevertheless understood the opportunity, blessed the marines' efforts, and bankrolled a larger program that ultimately wrested Anbar province from AQI.[72]

Although it was successful in accomplishing its first objective of reducing violence in Baghdad and Anbar, the effects of the surge took time to realize. The only way to secure the population was to have US forces patrolling and living among the citizens. The result was an increase in the number of American casualties. Petraeus was willing to accept a higher casualty rate if it meant convincing the Iraqi population that US forces could be trusted to act in their best interests. Over time, tips from local Iraqis about the location and movement of insurgent forces, weapons caches, and bomb-making factories increased. By the end of the year, the level of violence in Iraq fell precipitously.[73]

As the security situation stabilized, and as the UN authorization of a US military presence in Iraq was set to expire at the end of 2008, Washington and Baghdad entered into negotiations over a longer-term Status of Forces Agreement (SOFA). Under pressure from Sistani and Sadr, Maliki rejected any agreement that included the permanent presence of American forces in Iraq. Determined to put US-Iraq relations on a normal footing before he left office, Bush acceded to two key Iraqi demands: that all US forces be deployed to bases outside Iraq's cities by June 2009, and that all US forces be withdrawn from the country by the end of 2011.[74] Bush and Maliki signed the SOFA in a ceremony in Baghdad on December 14, 2008.

The Struggle for Strategic Solvency

America went to war in Iraq with a fundamentally flawed strategy. The Bush administration woefully underresourced a war effort aimed at establishing a stable and democratic Iraq. Strategic insolvency was caused in part by

Bush's willingness to let his untethered aspirations guide his thinking about warfare. Yet within the administration, this problem was neither unique to Bush nor universal. A more important cause of strategic insolvency was the broken decision-making system that bred undisciplined thought and dysfunctional behavior. Under this system, the war planning process was both myopic, focusing solely on the conventional battle, and short term, ignoring the widely forecast challenges that US forces would confront in the aftermath of major combat operations. Tragically, the administration's decision-making capacity further atrophied after the invasion, resulting in actions and policies that compounded the initial mistakes.[75]

Yet Bush learned and adapted. The surge was a critical course correction that led to dramatic improvements in the security environment in Baghdad and Anbar. Aided by Hadley and a talented team at the NSC, Bush entertained new ideas, considered trade-offs and risk in a more systematic fashion, and acted decisively in the face of uncertainty. Importantly, the surge was not the president's brainchild but was the product of various ideas originating from inside and outside the government. It was also the result of pulling and hauling among the bureaucracy and the White House. Though imperfect, the strategic decision-making process of 2006–2007 proved superior to that of 2002–2003 because it allowed a greater range of information and analysis to reach the principals and the president. The surge was an approach that more closely aligned resources with objectives by increasing the quantity and quality of the political and military assets committed to the war. By the end of 2007, American strategy was more solvent than it had been at any point prior.[76]

Still, the gap between means and ends remained unbridged. According to Lute, who was tapped for the NSC staff in May 2007 to oversee the wars in Iraq and Afghanistan, the surge had only tactical effects. Translating its gains into meaningful strategic progress proved elusive. "Strategically, the security effort outstripped the ability of Iraqi politics to keep up and solidify, [to] consolidate those security effects," Lute recalled. "There was no reconciliation [between Iraq's Sunnis and Shias]. . . . It was a losing fight, because we could not generate the political counterpart." By resolving the security challenges so effectively, the surge had the unintended consequence of reinforcing the very dysfunctions of Iraqi politics and institutions that spurred the civil conflict in 2005–2006.[77] As Lute concludes, "increasingly over time Maliki went back to his roots, which were sectarian and sponsored by Iran, and not what our image of Iraqi politics could be."

The American experience in Iraq is inextricably connected to the promotion of democracy, the objective Bush set at the outset and never abandoned. Gates understood the inescapable strategic problem created by the president's ambitious objective. Bush, Rice, and Hadley were, according to Gates, "true believers. They still think this Freedom Agenda is a huge part of Bush's legacy. Maybe someday it will be, but as we were fighting the wars, I thought that to articulate it as our near-term goal was setting ourselves up for failure." Presidents bear the ultimate responsibility for determining the ends for which wars are fought. For George W. Bush, America's interests and values were fused in Iraq. The result was a war the United States would never win.

Iraq and US National Security Policy

The scale, scope, and duration of the Iraq War posed challenges to the Bush administration's broader national security policy. As a theater in the expansive global war on terror, Iraq had effects, both dramatic and subtle, on the course of the war in Afghanistan. The subtler consequences were experienced early, from the moment Kabul fell in December 2001 to the second half of 2005—a period when administration officials believed the war against al Qaeda and the Taliban had largely been won. Afghanistan "looked almost too easy," Lute recalled. "The Taliban were brittle; they fell quickly; they didn't stick around to make trouble; they went to Pakistan. Al-Qaeda, after Tora Bora, were dispersed, and largely in Pakistan and not in Afghanistan. Karzai looked the part as a national leader. The constitution came together pretty quickly. There was pretty broad-based support with the UN mission and so forth. Violence levels were relatively low." In that context, Zelikow observed, "the Bush administration had already concluded Afghanistan was done."

The consequences of what turned out to be significant misperceptions of the Taliban's intentions and resilience were twofold. First, America's strategic objectives in Afghanistan, already poorly defined, became incomprehensible to the deployed units. As one officer in the Eighty-Second Airborne Division lamented, "My soldiers wanted to know if we were going there [Afghanistan] for humanitarian assistance, or were we going there to—in the soldier's vernacular—kill people."[78] Lacking clearly articulated strategic objectives from the White House and the Pentagon, US officials in Afghanistan surmised that their mission was merely to avoid defeat. Second, because senior American policymakers and officers believed the war in Afghanistan was well under control, they thought they could send higher-quality personnel to the war in Iraq. As the senior US commander in Afghanistan Gen. David Barno recalled, "None of the people the Army sent me were people who would ever grow up to be generals. The Army was unhelpful, to be generous. . . . They clearly had Iraq on their minds, but there was no interest whatsoever in providing us with anything but the absolute minimum level of support."[79] The result was strategic incoherence in the war—gauzy objectives, paltry resources, and uncoordinated military and diplomatic efforts, all compounded by a shallow understanding of the strategic environment in Afghanistan and the region.

The Iraq War had its most dramatic consequences on the Afghanistan War beginning in the fall of 2006. At the precise moment the war in Iraq was at its worst, the Taliban in Afghanistan reemerged as a potent insurgent force, particularly in Kandahar province. From his position as deputy national security adviser for Iraq and Afghanistan, Lute ascertained at the outset that, notwithstanding the deterioration of the war in Afghanistan, Iraq would take precedence. "We were managing, in Afghanistan, with maybe 20,000 U.S. troops, and there were 150,000 to 170,000 in Iraq. Our casualties were just off the charts, much worse in Iraq. So, all the indicators were that Iraq was the focal point, the main effort." Insofar as there were no spare combat units beyond the additional five combat brigades slated for Iraq, the surge significantly limited America's ability to respond effectively to the Taliban's growing strength. "My intent upon becoming secretary had been to give our commanders in Iraq and Afghanistan everything they needed to be successful," Gates later recalled. "I realized on this initial visit to Afghanistan [in mid-January 2007] that I couldn't deliver in both places at once."[80] The Bush administration's inability to respond effectively to the Taliban insurgency at a relatively early phase saddled the Obama administration with an even more complex strategic challenge—one that it too would fail to address satisfactorily.

Additionally, the Iraq War significantly complicated US relations with its European allies. Disputes between the United States and Britain, on the one hand, and France and Germany, on the other, erupted prior to the outbreak of the Iraq War, leading many to question whether some of America's key allies now saw it as a destabilizing force in the international system. US "hyperpower" was already a concern of French diplomats, who maintained that determined multilateralism was necessary to check America's penchant for unilateralism.[81] In the run-up to war, France led a coalition against the United States and Britain at the United Nations and other international forums to block the use of force against Iraq. French efforts denied the United States the opportunity for a UN Security Council resolution that explicitly sanctioned the use of force after Iraq's unsatisfactory report on its WMD programs. French president Jacques Chirac took his antiwar coalition-building agenda to the European Union and to a summit of fifty-two African leaders in Paris, where the French position opposing the march to war was endorsed.[82] In spring 2003 the prospects of another war in the Persian Gulf created "the most serious crisis in transatlantic relations since the mid-1950s," a crisis marked by genuine displays of mutual ill will and hostility.[83]

America's European allies were unable to thwart the march to war, however, in part because one member of the antiwar coalition proved less than steadfast. Chinese policymakers believed that US objectives in 2003 were the same as they had been in 1991: global hegemony by means of controlling the world's oil supply. Yet because of America's power and professed determination to target Saddam, Chinese leaders reasoned that war against Iraq was inevitable. Two policy tracks flowed from these assessments: China needed to be on record as opposing US aggression, but it had to do so in such a way that kept the war short and minimally disruptive to China's interests. As such, China took steps to work against its putative antiwar partners (France, Germany, and Russia) at key moments to dampen the effects of their obstructionism. Most important, China acceded to Resolution 1441 on November 8, 2002, a move that cleared the way for war, given the UN's explicit warning that Iraq would "face serious consequences" if it failed to fully cooperate with international weapons inspectors. Moreover, in the aftermath of the Baathist regime's downfall, China moved to quickly legitimate the American occupation.[84]

For its part, the Bush administration gave China little reason to abandon its qualified accommodationist stance. "Asia policy between 2001 and 2008 reflected a different strategic impulse from that of Iraq," historian Michael Green maintains. Not only did the Bush administration's approach to Asia exhibit a higher degree of multilateralism, but its objectives were also much more circumscribed. Rather than promoting democracy as the solution to a global terrorist threat, Washington sought stability and the gradual creation of "a favorable geopolitical equilibrium in the region."[85] Finally, the decisiveness of the conventional phase of the Iraq War did not come as a massive shock to the People's Liberation Army (PLA). The Chinese military assessed US military dominance in Iraq to be an improvement over its previous resounding performance in the 1991 Gulf War. PLA strategists already knew that China's military was outclassed, and they were taking steps to redress the imbalance. The Iraq War provided incentive to continue those efforts.[86]

As troubled as US relations with France and Germany were in 2002–2003, the Iraq War did not ultimately cause a rupture in the transatlantic alliance. On numerous issues—counterterrorism, the war in Afghanistan, the Iranian nuclear program, and crises in the Balkans, Côte d'Ivoire, and Haiti—cooperation among the United States, France, and other European countries was strong. By 2005, Washington and Paris were in reconciliation mode, facilitated by Chirac's determination to show that France's objections were specific to Iraq and Bush's belated understanding that moderation in his foreign policy was necessary.[87]

Viewed from Moscow, the Bush administration's handling of the war in Iraq demonstrated two problematic American tendencies ten years into the post–Cold War era. First, the decision to oust Saddam from Iraq typified America's desire to maximize its power at the expense of regimes seen as hostile to the United States. In this sense, US policy in the Middle East seemed little different from the December 2001 decision to pull out of the 1972 Anti-Ballistic Missile Treaty. From Russian president Vladimir Putin's perspective, US assurances that its theater and national missile defense systems were aimed solely at so-called rogue states, and not at Russia, were not to be believed. Second, after 9/11, the United States was emotionally driven and incompetently led. After years of warning Washington that al Qaeda in Afghanistan posed a common threat and relaying intelligence that Saddam had no viable WMD programs, Bush's decision to invade Iraq on the flimsy pretext of a WMD threat was, to Putin, incomprehensible.[88]

The eastward expansion of the North Atlantic Treaty Organization (NATO) and US support for the "color revolutions" in Ukraine and Georgia during Bush's presidency were even more troubling to Putin. In March 2004 a second round of NATO expansion brought seven eastern European states into the alliance: Bulgaria, Romania, Slovakia, Slovenia, Latvia, Lithuania, and Estonia. The Czech Republic, Hungary, Poland, Slovakia, Slovenia, and the three Baltic states were also admitted into the European Union that same year. The encroachment of Western military and economic power challenged Russia's sense of security and impinged on its freedom of maneuver in a region long deemed vital to Moscow. Even more central to Russia's sense of security were Georgia and Ukraine, two neighboring states that experienced social and political movements in 2003–2004 that reduced Russian influence in their political affairs. When demonstrators in Ukraine and George called for more democracy and less corruption, the Kremlin viewed this as foreign-inspired (if not -orchestrated) challenges to the Putin regime. The Russian president drew this connection seamlessly as US officials, most prominently Vice President Cheney, cast support for the two states' political progress in terms of Bush's Freedom Agenda—the very rationale that guided US efforts in Iraq and Afghanistan.[89] In 2008 Russia and Georgia were at war, and US-Russian relations were at their lowest point since the end of the Cold War.

The Bush administration's decision to wage war in Iraq had wide-ranging and, on balance, negative consequences for its broader national security policy. Iraq was to be the centerpiece of Bush's global Freedom Agenda. Instead, the war directly and indirectly undermined US efforts in Afghanistan and complicated US relations with other significant powers. Bush bequeathed to Obama an extraordinarily complex foreign policy agenda. At its core, Obama's challenge would be to find some balance between American objectives and resources, to scale back from Bush's grandiose ambitions and recapitalize the instruments of national power that had been strained after nearly eight years of war.

Notes

I would like to thank Michael Nelson, Robert Strong, and this book's two anonymous reviewers for their trenchant comments and suggestions on an early draft of this chapter. I am grateful to Russell Riley and Barbara Perry for their leadership of this vital oral history project.

1. James Mann, *The Great Rift: Dick Cheney, Colin Powell, and the Broken Friendship that Defined an Era* (New York: Henry Holt, 2020), 200–210.

2. "October 11, 2000 Debate Transcript," Commission on Presidential Debates, https://www.debates.org/voter-education/debate-transcripts/october-11-2000-debate-transcript/.

3. Condoleezza Rice, "Campaign 2000: Promoting the National Interest," *Foreign Affairs* 79, 1 (January–February 2000).

4. Christopher Hemmer, *American Pendulum: Recurring Debates in U.S. Grand Strategy* (Ithaca, NY: Cornell University Press, 2015), 138–142.

5. Melvyn P. Leffler, "The Foreign Policies of the George W. Bush Administration: Memoirs, History, Legacy," *Diplomatic History* 37, 2 (April 2013): 11.

6. James H. Lebovic, *Planning to Fail: The US Wars in Vietnam, Iraq, and Afghanistan* (New York: Oxford University Press, 2019), 70, 81.

7. Lebovic, 97–101.

8. John Gans, *White House Warriors: How the National Security Council Transformed the American Way of War* (New York: Liverlight, 2019), 155–163.

9. Richard K. Betts, "A Disciplined Defense: How to Regain Strategic Solvency," *Foreign Affairs* 86, 6 (November–December 2007): 68.

10. John Lewis Gaddis, *On Grand Strategy* (New York: Oxford University Press, 2018), 21.

11. Melvyn P. Leffler, *Safeguarding Democratic Capitalism: U.S. Foreign Policy and National Security, 1920–2015* (Princeton, NJ: Princeton University Press, 2017), 282.

12. Max Boot, *War Made New: Technology, Warfare, and the Course of History, 1500–Today* (New York: Gotham Books, 2006), 352–384.

13. Donald Rumsfeld, *Known and Unknown: A Memoir* (New York: Sentinel, 2011), 356.

14. Robert Draper, *To Start a War: How the Bush Administration Took America into Iraq* (New York: Penguin Press, 2020), 48.

15. All quotations in this chapter relating to the Bush presidency are from interviews conducted for the George W. Bush Oral History, unless otherwise noted. The interviews are available at the Miller Center's website: https://millercenter.org/the-presidency/presidential-oral-histories/george-w-bush.

16. George W. Bush, *Decision Points* (New York: Crown, 2010), 228.

17. Russell A. Burgos, "Origins of Regime Change: 'Idealpolitik' on the Long Road to Baghdad, 1993–2000," *Security Studies* 17 (April 2008).

18. Quoted in Terry H. Anderson, *Bush's War* (New York: Oxford University Press, 2011), 94–95.

19. Rumsfeld, *Known and Unknown*, 498. On this point, Secretary of State Colin Powell agreed.

20. Dick Cheney, *In My Time: A Personal and Political Memoir* (New York: Threshold Editions, 2011), 387; emphasis added.

21. Bush, *Decision Points*, 232. On the importance of freedom and democracy to Bush, see Philip Zelikow and Condoleezza Rice, *To Build a Better World: Choices to End the Cold War and Create a Global Commonwealth* (New York: Twelve, 2019), 403.

22. Draper, *To Start a War*, 173.

23. George W. Bush, "President's Remarks at the United Nations General Assembly," September 12, 2002, https://georgewbush-whitehouse.archives.gov/news/releases/2002/09/20020912-1.html.

24. UN Security Council Resolution 1441 (2002), https://undocs.org/S/RES/1441.

25. Alexander Thompson, *Channels of Power: The UN Security Council and U.S. Statecraft in Iraq* (Ithaca, NY: Cornell University Press, 2009), 144.

26. Farrah Hassen, "New State Department Releases on the 'Future of Iraq' Project," Briefing Book 198, National Security Archive, September 1, 2006, https://nsarchive2.gwu.edu/NSAEBB/NSAEBB198/index.htm.

27. Spencer D. Bakich, *Success and Failure in Limited War: Information and Strategy in the Korean, Vietnam, Persian Gulf, and Iraq Wars* (Chicago: University of Chicago Press, 2014), 214–217.

28. Michael R. Gordon and General Bernard E. Trainor, *Cobra II: The Inside Story of the Invasion and Occupation of Iraq* (New York: Pantheon, 2006), 24–54.

29. Dale R. Herspring, *Rumsfeld's Wars: The Arrogance of Power* (Lawrence: University Press of Kansas, 2008), 128.

30. Tommy Franks with Malcolm McConnell, *American Soldier* (New York: Reagan Books, 2004), 441; emphasis in original.

31. Nora Bensahel et al., *After Saddam: Prewar Planning and the Occupation of Iraq* (Santa Monica, CA: Rand, 2008), 11, 50.

32. Bradley Graham, *By His Own Rules: The Ambitions, Successes, and Ultimate Failures of Donald Rumsfeld* (New York: PublicAffairs, 2009), 348–352.

33. Rumsfeld, *Known and Unknown*, 483–485.

34. Draper, *To Start a War*, 233–237.

35. Stephen Robinson, *The Blind Strategist: John Boyd and the American Art of War* (Chatswood, Australia: Exisle, 2021), 273–279.

36. Williamson Murray and Robert H. Scales Jr., *The Iraq War: A Military History* (Cambridge, MA: Harvard University Press, 2005), 176–177.

37. Bensahel et al., *After Saddam*, 53–69.

38. Anthony H. Cordesman, *Iraq's Insurgency and the Road to Civil Conflict*, vol. 1 (Westport, CT: Praeger Security International, 2008), 47–50.

39. Rajiv Chandrasekaran, *Imperial Life in the Emerald City: Inside Iraq's Green Zone* (New York: Knopf, 2007), 169.

40. Bremer takes responsibility for handing over implementation of de-Baathification to the Iraqi Governing Council, which then outsourced it to Chalabi.

41. James P. Pfiffner, "US Blunders in Iraq: De-Baathification and Disbanding the Army," *Intelligence and National Security* 25 (February 2010): 83. In his interview, Bremer recalls that he believed the order "had been cleared appropriately" at the time.

42. Col. Joel D. Rayburn and Col. Frank K. Sobchak, eds., *The U.S. Army in the Iraq War*, vol. 1, *Invasion, Insurgency, Civil War, 2003–2006* (Carlisle, PA: US Army War College Press, 2019), 146–147.

43. Michael R. Gordon and Gen. Bernard E. Trainor, *The Endgame: The Inside Story of the Struggle for Iraq, from George W. Bush to Barack Obama* (New York: Vintage, 2012), 20.

44. Edelman maintains that the atomization of Iraqi society was a reason for the early reliance on Iraqi externals.

45. David Rothkopf, *Running the World: The Inside Story of the National Security Council and the Architects of American Power* (New York: PublicAffairs, 2005), 406–414.

46. Ivo H. Daalder and I. M. Destler, *In the Shadow of the Oval Office: Profiles of the National Security Advisers and the Presidents They Served—From JFK to George W. Bush* (New York: Simon & Schuster, 2009), 277; Feith interview.

47. Condoleezza Rice, *No Higher Honor: A Memoir of My Years in Washington* (New York: Crown, 2011), 16–17; Powell and Armitage interview.

48. Rumsfeld, *Known and Unknown*, 327.

49. Bakich, *Success and Failure in Limited War*, 209–213.

50. Robinson, *Blind Strategist*, 273–281.

51. Joshua Rovner, *Fixing the Facts: National Security and the Politics of Intelligence* (Ithaca, NY: Cornell University Press, 2011), 142–162.

52. Gordon and Trainor, *Endgame*, 14–42.

53. George Packer, *The Assassins' Gate: America in Iraq* (New York: FSG, 2005), 445–446.

54. Brian Burton and John Nagl, "Learning as We Go: The US Army Adapts to Counterinsurgency in Iraq, July 2004–December 2006," *Small Wars and Insurgencies* 19, 3 (2008): 319.

55. John D. Banusiewicz, "'As Iraqis Stand up, We Will Stand down,' Bush Tells Nation," American Forces Press Service, June 28, 2005, https://archive.defense.gov/news/newsarticle.aspx?id=16277.

56. John R. Ballard, David W. Lamm, and John K. Wood, *From Kabul to Baghdad and Back: The U.S. at War in Afghanistan and Iraq* (Annapolis, MD: Naval Institute Press, 2012), 148–149.

57. Lebovic, *Planning to Fail*, 91–92.

58. Gordon and Trainor, *Endgame*, 185–187.

59. Ballard, Lamm, and Wood, *From Kabul to Baghdad and Back*, 149–150.

60. Gordon and Trainor, *Endgame*, 191–195.

61. Ballard, Lamm, and Wood, *From Kabul to Baghdad and Back*, 153–154.

62. Bob Woodward, *The War Within: A Secret White House History, 2006–2008* (New York: Simon & Schuster, 2008), 72–79.

63. Quoted in Stephen Hadley, Meghan O'Sullivan, and Peter Feaver, "How the 'Surge' Came to Be," in *The Last Card: Inside George W. Bush's Decision to Surge in Iraq*, ed. Timothy Andrews Sayle et al. (Ithaca, NY: Cornell University Press, 2019), 217.

64. Fred Kaplan, *The Insurgents: David Petraeus and the Plot to Change the American Way of War* (New York: Simon & Schuster, 2013), 235–236.

65. George W. Bush, "President's Address to the Nation," January 10, 2017, https://georgewbush-whitehouse.archives.gov/news/releases/2007/01/20070110-7.html.

66. Kaplan, *Insurgents*, 213–222.

67. Benjamin M. Jensen, *Forging the Sword: Doctrinal Change in the U.S. Army* (Stanford, CA: Stanford University Press, 2016), 132.

68. US Department of Defense, *FM 3-24 Counterinsurgency* (Washington, DC: Department of the Army, 2006), 1–22.

69. Quoted in Sayle et al., *Last Card*, 190.

70. Thomas E. Ricks, *The Gamble: General David Petraeus and the American Military Adventure in Iraq, 2006–2008* (New York: Penguin, 2009), 139; Hadley, O'Sullivan, and Feaver, "How the 'Surge' Came to Be," 220–221.

71. Kimberly Kagan, *The Surge: A Military History* (New York: Encounter Books, 2009), 27–31.

72. Gordon and Trainor, *Endgame*, 248–254, 346–350.

73. Kagan, *Surge*, 196–197.

74. Lebovic, *Planning to Fail*, 105.

75. William J. Burns, *The Back Channel: A Memoir of American Diplomacy and the Case for Its Renewal* (New York: Random House, 2019), 174.

76. Hal Brands and Peter Feaver, "The Case for Bush Revisionism: Reevaluating the Legacy of America's 43rd President," *Journal of Strategic Studies* 41, 1–2 (2018): 250.

77. Joshua Rovner, "Strategy and the Surge," in Sayle et al., *Last Card*, 312.

78. Quoted in Craig Whitlock, *The Afghanistan Papers: A Secret History of the War* (New York: Simon & Schuster, 2021), 47.

79. Quoted in Whitlock, 49.

80. Robert M. Gates, *Duty: Memoirs of a Secretary at War* (New York: Knopf, 2014), 200.

81. "To Paris, U.S. Looks Like a 'Hyperpower,'" *International Herald Tribune*, February 5, 1999, https://www.nytimes.com/1999/02/05/news/to-paris-us-looks-like-a-hyperpower.html.

82. T. V. Paul, "Soft Balancing in the Age of U.S. Primacy," *International Security* 30, 1 (Summer 2005): 64–70.

83. Simon Serfaty, *Architects of Delusion: Europe, America, and the Iraq War* (Philadelphia: University of Pennsylvania Press, 2007), 3.

84. John W. Garver, *China's Quest: The History of the Foreign Relations of the People's Republic of China* (New York: Oxford University Press, 2016), 567–570.

85. Michael J. Green, *By More than Providence: Grand Strategy and American Power in the Asia Pacific since 1783* (New York: Columbia University Press, 2017), 482–486.

86. M. Taylor Fravel, *Active Defense: China's Military Strategy since 1949* (Princeton, NJ: Princeton University Press, 2019), 187, 226–228; Dean Cheng, "Chinese Lessons from the Gulf Wars," in *Chinese Lessons from Other Peoples' Wars*, ed. Andrew Scobell, David Lai, and Roy Kamphausen (Carlisle, PA: Strategic Studies Institute, 2011), 158–191.

87. Frédéric Bozo, *A History of the Iraq Crisis: France, the United States, and Iraq, 1991–2003* (New York: Columbia University Press, 2016), 289–300.

88. Fiona Hill and Clifford G. Gaddy, *Mr. Putin: Operative in the Kremlin* (Washington, DC: Brookings Institution Press, 2015), 303–304.

89. Hill and Gaddy, 304–309; Angela E. Stent, *The Limits of Partnership: U.S.-Russian Relations in the Twenty-First Century* (Princeton, NJ: Princeton University Press, 2015), 82–83.

CHAPTER NINE

George W. Bush and the Financial Crisis of 2008

Robert F. Bruner

The financial crisis of 2008 ranks among the premier episodes of government intervention in the US economy. This chapter explains why and addresses the following questions about policymaking, implementation, and presidential leadership:

- What distinguished the Bush administration's crisis response? Its policies marked a sharp—and innovative—departure from previous presidents, especially Republicans.
- What characterized the Bush administration's management of the crisis response? The record suggests that the president retained authority over major policy decisions but extensively delegated policy implementation. In addition, the team of policymakers showed relatively close alignment in their thinking, in contrast to policymakers in previous financial crises.
- To what extent did rational calculation, as opposed to emotional impulse, motivate the policy changes? The abundance of oral histories and memoirs opens a window into the minds of decision makers—the first financial crisis for which we have this opportunity. The evidence reveals an intense struggle to act rationally and decisively in the face of fear. Moreover, it reminds us of the importance of human agency in the context of larger economic and political forces.
- What issues do the precedents of 2008 raise for presidential discretion and democratic rule? Crisis conditions and government structures make it extremely difficult to mobilize collective action and

respect democratic process. The use of exceptional powers during crises emerges as the primary dilemma for democracy.

These questions and their answers underscore the significance of the financial crisis of 2008 to the overall assessment of the Bush administration. Part I of this chapter summarizes the main events of the crisis. Part II surveys pivots in long-standing policy made by the Bush economic team and compares these policy pivots to Republican economic orthodoxy forged in previous crises. Part III addresses two notable attributes of policymaking during the crisis: delegation and alignment. Part IV recounts the motivations of the principal policymakers. Finally, part V reflects on the implications for crisis leadership in a democracy.

I: Overview of the Financial Crisis of 2008

The market for subprime home mortgages grew rapidly in the 2000s, as did their delinquency rate.[1] Analysts attributed the growth in subprime mortgage lending to the originate-and-distribute model of mortgage lending, lax regulation, overconfident rating agencies, securitization, the use of special-purpose vehicles, mark-to-market accounting, aggressive incentives, shadow banking, growing leverage, and the increasing complexity of financial markets, institutions, instruments, and services. Given the many kinds of financial institutions in the United States and their many regulators, it was difficult for regulations to keep up with developments in innovation, complexity, and opacity in the financial sector.

Home prices peaked in April 2006. The subsequent price decline commenced a pernicious debt-deflation cycle. Economic growth slowed. Job losses increased. In the summer of 2007 hedge funds that specialized in investing in subprime debt began to collapse. Mortgage loan originators then lost money and went bankrupt. Fears arose about the stability of banks. Credit market conditions deteriorated. To stem the declining flow of credit, central banks in the United States and Europe began to provide liquidity to the capital markets. An economic recession began in December 2007.

The ability of the Federal Reserve System (the Fed) to serve as a lender of last resort had been common knowledge since its founding in 1913. In 1932 Congress amended the original Federal Reserve Act by adding paragraph 3 to section 13, which allowed the Fed to lend through the discount window "in unusual and exigent circumstances . . . to any individual, partnership, or corporation."[2] The law also required collateral to secure any loans to the satisfaction of the Fed, sufficient to ensure full repayment, and without losses for taxpayers. What section 13(3) did not permit was for the Fed to invest in the capital stock of a bank or guarantee the value of assets. During the Great Depression, the Fed had assisted financial institutions in this way, lending $280 million, or nearly 0.43 percent of gross national product (GNP),[3] when it made 123 such loans from 1932 to 1936.[4] From that time until 2008, the Fed made no more section 13(3) loans. Fed officials justified this hiatus as resisting "mission creep" and avoiding inflationary increases in credit.

On Friday, March 14, 2008, the financial firm Bear Stearns told regulators that it would likely be unable to roll over (that is, re-fund) its wholesale financing on Monday, March 17. The prospective failure of Bear—the fifth-largest investment bank in the United States—threatened the stability of other large investment banks, commercial banks, and shadow banks.

Over the weekend of March 15–16, Ben Bernanke (chairman of the Fed), Hank Paulson (secretary of the treasury), and Timothy Geithner (president of the New York Fed) implored, cajoled, and threatened the CEOs of the nation's largest banks to find a private-market solution in the form of a takeover or a jointly funded rescue of Bear. One by one, the prospective suitors fell away, asserting that Bear was too big and a rescue too risky. The US Treasury Department did not have congressional authorization to inject capital into Bear. In addition, because Bear was not a member bank, the Fed could not lend to Bear through the discount window. In the final hours before the Asian markets opened on Monday morning, Bernanke, Geithner, and Paulson announced an agreement to help J. P. Morgan acquire Bear. Critics immediately charged that the rescue set a precedent of intervention, creating moral hazard, and that the Fed's actions exceeded its legal authority. Bear's stock price plunged 47 percent on the day of the announcement, prompting a hostile reaction from shareholders. The Senate and House convened hearings, where critics lambasted the Fed and the Treasury for the bailout. Nevertheless, Bernanke, Paulson, and Geithner argued that they could not let Bear default— not because it was too big but because it was too *interconnected* to fail. Bear's failure could commence a run on other financial institutions.

During the summer of 2008, home values continued to decline and mortgage defaults rose. Government-sponsored entities (GSEs)—the Federal National Mortgage Association (Fannie Mae) and the Federal Home

Loan Mortgage Corporation (Freddie Mac)—saw their share prices drop 20 percent as investors lost confidence in their ability to fund their assets.[5] This run marked a significant worsening of the crisis, as previous runs had affected private firms (not GSEs) and subprime debt (not government-guaranteed debt). On July 14 Paulson proposed extending a $300 billion credit line to the GSEs and appealed to Congress for the authority to purchase their debt securities and shares. Justifying this huge request to backstop the GSEs, Paulson said, "If you've got a squirt gun in your pocket, you may have to take it out. If you've got a bazooka, and people know you've got it, you may not have to take it out."[6] On July 24 Congress enacted new legislation to support the GSEs, which President Bush immediately signed. The authority to inject capital into the GSEs made *explicit* the previously implicit government guarantee. Hostility toward financial market rescues was rising, based on claims that they stoked moral hazard, but as Bernanke said, "Invoking moral hazard in the middle of a major financial crisis was misguided and dangerous."[7] Evidence of the shift in sentiment appeared in the platforms of the two major political parties at their 2008 national conventions, both of which condemned the rescues as "bailouts" of private enterprises by the federal government. Moreover, in the next two weeks, both candidates for the presidency announced their opposition to more public-money bailouts of troubled financial institutions.[8]

As the crisis unfolded, it became apparent that the government had limited authority to act.[9] Then Lehman, Merrill Lynch, and Wachovia disclosed their own financial distress to the Fed and the Treasury Department. The strategy devised by Paulson, Bernanke, and Geithner was to find a buyer for the three firms. Paulson added another condition: no public funds could be used. As he said, "I never once considered it appropriate to put taxpayer money on the line in resolving Lehman Brothers."[10] This proved to be one of the administration's most controversial policy statements during the financial crisis.[11] Bernanke later wrote, "We very much wanted the private sector to take the lead in rescuing Lehman. . . . But the private sector would have little incentive to incur the costs of a solution if they were sure that the government would ultimately step in. Hence the need to talk tough."[12] Paulson's reservations stemmed from an antipathy toward moral hazard and "socialistic" policies. Bernanke wrote, "House Republicans would never accept a plan that looked like a government takeover of banks. . . . [Paulson] also worried that proposing government capital injections would panic existing bank shareholders. . . . Finally, [Paulson] was concerned (as we all were) that banks that were partially or fully nationalized might find it difficult to reestablish profitability and return to private status."[13]

On September 6 the federal government assumed direct control (conservatorship) of Fannie Mae and Freddie Mac, in effect, nationalizing the ownership of $5 trillion worth of mortgage loans.[14] Investors' fears soon turned to Lehman, the fourth-largest investment bank in the United States. With no private buyer in sight, and with the government opposed to a capital injection, Lehman declared bankruptcy on Monday, September 15.

Lehman's bankruptcy and the government's decision not to lend support shocked global markets. The government was condemned for failing to rescue Lehman, and critics used terms such as "horrendous" and "a calamity."[15] That day, the Dow Jones Industrial Average plunged 504 points (4.4 percent), its largest one-day percentage decline in six years. Lehman's failure resulted in the termination of twenty-six thousand employees, triggered $873 billion in claims, and proved to be the "largest, most complex, multifaceted and far-reaching bankruptcy case ever filed in the United States."[16]

Also on September 15, Merrill Lynch, by some measures the largest investment bank, agreed to be acquired by Bank of America. Earlier in the decade, Merrill had taken a major plunge into collateralized debt obligation underwriting and mortgage financing. It held a large portfolio of collateralized debt obligations and subprime debt.

On September 16 the Fed extended an emergency loan of $85 billion to AIG, a large insurance and financial services company, under the "unusual and exigent circumstances" provision of section 13(3). Unlike Lehman, the Fed deemed that AIG had sufficient collateral to qualify for a loan. In October the Fed extended more loans to AIG, and in November the government announced that it would buy stock in the company, effectively nationalizing it.

On September 16 the Reserve Primary Fund, a money market mutual fund, "broke the buck" when its net asset value per share fell below $1, reflecting the write-off of a commercial paper investment in Lehman. This failure shocked the financial markets and triggered runs on many similar mutual funds. Three days later, the Fed and the Treasury announced measures to support money market mutual funds.

Finally, on September 25, regulators closed Washington Mutual and sold its operations to J. P. Morgan. Washington Mutual was the largest savings and loan (S&L) association in the United States, the third-largest mortgage originator, and the sixth-largest banklike institution. It held a large portfolio of subprime debt, and depositors that knew this fact commenced a run on the bank. In a divergence from previous practice involving Bear, Fannie Mae, Freddie Mac, and AIG, Federal Deposit Insurance Corporation (FDIC) chair Sheila Bair publicly objected to this rescue, declaring that the creditors of Washington Mutual's holding company would not be made whole. This departed from the approach of calming the markets and triggered angry exchanges with Geithner and Paulson.

Bair's decision spooked lenders and investors in Wachovia, the fourth-largest bank in the United States, which had acquired Golden West Financial Corporation, a big mortgage loan originator, in 2006. A run on Wachovia began on September 26. It lost $5 billion in deposits that day, and its stock price fell 27 percent. Over the weekend of September 27–28, the Fed, FDIC, and Treasury searched for a private buyer for Wachovia. When the markets opened on Monday, September 29, the regulators announced that Citigroup would buy Wachovia. Then, on Thursday, October 2, Wells Fargo entered a bid that required no government support at all. Ultimately, Wells Fargo bought Wachovia, creating the second-largest bank in the United States, as measured by deposits.[17]

Within a week, the crisis had transformed the financial services industry in the United States. Certainly, the mood among investors had worsened dramatically, and measures of market anxiety, such as the Treasury–Eurodollar (TED) spread, had spiked.[18]

Paulson, Bernanke, and Geithner struggled to find a response that would restore confidence and calm. Reverting to Paulson's "bazooka" idea, they opted to ask Congress for a huge appropriation to invest directly in mortgage-backed securities. They hoped this would stabilize the market. In late September Paulson sent Congress a three-page document proposing the creation of a Troubled Asset Relief Program (TARP). This would authorize the secretary of the treasury to purchase mortgage-related assets, an unprecedented grant of executive discretion.

Bush addressed the nation on prime-time television to endorse the rescue proposal: "I [understand] the frustration of responsible Americans who pay their mortgages on time, file their tax returns every April 15, and are reluctant to pay the cost of excesses on Wall Street. But given the situation we are facing, not passing a bill now would cost these Americans much more later."[19]

Legislators criticized Paulson for the brevity and offhand preparation of the TARP proposal.[20] It made no provision for judicial review and gave the secretary of the treasury broad discretion to dispense the funds. Some legislators wanted the act to include restrictions on financial executives' compensation, which the proposal completely ignored. Paulson had not prepared the way by building a case with the public or other constituencies. The recent bailouts and the suddenness of the TARP proposal ignited a firestorm of opposition in the House of Representatives.[21] Rep. Barney Frank, a supporter of the proposal and chair of the House Financial Services Committee, observed, "I think it's . . . inappropriate in a democracy to have [Bernanke and Paulson] in this position where they were sort of doing this stuff unilaterally."[22] Frank also supported the Democrats' view that approval of the bill should be contingent on reining in CEO pay. Paulson opposed such an amendment, claiming that it added an unnecessary complication and would cause loss of support among Republicans.

On September 25 presidential nominees John McCain and Barack Obama met with Bush at the White House, but the discussion produced no new policy. McCain had requested the meeting the day before, claiming he wanted to put aside politics and broker a bipartisan response to the crisis. The *New York Times* reported that McCain "sat silently for more than 40 minutes, more observer than leader, and then offered only a vague sense of where he stood."[23] Bush described the meeting as "the marquee event in Washington's political theater. . . . [But] what had started as a drama quickly descended into a farce . . . a verbal food fight."[24]

On September 29 the TARP bill was defeated in the House by a vote of 228–205. A majority of Democrats supported the bill (140–95), but the Republicans rejected it (133–65). Almost immediately, the stock market swooned. The Dow dropped 777 points (7 percent), the largest one-day point plunge in its history. One trader said, "You just felt like the world was unraveling. People started to sell, and they sold hard. It didn't matter what you had—you sold."[25] Bernanke later wrote, "I felt like I had been hit by a truck."[26]

On October 3 Congress enacted a revised version of the TARP legislation: the House approved it, 263–171, and the bill passed the Senate by a vote of 74–25. Over the next seven days, the stock market declined an additional 18 percent, one of its worst weeks ever.[27]

Meanwhile, Paulson had changed his mind about how to use TARP funds. The Treasury would invest directly in the struggling financial firms and corporations, as the initial strategy of investing in mortgage-backed securities would take too long to implement. Therefore, on October 13, Paulson, Bernanke, Geithner, John Dugan (comptroller of the currency), and Bair convened a meeting with the CEOs of the nine largest banks to inject

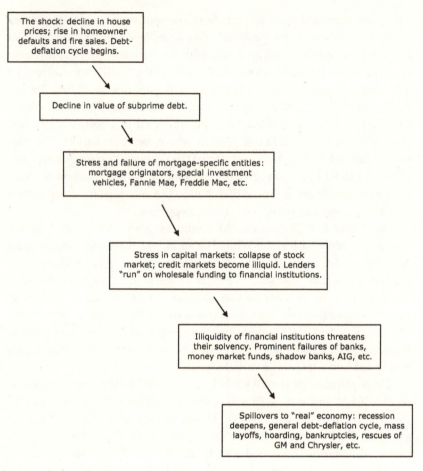

Figure 9.1. Cascade of events in the 2008 financial crisis

$250 billion into the banks' equity in the hope of restoring confidence and stabilizing the system.[28]

November and December 2008 revealed more restructuring of the US financial sector. Joint action by several government agencies rescued Citigroup with a package of guarantees, liquidity access, and capital. CIT Group, a consumer finance concern, applied to become a bank holding company, as did General Motors Acceptance Corporation. Detroit's Big Three automakers appealed to Congress for emergency financing. Congress denied them, but the Treasury agreed to extend emergency loans under

TARP. On November 25 the Fed announced that it would start purchasing GSE-guaranteed mortgage securities in the open market and commenced a quantitative easing program.[29] On December 1 the Fed cut its target for the effective federal funds rate to between 0 and 0.25 percent.

In the presidential race, voter sentiment shifted at the nadir of the crisis away from the incumbent-party candidate (McCain) and toward the challenger (Obama). The November election returned a Democratic majority to both houses of Congress and a Democrat to the White House. In early 2009 the Obama administration sought more funding from Congress, not only to rescue the financial system but also to provide a fiscal stimulus to the economy.

By one estimate,[30] the federal government committed some $32 trillion of public resources to fighting the crisis—more than double the 2008 gross domestic product (GDP) of $14.72 trillion. In addition, decision makers in the private sector of the economy anxiously withheld commitments for capital spending and growth, pending a restoration of economic confidence. In early 2009 the spillovers from the panic were stark: economic output was falling, the economy was shedding jobs, bankruptcies were rising, and financial markets were severely depressed. The Panic of 2008 had reshaped the financial system.

This crisis was a long-running cascade of developments, as depicted in figure 9.1, rather than a crisis moment. Events built on one another; the crisis gathered and grew in intensity, threatening a systemic collapse of the financial structure at home and abroad.

II: Pivots in Policy

History suggests that it is easier for presidents to comply with the norms and policies their political party and the electorate expect them to follow than it is to break from those expectations. In times of crisis, however, a policy pivot may be warranted or unavoidable, and it may be the path toward better goals. As the cynical maxim puts it, "Never let a crisis go to waste."[31]

The Bush administration pivoted from earlier administrations' policies in nine dimensions, as summarized in table 9.1. The policymakers exploited existing but unused authority under the Fed's section 13(3) and the FDIC's systemic risk exception. This enabled financial interventions in private firms, bank recapitalizations, and rescues of automakers. The crisis response

Table 9.1. Significant Policy Pivots by the Bush Administration during the Financial Crisis of 2008

Policy Pivot	What, When	Significance
1. Emergency provisions used: Federal Reserve Act section 13(3) "unusual and exigent circumstances" exception	Fed loan to J. P. Morgan in support of acquisition of Bear Stearns, March 2008	First use since 1930s. First deployment of such funds to prevent bankruptcy of a non-Fed-regulated institution. "The decision to treat Bear Stearns as if it were a commercial bank appears to have marked a permanent shift in the governance of financial services firms."[1] Expanded the scope of government intervention in the US financial system.
2. Federal Deposit Insurance Corporation (FDIC) "systemic risk" exception in Federal Deposit Insurance Corporation Improvement Act of 1991	Secretary Paulson invoked the exception to authorize the FDIC to assist the sale of Wachovia to Citigroup, September 29, 2008. Paulson invoked the exception again to provide assistance to various banks, October 2008. A third exception enabled the FDIC to assist Citigroup and Bank of America (BofA), January 2009.	First use of that provision by FDIC.[2] The systemic risk exception exempts the FDIC from pursuing the least costly method of closing or assisting an insured institution. Generally, these actions affirmed the doctrine of "too big to fail" and expanded the government's role as a lender of last resort. In addition, these actions signified a heightened focus on systemic risk, not just risk involving individual institutions.
3. Federal assumption of conservatorship for government-sponsored entities	Fannie Mae and Freddie Mac, August 2008	First exercise of the implicit federal guarantee of government-sponsored entities and first effective nationalization of financial intermediaries.
4. Apparent reversal of "too big to fail" doctrine	Rescue support of Lehman Brothers denied based on inadequate collateral, September 15, 2008	Affirmed a condition in section 13(3) of the Federal Reserve Act that limited the "too big to fail" doctrine: loans were to be extended only against good collateral. The rescue of Continental Illinois Bank in 1984 implied that the federal government would rescue any systemically important financial institution (i.e., too big to fail). Lehman's failure added uncertainty to the market and raised fundamental questions: In a financial crisis and in the context of complex

5. Concern for systemic stability dominates antitrust considerations	Approval of major mergers: BofA–Merrill Lynch, September 15, 2008; J. P. Morgan–Washington Mutual, September 26, 2008; Wells Fargo–Wachovia, October 3, 2008	Peer rescues led to significant industry concentration. The approval of major deals in 2008 was motivated more by systemic stability and expediency than by considerations of market concentration and competition.
6. Recapitalization of banks	TARP: pivot away from purchasing subprime debt in favor of direct purchases of bank preferred stock, November 12, 2008	First occurrence since 1930s. Policy change differed from intentions presented to Congress. Funds deployed by Treasury, not regulators.
7. Investment in industrial firms	GM and Chrysler, December 2008, January 2009	First occurrence since 1930s. Recognition of "too big to fail" industrials. Pressure from unions. Avoidance of pension and social relief costs dominated over free-market rationalization.
8. Global coordination	G7 and G20 meetings, October 11 and November 14, 2008, respectively. Dollar swap lines: Fed and other central banks, September 29, 2008. Simultaneous announcement of central bank actions in US, Europe, UK, and Japan, October 8, 2008.	Recognition of tight connectivity among institutions and national economies and that the crisis was international in nature.
9. Sheer size of interventions	$32 trillion total US government commitment (217% of US GDP in 2008), March–December 2008, with heaviest commitments in August–November 2008	Mostly occurred outside of congressional authority. Showed that the federal government is the most powerful intervener and expanded the scope of government intervention in the US credit system to include institutions in the shadow banking sphere.

institutions and instruments, what constitutes good collateral? Does collateral matter if the bank's collapse threatens the entire system?

1. David A Skeel Jr, "Governance in the Ruins," *Harvard Law Review* 122, 2 (December 2008): 740.

2. US Government Accountability Office, "Federal Deposit Insurance Act: Regulators' Use of Systemic Risk Exception Raises Moral Hazard Concerns and Opportunities Exist to Clarify the Provision," GAO-10-100, April 2010, https://www.gao.gov/new.items/d10100.pdf.

invoked the first actual recognition of the implicit federal guarantee of GSEs. The policy team suspended antitrust concerns to allow institutions to rescue their failing peers. They massively increased international coordination with and support for foreign countries' central banks by means of currency swap lines. The sheer size of the federal government's commitments obliterated any sense of limits on governmental intervention. And the signals of rescue–no rescue–rescue in the successive cases of Bear Stearns, Lehman, and AIG added a new condition to the doctrine of "too big to fail": rescue would occur only if congressional authority permitted it.

These pivots revealed a new set of priorities. Clearly, the first priority was to stabilize the financial system through rescue: assisted takeovers (Bear Stearns), conservatorship (or nationalization) of Fannie Mae and Freddie Mac, and capital injections (purchases of banks' preferred stock with TARP funds). Characterized by some as bailouts, these actions became the lightning rod for critics on both the left and the right wings of the political spectrum. Yet these rescues recognized—as did 150 years of judicial opinion—that in the middle of a financial panic, it is hard to tell whether a financial institution is in distress because it is insolvent or merely illiquid. Thus, the intent was to stabilize the financial system first and then deal with errant institutions through stress tests, heightened capital requirements, and changes in governance.

A distant second priority was reform of the financial system. The Bush administration promoted few legislative initiatives, although policy pivots did implement institutional reforms through the dramatic consolidation of the largest financial institutions. Efforts to control or even claw back executive compensation were largely ineffective. TARP created the Financial Stability Oversight Council (FSOC), which institutionalized greater coordination among federal agencies. However, a greater reform effort would occur under the Obama administration, in the form of stress tests and the Dodd-Frank Act of 2010.

A modest third priority was social relief. The original TARP proposal included government purchase of subprime mortgages, which opened the possibility of government forbearance on foreclosures. However, the mortgage purchase program was abandoned in favor of direct injection of capital into banks, reflecting that relief was a lower priority than rescue. Although the TARP Act included a provision for foreclosure relief, the program had not yet gained traction when the Bush administration transitioned to the Obama administration. Previously established relief programs, such as food stamps and unemployment insurance, provided some assistance for the unemployed and underemployed.

Economic recovery ranked fourth on the list of priorities. There were no new initiatives to support economic growth beyond existing programs and actions by the Fed to reduce interest rates and adjust other monetary policies. To be fair, this ranking of priorities reflected the exigencies of the crisis. Quenching the fire had to take precedence over improving the fire department or the neighborhood.

Overall, the Bush administration's policy innovations were exceptional when compared with the Republican economic orthodoxy of the preceding century. Oral history interviewees asserted that Bush wanted to deal with the financial crisis in a way that was independent of political interests. He wanted to do what was best for the country, not simply the party. And he wanted to meet the crisis as it occurred rather than kick difficult policy questions down the road. Yet it is impossible to size up the president's policy innovations apart from the norms, practices, and values that came before.

From 1907 to 2007 the US financial system experienced eight prominent episodes of instability, most of which occurred during Republican presidencies.[32] This created a policy precedent that framed the actions of the Bush administration.

Table 9.2 presents an overview of previous crisis responses. The administrations of Theodore Roosevelt[33] and Warren Harding[34] characterized the classic crisis policy through the early 1920s: little or no provision for liquidity or reforms. The Herbert Hoover administration initially met the onset of the Great Depression with traditional Republican economic orthodoxy: protectionist trade legislation, fiscal austerity, tax and debt reduction, increased public works spending, calming statements, and an appeal for local organizations to provide social relief. In the 1930 midterm elections, Hoover and the Republicans took a severe beating as the economic contraction accelerated. Over the next two years, Hoover pivoted somewhat. He promoted direct government investment in banks and businesses through the newly created Reconstruction Finance Corporation (RFC), and he authorized the RFC to invest in direct social relief programs. In addition, he endorsed expansion of the Fed's power to conduct operations in markets and to discount loans to member banks backed by government bonds as well as commercial paper. Nonetheless, Hoover's moves proved to be too little, too late. In the 1932 presidential election, voters sent him packing in favor of Franklin D. Roosevelt.

Table 9.2. US Government Responses to Financial Crises under Republican Presidents

Response	Panic of 1907 (Theodore Roosevelt)	Depression of 1920–1921 (Warren G. Harding)	Great Depression, 1929–1933 (Herbert Hoover)	Run on Gold, 1971 (Richard Nixon)	S&L Crisis, 1986–1992 (Ronald Reagan, George H. W. Bush)	Dot-com Bust, 2001–2002 (George W. Bush)	Financial Crisis of 2008 (George W. Bush)
Financial commitment:							
Total committed[1]	$0.137 billion	Negligible	$4.48 billion	Negligible	$132 billion	Negligible	$32 trillion
Months[2]	13	42			24		10
Annualized current $[3]	$0.126 billion	Negligible	$1.28 billion	Negligible	$22 billion	Negligible	$38 trillion
Annualized current $/GDP[4]	0.4%	Negligible	1.2%	Negligible	0.5%	Negligible	261%
Annualized current $ in 2008 $[5]	$2.9 billion	Negligible	$16 billion	Negligible	$43 billion	Negligible	$38 trillion
Rescue	Negligible	Negligible	Reconstruction Finance Corp. (RFC) investment in banks and businesses. Fed makes 132 section 13(3) loans	Negligible	Negligible	Negligible	Rescue loans and TARP investments in dozens of large banks and businesses. Nationalization of Fannie Mae and Freddie Mac. Massive liquidity

Recovery	Negligible	Negligible	Public works spending. Protectionist legislation	Negligible	Negligible	Negligible	Negligible	injections into markets. Negligible
Reform	Chartered National Monetary Commission to study systemic instability	Negligible	Creation of RFC Expansion of Fed authority	Negotiations to reform international currency system	Legislation to reform S&L industry, regulations, deposit insurance	Corporate Fraud Task Force Sarbanes-Oxley Act	Structural revision of financial sector, TARP established Financial Stability Oversight Council
Relief	Negligible	Negligible	RFC support for state social relief	Negligible	Negligible	Negligible	Negligible

1. Sum of grants, loans, subsidies, guarantees, and other financial commitments during the term. Figure for 2008 is from a report by the special inspector general for TARP, US Treasury. For 1986–1992, the estimate draws from a report by the US General Accounting Office. Figure for 1929–1933 is a liberal estimate, the cumulative excess of federal spending over 1928 levels.

2. Number of months from the onset of the crisis to the end of the president's term.

3. The financial commitment during the president's term, annualized by multiplying the financial commitment by 12/months.

4. The ratio of annualized current spending to gross domestic product (GDP), where GDP is measured at the year ending before the onset of the crisis.

5. The annualized current spending expressed in constant 2008 dollars. This is the basis for an apples-to-apples comparison over time, controlling for inflation in the currency and variations in the length of the crisis.

Richard Nixon faced a different kind of crisis in the form of a run on the US Treasury's gold reserves in August 1971.[35] He suspended the convertibility of paper dollars into gold, froze wages and prices to quell inflation, implemented a tax on imports, and lowered taxes. The Ronald Reagan and George H. W. Bush administrations used the orthodox Republican playbook to deal with the long-running S&L crisis: let the insolvent institutions fail, and then resolve the depositors' claims through insurance reserves and a special Resolution Trust Corporation. The Bush 41 administration, however, advanced new legislation to reform the S&L industry, its regulations, and insurance for depositors.

George W. Bush entered the White House during a sharp slump in the stock market and US economy. The NASDAQ stock market index fell 78 percent from its peak in March 2000 to its nadir in October 2002. A recession began two months after Bush's inauguration and ended seven months later. The period from 2000 through 2002 marked a dramatic downturn in measures of economic well-being after a long period of economic growth, as gauged by indexes of consumer and executive confidence.

In October–December 2001 the United States verged on financial crisis after the exposure of fraud at Enron Corporation, the seventh-largest public company in America, followed by its sudden bankruptcy. Headquartered in Houston, Enron and its executives were well known to Bush and his circle. The company was the nexus of a large network of energy traders and had virtually invented the system of digital trading for energy products and other commodities. As journalists and hedge funds exposed the fraud, trading partners shunned Enron, withdrawing credit from its trading system and producing a "run on the bank." Enron appealed to the Bush administration for a government rescue. However, Bush opposed government assistance to distressed private companies and advised Enron to seek private sources of support. The threat of market runs ended when Enron filed for bankruptcy in December 2001.

The crisis then morphed as revelations of fraud and misrepresentation among other public companies emerged. From May 2001 to July 2002, investigations disclosed that twenty-six public corporations had fraudulently reported their financial results. Enron was just one prominent case in a larger crisis of public trust. All segments of American society expressed outrage at the events and looked to the federal government to fix the mess. The *Economist* opined, "The Enron case still embodies many of the doubts that Americans have about [the president]: that he is too close to Big Business (and the energy industry in particular), and that his concerns are not the concerns of ordinary Americans."[36]

On March 6, 2002, Bush announced his "Ten-Point Plan to Improve Quarterly Reporting and Protect America's Shareholders." He asserted that the Securities and Exchange Commission (SEC) could meet most of these goals and pledged to work with Congress to produce any necessary enabling legislation.[37] Then, three months later, Bush announced an executive order to create the interdepartmental Corporate Fraud Task Force. Meanwhile, Congress gained momentum on the issue of corporate fraud. On July 30, 2002, Sen. Paul Sarbanes and Rep. Michael Oxley shook hands after Bush signed the Sarbanes-Oxley Act of 2002. Just before signing, the president declared that this legislation was the most significant new financial regulation in seventy years. The act had passed with large majorities in both houses of Congress. In the November 2002 elections the Democrats retained their House majority, but the Republicans won control of the Senate.

As table 9.2 indicates, the crisis response in 2008 stands out for its rescues of faltering institutions and interventions to inject liquidity into freezing markets—far exceeding even Hoover's responses to the Great Depression in both number and dollar value. Economic recovery was not the immediate priority of the Bush administration, but it was addressed by Obama's American Recovery and Reinvestment Act of February 2009. The Bush administration took some preliminary steps toward relief for mortgage-distressed homeowners, although it did so in a way consistent with Republican orthodoxy by looking to states and localities to fund and implement social relief. Finally, reform of the financial sector in 2008 was modest and awaited the Obama administration's stress-testing of financial institutions in 2009 and the Dodd-Frank Act of 2010 to address the weaknesses that emerged from the crisis.

Notably, these policy innovations took place in compressed moments. For instance, leading up to the failure of Bear Stearns in March 2008, President Bush asked Secretary Paulson, "We're not going to do a bailout are we?" expressing the traditional Republican economic orthodoxy of letting failures happen.[38] However, by the following weekend, the federal government had assisted in J. P. Morgan's acquisition of Bear Stearns, a rescue operation that prevented a cascade of credit defaults throughout the financial markets. After the rescue of Bear Stearns, John McCain and Sarah Palin penned an op-ed in the *Wall Street Journal* titled "We'll Protect Taxpayers from More Bailouts."[39] During the first vote on the TARP legislation, one

Republican member of Congress told Paulson, "I've been talking about deregulation and free markets my whole life. You're asking me to change my view, and there is no way I can do that."[40] Nevertheless, the federal government injected rescue funds into numerous financial institutions and two large auto manufacturers.

Even within the Bush administration, advisers were initially reluctant to take the plunge into heavy government intervention in markets and firms. As Karl Zinsmeister, director of the Domestic Policy Council, observed in an interview:

> There were lots of times I think things could have been punted and the president decided to just do it now. . . . The worst damage was the precedent it set. . . . The terrifying scale of the government interventions into our private economy—several trillion dollars added to the Federal Reserve balance sheet. Stepping in to preserve some companies, but not others. Thing's I've argued against my whole life. The only way we could justify these things was via a war metaphor. The entire nation was in great danger, and the well-being of innocent people was threatened, so the government had to take extreme and odious measures, as in wartime.[41]

Keith Hennessey, director of the National Economic Council, described the reaction of legislators in the House Republican conference when the original TARP proposal was presented:

> They were *angry*. It was one of the more painful things I have had to go through as a policy staffer. They were just chewing me out. It was just one after another, and it was terrible. They wanted to not have to deal with this. . . . [They said,] "The idea that you want us to write a $700 billion check to bail out Wall Street offends every free market sensibility I have, and you haven't convinced me that the world is going to end unless we do this."

In his oral history interview, Bush's chief of staff Josh Bolten summed up the opposition to TARP this way: "Republicans were against it because it was a bailout. Democrats were against it because it was a bailout for the banks. Find me the politician who stands up and proudly says, 'I was for that, and it was the best thing I ever did.'"

In short, the policy innovations of the Bush administration—principally the rescue of the faltering financial system and injections of liquidity into financial markets—represented a major departure from precedents of government aid and intervention. The size and scope of the 2008 rescue dwarfed all earlier efforts. They also represented a major departure from the Republican orthodoxy of reverting to private firms to assist distressed institutions, limiting the exposure of taxpayer funds and government intrusions into markets, and accepting failures and bankruptcies as normal workings of the market economy.

III: Dynamics of the Crisis Response Team: Delegation and Alignment

The idiosyncratic nature of crises challenges leaders to organize an appropriate response. Two opposing theories about financial crises suggest very different strategies.

One theory, advanced by economist Hyman Minsky,[42] characterizes a financial crisis as a point in time at which the sentiment of financial markets turns from euphoria to revulsion. In this view, the crisis happens at once and then subsides. Mitigating the effects of the crisis requires a one-time response because once the crisis has happened, it will not repeat itself. To view a financial crisis as just a moment tends to invite a rote solution, a belief in the sufficiency of the information at hand, top-down decision making, and overconfidence in the efficacy of the policy response.

As the narrative of the 2008 crisis illustrates, sentiment did not turn at one specific moment; rather, it happened gradually over a series of events. Thus, an alternative theory posits that financial crises are a cascade of adverse occurrences, as shown in figure 9.1. In this view, the policymakers' challenge is to anticipate the approaching crescendo of a series of smaller events. Crisis conditions vary in intensity—rising, falling, and rising again. A crisis response therefore must entail a mind-set of learning, agility, and resilience. Policy must adapt to rapidly changing conditions in financial markets: one size does not fit all. Policy must also emphasize the effectiveness and efficiency of staged actions. Leaders must delegate decision making to those who are best informed. The response team must anticipate various scenarios of failure, resist simplification, remain vigilant, and commit to a resilient response.

These two theories about crisis distinguish between a fixed mind-set (the moment) and a learning mind-set (the cascade). Research by Carol Dweck and others suggests that a learning mind-set leads to better decision making.[43] For instance, studies of the causes of and responses to industrial accidents by Karl Weick and Kathleen Sutcliffe and others link attributes of the fixed mind-set with disasters.[44] The Bush administration's crisis response team generally displayed a learning mind-set.

The memoirs and oral histories of the Bush administration during this crisis reveal a receptivity to new information and a willingness to adjust the frame of thinking as new facts arrived, to value inquiry, and to take actions based on learning. President Bush decided on policy and then delegated its implementation to those who were best informed and at the front line of the crisis. The crisis response team was preoccupied with the prospect of failure rather than being overconfident of success. With one exception,[45] the crisis response team displayed remarkable cohesion. In his oral history, Henry Paulson sketched his relationship with President Bush:

> It took very little time [for me] to convince him. He's told me repeatedly he trusted me, which made it easier for me, but the point I have made repeatedly and people are skeptical about, but I just will tell you is absolutely true—It wasn't blind trust, because he understood what the issues were better than anyone in the White House and most of the people in Treasury. He understood markets; he understood fear. He used analogies; he totally got it. He had a very good memory. He understood how to manage me, and that I needed bucking up and encouragement. I could not have done this—There's no way that we could have gotten through the crisis if we had not worked so well together. He delegated much to me—Told me and his staff that I was his "wartime general." I will assure you that if I had had to go through a process where every single thing was vetted, where you prepared memos, where you let people debate and let the free-market people debate and whatever, we never would have gotten from here to there. He was able to figure out how to make it work and he knew how to ask the right questions. It was amazing to me, when I think back on it. I didn't think about it that much at the time, but I thought back on it—He would ask me three or four questions, and they were the perfect questions. Before Lehman Brothers weekend he'd said to me, "Listen, there is huge resistance from Capitol Hill and from the public and all

kinds of people, to not bail them out, after what the Fed did for Bear Stearns." I said, "We're going to try to do a private sector solution," and he said to me, "If you're going to bail them out, come back and talk to me first." I never worried for one second in terms of whether the President would approve it if we could put together an effective rescue for Lehman where there was Fed assistance. When I came back and told him, despite our efforts, we'd been unable to save Lehman, he immediately said—which was the obvious thing—"You're going to have to be prepared to explain someday how the Fed was able to rescue Bear Stearns but not Lehman." And I said, "It's very simple. We had a buyer for Bear Stearns to inject capital and not for Lehman," et cetera, and he said, "You will have to explain that." On the illiquid assets, he understood the political ramifications; he understood the market stuff. He's not of Wall Street. He had a disdain for Wall Street, so that's another interesting question you'll have to ask him: why did he recruit me, coming from Wall Street, because there's no doubt he had an absolute disdain for Wall Street.

In August 2006 Paulson organized the President's Working Group on Financial Markets, which included the chairs of the Fed, the SEC, the Commodity Futures Trading Commission, the New York Fed (Geithner), and the comptroller of the currency (John Dugan). Paulson wrote, "I was determined to form a cohesive group with close working relationships—it would be critical to how we performed in a crisis." The group met almost monthly. Tensions surfaced among Bair, Paulson, and Geithner. Paulson explained, "We usually agreed on policy, but she [Bair] tended to view the world through the prism of the FDIC—an understandable but at times narrow focus."[46]

Zinsmeister explained that Paulson drove the policy meetings and "knew what he was doing." He was "very dominant and not much of a listener." According to Zinsmeister:

It was so much the Hank Paulson show . . . everything else in the White House was this very careful, consultative process. . . . When Hank came to the Treasury Department, he had been the cock of the walk for a long time. He had not been socialized with any chain of command that restrained action. And they told him, "You're the czar, fix it." Maybe that was the right thing for the moment, but man, he didn't respect any of those procedural limits that the rest of us lived with and worked through.

Zinsmeister acknowledged the "fog of war" conditions:

All of us were not confident that we had an accurate grasp on the facts. . . . This was an extremely opaque area. The honest people on Wall Street would tell you none of them had a clue. Bernanke didn't have a clue, and he is one of the most sage scholars on these panics. . . . [Even] Paulson didn't know. He did a very good impersonation of someone who might know, but he didn't know, by any means. We all fumbled through this. There were all kinds of subjective judgments.

With regard to the perceived detachment of President Bush, Zinsmeister said, "I never got the sense that the president was in any way derelict. I do remember feeling a few times like he was a little detached. . . . The president had some good calls from his gut; he had good gut instincts. . . . I gave him credit that he didn't dodge the bullet."

Regarding Paulson's relationship with Bush, Zinsmeister commented: "Paulson had a special dispensation. He had this very aggressive, very strange, and flummoxing way of hijacking conversations and dominating decision making. He was not a good public speaker. . . . If people say that Hank Paulson had a blank check or something, that's not accurate. The president made the final decisions and there were other people involved. . . . I definitely don't think he had a blank check."

Hennessey said that while the president made policy, those policies were implemented by the senior department or agency leaders. For instance, in the rescue of Bear Stearns:

It is Bernanke, Geithner, and Paulson who are in constant conversation . . . if the three of them reach an agreement and if something is going to be done, it will have to be done by the Fed guys. But Hank can't do that by himself. He's got to get the President to sign off. . . . President Bush grants Paulson a lot of authority to implement policy decisions in specific cases. . . . When there was a fundamental question about something to be done or a directional shift or a policy initiative or some fundamental policy choice to be made, Paulson would go to the President and say, "Here is what I want to do. Here is what I recommend you give me the go-ahead to do. Are you OK with it?" Nine times out of ten or 99 times out of 100 President Bush would say yes. I think the key distinction is that from my standpoint there was a pretty clear delineation that we wanted, the President wanted, to try to keep the application of those policy decisions to specific firms outside of the White House. We didn't want to have the President deciding that this firm would get a loan and that firm would not get a loan.

Similarly, regarding the decision to take Fannie Mae and Freddie Mac into conservatorship, Hennessey said:

It was the president's decision. It wasn't a substantively hard decision because there was a consensus among at least everybody we had involved that this made sense to do. . . . The only hard part was the president was taking on a big political risk for it, and the neat thing about it was his treatment of that was, "Look, you guys all think this is the right thing to do. You've convinced me that this is the right thing to do. I understand how serious this is and how significant are these policy changes that we're making. Let's not worry about the politics. Let's do the right thing."

The variety of pivots and their significance raised questions about the policies that, over the next decade, crystallized into criticisms, protests, and political platforms that focused on at least four issues:

1. *Policy inconsistency:* The pivot about the use of TARP funds and the willingness (or ability) to rescue AIG and Citigroup but not Lehman Brothers gave some critics the impression that leaders were making up policy as they went along, rather than governing consistently. The memoirs of Bush, Paulson, Geithner, and Bernanke argue vehemently that their actions were consistent but constrained by the crazy quilt of US laws, regulations, and regulators.
2. *Poor policy development:* The prime example is the first TARP proposal—all three pages of it. Critics also point to the invocation of section 13(3) provisions over the course of a weekend. Paulson, Geithner, and Bernanke have argued that the brief document was meant to serve as an initial outline from which legislators and the administration would draft the final law. Congressional leaders, however, expected a definitive proposal from the administration.

Paulson wrote, "We were pilloried for the proposal—not least because it was so short and hence appeared to some critics as if it had been done offhandedly. . . . Nonetheless, we could have managed our introduction of the TARP legislation more adroitly."[47]

3. *Lack of foresight and early response:* If the laws, regulations, and regulators were inadequate to the task, why didn't leaders fix the system before the crisis? Overconfidence was endemic in the years before 2007, as indicated by analysts' belief in the "great moderation" that would permit more relaxed oversight of the financial sector. In addition, incoming data are noisy: it is difficult to separate genuine signals from noise. Yet, in reviewing the Panic of 2008, the Financial Crisis Inquiry Commission wrote, "We conclude this financial crisis was avoidable. The crisis was the result of human action and inaction, not of Mother Nature or computer models gone haywire. The captains of finance and the public stewards of our financial system ignored warnings and failed to question, understand, and manage evolving risks."[48] Bernanke recounted, "We failed to understand—'failed to imagine' might be a better phrase— how those pieces would fit together to produce a financial crisis that compared to, and arguably surpassed, the financial crisis that ushered in the Great Depression."[49] Geithner noted, "Our failures of foresight were primarily failures of imagination. . . . We certainly could have been more prescient, more forceful, more imaginative."[50] Paulson recalled that at a meeting with President Bush in August 2006, "I misread the cause and the scale of the coming disaster. Notably absent from my presentation was any mention of problems in housing or mortgages."[51]

4. *Poor communication:* Abrupt changes in policy during a crisis can create relief—or fear and confusion. It seems that investors reacted to the announcement of the Bear Stearns acquisition by J. P. Morgan Chase in March 2008 with relief. However, the failure to follow up in the ensuing weeks with robust communications to build broad alignment allowed adverse reactions to accumulate. Then came the conservatorship for Fannie Mae and Freddie Mac in August and the Lehman Brothers weekend in September, which left no time for considered explanations. Similarly, the presentation of the first proposal for TARP failed to sway skeptical legislators; nor did communications to the public provide a compelling rationale.

Less well understood by the public were the constraints under which the crisis responders operated. The US Treasury could spend funds only with congressional authorization. The Fed could lend under section 13(3) only upon receiving sufficient collateral to protect taxpayers from loss. The FDIC could draw on only its insurance reserve fund. All told, eight federal regulators had some input into the crisis response, making coordination and respect for the others' prerogatives a challenge.

IV: Motivations of the Policymakers

The gravity of the crisis spurred the development of policy. Was the crisis response simply a fear-driven reaction, as some critics claimed, or a recognition of threat? All the actors involved recognized the profound danger to the nation. In his oral history interview, Zinsmeister referred to the financial crisis as a "national emergency . . . the financial equivalent of wartime."

At the same time, the participants' memoirs offer abundant evidence of an emotional component to their work. Bush's memoir relates, "I was furious the situation had reached this point. . . . I was surprised by the sudden crisis. . . . All Hell broke loose . . . a breathtaking intervention [that] flew against all my instincts."[52] "It is hard to overstate just how chaotic and frightening the crisis became," wrote Bernanke, Geithner, and Paulson. They describe the episode with highly charged language: "most aggressive," "first ever," "highly unprecedented," "market-crushing," "emotions certainly ran high," "fog of uncertainty," and "panic."[53] In explaining his attempts to persuade the Republican caucus to support the TARP legislation, Paulson recalled, "Halfway through the session, I hit the wall. I had been going for days with little sleep and no exercise, hustling from one difficult meeting or conversation to another, and I ran out of gas. I realized I was going to get the dry heaves, and if I did that in front of people, it would make for a bad news story to say the least," at which point he stepped out of the meeting.[54] Geithner's memoir echoes many of the same emotions and emphasizes the stress arising from the rapidly changing conditions and the lack of good information.

V: Multiple Crises of Economics, Politics, and Democracy

The financial crisis of 2008 ranks among the leading economic disasters in US history. It summoned a massive reaction by the federal government. The Bush administration's response displayed innovation, delegation, cohesion, and a learning mind-set. The administration set new precedents for the size, scope, and focus of government intervention into financial markets and firms.

To observers on the sidelines during the crisis, the Bush administration's improvisations seemed desperate and rather impulsive. Repeatedly, the crisis team contended with new developments—the cascade of crises described in part I—and improvised in the face of constraints wrought by laws and political norms. The reality was that administrative conditions were messy. Paulson, Geithner, Bernanke, and others seemed to be playing "whack-a-mole" as each new wave of problems arose. The nine pivots outlined in table 9.1 prompted outraged critics to charge inconsistency (and worse).

In a classic article, political scientist Charles E. Lindblom characterized this kind of leadership as "muddling through" and praised it as "superior to any other decision-making method available for complex problems in many circumstances, certainly superior to a futile attempt at superhuman comprehensiveness."[55] "Muddling" may imply disorder, but Lindblom seemed to be advocating pragmatic experimentation, solving a problem in parts rather than all at once and trusting in the virtue of persistent determination. History suggests that each financial crisis differs in unexpected ways from previous crises. Therefore, some creative policymaking should be expected and desired. As Bernanke asserted, "There are no atheists in foxholes or ideologues in a financial crisis."[56] Of course, bending or abandoning long-standing precedents and norms will raise concerns, as happened both during and after the financial crisis.

The primary source materials cited in this chapter—biographies, memoirs, and oral histories—show the profound influence of human agency on the course of the crisis. Zinsmeister and others pointed to the commanding personality of Paulson. Hennessey referred to the expertise of Bernanke. All the interviewees noted Bush's determination to do the right thing right now, rather than punt difficult choices to his successor. In their classic treatise on the history of US monetary policy, Milton Friedman and Anna Schwartz emphasize the importance of human agency:

The detailed story of every banking crisis in our history shows how much depends on the presence of one or more outstanding individuals willing to assume responsibility and leadership. It was a defect of the financial system that it was susceptible to crises resolvable only with such leadership.... In the absence of vigorous intellectual leadership ... the tendencies of drift and indecision had full scope. Moreover, as time went on, their force cumulated. Each failure to act made another such failure more likely.[57]

Finally, this episode highlights some leadership attributes of President George W. Bush that are worthy of future research:

- *Apparent detachment and delegation of action to others:* "One measure of the gravity of an issue is presidential involvement," said Barney Frank, chairman of the House Financial Services Committee, and "the absence of any presidential speech was hurting."[58] Harry Reid, Senate majority leader, said, "This [TARP proposal] is the Bush plan. It's time for him to take ownership and demonstrate leadership. He's our president, it's time for him to realize that the buck stops with him."[59] These criticisms notwithstanding, authorities on crisis response urge leaders to defer to those with expertise at the site of the crisis and to delegate the authority to respond.[60] Extremely sophisticated financial instruments and complicated financial institutions stood at the heart of the panic. It would have been unimaginable for a career politician to diagnose and remediate the financial problems quickly. That said, the charge of detachment seems extreme: the memoirs of both Bush and Paulson reveal that they communicated about the crisis daily, if not more frequently. Presidential history is no stranger to micromanagers who intervene unnecessarily or in matters beyond their grasp: for instance, FDR (setting the dollar price of gold), Jimmy Carter (making reservations for the White House tennis court), and Donald Trump (COVID-19 policies, among others). The ability to delegate some decision making and implementation to others suggests a respect for advisers' expertise, a realistic sense of how much a president can accomplish alone, self-control over the addictive qualities of power, and, ultimately, the humility to accept that no one person has all the answers.
- *Listening and flexibility:* In his memoir and in his speech of Septem-

ber 24, Bush explained that he resisted rescuing banks and companies in the belief that "firms that fail should go out of business."[61] However, Paulson and others presented compelling evidence that the failure of major institutions would make the crisis worse, not better. Bush was an economic conservative, but he was not doctrinaire in the face of new and better information. This mirrors a famous statement by John Maynard Keynes: "When my information changes, I alter my conclusions. What do you do, sir?"[62]

- *Sacrifice:* The interviews and various memoirs note that Bush acknowledged that the financial crisis and the government's controversial response would probably stain his record—yet he proceeded. Facing the possible collapse of General Motors and Chrysler, Bush declared, "I won't dump this mess on [Obama]."[63] In addition, he urged leaders in both political parties to suspend politics and posturing in order to establish laws and policies that would end the crisis quickly. Perhaps this was making a virtue out of necessity or attempting to signal virtues that would gloss his legacy. Nevertheless, the pressure to skirt controversial remedies was palpable—yet he went ahead with them.

- *Communications skills:* During the height of the crisis, Bush addressed the nation on television on September 18, 19, and 24; at press conferences on September 18 and 19; on the radio on September 20; and in public speeches on October 17 and November 13. His frequent outreach to the public belies charges of detachment. Though he had connected successfully with the American public following the 9/11 terror attacks, in 2008 he struggled to rally the nation. He seemed fatigued and somewhat uncomfortable during these addresses. His presentations gave effective and simple descriptions of the crisis and conveyed his engagement with the situation. However, the cascade of bad economic news called for a stronger rhetorical expression of resolve, a plan of action to reverse the gloom, and some evidence of impact. Unfortunately, the ongoing bad news (and his status as a lame-duck president) weakened any claim to immediate and lasting impact. The generality of his comments about planned actions invited doubt rather than confidence. For instance, in his statement on November 13, Bush said he would convene a conference of world leaders without expressing what they would do or what he hoped the conference would achieve.

The financial crisis of 2008 raised profound questions about democracy. When Congress was considering the TARP legislation, presidential candidate John McCain remarked, "I am greatly concerned that the plan gives a single individual the unprecedented power to spend one trillion—trillion—dollars without any meaningful accountability. Never before in the history of our nation has so much power and money been concentrated in the hands of one person."[64] The risk-taking and rapid deployment of massive public assets by unelected officials under generally worded congressional authority became a lightning rod for new protest movements, particularly the Tea Party and Occupy Wall Street. The crisis resurrected latent constitutional questions about delegating the authority to make consequential decisions on behalf of the public. At the same time, incomplete information, the "fog of war," cognitive biases, competing interests, different ideologies, and a balkanized regulatory structure rendered the mobilization of collective action and the respect for democratic processes extremely difficult. The use of exceptional powers during crises emerges as an unresolved issue for the future of American democracy.

Notes

1. Paul Mizen, "The Credit Crunch of 2007–2008: A Discussion of the Background, Market Reactions, and Policy Responses," *Federal Reserve Bank of St. Louis Review* (2008): 540.

2. Absent a section 13(3) exception, the "discount window" was open only to member banks of the Federal Reserve System—the Fed would "haircut" or discount the collateral required when determining the amount to be loaned.

3. David Fettig, "Lender of More than Last Resort," Federal Reserve Bank of Minneapolis, https://www.minneapolisfed.org/publications/the-region/lender-of-more-than-last-resort (accessed July 11, 2018).

4. Ben S. Bernanke, *The Courage to Act: A Memoir of a Crisis and Its Aftermath* (New York: W. W. Norton, 2015), 205.

5. From February 25 to August 21, 2008, Fannie Mae's stock price fell 79 percent; Freddie Mac's stock price fell 88 percent. Data from NASDAQ Historical Prices, https://www.nasdaq.com/symbol/fmcc/historical (accessed July 11, 2018).

6. Mizen, "Credit Crunch," 234.

7. Bernanke, *Courage to Act*, 260.

8. Timothy Geithner, *Stress Test* (New York: Crown, 2014), 175.

9. Principal regulators during the crisis were the Federal Reserve, the FDIC, the Office of Thrift Supervision, the comptroller of the currency, the Treasury, the SEC, the Commodities and Futures Trading Commission, and the Justice Department.

10. Henry Paulson, *On the Brink* (New York: BusinessPlus, 2010), 225.

11. Paulson later expressed regret: "I've come to see that I ought to have been more careful with my words. Some interpreted them to mean that we were drawing a strict line in the sand about moral hazard, and that we just didn't care about a Lehman collapse or its consequences. Nothing could have been further from the truth . . . few understood what we did—that the government had no authority to put in capital, and a Fed loan by itself wouldn't have prevented a bankruptcy." Paulson, *On the Brink*, 225.

12. Bernanke, *Courage to Act*, 289.

13. Bernanke, 302–303.

14. The estimate of the amount of nationalized mortgage loans is from David Ellis, "U.S. Seizes Fannie and Freddie," CNN Money, September 7, 2008, http:// money .cnn.com/2008/09/07/news/companies/fannie_freddie/index.htm?postversion=200809 0711.

15. Christine Lagarde, French finance minister, quoted in John Cassidy, "Anatomy of a Meltdown," *New Yorker*, December 1, 2008, https://www.newyorker.com/magazine /2008/12/01/anatomy-of-a-meltdown; "September 2008: The Bankruptcy of Lehman," in *The Financial Crisis Inquiry Report* (Washington, DC: Financial Crisis Inquiry Commission, 2011), 339.

16. "September 2008," 340.

17. Data on the ranking of bank size by deposits are drawn from "United States' Largest Banks 2012," Infoplease, http://www.infoplease.com/ipa/A0763206.html (accessed July 11, 2018).

18. *Eurodollar* is the term for dollars traded in European or other non-US-domiciled markets. The size of the TED spread, or the difference in yields between US Treasury bills and short-term interbank loans in the unregulated Eurodollar market, is one widely used gauge of uncertainty in financial markets.

19. George W. Bush, *Decision Points* (New York: Crown, 2010), 460.

20. Paulson, *On the Brink*, 267.

21. Statement by Rep. Jeb Hensarling, *Congressional Record*, October 3, 2008.

22. "The Foreclosure Crisis and Older Americans," AARP Solutions Forum, September 19, 2008; Brian Blackstone and Patrick Yoest, "Bailouts Turn up Heat on Fed Chief," *Wall Street Journal*, September 19, 2008, https://www.wsj.com/articles/SB12217644408 8253287.

23. Adam Nagourney and Elisabeth Bumiller, "McCain Leaps into a Thicket," *New York Times*, September 25, 2008, https://www.nytimes.com/2008/09/26/us/politics/26 campaign.html.

24. Bush, *Decision Points*, 462, 463.

25. Vikas Bajaj and Michael M. Brynbaum, "For Stocks, Worst Single-Day Drop in Two Decades," *New York Times*, September 29, 2008, http://www.nytimes.com/2008/09/30 /business/30markets.html.

26. Bernanke, *Courage to Act*, 334.

27. Pietro Veronesi and Luigi Zingales, "Paulson's Gift" (working paper, National Bureau of Economic Research, University of Chicago, December 2009), 3.

28. Included at the meeting were the CEOs of J. P. Morgan, Citigroup, Wells Fargo,

Bank of America, Bank of New York Mellon, State Street, Goldman Sachs, Morgan Stanley, and Merrill Lynch (soon to be acquired by Bank of America).

29. Quantitative easing aimed to inject liquidity into the markets for debt securities and lower interest rates to stimulate the economy.

30. Estimate by the special inspector general for TARP in July 2009, as reported in "The Financial Crisis Response in Charts," US Department of the Treasury, April 2012, 11, https://www.treasury.gov/resource-center/data-chart-center/Documents/20120413_Fi nancialCrisisResponse.pdf.

31. Rahm Emanuel said in 2008, "You never want a serious crisis to go to waste." Rahm Emanuel, *Wall Street Journal* video interview, YouTube, November 19, 2008, https://video.search.yahoo.com/yhs/search. The maxim has also been attributed to Saul Alinsky, Machiavelli, and Winston Churchill.

32. The eight prominent episodes refer to crisis conditions in the United States in 1907, 1914, 1920–1921, 1929–1933, 1971, 1986–1994, 1998, and 2001.

33. In October 1907 the financial sector was rocked by a bank panic that started in New York City and spread nationally. The secretary of the treasury shifted $50 million in gold reserves to the New York Sub-Treasury, although the additional specie proved insignificant. President Theodore Roosevelt issued calming statements to the press, and near the end of the panic he approved the merger of two steel companies in an effort to stem a resurgence of financial sector instability. Roosevelt's administration made no attempts to stimulate economic recovery or provide social relief. Consistent with crisis-fighting norms of the previous century, rescues of financial institutions were left to private parties such as J. P. Morgan and his circle of financiers.

34. In the first half of 1920 the Fed sharply raised interest rates to quell inflation. Industrial production slumped and unemployment skyrocketed. In the 1920 presidential election, the Democratic Party lost the White House to Warren G. Harding, who vowed a return to normalcy. Questions of whether and how to respond to the deep economic contraction stimulated sharp division within the Fed and within Harding's administration. The debates led to a reaffirmation of the Republican economic orthodoxy that had prevailed since the Civil War: deficit reduction, low taxes, spending on public infrastructure, protectionism, adherence to the gold standard, and a sound dollar. Ultimately, that orthodoxy relied on the self-corrective powers of a free-market economy. By July 1921, the economic contraction ended and the Roaring Twenties began. James Grant, a historian of this crisis, wrote, "The successive administrations of Woodrow Wilson and Warren G. Harding met the downturn by seeming to ignore it." James Grant, *The Forgotten Depression: 1921: The Crash that Cured Itself* (New York: Simon & Schuster, 2014), 1–2.

35. The United States largely brought the crisis on itself by flooding the global economy with dollars to pay for European reconstruction after World War II, the Great Society, and the Vietnam War. Nixon organized a secret meeting with economic advisers at Camp David, where two strategies competed for adoption. One called for "shock therapy," a comprehensive response that included freezing wages and prices to slow inflation, closing the gold window to stop the run on gold reserves, implementing a 10 percent import tax surcharge to reduce the trade deficit, and stimulating job creation by granting an investment tax credit and removing the excise tax on automobiles. The tax surcharge was

meant to get the attention of foreign governments and send the message that unless they revalued, the United States might make it more difficult for their products to compete in US markets. The second strategy entailed a more gradual approach—implementing an import tax surcharge, wage and price controls, and changes in the tax code that would spur capital investment and job creation; seeing how the markets responded; and closing the gold window only if necessary. Nixon decided to accept the "shock therapy" recommendation and crafted tough rhetoric to explain the new policy. In reality, the speech was aimed at three constituencies: trading partners, particularly Japan and Germany; southern voters whose local industries had been hurt by the incursion of cheaper foreign goods; and unions and protectionists in the Democratic Party. The decision to close the gold window began the process that unhitched currencies from gold and established today's regime of floating currency exchange rates.

36. "Bush and Enron's Collapse," *Economist*, January 11, 2002, http://www.economist .com/node/938154.

37. For the full White House press release, see http://www.wsj.com/articles/SB101 5460971646141720 (accessed July 13, 2017).

38. Paulson, *On the Brink*, 92.

39. John McCain and Sarah Palin, "We'll Protect Taxpayers from More Bailouts," *Wall Street Journal*, September 9, 2008, https://www.wsj.com/articles/SB122091995349512749.

40. Paulson, *On the Brink*, 287.

41. All unattributed quotations in this chapter are from the Miller Center Oral History.

42. See, for instance, Hyman Minsky, *Stabilizing an Unstable Economy* (New York: McGraw-Hill, 2008).

43. See, for instance, Carol Dweck, *Mindset: The New Psychology of Success* (New York: Random House, 2006).

44. See Karl E. Weick and Kathleen M. Sutcliffe, *Managing the Unexpected: Assuring High Performance in an Age of Complexity* (San Francisco: Jossey-Bass, 2001).

45. Sheila Bair, chair of the FDIC, took exception to policy approaches recommended by Paulson, Bernanke, and Geithner, such as the rescue of Citigroup and the use of TARP funds. See Paulson, *On the Brink*, 376–379, 411; Sheila Bair, *Bull by the Horns: Fighting to Save Main Street from Wall Street and Wall Street from Itself* (New York: Simon & Schuster, 2012), 115–117, 122–125.

46. Paulson, *On the Brink*, 262.

47. Paulson, 267.

48. *Financial Crisis Inquiry Report*, xvii.

49. Bernanke, *Courage to Act*, 82.

50. Geithner, *Stress Test*, 111–115.

51. Paulson, *On the Brink*, 47.

52. Bush, *Decision Points*, 440, 453, 457, 458.

53. Ben S. Bernanke, Timothy F. Geithner, Henry M. Paulson Jr., and J. Nellie Liang, eds., *First Responders: Inside the U.S. Strategy for Fighting the 2007–2009 Global Financial Crisis* (New Haven, CT: Yale University Press, 2020), 4.

54. Paulson *On the Brink*, 289–290.

55. Charles E. Lindblom, "The Science of 'Muddling Through,'" *Public Administration Review* 19, 2 (Spring 1959): 88.

56. Bernanke, *Courage to Act*, 164.

57. Milton Friedman and Anna Jacobson Schwartz, *A Monetary History of the United States, 1867–1960* (Princeton, NJ: Princeton University Press, 1964), 418.

58. Jeanne Sahadi, "Financial Crisis," CNN Money, September 24, 2008, https://money.cnn.com/2008/09/24/news/economy/bush_address_financialcrisis/index.htm.

59. Michael S. James, "Bush: Bail out Economy, or Face 'Long and Painful Recession,'" ABC News, September 24, 2008, https://abcnews.go.com/Politics/Vote2008/story?id=5879591&page=1.

60. Karl E. Weick and Kathy Sutcliffe, *Managing the Unexpected: Resilient Performance in an Age of Uncertainty*, 2nd ed. (New York: Jossey-Bass, 2007).

61. Bush, *Decision Points*, 453.

62. James S. Earley, "Review of Collected Writings of John Maynard Keynes," *Journal of Economic Literature* 17, 2 (1979): 539–541.

63. Bush, *Decision Points*, 468.

64. John McCain quoted in Paulson, *On the Brink*, 279.

CHAPTER TEN

George W. Bush, Presidentialism, and the Fracturing of America

Sidney M. Milkis

The contributors to this volume have grappled to ascertain George W. Bush's place in history. Russell Riley's introduction sets the tone for this difficult task. "No presidency in the lifetime of the republic will be more difficult for history to get right than the forty-third," he argues. Perhaps the most confounding factor in trying to put Bush in context, Riley suggests, is the "extraordinarily controversial nature of his tenure." Such controversy could not have been foretold in 1999, at the start of Bush's bid for the presidency, when he presided over what Riley calls a "balanced system." As Jesse Rhodes notes in his chapter on domestic policy, Bush envisioned "compassionate conservatism"—the idea that policymakers should "put conservative values and conservative ideas into the thick of the fight for justice and opportunity," as Bush put it when he launched his campaign. He believed "compassionate conservatism would appeal to moderate voters alienated by the usual themes of individual achievement and material success featured in Republican rhetoric."

In the end, Bush's promise that he would be a "uniter, not a divider" was dashed by the highly controversial 2000 election, which Democratic activists claimed was "stolen," and more decidedly by the aftermath of 9/11, especially the controversial extension of the war on terror to Iraq. The battle against radical Islamic terrorism transformed "homeland security"—a new federal responsibility—into a highly charged partisan issue. The visceral opposition to Bush's leadership was further agitated by his economic team's response to the 2008 financial crisis in the final frantic months of his administration. As Robert Bruner reports in the conclusion of his chapter on the crisis, "The risk-taking and rapid deployment of massive public assets by unelected officials under generally worded congressional authority became a lightning rod for new protest movements, particularly the Tea Party and Occupy Wall Street."

The fractious politics aroused by Bush's response to these two major crises indeed makes the sort of "clear-eyed and dispassionate analysis required of those who endeavor to commit a president to history" very challenging, notes Riley. The tumultuous four years of the next Republican president administration encouraged a competing narrative that also may cloud judgment. As Rhodes concludes, considering what happened to the Republican Party under the spell of Donald Trump, "it is hard not to look back on the compassionate conservative agenda with nostalgia."

Yet this volume contains considerable evidence that Bush's two terms in office contributed to two critical developments that helped set the stage for Trump's highly disruptive presidency: executive aggrandizement and rancorous partisanship. Clearly, presidentialism did not begin with Bush, but as Andrew Rudalevige's chapter reveals, "a strengthened administrative presidency became a crucial aspect of the Bush administration and his legacy." Presidential unilateralism has been a chronic temptation of the modern executive, and it was consolidated during the protracted presidency of Franklin Roosevelt. The Bush White House was determined to restore grandeur to an office diminished by the Watergate scandal.

Ronald Reagan saw the post-Watergate constraints on the presidency as an obstacle to his ambition to forge a new conservative political order amid the disintegration of the New Deal coalition. He had already embraced aggressive executive administration as a remedy, not only to circumnavigate presidency-curbing legislation but also to slice through the Gordian knot of partisan warfare that began in the late 1960s. Nor was the promise of unilateralism limited to ambitious Republican presidents. In 2001 Elena Kagan, a former Clinton staffer, wrote a widely read article in the *Harvard Law Review* that offered an elaborate defense of energetic presidential leadership in an "inhospitable political environment" characterized by gridlock between the branches of government and even within the executive branch. But Kagan's notion of "presidential administration," Rudalevige argues, became particularly important during the Bush administration.

What distinguished Bush's advance of the "unitary executive" doctrine was his administration's pioneering efforts to join presidential prerogative to party politics. Especially after the September 11 attacks, Bush advanced a form of the executive-centered partisanship that had roiled the Reagan and Clinton presidencies. With the country fractured by high-stakes battles over domestic and foreign policy, Democrats and Republicans became increasingly dependent on presidents to pronounce party doctrine, raise funds, campaign on behalf of partisan allies, mobilize grassroots support, and advance party programs.

As Michael Nelson shows in chapter 1, Bush's leadership initially earned him and the Republican Party considerable political success, culminating in a narrow but decisive victory in 2004 that became a de facto referendum on the president's leadership in the war on terror. By 2006, however, the growing unpopularity of the war in Iraq and other policy failures had thrown the Bush administration into political free fall. In 2008 Bush was a political albatross for the Republican candidate hoping to succeed him: Sen. John McCain of Arizona. The Democrats' strong comeback in the 2006 midterm elections, in which they regained control of Congress for the first time in twelve years, and the victory of their presidential nominee, Sen. Barack Obama of Illinois, in 2008 badly compromised Bush's accomplishments. More broadly, Nelson concludes, the Bush presidency left a fractured nation. Under Obama, the GOP regained control of the House in 2010, the Senate in 2014, and the presidency in 2016. Indeed, in the aftermath of the 2014 midterm elections, there were more Republicans in the House than in any Congress since 1946. "The New Deal Democratic realignment of the 1930s was long gone," Nelson writes, "but no other realignment has arisen to take its place."

The fracturing of America was compounded by partisan battles that have become increasingly animated by issues of race, religion, and sexual identity that go to the heart of what it means to be an American. The fight for the soul of the nation became a routine feature of American politics starting with the culture wars of the 1960s. But as Rhodes notes, the Bush administration aggravated identity politics when it accompanied compassionate conservativism with a politics of fear that manifested in the harsh treatment of marginalized groups in three important areas: erosion of federal enforcement of minority voting rights, failed leadership in the aftermath of Hurricane Katrina, and presidential support for a constitutional amendment to prevent same-sex marriage. The attack on same-sex marriage became a leading issue in the 2004 campaign, which Bush heralded as a crusade to protect the "most fundamental institution of civilization." This crusade exemplified the Bush White House's partnership with the Christian

Right movement, a Republican mainstay since the Reagan era. Bush and, to a much greater degree, Trump exploited the toxic combination of messianic politics and executive aggrandizement in ways that severely tested the resilience of American democracy.[1]

The successes and failures of the Bush presidency thus invite us to consider whether his two terms represent the birth of an uplifting conservatism or the advent of ideological and institutional developments that paved the way for a right-wing populist to severely test the foundations of constitutional government. A careful reading of the chapters in this volume suggests that the Bush administration cannot be easily cast in either role, but collectively, the authors make it clear that Bush was a consequential president whose momentous tenure provides important lessons about the causes of America's present discontents.

Executive-Centered Partisanship

The national security and economic crises faced by the Bush administration raised a familiar dilemma: how can the country maintain an executive that is strong enough to meet difficult challenges at home and abroad but not so strong as to defy accountability to Congress and the public? This dilemma is as old as the republic. But Bush's joining of partisanship to the unilateral powers of the presidency, some of them widely disputed, raised the issue in an especially extreme form.

Executive-centered partisanship in the United States sits at the crossroads of two related phenomena in American political development. First were the organizational and electoral reforms of the late 1960s and early 1970s that weakened the decentralized, patronage-based parties that formed during the nineteenth century. Throughout the twentieth century, both parties were pressured by insurgent movements to alter the rules governing presidential selection—ostensibly to give "the people" more power to choose candidates for office and determine party priorities. However, the pursuit of "participatory democracy," culminating with the McGovern-Fraser reforms of the 1970s, did not empower the average voter; rather, the weakening of traditional party organizations enhanced the influence of donors, interest groups, and social activists who scorned the pragmatic politics and compromises credited with forging majority coalitions.[2] Republican shifted further to the right, and Democrats followed suit on the left.

The effect of these reforms was enhanced by a second development: elaboration of the presidential institution in pursuance of the 1939 Executive Reorganization Act. With the creation of the Executive Office of the President, comprising the White House Office (the West Wing) and important staff agencies such as the Office of Management and Budget (OMB), the president could form alliances with activists and outside groups that disdained the party "establishment," thus subordinating decentralized and pluralistic party coalitions to the more national and programmatic networks that later shaped contemporary partisan politics.

Support for an executive-centered administrative state was consolidated by the programmatic commitments of New Deal liberalism. As FDR argued in his 1941 State of the Union message, traditional freedoms such as speech and religion needed to be supplemented by two new ones: "freedom from want" and "freedom from fear." These new freedoms—representing, for all intents and purposes, the charter of the modern American state—were given institutional form by new or expanded welfare and national security agencies. FDR's "Four Freedoms" speech ushered in a new understanding of rights whereby domestic programs such as Social Security and international causes such as the Cold War called not for partisan debate but for what he called "enlightened administration." Politics became a search for pragmatic solutions to America's challenging responsibilities in the wake of the Great Depression and World War II.[3] From then until the late 1960s, party politics was subordinated to a policymaking state.[4]

Even so, changes in the dynamics of partisanship in the 1960s encouraged the White House to deploy executive power in the service of partisan objectives. Beginning with the presidency of Richard Nixon, party conflict roiled the administrative state forged during the New Deal. Most accounts of contemporary politics emphasize polarization in Congress, but the modern executive has also embraced partisan polarization as presidents have become divisive rather than unifying figures. The fractious politics within Congress has made the parties even more dependent on presidents to advance their objectives.

Reagan pioneered the art of mobilizing partisan fervor and exploiting administrative power for partisan objectives.[5] But as Rhodes and Nelson illustrate, Bush came to office planning to make his own mark on the conservative movement in a political environment where electoral margins were razor thin, old campaign strategies were cast in doubt, comparative organizational weaknesses were strongly perceived, and unified party government presented the possibility of more cooperative partisan decision making. The combination of these incentives drove Bush and political adviser Karl Rove to a new level of party leadership—to make, as Nelson details, the Republican Party an enduring governing majority. As such, Bush surpassed Reagan in showing how a strongly partisan president can use the expanded powers of the office for party-building purposes.

As Rhodes points out, Bush embraced compassionate conservatism for both principled and practical reasons. A born-again Christian, he was strongly committed to softening his party's harsh antigovernment edge. His rhetoric and policy proposals, Rove claimed, were a deliberate attempt to play to conservative values "without being reflexively antigovernment."[6] In fact, as Michael Gerson, Bush's principal speechwriter, argued, the president's rhetoric did not try to "split the difference between liberalism and conservatism"; rather, it conveyed how "activist government could be used for conservative ends."[7]

Bush's willingness to exploit the power and independence of the modern presidency to broaden his party's political appeal transformed American politics. Since Nixon, Republicans and their conservative allies had begun to view the modern executive—cast originally as the vanguard of a liberal state—as a double-edged sword that could cut in a conservative as well as a liberal direction. Bush's commitment to reimagining Republican conservatism, along with his administration's embrace of the unitary executive doctrine, consolidated the GOP's commitment to building a conservative state. Partisanship would no longer be a struggle over the size of government. It became instead an executive-centered struggle over whether national administrative power would be deployed on behalf of Democratic social welfare policies or Republican efforts to promote homeland security, border protection, local policing, and market-oriented policies involving education and climate change.[8]

Rather than curtailing New Deal and Great Society entitlement programs, as Reagan and the Republican 104th Congress (during the Clinton presidency) tried to do, Bush sought to recast these programs in conservative form. His goal was to cement ties between the Republican Party and groups whose members embraced generally conservative values but also relied on government help. Bush's faith-based social services initiative was, in part, a response to religious organizations' belief that they were unfairly disadvantaged in obtaining federal funds to help the poor, the uneducated, and the addicted. No Child Left Behind promised to enhance educational opportunities for marginalized groups—as Bush put it, "to overcome the soft bigotry of low expectations." However, as Rhodes reveals, this objective was compromised when Bush sought to make public schools more accountable not only through standardized testing but also through the expansion of government support for charter schools and other educational institutions that would teach "traditional values." Finally, to win support from senior citizens, in 2003 Bush secured congressional approval of a costly prescription drug program as part of Medicare. As Rhodes shows, Medicare expansion "introduced new privatizing features such as . . . private prescription drug programs and . . . private health savings accounts."

Even Bush's most spectacular domestic policy failure—his attempt to reform Social Security—reflected his commitment to deploying the federal government for conservative objectives. Unlike Reagan, Bush proposed not to cut Social Security benefits but to privatize them by allowing workers to divert some of their payroll taxes into personal retirement accounts. This reform, the president claimed, would yield a better rate of return on individuals' contributions by encouraging them to assume greater responsibility for planning their own retirement.[9] The plan foundered after Democrats won control of Congress in 2006, although by then, even Republicans had little interest in taking on this cause.

The most dramatic example of Bush's "big government conservatism" was his foreign policy, especially the controversial Bush doctrine of launching preemptive wars against terrorist or terrorist-harboring states that might pose a threat to the United States. "If we wait for threats to materialize," the president declared in a June 1, 2002, graduation address at West Point, "we will have waited too long." Because "the war on terrorism will not be won on the defensive," he added, "we must take the battle to the enemy, disrupt his plans, and confront the worst threats before they emerge." Bush left little doubt that he intended to use his new doctrine to justify a war against Saddam Hussein's regime in Iraq.[10]

Campaigning on the war issue, Bush threw himself into the 2002 midterm election campaign earlier and more energetically than any president in history. Recognizing the country's obsession with homeland security and reluctant to thwart a popular president as the midterm elections approached, Congress passed, with substantial Democratic support, a resolution in October 2002 authorizing the president to use military force against Iraq "as he determines to be necessary." Nevertheless, the Iraq War became an inflection point for the fracturing of America—a decisive moment that defined Bush's wartime leadership as divisive rather than unifying.

The Democrats' inept handling of legislation establishing the Department of Homeland Security delayed its passage until after the election (there was a dispute over unionized government workers). This gave Bush and Republican congressional candidates another issue to exploit in several close Senate elections. As John Pitney observes in his chapter on Bush and Congress, "The squabble over collective bargaining was not the only indication that partisan polarization would soon reemerge." Most controversially, Bush made this issue a cause célèbre by championing Saxby Chambliss's successful challenge of Georgia Democrat Max Cleland, who had lost both legs and an arm in Vietnam. The attack on Cleland for "voting against the president's vital homeland security efforts" featured a campaign ad showing footage of Osama bin Laden and Saddam Hussein with an unflattering shot of the Democratic incumbent. This infuriated his partisan brethren in Washington. The ad was perhaps the "single largest contributor to the post-September revival of partisan acrimony on the Hill."[11]

Although harsh partisanship eventually engulfed the Bush presidency, the results of the midterm election appeared to vindicate his decision to become actively involved in the campaign. The Republicans gained two seats in the Senate in 2002, moving them from minority to majority status, and also increased their majority in the House of Representatives. Political analysts were quick to note the historic nature of the Republican victory. As Nelson points out, it marked the first time in more than a century that the president's party regained control of the Senate in a midterm election. And it was the first election since 1934—and the first ever for a Republican—in which the president's party gained seats in both houses of Congress midway through his first term.

Bush's presidency-centered partisanship was reaffirmed in 2004. Eschewing the "soft focus" issues that had dominated Reagan's 1984 reelection campaign—"It's morning again in America"—the Bush White House made personal leadership a partisan issue. The president's strong leadership in Iraq and in the war on terror, campaign strategist Matthew Dowd argued, was championed not to elevate Bush as a commander in chief who stood above partisan conflict but to highlight the Republicans' advantage over Democrats on matters of national security.[12] John Kerry's campaign, for its part, emphasized the Democratic nominee's military service in Vietnam.

The Democratic convention presented him as the candidate who displayed the "strength required of a leader in post-9/11 America."[13]

Kerry's electoral chances suffered when a group calling itself the Swift Boat Veterans for Truth sponsored a devastating television ad claiming that Kerry lied about actions in Vietnam for which he had been awarded medals. Legally, the group had no official ties to the Bush campaign, but the White House maintained a deafening silence for more than a week after the assault on Kerry's war record. In other ads, the group denigrated Kerry's patriotism, claiming the Massachusetts senator, who became an outspoken critic of the Vietnam War, dishonored troops with his 1971 Senate testimony alleging American atrocities in Vietnam. These commercials reopened wounds left raw by the cultural conflicts of the 1960s, abetting the Bush administration's ambition to expand a Republican base dedicated to traditional values.

Republicans amplified the loyalty issue by characterizing Kerry's erratic support for the war in Iraq as "flip-flopping," which also appeared to defy the emphasis on his strength of character. Like many Democrats in Congress, Kerry justified his vote for the 2002 Iraq resolution by claiming that he was merely voting to authorize the president to make the decision whether to go to war. Kerry maintained throughout the campaign that he would have cast the same vote, even after seeing how frustrating the situation in Iraq became. After all, he said, "I believe it's the right authority for the president to have."[14] In that sense, Kerry's acceptance of executive aggrandizement was not all that different from Bush's.

The extraordinary Bush-Cheney get-out-the-vote effort highlighted executive-centered partisanship with innovative appeals to the party's base of supporters. Rather than merely focusing on swing voters, the campaign's grassroots organization, in coordination with the Republican Party committees, mobilized "lazy Republicans" who were predisposed to vote for the GOP at all levels but whose voting habits were unreliable.[15] As Nelson illustrates, the grassroots organization was extremely successful in locating, targeting, and turning out these Republicans. The emphasis was on Bush as a wartime leader. As Dowd put it, "People want someone they can count on in tough times, and Bush filled this paternalistic role."[16]

The 2004 election, widely regarded as a referendum on the Bush presidency, appeared to sanction his approach to homeland security and the war on terror. In fact, the White House's mobilization and expansion of the Republican base emphasized a personal connection with the president. Much of the grassroots organizing was run out of the Bush-Cheney campaign office, although the Republican National Committee played an important ancillary role. Campaign officials admitted that they bypassed uncooperative or incompetent state and local party organizations and created new political operations to maximize the effectiveness of their grassroots efforts.[17] The success of the grassroots effort in Ohio, which gave Bush his margin of victory in the Electoral College, was due in large part to the "volunteers' admiration for and loyalty to George W. Bush."[18] Significantly, as Dowd acknowledged, "Both parties' organizing force focused on President Bush—the Republicans in defense of his leadership; the Democrats in opposition—hostility—to it."[19]

Just as Reagan laid the philosophical and political foundation that enabled the GOP to become a solidly conservative and electorally competitive party by 1984, Bush helped enlarge the party's ranks of core supporters by 2004. With crucial support from the Republican organization, Bush won 51 percent of the popular vote to Kerry's 48 percent, and his party gained three seats in the House and four in the Senate. Although, as Nelson notes, Reagan never converted his personal popularity into Republican control of Congress or in a majority of states, Bush approached his second term with his party in charge of the House, the Senate, and most governorships. Indeed, the Republican Party controlled more governing institutions than at any time since the 1920s.

The Hazards of Centralized Administration

The 2004 campaign, Nelson argues, had the potential to forge a critical party realignment—the first since the rise of the New Deal political order in the 1930s. Instead, the Bush administration's consolidation of a presidency-centered party marked a potential milestone in the development of a new party system characterized by presidential unilateralism, social activism, and polarizing questions about national identity that sharply divide the nation by race, ethnicity, and religion. The emergence of presidential partisanship since the late 1960s had already strengthened party discipline in Congress, and it was a valuable source of campaign funds and other services for candidates. But it failed to stir the passions and allegiance of the American people, as evidenced by declining voter turnout from the 1960s to 2000. In contrast, the 2004 campaign was passionate, polarized, and participatory. Significantly, both the Republicans' grassroots organizations and the get-out-the-vote campaign of Americans Coming Together (ACT), the group largely responsible for Kerry's voter mobilization effort, were organized outside the regular state and local party organizations.[20] Voter turnout rose from 51 percent in 2000 to 55 percent in 2004, allowing Bush to win 11.5 million more popular votes in 2004 than he had in his first victory, the largest increase for a president from one election to the next.[21]

Beyond its immediate effectiveness in securing Bush's reelection, the Republicans' White House–inspired mobilization effort in 2004 might have provided a plausible blueprint for a revitalized party politics that could draw in more people—one that was less about whether to expand or dismantle the government and more about what objectives the government should serve. Nevertheless, the centrality of the Bush White House in policymaking, as well as in mobilizing support and framing issues in the 2002 and 2004 campaigns, meant that presidential politics ultimately subordinated partisan responsibility to executive primacy. As Rove argued at the time, the executive-centered parties that have emerged since the 1980s are "of great importance in the tactical and mechanical aspects of electing a president." But they are "less important in developing a political and policy strategy for the White House." In effect, parties serve as a critical "means to the president's end."[22]

Bush's presidency-centered partisanship was linked to his heavy reliance on the administrative presidency. Reagan made extensive use of executive administration at a time when Congress was usually in Democratic hands. That Bush also utilized administrative mechanisms to achieve his goals, even when his party controlled both houses of Congress, indicated that the administrative presidency impeded the emergence of a more collaborative, party-centered policy process, even under the most favorable circumstances. Indeed, as a subscriber to the unitary executive theory, Bush became a more zealous defender of presidential prerogatives than his Republican predecessors, and his position only hardened as he fought the war on terror.

In domestic policy, the president's staffing practices and aggressive use of the OMB's regulatory review powers were designed to maximize presidential control over the civil service. Particularly in areas such as environmental and health and safety regulation, Bush made extensive use of executive orders, signing statements, and regulatory rule making to change existing policies. The president also used executive orders to make headway on controversial social issues, such as launching a faith-based initiative, limiting federal funding for stem cell research, and denying funds to overseas family-planning organizations that offered abortion counseling. As Rudalevige details, White House management dovetailed with the Bush administration's "plot" to remake the bureaucracy, an effort that targeted more liberal departments and agencies such as the Environmental Protection Agency, the Office of Civil Rights in the Department of Education, and the Civil Rights Division of the Justice Department. Although these efforts often enjoyed the support of congressional Republicans, the administration's heavy-handed approach to Congress elicited resentment among GOP legislators. For example, Vice President Cheney, sometimes with Rove in tow, frequently attended the Senate Republicans' weekly strategy sessions, an unusual intrusion that attested to the Bush administration's determination to make the Republican Party on Capitol Hill an arm of the White House.[23]

Bush's partisan approach to administration tied the party's fortunes to his personal support, which declined after 2004. For the GOP, the negative consequences of Bush's administrative overreach were most evident in the White House's imperious management of the war in Iraq and the broader war on terror. The creation of a new cabinet department signified that homeland security had become an ongoing responsibility of the national government. An important institutional consequence was the blurring of the boundary between traditional executive prerogatives in foreign affairs and the White House's previously more limited authority in domestic matters.[24]

The Bush administration readily embraced this expansion of executive power. Determined to wage war on its own terms, the White House, bolstered by solid and largely passive Republican congressional support, made a series of unilateral decisions that departed from historical and legal conventions. It chose to deny "enemy combatants" captured in the war on terror access to civilian courts, to abrogate the Geneva Conventions and sanction rough treatment (or torture) of detainees during interrogations, and to engage in warrantless surveillance of American citizens suspected of communicating with alleged terrorists abroad. When these controversial decisions were revealed, they provoked widespread condemnation. More broadly, the administration's insistence on a free hand to manage the war in Iraq ultimately resulted in the erosion of public confidence in the Republican Party as it became clear that the administration had badly botched postwar reconstruction efforts.

Well before the financial crisis of 2008 overwhelmed all other issues, the 2006 midterm elections revealed that the Bush administration's and the Republican Party's prestige had been severely (and, in the case of the president, irreparably) wounded by the war. The elections also confirmed the trend toward president-centered partisan voting, even in a nonpresidential year. The Democrats based their victorious campaign on opposition to a president who had become increasingly unpopular because of the violent aftermath of the war in Iraq, his failed Social Security reform effort, and the administration's ineffective response to the devastation wrought by Hurricane Katrina in August 2005—even though he would not be on the ballot in 2008.[25] Even after the election, attitudes toward Bush and the parties remained closely interwoven, both in Congress and throughout the country. An April 2007 *New York Times*–CBS News poll found that Bush's approval rating among all voters was 32 percent, but among Republicans it was more than twice as high—66 percent.[26] That same month, in a crucial vote on continued funding for the Iraq War, House and Senate Republicans voted 195–2 and 45–2, respectively, against a bill to tie the appropriation to a schedule for military withdrawal. House and Senate Democrats voted 216–13 and 49–0, respectively, in favor of the bill.[27] When Bush vetoed the legislation, Republican loyalists in Congress united to prevent the Democrats from attaining the two-thirds majority needed to override the veto.

Bush's command of his party, even though it deprecated collective partisan responsibility, enabled him to "muddle through" the last two, highly contentious years of his presidency, as Bruner puts it. As unpopular as Bush was in early 2007, his reliance on executive authority left him far from powerless. The Democrats won the midterm elections by promising to end the war in Iraq, but that meant nothing to a president whose willingness to resort to unilateral executive action characterized his entire administration. To the president's credit, as Spencer Bakich writes in his account of the Iraq War, Bush demonstrated a remarkable capacity to learn and adapt. "Aided by [national security adviser Steve] Hadley and a talented team at the NSC, Bush admitted errors, entertained new ideas, considered trade-offs and risk in a more systematic fashion, and acted decisively in the face of uncertainty." The day after the 2006 "shellacking," as the president called his party's midterm disaster, Bush fired Secretary of Defense Donald Rumsfeld, signaling his desire for a new strategy to achieve success in the war. He found such a strategy in the counterinsurgency approach championed by Gen. David Petraeus, who argued that American forces could bring stability to Iraq only by protecting the Iraqi people in the neighborhoods where they lived. Whereas Rumsfeld's objective of turning the war effort over to the Iraqis would have required fewer US troops, Petraeus's strategy required more. Relying on his authority as commander in chief, Bush sent an additional twenty thousand soldiers to Iraq—the so-called surge. Congressional Democrats sputtered but acquiesced, pinning their hopes on the election of a Democratic president in 2008 who would use his or her own unilateral authority to bring US involvement in Iraq to a speedy conclusion.

Although the Bush administration's pivot to the surge stabilized conditions in Iraq somewhat, it left the country mired in a sectarian struggle between Sunni and Shia Muslims. In fact, as Bakich observes, "By resolving the security challenges so effectively, the surge had the unintended consequence of reinforcing the very dysfunctions of Iraqi politics and institutions that spurred the civil conflict in 2005–2006." This internecine struggle in Iraq and elsewhere in the Middle East undermined Bush's commitment to advance democracy throughout the region. In the 2000 campaign Bush had promised that the US military's focus would no longer be on nation building and humanitarian interventions in parts of the world that had no bearing on the national interest. But his post-9/11 ambition to make the war on terror a core partisan objective, his commitment to the consolidation of presidential power, and the shock of presiding over the first attack on American soil since the War of 1812 inspired his later transformative objectives.

Bush, Condoleezza Rice (who served as first-term national security adviser and second-term secretary of state), and Hadley were, according to Secretary of Defense Robert Gates, "true believers. . . . But as we were fighting the wars, I thought that to articulate it as our near-term goal was setting ourselves up for failure." "The result," Bakich concludes, "was a war the United States would never win"—a seemingly permanent struggle against not just a country but an idea—radical Islamic terrorism—that diminished the United States' reputation in the world.

Bush's final exercise of power came in response to the worst economic crisis since the Great Depression. It required the full involvement of the White House, Congress, the Treasury Department, the Federal Reserve Board, and other independent financial agencies. In September 2008 several of the nation's largest banks, insurance conglomerates, and investment firms teetered on the verge of bankruptcy, the result of rampant speculation and loose lending in the home mortgage market, facilitated by passage of the Gramm-Leach-Bliley Act and other deregulatory measures in the 1990s.

Although Bush did not know how to avert what appeared to be a looming depression, he relied on those who did—notably, Secretary of the Treasury Henry Paulson and Federal Reserve chair Ben Bernanke.

Bruner's account of the response to this cascading crisis shows that congressional Republicans and even some members of the Bush administration "were initially reluctant to take the plunge into heavy government intervention in markets and firms." Eschewing the example of Herbert Hoover, who refused to undertake a full-scale federal intervention to redress the collapse of the stock market and the banking system during the Great Depression, Bush, who was in the twilight of his presidency, refused to punt. Indeed, his big-government brand of conservatism relegated the GOP's traditional antistatism, already seriously compromised by the Reagan administration's heavy investment in defense and acceptance of massive deficit spending, to empty rhetoric. Having put the country on a war footing in response to 9/11, Bush was prepared to extend his crisis presidency to the domestic front. As director of the Domestic Policy Council Karl Zinsmeister remembered, "The entire nation was in great danger, and the well-being of innocent people was threatened, so the government had to take extreme and odious measures, as in wartime."

Through the fog of war, the Bush economic team, led by Paulson, used the nearly blank check reluctantly bestowed by Congress to pursue an unprecedented bailout initiative: the Troubled Asset Relief Program (TARP), with a budget of $700 billion. Democrats in Congress had been reluctant to pass a bill from a lame-duck Republican president, and congressional Republicans blanched at any massive market intervention by the federal government. On September 29 the House voted down the measure, and the Dow Jones Industrial Average immediately fell 777 points, the largest single-day drop in history. To avert a panic, the Senate passed the bill on October 1, and the chastened House followed suit on October 3; the president signed it into law later that same day.[28] TARP stopped the bleeding and stabilized the financial system.

The dampening effects of the financial crisis on the nation's economy persisted, awaiting the incoming Obama administration. But as Bruner notes, "The sheer size of the federal government's commitments obliterated any sense of limits on governmental intervention." Moreover, this massive program marked important departures from past government responses to economic crises. The rapid response exploited existing but unused legal authority under the Fed's section 13(3) and the FDIC's systemic risk exception. As Bruner summarizes, this enabled the Bush administration to intervene in private firms, recapitalize banks, and rescue automakers; to recognize the federal guarantee of government-sponsored entities (Fannie Mae and Freddie Mac); to suspend antitrust concerns, allowing institutions to rescue their failing peers; and to massively increase international coordination and support for foreign countries' central banks by means of currency swap lines.

In sum, the Bush administration's war against the terror of economic collapse put a premium on rescuing financial markets—a bold but conservative response that de-emphasized economic reform and social relief. These actions, demonized as "bailouts," continued after Obama took office and became a lightning rod for critics from both the Right and the Left. Just as the Iraq War discredited the foreign policy establishment, TARP led many to charge that the system was "rigged," a rallying cry that later sparked movements as diverse as the Tea Party and Occupy Wall Street and, in 2016 and 2020, presidential candidates as disparate as Donald Trump and Bernie Sanders.

How Should George W. Bush Be Remembered?

Although Bush's presidency advanced a form of executive-centered partisanship that helped fracture the country, the hindsight afforded by Trump's disruptive leadership cast Bush's tenure in a more positive light. By early 2018, six in ten Americans (61 percent) expressed a favorable view of Bush, nearly double the 33 percent who judged him favorably when he left office in January 2009. Significantly, much of this increase came from Democrats, rising from 11 percent in February 2009 to 54 percent less than a decade later. By the same token, although most Republicans still had a favorable view of Bush in 2018 (76 percent), their disapproval of him had tripled from 7 percent to 21 percent. Much of this change in attitude can be attributed to Trump. Some pro-Trump Republicans did not appreciate Bush's comment in 2017 that "bigotry seems emboldened. Our politics seems more vulnerable to conspiracy theories and outright fabrication."[29] In contrast, many Democrats and independents identified Bush as the kind of Republican they found acceptable—a political opponent, but not someone who posed an existential threat to American democracy.[30] They contrasted Bush's 9/11 outreach to Muslims with Trump's anti-Muslim bigotry.

In 2021 the death of Donald Rumsfeld—the point man for the Iraq disaster—prompted reflection about the tragic nature of the Bush presidency, characterized by dedicated public servants with idealistic intentions leading America down a disastrous path. Like other well-intentioned public servants in the Bush administration, Rumsfeld abetted the White House in centralizing power and politicizing the bureaucracy.

Overall, Bush advanced the executive-centered partisanship that the Reagan administration—the template for the Bush presidency—first brought into sharp relief. Bush "extended the precedents of his predecessors," Rudalevige concludes, and "bequeathed to his successors a stronger office in institutional, administrative terms." More concretely, under Bush, a conservative state apparatus began to take shape in Washington that embodied a centralizing ambition to advance traditional values at home and abroad.

Fierce partisan conflict in the United States is not new. Throughout American history, there have been polarizing struggles over fundamental questions about the meaning of the Declaration of Independence and the Constitution and the relationship between the two. When added to battles over what it means to be an American, these struggles over ideals have become all-encompassing—conflicts that have become more regular and dangerous with the rise of the administrative state. The idea of the "state" cuts more deeply than suggested by Max Weber's definition: "a human community that (successfully) claims the monopoly of the legitimate use of physical force within a given territory."[31] Beyond the powers of government, the state represents a centralizing ambition to impose a vision of citizenship on its people. This vision is symbolized less by the Declaration and the Constitution than by rallying emblems such as the flag. A key state mobilizing force is patriotism, a concept at once centralizing and conflictual.[32]

In the end, as the 2002 midterm and 2004 presidential campaigns showed, the war on terror became a crusade that tested the meaning of patriotism in the United States. The presidency's increasing tilt toward unilateralism in foreign affairs had been a growing concern since the travails of Vietnam. Nixon's pioneering but corrupt advancement of executive-centered partisanship resulted in efforts to restore the guardrails of constitutional government, but since the 1980s, public concerns about an "imperial presidency" have typically diminished when a president of one's own party is in office.[33] As a result, Bush was able to conduct the war on terror in an ideological environment primed by modern conservatism's embrace of a presidency-centered state when the power is in Republican hands. His legal team built a fortress of theoretical support—the unitary executive—for the presidency's constitutional independence, and the White House took innovative steps to centralize the Republican Party's messaging in ways that transformed the 2002 and 2004 elections into referenda on Bush's leadership in that war.

To be sure, Trump's right-wing populism was not the lineal descendant of Bush's big-government conservatism. In 2005, for example, efforts to nominate the moderate Harriet Miers to the Supreme Court failed when Bush and Rove were blindsided by the conservative Republican base's determination to select only militant conservatives. As Barbara Perry's account of this episode shows, Bush's view that Miers—his legal counsel and longtime political ally, an adept problem solver, and the first woman to head the Texas Bar—was an appropriate successor to Sandra Day O'Conner was rejected by the highly mobilized conservative activists who had become such an important force in judicial politics. Although Bush had encouraged these activists, their rebellion clearly showed that there were limits to his executive-centered party building.

Bush embraced and extended the uplifting conservatism expressed by Reagan—a conservatism that, in opposition to post-1960s liberalism, saw America as a "city on a hill." Reagan's message of national resilience and religious tolerance inspired the position Bush took in the wake of 9/11. The first sentence of the 2016 Republican platform read: "We believe in American exceptionalism," an uplifting sentiment exalted by Bush in his quest to bring democracy to the Middle East.

Nevertheless, under Reagan and Bush, the Republican Party built a conservative base whose foot soldiers, most notably those in the Christian Right, were fixated on the potential threats posed by radical Islamic terrorism and illegal immigration. Bush resisted these nativist tendencies. Indeed, he and Rove considered the support of a surging Latino population critical to building a new Republican majority. In courting Latino voters in 2000 and 2004, Bush emphasized his deep cultural ties to Mexico, reminding Latinos that he spoke Spanish; that his brother Jeb, then Florida's governor, was married to a Mexican American woman; and that as governor of Texas he had met with Mexican officials along the border to improve political relations and spur economic development. These efforts appeared to bear fruit in the president's 2004 reelection effort. Exit polls indicated that he won 44 percent of the Hispanic vote, the best showing for a Republican candidate in a presidential election. In his 2005 State of the Union speech,

Bush announced that comprehensive immigration reform would be a top priority of his second term. The president's plan was to knit together a bipartisan coalition in support of a bill that tied tough border security and workplace enforcement to creation of a path to citizenship for the estimated twelve million illegal immigrants. However, in contrast to the war on terror, Republicans refused to follow Bush's lead on immigration, and after a protracted struggle, Congress failed to pass his immigration reform bill. In an indication of where the party was headed, most Republicans saw Bush's plan as an amnesty program that violated their commitment to law and order, a Republican trope since the Nixon administration.

Then and later, Bush expressed deep regret for failing to achieve immigration reform, calling this defeat one of the biggest disappointments of his presidency. But as his party's opposition indicated, grassroots Republicans were ready for a different kind of conservatism that was nativist rather than welcoming, populist rather than establishment, and angry rather than compassionate. John McCain and Mitt Romney, the GOP's losing presidential candidates in 2008 and 2012, respectively, did not satisfy this desire any more than Bush did. In 2016, however, the party's grass roots found their leader in Donald Trump.

The Trump-led Republican Party continued to embrace some of the most controversial features of Bush's presidency: executive aggrandizement, harsh partisanship, and direct ties to social activists who resisted the surging diversity in America. Moreover, the Republican base Bush cultivated has given succor not just to Trump but also to members of Congress who, like him, are purveyors of polarizing issues that divide red and blue America.

In the final analysis, Bush's fusion of presidential prerogative and partisan politics weakened the institutions that might have forestalled Trump's capture of the Republican Party. According to William Mayer, during their eight years in the White House, Bush and Rove, his chief strategist, added to the "substantial delegitimization of the Republican establishment, which allowed Trump to win the nomination even though he was supported by virtually no major Republican Party leaders or elected officials."[34]

Ironically, Bush was the choice of the rearguard GOP leaders whose power had been greatly weakened by party reforms, most notably the McGovern-Fraser reforms, since the late 1960s. They knew that, to defeat Vice President Al Gore, they needed a moderate conservative candidate, so the large-state Republican governors united behind their Texas colleague and his record as a problem solver. The governors' display of solidarity was evidence that, even though candidate-centered politics had supplanted party-centered politics since the waning of the New Deal, it was still possible to put the party's political well-being first.

As the contributors to this volume clearly show, Bush turned out to be neither a pragmatist nor a champion of the Republican establishment. To the contrary, he oversaw a national party offensive that accelerated the displacement of state and local Republican organizations. He and his staff advanced an executive-centered partisanship that weakened the constitutional system of checks and balances, diminished the integrity of decentralizing institutions such as Congress and the states, and eroded citizens' trust in the competence and fairness of the national government.

In an era marked by vigorous party competition, divided government, and bitter struggles to control the judiciary, these dangerous trends are likely to continue.[35] Trump's disruptive presidency was testament to the political developments that fused executive prerogative with fierce partisanship and instilled in the country the false hope that a single individual can be the sole steward of the public welfare. Bush and his political allies did much to advance the myth of presidentialism. Until this misplaced faith in a presidency-centered democracy is decisively disabused, the prospect of revitalizing a more sober form of conservatism or restoring the constitutional norms and institutions of the American republic will be a chimera.

Notes

1. Steven Levitsky and Daniel Ziblatt, *How Democracies Die* (New York: Crown, 2018).

2. Morton Keller, *America's Three Regimes: A New Political History* (Oxford: Oxford University Press, 2007).

3. Sidney M. Milkis, "Ideas, Institutions, and the New Deal Constitutional Order," *American Political Thought* 3, 1 (Spring 2014): 167–176.

4. Sidney M. Milkis, *The President and the Parties:The Transformation of the American Party System since the New Deal* (New York: Oxford University Press, 1993), 143; Karen Orren and Stephen Skowronek, *The Policy State: An American Predicament* (Cambridge, MA: Harvard University Press, 2017).

5. Daniel Galvin, "Presidents as Agents of Change," *Presidential Studies Quarterly* 44, 1 (March 2014): 95–119.

6. Karl Rove, director of Office of Strategic Initiatives and chief adviser to President George W. Bush, interview with Sidney Milkis and Jesse Rhodes, November 15, 2001.

7. Michael Gerson, chief speechwriter for President George W. Bush, interview with Sidney Milkis and Jesse Rhodes, November 15, 2001.

8. Nicholas F. Jacobs, Desmond King, and Sidney M. Milkis, "Building a Conservative State: Partisan Polarization and the Redeployment of Administrative Power," *Perspectives on Politics* 17, 2 (June 2019): 453–469.

9. Stephen Mufson, "FDR's Deal in Bush's Terms," *Washington Post*, February 20, 2005.

10. "The Bush Doctrine," in Michael Nelson, *Evolving Presidency: Landmark Documents*, 6th ed. (Los Angeles: Sage, 2019), 283–287.

11. Gary Jacobson, *A Divider, Not a Uniter: George W. Bush and the American People*, 2nd ed. (Boston: Longman, 2010), 71.

12. Matthew Dowd, interview with Sidney Milkis and Jesse Rhodes, July 20, 2005.

13. Tad Devine, political strategist, John Kerry–John Edwards 2004 campaign, interview with Sidney Milkis, July 2004.

14. Comment by John Kerry on CNN's *Inside Politics*, August 9, 2004.

15. Dowd interview; Terry Nelson, political director, George W. Bush–Richard Cheney 2004 campaign, interview with Sidney Milkis and Jesse Rhodes, August 19, 2005.

16. Dowd interview.

17. Nelson interview.

18. Darrin Klingler, Ohio executive director, George W. Bush–Richard Cheney 2004 campaign, interview with Sidney Milkis, July 27, 2005.

19. Dowd interview.

20. The Democratic Party's tendency to rely on auxiliary organizations such as labor unions was reinforced by enactment of the Bipartisan Campaign Finance Reform Act of 2002, which proscribed party organizations but not independent interest groups from raising and spending "soft" money. These so-called 527 groups, named for the section of the tax code that regulates them, were formed outside the regular party organization in part to circumvent campaign finance regulations. No less important, however, was the view of some leaders of the 527 organizations that the Democratic National Committee and state parties were not capable of mobilizing base support for liberal causes. ACT official, interview with Sidney Milkis, August 19, 2005. These groups formed an alliance to build an impressive media and ground campaign to match the efforts of the Republican Party.

21. Paul R. Abramson, John H. Aldrich, and David W. Rohde, *Change and Continuity in the 2004 and 2006 Elections* (Washington, DC: CQ Press, 2007), 85.

22. Rove interview.

23. Jonathan Mahler, "After the Imperial Presidency," *New York Times Magazine*, November 9, 2008, 44.

24. Jennifer Merolla and Paul Pulido, "Follow the Leader: Major Changes to Homeland Security and Terrorism Policy," in *The Politics of Major Policy Reform in Postwar America*, ed. Jeffery A. Jenkins and Sidney M. Milkis (New York: Cambridge University Press, 2014), 257–258; Aaron Wildavsky, "The Two Presidencies," *Society*, January–February 1998, 24–31 (first published in 1966).

25. The 2006 elections are discussed in Abramson, Aldrich, and Rohde, *Change and Continuity*, and in Larry J. Sabato, *The Sixth Year Itch: The Rise and Fall of the George W. Bush Presidency* (New York: Longman, 2007).

26. Janet Elder, "For Most Bush Voters, No Regrets after 2 Years," *New York Times*, May 2, 2007.

27. "Senate Passes Iraq Withdrawal Bill; Veto Threat Looms," CNN.com, April 26, 2007, http://www.cnn.com/2007/POLITICS/04/26/congress.iraq/index.html.

28. Peter Baker, *Days of Fire: Bush and Cheney in the White House* (New York: Doubleday, 2013), chap. 35.

29. Rebeca Saransky, "George W. Bush: 'Bigotry Seems Emboldened' in US," The Hill, October, 19, 2017, https://thehill.com/homenews/news/356212-george-w-bush-bigotry -seems-emboldened-in-us.

30. Ryan Stuyk, "George Bush's Favorability Rating Has Pulled a Complete 180," CNN.com, January 22, 2018, https://www.cnn.com/2018/01/22/politics/george-w-bush -favorable-poll/index.html.

31. Max Weber, "Politics as a Vocation," in *From Max Weber: Essays in Sociology*, ed. H. R. Gerth and C. Wright Mills (New York: Oxford University Press, 1946), 78:77–128.

32. Randolph Bourne, "The State," 1918, http://fair-use.org/randolph-bourne/the -state/ (accessed January 3, 2018).

33. Andrew Rudalevige, *The New Imperial Presidency: Renewing Presidential Power after Watergate* (Ann Arbor: University of Michigan Press, 2006).

34. William G. Mayer, *The Uses and Misuses of Politics: Karl Rove and the Bush Presidency* (Lawrence: University Press of Kansas, 2021), 48.

35. Frances E. Lee, *Insecure Majorities: Congress and the Perpetual Campaign* (Chicago: University of Chicago Press, 2018).

APPENDIX ONE

Timeline of the George W. Bush Presidency

Compiled by Justin Peck and Bryan Craig, drawing on the *Washington Post*, the Miller Center, and other sources.

1999

Mar 2   Bush announces formation of an exploratory committee.

Jun 12   Bush declares his candidacy in Iowa and introduces "compassionate conservatism."

Nov 19   Bush outlines his foreign policy perspective.

Dec 1   Bush proposes a five-year, $483 billion tax plan.

2000

Jan 24   Bush wins the Iowa caucus.

Feb 1   Bush loses the New Hampshire primary to John McCain.

Mar 9   After Super Tuesday, McCain drops out of the campaign, clearing the way for Bush.

Jul 25   Bush selects Richard Cheney as his running mate.

Aug 3   Bush accepts the Republican Party's presidential nomination.

Nov 7   Election is too close to call; recount begins in Florida.

Nov 26   Florida's state canvassing board certifies Bush the winner by a 537-vote margin.

Dec 8   Florida Supreme Court overrules a county circuit court ruling to ensure that the recount continues; Bush campaign appeals to US Supreme Court.

Dec 12   Supreme Court rules in *Bush v. Gore*, halting the Florida recount and ensuring Bush's victory.

Dec 13   Al Gore concedes.

2001

Jan 20   Bush is inaugurated as forty-third president of the United States.

Jan 22   President Bush reinstates a Reagan-era ban on aid to international groups performing or counseling on abortion.

Jan 23   President Bush announces the No Child Left Behind proposal that holds states accountable for students' performance based on annual assessments and provides private school vouchers for students in failing schools.

Jan 29   President Bush creates White House Office of Faith-Based and Community Initiatives.

Feb 16   US airplanes attack Iraqi radar sites to enforce a no-fly zone.

Mar 29   President Bush announces the United States will not ratify the Kyoto Protocol.

Apr 1   US spy plane collides with Chinese aircraft over China and is forced to make an emergency landing.

May 24   Jim Jeffords announces that he will caucus with Democrats, giving them control of the Senate.

May 26   Congress passes President Bush's $1.35 trillion tax cut proposal.

Jun 16   President Bush meets with Vladimir Putin for the first time.

Aug 9   President Bush outlines his policy on stem cell research, allowing government funding for research on already extracted stem cells but prohibiting the extraction of additional stem cells from human embryos.

Sep 11   Terrorist attacks by al Qaeda kill more than 3,000 in New York City and Washington, DC.

Sep 18   President Bush signs Authorization for Use of Military Force Act, which allows him to use force against those responsible for the 9/11 attacks. Bush uses this legislation to engage in warrantless surveillance of possible terrorists and to detain suspects indefinitely.

Sep 20   President Bush addresses a special joint session of Congress to outline his plan for a global war on terror, declaring there is no longer any meaningful distinction between those nations that launch attacks and those that harbor terrorists.

Oct 7   United States launches air strikes against Taliban outposts in Afghanistan.

Oct 17   The Capitol shuts down amidst an anthrax scare. President Bush calls for $1.5 billion to fight bioterrorism.

Oct 26   President Bush signs the USA Patriot Act.

Nov 13   President Bush authorizes the use of military tribunals to try captured terrorists.

Dec 2   Enron files for bankruptcy; a criminal investigation leads to the eventual breakup of Arthur Anderson Consulting and the conviction of CEO Kenneth Lay and COO Jeffrey Skilling.

Dec 9   US forces capture Kandahar, the former citadel of Taliban power.

Dec 13   President Bush announces US withdrawal from 1972 Anti-Ballistic Missile Treaty.

2002

Jan 8   President Bush signs No Child Left Behind Act.

Jan 11   First detainees arrive at Guantánamo Bay, Cuba.

Jan 29   President Bush delivers the State of the Union address that becomes known as the "Axis of Evil" speech.

Feb 7   President Bush declares al Qaeda and Taliban fighters will not receive POW protection under the Third Geneva Convention.

Mar 22   President Bush renews his call on Palestinian leader Yasir Arafat to end attacks on Israel.

Mar 27   President Bush signs the Bipartisan Campaign Reform Act of 2002, which eliminates all soft-money donations to national party committees and curtails ads by nonparty organizations.

May 16   Congress presses the Bush administration for information on warnings about the 9/11 attacks. National security adviser Condoleezza Rice insists there was no lapse in intelligence.

May 20   President Bush announces continuation of forty-year-old trade embargo until Cuba has free and fair elections.

May 24 Presidents Bush and Putin sign a nuclear arms treaty, vowing to reduce their nations' arsenals by two-thirds over ten years.

Jun 1   In a speech at West Point, President Bush lays out the Bush doctrine on military preemption.

Jun 6   President Bush announces the Office of Homeland Security will coordinate a wide range of functions and oversee more than 100 organizations.

Jun 10 Federal agents arrest Jose Padilla for allegedly intending to detonate a radioactive "dirty bomb" in an American city.

Jun 13 Hamid Karzi is elected president of Afghanistan.

Jun 24 President Bush calls for an independent Palestinian state and encourages the Palestinian people to replace Yasir Arafat.

Jul 30 Following the Enron and WorldCom scandals, President Bush signs a corporate reform law creating a federal accounting oversight board.

Aug 26 In a speech to the Veterans of Foreign Wars, Vice President Cheney asserts there is "no doubt" that Saddam Hussein has weapons of mass destruction (WMD).

Sep 4   Seeking support for action against Iraq, President Bush addresses Congress, identifying Saddam Hussein as a threat.

Sep 12 President Bush calls for regime change in Iraq in an address before the United Nations.

Oct16   President Bush signs a joint resolution authorizing the use of military force against Iraq.

Nov 5   Republicans expand their majorities in midterm elections.

Nov 25 President Bush signs legislation creating the Department of Homeland Security.

2003

Jan 7   President Bush reveals a plan to cut taxes $674 billion over ten years.

Jan 28 In the State of the Union address, President Bush declares the United States is ready to attack Iraq.

Feb 5   Colin Powell appears before UN Security Council to present the US case for invading Iraq.

Feb 12   CIA director George Tenet announces that North Korea possesses a nuclear ballistic missile capable of hitting the United States.

Mar 17   President Bush delivers a national address giving Saddam 48 hours to leave Iraq or face military action.

Mar 19   US and coalition forces launch air strikes against Iraq.

Apr 9   US and coalition forces reach and occupy Baghdad. The statue of Saddam is toppled in Firdos Square.

Apr 10   President Bush and British prime minister Tony Blair air a joint address on Iraqi television describing the goals of coalition forces.

May 1   President Bush appears on the deck of the USS *Abraham Lincoln* to declare the end of major combat operations in Iraq.

May 27   President Bush signs the $15 billion US Leadership against HIV/AIDS, Tuberculosis, and Malaria Act.

May 28   President Bush signs a ten-year, $330 billion tax cut; congressional Democrats argue that it benefits the wealthy.

Jun 4   President Bush meets with Israeli prime minister Ariel Sharon and Palestinian prime minister Mahmoud Abbas in Aqaba, Jordan, to discuss peace in the region.

Jun 17   President Bush issues guidelines forbidding federal law enforcement from considering race or ethnicity in patrol duties, with the exception of national security.

Jul 7   Tommy Franks resigns as head of US Central Command (CENTCOM) and is replaced by Gen. John Abizaid.

Jul 11   Regarding President Bush's remarks in his State of the Union address, CIA director George Tenet says the intelligence regarding Iraq's alleged effort to obtain uranium from Africa was discredited.

Jul 14   Writing in the *Washington Post,* Robert Novak "outs" CIA agent Valerie Plame to discredit her husband's accusations about prewar intelligence.

Jul 22   Saddam's sons Uday and Qusay are killed in Iraq.

Sep 30   Justice Department announces a criminal investigation into allegations that Bush administration officials leaked the name of a covert CIA operative to the media in July. President Bush urges full cooperation.

Oct 2   Chief US weapons inspector David Kay reports that the Iraq Survey Group failed to find any WMD in Iraq.

Nov 5   President Bush signs a ban on late-term abortion; the Supreme Court later upholds the ban.

Nov 6   President Bush signs an $87.5 billion reconstruction effort for Iraq and Afghanistan.

Dec 4   President Bush withdraws steep tariffs on imported steel.

Dec 8   President Bush signs the Medicare Modernization Act, including prescription drug benefits.

Dec 13 US troops capture Saddam Hussein.

2004

Jan 7   President Bush proposes major changes to US immigration law, calling for a guest worker program and permanent residency.

Jan 14 President Bush outlines his space program, including an eventual manned trip to Mars and $1 billion for NASA over five years.

Jan 16 President Bush recess-appoints Judge Charles Pickering to the federal appeals court due to the Senate standstill on his judicial nominees.

Feb 6   President Bush names a bipartisan commission to investigate intelligence failures related to the war in Iraq.

Feb 24 President Bush announces support for a constitutional amendment banning gay marriage.

Apr 4   US forces in Iraq confront violent uprisings in Baghdad and Fallujah.

Apr 28 First Abu Ghraib photos appear on *60 Minutes II*.

Jun 3   President Bush accepts the resignation of CIA director George Tenet. Porter Goss is nominated to replace him in August.

Jun 8   Attorney General John Ashcroft appears before Senate Judiciary Committee regarding the use of torture.

Jun 10 President Bush hosts the G8 summit at Sea Island, Georgia.

Jun 28 Supreme Court issues a ruling in *Hamdi v. Rumsfeld*, which recognizes the government's right to detain unlawful combatants but finds that US citizens must be able to challenge their detention before an impartial judge.

Jun 28 Sovereignty is transferred to Iraq's interim government.

Jul 22 9/11 Commission issues its final report.

Sep 2   President Bush accepts the Republican nomination for president.

Oct 7   Chief US weapons inspector Charles Duelfer issues a report
          contradicting most prewar claims regarding Iraq's WMD
          program.
Oct 22   President Bush approves tax breaks totaling $136 billion.
Nov 2   President Bush is reelected, and the Republican Party adds
          slightly to its majorities in the House and Senate.
Nov 8   US troops launch an assault to retake the rebel-controlled city of
          Fallujah.
Nov 15   Colin Powell resigns as secretary of state.
Nov 16   President Bush names Condoleezza Rice as his new secretary of
          state.
Dec 26   Tsunami strikes the Philippines; four days later, Bush pledges aid.

2005

Jan 3   President Bush asks his father and former president Clinton to
          lead a nationwide fund-raising campaign for tsunami victims.
Jan 20   President Bush is inaugurated for a second term.
Jan 30   Iraq holds elections to choose a 275-member National Assembly
          charged with drafting a new constitution.
Feb 2   In the State of the Union address, President Bush calls for massive
          restructuring of the Social Security system to allow for private
          accounts.
Feb 20   President Bush travels to Europe to meet with French president
          Jacques Chirac, German chancellor Gerhard Schroeder, and
          Putin.
Mar 21   President Bush signs legislation to allow a federal court to
          intervene in the case of Terri Schiavo.
Jun 10   President Bush meets with South Korean president Roh Moo
          Hyun to discuss North Korea's pursuit of nuclear weapons.
Jun 21   Vietnamese premier Phan Van Khai meets with President Bush
          to discuss human rights in Vietnam—the first US visit by a
          Vietnamese premier since 1975.
Jul 1   Sandra Day O'Connor announces her retirement from the
          Supreme Court.
Aug 1   President Bush recess-appoints John Bolton to be ambassador to
          the United Nations.

Aug 2   President Bush signs the Central American Free Trade Agreement
          (CAFTA).

Aug 8   President Bush signs legislation providing incentives to encourage
          new nuclear plants, cleaner-burning coal facilities, wind and
          other renewable sources of energy, and the production of more oil
          and natural gas.

Aug 28   Hurricane Katrina strikes the Gulf coast.

Sep 3   Chief Justice William Rehnquist dies.

Sep 12   Federal Emergency Management Agency (FEMA) director
          Michael Brown resigns amidst the federal government's botched
          response to Katrina. Three days later, President Bush pledges
          to rebuild New Orleans and uncover the problems in the
          government's response.

Sep 29   John Roberts is sworn in as chief justice.

Oct 3   President Bush nominates White House counsel Harriet Miers to
          replace Justice O'Connor; Miers withdraws her nomination by the
          end of the month.

Oct 28   I. Lewis "Scooter" Libby is indicted for perjury, obstruction of
          justice, and making false statements to investigators looking into
          the Valerie Plame affair.

Oct 31   President Bush nominates Samuel Alito to replace Justice
          O'Connor.

Nov 2   The *Washington Post* reveals the existence of secret prisons for
          suspected terrorists.

Dec 17   President Bush asserts that wiretapping is both legal and
          necessary, in response to a *New York Times* article reporting that
          he authorized the National Security Agency (NSA) to wiretap
          American citizens without a warrant.

2006

Jan 26   After Hamas wins Palestinian elections, President Bush declares
          that he will not deal with the group until it renounces terrorism.

Jan 31   Samuel Alito is sworn in as Supreme Court justice.

Mar 9   President Bush renews the USA Patriot Act.

Mar 28   White House chief of staff Andrew Card resigns and is replaced
          by Joshua Bolten.

Apr 19 White House press secretary Scott McClellan resigns and is
        replaced by Tony Snow.
Apr 20 Bush meets with Chinese president Hu Jintao in Washington.
May 3   Iraq's parliament meets for the first time since 2005 elections.
May 3   Bush administration proposes a plan to minimize losses in the
        event of a deadly pandemic after several cases of avian influenza
        are reported in Central and Southeast Asia.
May 5   CIA director Porter Goss resigns and is replaced by Michael
        Hayden.
May 15 United States restores full diplomatic relations with Libya and
        removes it from the list of state sponsors of terrorism.
Jun 29 Supreme Court strikes down the military tribunal system in
        Hamdan v. Rumsfeld.
Jul 19 President Bush vetoes a bill that would have provided federal
        funding for stem cell research.
Jul 20 Responding to a Supreme Court ruling on the treatment of
        detainees, President Bush reverses course and announces that
        they are protected by the Geneva Conventions.
Sep 6   In a speech, President Bush acknowledges the existence of secret
        prisons and claims that the information gathered by intelligence
        operatives at these prisons has saved lives.
Oct 17 President Bush signs the Military Commissions Act, authorizing
        the military tribunal system.
Oct 26 President Bush signs the Secure Fence Act, authorizing a 700-
        mile fence along the US-Mexico border.
Nov 7   Democrats retake the House and the Senate in midterm elections.
Nov 8   Donald Rumsfeld resigns as secretary of defense.
Dec 6   Robert Gates is confirmed as the new secretary of defense. Iraq
        Study Group issues a final report calling the situation in Iraq
        "grave and deteriorating."
Dec 7   Seven US attorneys are fired.
Dec 30 Saddam Hussein is executed.

2007

Jan 8   United States launches an air attack on Islamist militias and
        suspected al Qaeda operatives in Somalia.

Jan 10   President Bush announces a "surge" of an additional 20,000 troops into Iraq.

Jan 26   Senate confirms Gen. David Petraeus as the new commander of forces in Iraq.

Feb 18   The *Washington Post* reveals substandard treatment of recovering troops at Walter Reed Medical Facility.

Mar 6   Congress holds its first hearings on the emerging scandal over the improper firing of US attorneys.

Mar 16   John Abizaid resigns his post at CENTCOM and is replaced by Adm. William J. Fallon.

Apr 9   President Bush gives a speech in Arizona to promote comprehensive immigration reform.

May 1   President Bush vetoes a war spending bill that sets a timetable for troop withdrawal from Iraq.

Jun 28   Senate kills the Bush-backed immigration reform proposal.

Jun 28   President Bush invokes executive privilege in withholding subpoenaed documents on fired US attorneys.

Jun 29   Supreme Court reverses an April decision and agrees to hear appeals from Guantánamo Bay detainees with no access to federal courts.

Jul 3   President Bush commutes the sentence of "Scooter" Libby.

Jul 10   President Bush expands the Foreign Intelligence Surveillance Act, making it easier to eavesdrop on terrorist suspects and giving immunity to telephone companies involved in the NSA's wiretapping program.

Jul 26   Congress passes an antiterrorism bill that allows screening of air and sea cargo and allocates more money to government antiterrorism grants.

Aug 13   Karl Rove resigns.

Aug 27   Attorney General Alberto Gonzalez resigns after facing sustained criticism over handling of the US attorney scandal.

Sep 11   General Petraeus tells Congress that the surge has made enough progress to allow the pullout of some troops by next summer.

Oct 3   President Bush vetoes S-CHIP expansion; he vetoes the bill a second time in December.

Nov 8   Michael Mukasey is confirmed as the new attorney general.

Nov 27   President Bush hosts a Mideast peace summit in Annapolis, Maryland.

Dec 6   President Bush announces an agreement with mortgage lenders to freeze interest rates for five years for financially troubled homeowners.

2008

Feb 13   President Bush signs a $145 billion economic rescue package.

Mar 5   President Bush endorses Republican John McCain for president.

Mar 8   President Bush vetoes legislation meant to ban the CIA from using waterboarding and other interrogation techniques.

Mar 11   Adm. William J. Fallon resigns his CENTCOM post and is replaced by Gen. David Petraeus.

Mar 16   Federal Reserve helps J. P. Morgan purchase Bear Stearns to prevent a widespread economic crisis.

May 22   House and Senate override President Bush's veto of the $307 billion farm bill providing subsidies to farmers.

Jun 5   Senate Select Committee on Intelligence finds that President Bush and other officials greatly exaggerated the evidence that Saddam Hussein had WMD.

Jul 5   President Bush travels to Japan for G8 summit.

Jul 14   President Bush lifts a presidential ban on offshore drilling.

Sep 7   US government places Fannie Mae and Freddie Mac under its control to prevent them from going under and endangering more than half the country's mortgages.

Sep 15   Lehman Brothers files for chapter 11 bankruptcy.

Sep 16   Federal Reserve lends $85 billion to American International Group (AIG).

Sep 25   Treasury Department seizes Washington Mutual in the largest bank failure in US history.

Oct 3   President Bush signs a $700 billion financial rescue bill.

Nov 4   Democrat Barack Obama is elected president.

Nov 25   Treasury Department and Federal Reserve agree to another $800 billion in lending programs to buy debt insured by Fannie Mae and Freddie Mac and to provide more small loans to consumers.

Dec 19   President Bush issues a $17.4 billion auto bailout to General Motors and Chrysler to prevent bankruptcy.

APPENDIX TWO

Interviewees for the George W. Bush Presidential History Project

Additional interviews remained closed as this book went to press, but as they are opened by the interviewees, they will be posted to the Miller Center's website: https://millercenter.org/the-presidency/presidential-oral-histories/george-w-bush.

Elliott Abrams, deputy national security adviser for global democracy strategy; special assistant to the president; senior director for democracy, human rights, and international operations, National Security Council (NSC); NSC senior director for Near East and North African affairs. Washington, DC, May 17–18, 2012.

Daniel J. Bartlett, White House communications director, counselor to the president. Washington, DC, January 30–31, 2014.

John Bellinger III, legal adviser, National Security Council; legal adviser, State Department. Charlottesville, VA, part I, March 8–9, 2013; part II, April 20, 2013.

Joshua Bolten (with Kristen Silverberg and Joel Kaplan), White House deputy chief of staff for policy; director, Office of Management and Budget; chief of staff. Washington, DC, part I, January 15–16, 2013; part II, July 13, 2016; part III, September 26, 2016; part IV, February 9, 2018.

L. Paul Bremer III, presidential envoy to Iraq; chief executive administrator, Coalition Provisional Authority. Charlottesville, VA, August 28–29, 2012.

John Bridgeland, deputy assistant to the president; director, White House Domestic Policy Council; assistant to the president and director, USA Freedom Corps. Charlottesville, VA, May 3–4, 2012.

Nicholas E. Calio (with David W. Hobbs, John W. Howard, and Ziad S. Ojakli), assistant to the president for legislative affairs. Charlottesville, VA, March 14–15, 2013.

George Casey, chief of staff, US Army; vice chief of staff, US Army; senior coalition commander, Iraq; director, Joint Staff; director of strategic plans and policy. Charlottesville, VA, September 25, 2014.

Elaine Chao (with Laura Genero and Tamara Somerville), secretary of labor. Washington, DC, January 17, 2019.

Michael Chertoff, secretary of homeland security; judge, US Third Circuit Court of Appeals; assistant US attorney general, Criminal Division. Washington, DC, January 31, 2012.

Ryan Crocker, US ambassador to Syria, Pakistan, and Iraq. Charlottesville, VA, September 9–10, 2010.

Mitchell E. Daniels Jr., director, Office of Management and Budget. West Lafayette, IN, May 2, 2014.

Mark R. Dybul, US global AIDS coordinator. Geneva, Switzerland, December 6, 2016.

Eric Edelman, undersecretary of defense for policy, ambassador to Turkey, principal deputy assistant to the vice president for national security affairs. Charlottesville, VA, June 2, 2017.

Peter Feaver, special adviser for strategic planning and institutional reform. Charlottesville, VA, January 10–11, 2012.

Evan A. Feigenbaum, deputy assistant secretary of state for South Asia, deputy assistant secretary of state for Central Asia, member of the secretary of state's policy planning staff for East Asia and the Pacific. Charlottesville, VA (recorded remotely), part I, November 20, 2020; part II, November 30, 2020.

Douglas J. Feith, undersecretary of defense for policy. Washington, DC, March 22–23, 2012.

Fred Fielding, White House counsel. Charlottesville, VA, March 8–9, 2011.

Ari Fleischer, White House press secretary. Charlottesville, VA, September 29, 2010.

Tommy Franks, commander in chief, US Central Command (CENTCOM). Hobart, OK, October 22, 2014.

Robert Gates, secretary of defense. Mount Vernon, WA, July 8–9, 2013.

Richard Gephardt, member, US House of Representatives (Missouri); House minority leader. Washington, DC, May 24, 2016.

Edward Gillespie, chair, Republican National Committee; chair, Virginia Republican Party; counselor to the president. Charlottesville, VA, January 24–25, 2012.

Alberto R. Gonzales, White House counsel, attorney general. Washington, DC, October 14–15, 2010.

Judd Gregg, US senator (New Hampshire). Rye Beach, NH, June 2, 2015.

Stephen J. Hadley (with Judy Ansley and J. D. Crouch), deputy national security adviser, national security adviser. Washington, DC, October 31–November 1, 2011.

J. Dennis Hastert, Speaker of the US House of Representatives (Illinois). Washington, DC, May 16, 2014.

Michael Hayden, director, National Security Agency; principal deputy director of national intelligence; director, CIA. Washington, DC, November 20, 2012.

Keith Hennessey, deputy director, National Economic Council; director, National Economic Council. Palo Alto, CA, January 8, 2015.

Clay Johnson, assistant to the president for presidential personnel; deputy director, Office of Management and Budget. Charlottesville, VA, February 11–12, 2014.

Jay Lefkowitz, general counsel, Office of Management and Budget; deputy assistant to the president for domestic policy; special envoy for human rights, North Korea. New York, NY, May 30, 2014.

Douglas Lute, director of operations, US Central Command (CENTCOM); director of operations, Joint Chiefs of Staff; assistant to the president and deputy national security adviser. Washington, DC, August 3, 2015.

William McGurn, assistant to the president for speechwriting. New York, NY, April 14, 2016.

Harriet Miers, White House staff secretary; deputy chief of staff for policy; White House counsel. Charlottesville, VA, January 31–February 1, 2013.

Michael Mukasey, attorney general. Washington, DC, October 8–9, 2012.

John Negroponte, US ambassador to the United Nations, US ambassador to Iraq, director of national intelligence, deputy secretary of state. Charlottesville, VA, September 14, 2012.

Theodore B. Olson, attorney for George W. Bush in *Bush v. Gore*, US solicitor general. Washington, DC, March 28, 2012.

Peter Pace, commander in chief, US Southern Command (SOUTHCOM);

vice chairman, Joint Chiefs of Staff; chairman, Joint Chiefs of Staff. McLean, VA, January 19, 2016.

Henry Paulson, secretary of the treasury. Charlottesville, VA, March 11–12, 2013.

Colin L. Powell, secretary of state, and Richard L. Armitage, deputy secretary of state. Alexandria, VA, March 28, 2017.

Karl Rove, senior adviser to the president, White House deputy chief of staff for policy. Washington, DC, part I, June 11–12, 2013; part II, November 8–9, 2013.

John Snow (with Chris Smith), secretary of the treasury. Charlottesville, VA, May 1–2, 2013.

Margaret Spellings (with Holly Kuzmich), director, Domestic Policy Council; secretary of education. Charlottesville, VA, August 5–6, 2010.

Kevin Sullivan, assistant secretary for communications and outreach, Department of Education; assistant to the president for communications. Charlottesville, VA, November 1–2, 2012.

James Towey, director, White House Office of Faith-Based and Community Initiatives. Ave Maria, FL, October 8, 2015.

Frances Townsend, deputy national security adviser, homeland security and counterterrorism adviser. Charlottesville, VA, August 26–27, 2010.

Peter Wehner, deputy director for speechwriting, deputy assistant to the president, head of White House Office of Strategic Initiatives. Charlottesville, VA, May 1, 2015.

John Yoo, deputy assistant attorney general. Charlottesville, VA, February 24, 2011.

Philip Zelikow, executive director, 9/11 Commission; counselor,

Department of State. Charlottesville, VA, part I, July 28, 2010; part II, October 4, 2010.

Karl Zinsmeister, director, Domestic Policy Council. Charlottesville, VA, July 25, 2016.

APPENDIX THREE

Interviewers for the George W. Bush Presidential History Project

Henry Abraham, University of Virginia
William Antholis, University of Virginia
Spencer Bakich, Virginia Military Institute
Stephen Bragaw, Sweet Briar College
Seyom Brown, Southern Methodist University
Emily Charnock, University of Virginia
Martha Derthick, University of Virginia
John Dinan, Wake Forest University
Jeffrey Engel, Southern Methodist University
Jasmine Farrier, University of Louisville
Paul Freedman, University of Virginia
Karen Hult, Virginia Tech University
Charles O. Jones, University of Wisconsin–Madison
Nancy Kassop, State University of New York at New Paltz
Steven Knott, United States Naval War College
Melvyn Leffler, University of Virginia
Stephen Long, University of Richmond
Guian McKee, University of Virginia
Sidney Milkis, University of Virginia
Michael Nelson, Rhodes College
Daniel Palazzolo, University of Richmond
Barbara A. Perry, University of Virginia
Jesse Rhodes, University of Massachusetts–Amherst
Russell L. Riley, University of Virginia
Patrick Roberts, Virginia Tech University

Peter Rodriguez, University of Virginia
Marc Selverstone, University of Virginia
Robert Strong, Washington & Lee University
Charles Walcott, Virginia Tech University
Stephen Weatherford, University of California–Santa Barbara
Sarah Wilson, Covington & Burling
Brantly Womack, University of Virginia

CONTRIBUTORS

Spencer D. Bakich is a professor of international studies and director of the National Security Program at the Virginia Military Institute, as well as a senior fellow at the University of Virginia's Miller Center. He is the author of *Success and Failure in Limited War: Information and Strategy in the Korean, Vietnam, Persian Gulf, and Iraq Wars.*

Robert F. Bruner is professor, dean emeritus, and senior fellow of the Miller Center at the University of Virginia.

Joel K. Goldstein is the Vincent C. Immel Professor of Law Emeritus at Saint Louis University School of Law. He is the author of *The White House Vice Presidency: The Path to Significance, Mondale to Biden* and *The Modern American Vice Presidency: The Transformation of a Political Institution.*

Sidney M. Milkis is the White Burkett Miller Professor of Politics and a Miller Center faculty fellow at the University of Virginia. His most recent book, coauthored with Nicholas Jacobs, is *What Happened to the Vita Center? Presidentialism, Populist Revolt and the Fracturing of America.*

Michael Nelson is the Fulmer Professor of Politics and Law at Rhodes College, senior fellow at the University of Virginia's Miller Center, and author of the Richard Neustadt Award–winning *Resilient America: Electing Nixon in 1968, Channeling Dissent, and Dividing Government* and the V. O. Key Award–winning *How the South Joined the Gambling Nation: The Politics of State Policy Innovation.*

Barbara A. Perry is the Gerald L. Baliles Professor and director of Presidential Studies at the University of Virginia's Miller Center, where she cochairs the Presidential Oral History Program. Her most recent book, coedited with Michael Nelson, is *The Presidency: Facing Constitutional Crossroads.*

John J. Pitney Jr. is the Roy P. Crocker Professor of American Politics at Claremont McKenna College.

Jesse H. Rhodes is professor of political science at the University of Massachusetts–Amherst, associate director of the UMass Poll, and the author of three books and numerous articles about representation, voting rights, and the presidency.

Russell L. Riley is the White Burkett Miller Center Professor of Ethics and Institutions at the University of Virginia, where he cochairs the Miller Center's Presidential Oral History Program.

Andrew Rudalevige is the Thomas Brackett Reed Professor and chair of the Government and Legal Studies Department at Bowdoin College and the author of *By Executive Order* and *The New Imperial Presidency.*

INDEX

state legislators, Republican victories of, 53

State of the Union address, 72, 307–308

Status of Forces Agreement (SOFA), 246

Stellarwind data-gathering program, 129

Stem Cell Research Enhancement Act of 2005, 158

Stevens, John Paul, 165, 177

Stevens, Stuart, 40

strategic solvency, 226–227, 246–248

Sullivan, Kevin, 328

Sunni population (Iraq), 241

Sununu, John E., 47, 140

Supreme Court
  Bush's legacy within, 188–189
  justice ages within, 165
  nomination process of, 171–175, 176–181, 307
  party division within, 182
  presidential nominations within, 165
  Republican Party and, 166–168
  timeline regarding, 320
  vacancy within, 168–171
  See also specific cases; specific justices

survival of government plan, 96–97, 104

suspense, significance of, 4

Sutcliffe, Kathleen, 276

Swift Boat Veterans for Truth, 51, 298

Taliban, 248, 249

Tarr, Ralph, 134n28

Tauzin, Billy, 154

tax credits, policy proposals regarding, 64

tax cuts, 9, 75–76, 146–147, 154, 316, 317

tax surcharge, 287–88n35

Taylor, Zachary, 14

Tea Party, 285, 305

Tenet, George, 16, 95, 318

Tennessee, 43

"Ten-Point Plan to Improve Quarterly Reporting and Protect America's Shareholders," 273

terrorism, 27n12. *See also* September 11

Terrorist Surveillance Program (TSP), 208, 212

Texas, 141, 186

Texas Rangers, 37

Thomas, Clarence, 165

Thompson, Fred, 195

Thune, John, 47, 155

Thurmond, Strom, 153

Tillman, Mark, 89, 90

time for a change penalty, 36

Timmons, Jay, 52

Towey, James, 123, 131, 205, 328

Townsend, Frances, 3, 86, 87, 102, 328

Trippi, Joe, 49

Troubled Asset Relief Program (TARP)
  challenges within, 22–23
  conditions of, 264–265
  criticism of, 262–263, 305
  overview of, 21, 304
  passage of, 159–160, 263
  policies within, 268–269
  proposal of, 262

Truman, Harry, 170

Trump, Donald, 84–85, 283, 293, 307, 308

Trump v. Hawaii, 186

Twenty-Second Amendment, 35–36

Ukraine, 252

unilateralism, 108, 111

unitary executive branch theory, 108, 109–115, 130, 291–292

United Flight 93, 93–94

United Nations, 229

USA Patriot Act, 13–14, 149, 315

US Capitol, January 6 attack on, 84–85, 104

US Central Command (CENTCOM), 230, 231

Vacancies Act, 10

vetoes, 14, 158

vice presidents, nomination of, 35–36. *See also* Cheney, Dick

Virginia, 46

VJ Day, 11–12

Voting Rights Act, 76, 186